GREEN LANTERNS

VOL.5 OUT OF TIME

SAM HUMPHRIES
writer

CARLO BARBERI * RONAN CLIQUET * JULIO FERREIRA
SCOTT GODLEWSKI * EDUARDO PANSICA * MATT SANTORELLI
artists

ULISES ARREOLA * BLOND
HI-FI * ALEX SOLLAZZO
colorists

DAVE SHARPE * TOM NAPOLITANO
letterers

BRANDON PETERSON
collection cover artist

MIKE COTTON Editor - Original Series ✴ **ANDREW MARINO** Assistant Editor - Original Series ✴ **JEB WOODARD** Group Editor - Collected Editions
BETSY GOLDEN Editor - Collected Edition ✴ **STEVE COOK** Design Director - Books ✴ **LOUIS PRANDI** Publication Design

BOB HARRAS Senior VP - Editor-in-Chief, DC Comics ✴ **PAT McCALLUM** Executive Editor, DC Comics

DIANE NELSON President ✴ **DAN DiDIO** Publisher ✴ **JIM LEE** Publisher ✴ **GEOFF JOHNS** President & Chief Creative Officer
AMIT DESAI Executive VP - Business & Marketing Strategy, Direct to Consumer & Global Franchise Management
SAM ADES Senior VP & General Manager, Digital Services ✴ **BOBBIE CHASE** VP & Executive Editor, Young Reader & Talent Development
MARK CHIARELLO Senior VP - Art, Design & Collected Editions ✴ **JOHN CUNNINGHAM** Senior VP - Sales & Trade Marketing
ANNE DePIES Senior VP - Business Strategy, Finance & Administration ✴ **DON FALLETTI** VP - Manufacturing Operations
LAWRENCE GANEM VP - Editorial Administration & Talent Relations ✴ **ALISON GILL** Senior VP - Manufacturing & Operations
HANK KANALZ Senior VP - Editorial Strategy & Administration ✴ **JAY KOGAN** VP - Legal Affairs
JACK MAHAN VP - Business Affairs ✴ **NICK J. NAPOLITANO** VP - Manufacturing Administration ✴ **EDDIE SCANNELL** VP - Consumer Marketing
COURTNEY SIMMONS Senior VP - Publicity & Communications ✴ **JIM (SKI) SOKOLOWSKI** VP - Comic Book Specialty Sales & Trade Marketing
NANCY SPEARS VP - Mass, Book, Digital Sales & Trade Marketing ✴ **MICHELE R. WELLS** VP - Content Strategy

GREEN LANTERNS VOL. 5: OUT OF TIME

Published by DC Comics. Compilation and all new material Copyright © 2018 DC Comics. All Rights Reserved. Originally published in single magazine
form in GREEN LANTERNS 27-32. Copyright © 2017 DC Comics. All Rights Reserved. All characters, their distinctive likenesses and related elements
featured in this publication are trademarks of DC Comics. The stories, characters and incidents featured in this publication are entirely fictional.
DC Comics does not read or accept unsolicited submissions of ideas, stories or artwork.

DC Comics, 2900 West Alameda Ave., Burbank, CA 91505
Printed by LSC Communications, Kendallville, IN, USA. 2/23/18. First Printing.
ISBN: 978-1-4012-7879-3

Library of Congress Cataloging-in-Publication Data is available.

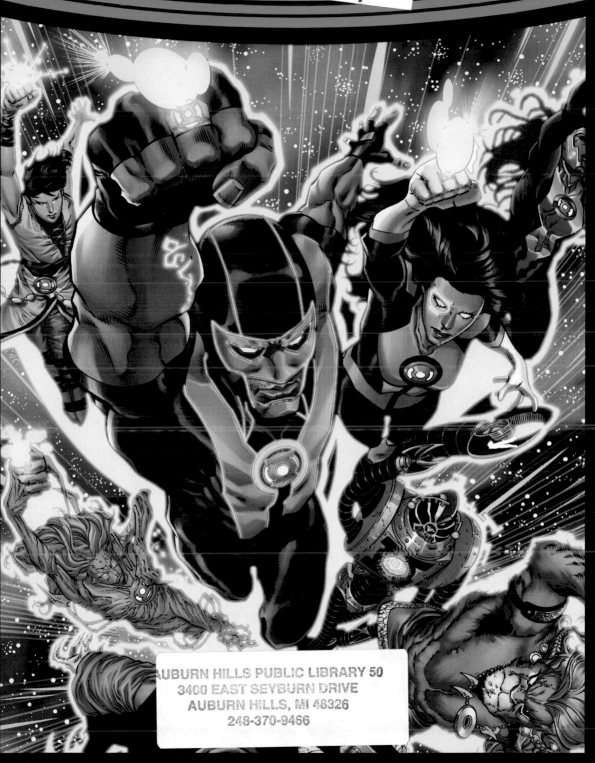

GREEN LANTERNS
VOL.5 OUT OF TIME

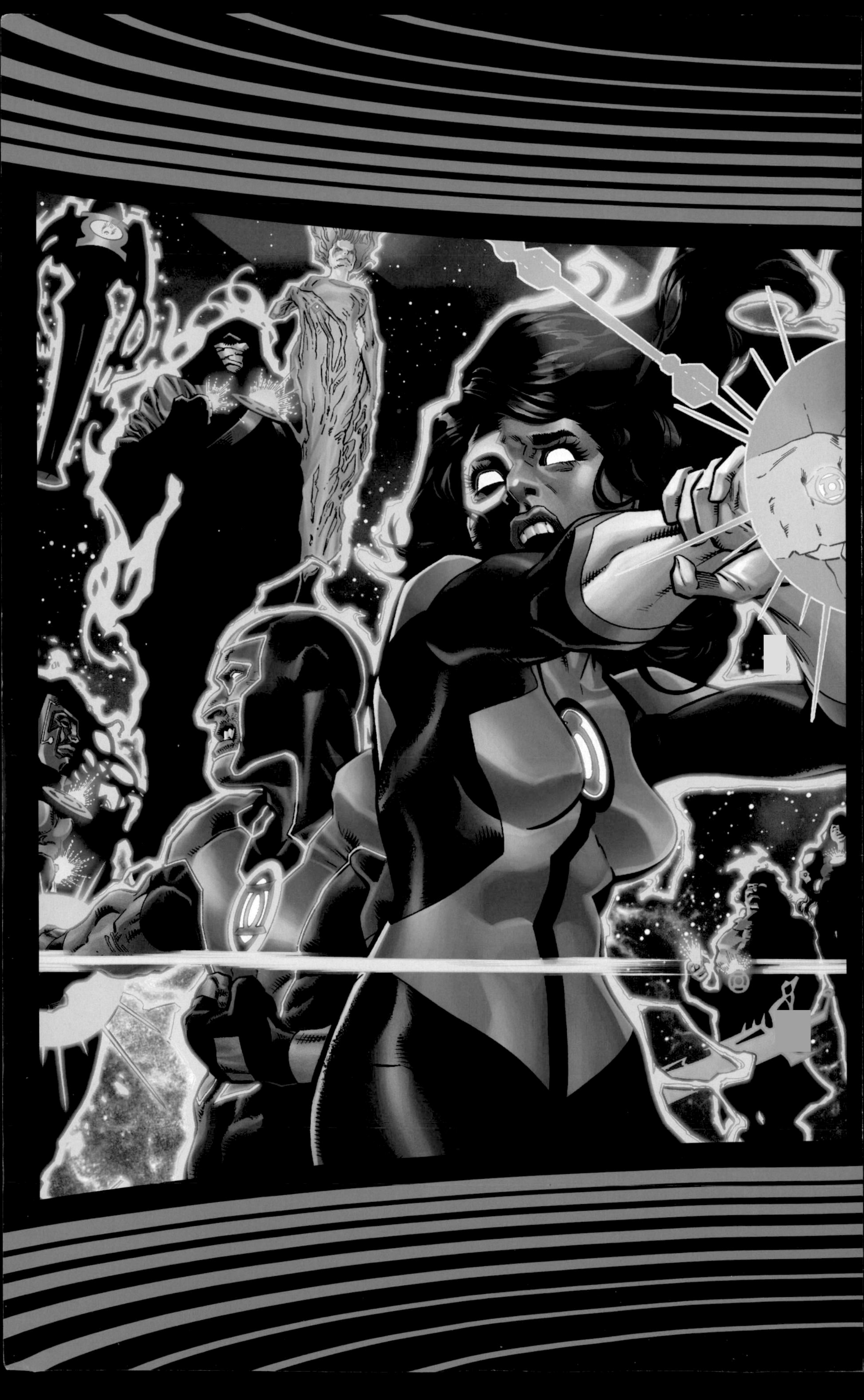

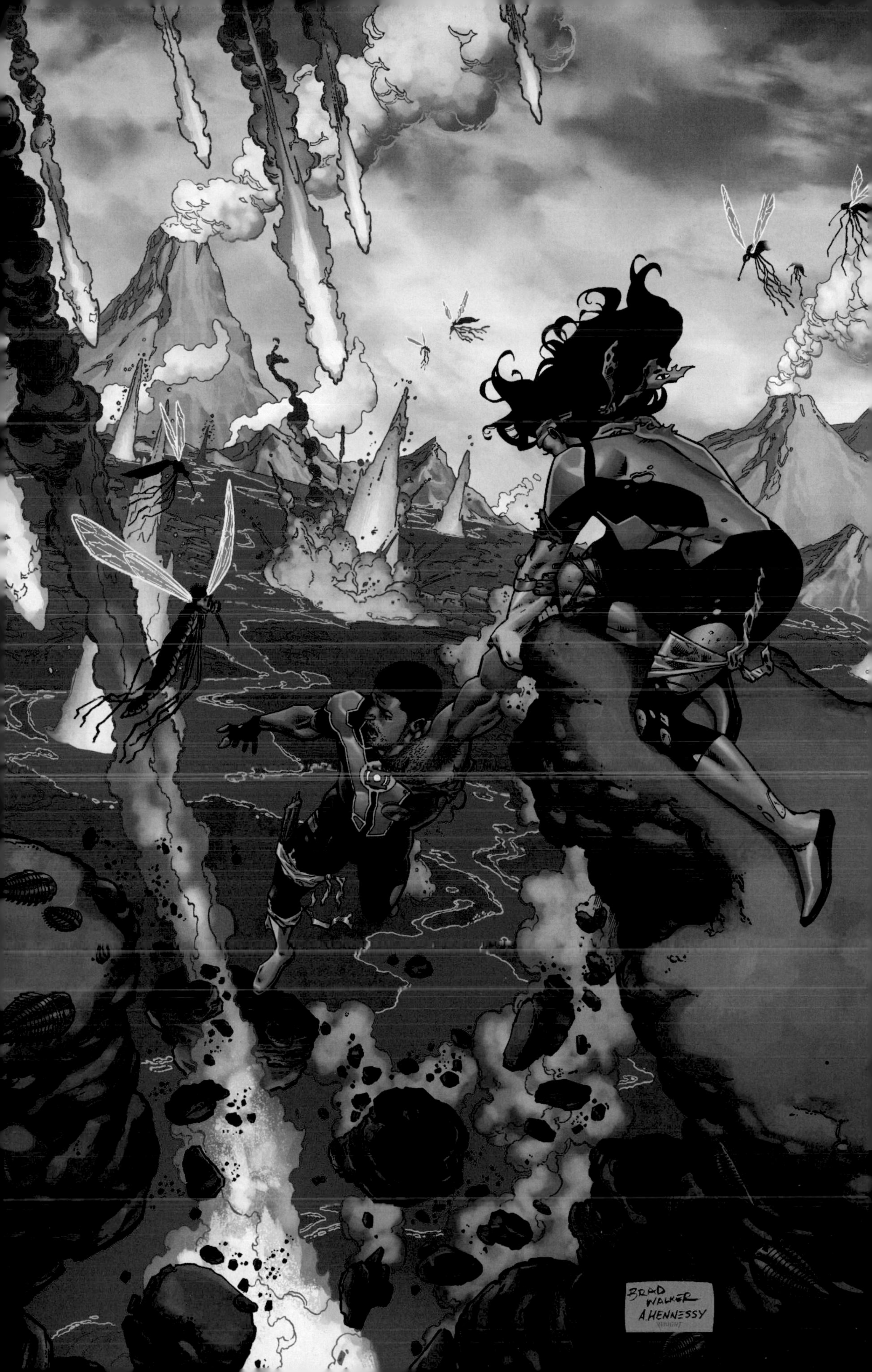
BRAD WALKER
A.HENNESSY

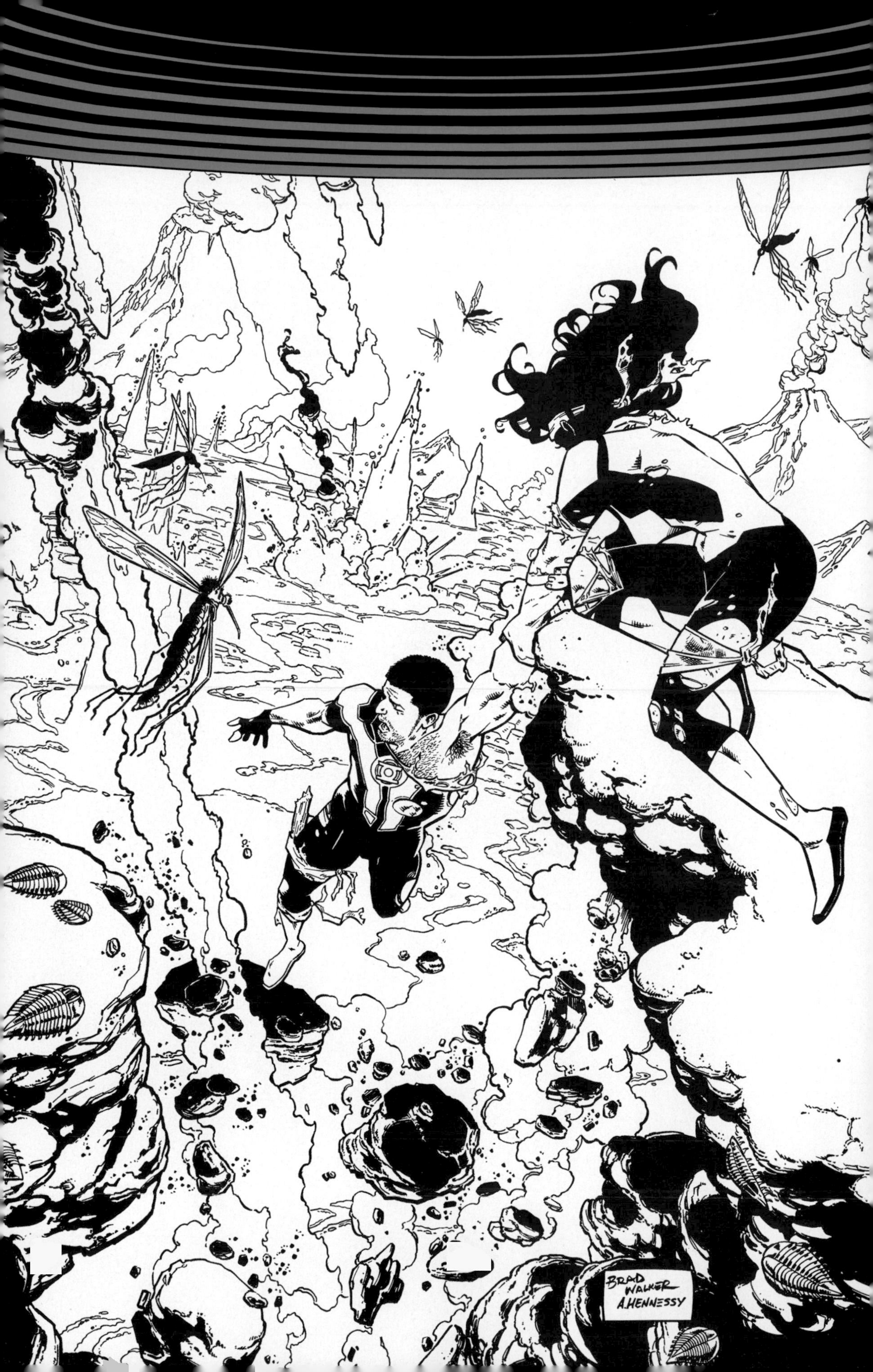
BRAD WALKER
A.HENNESSY

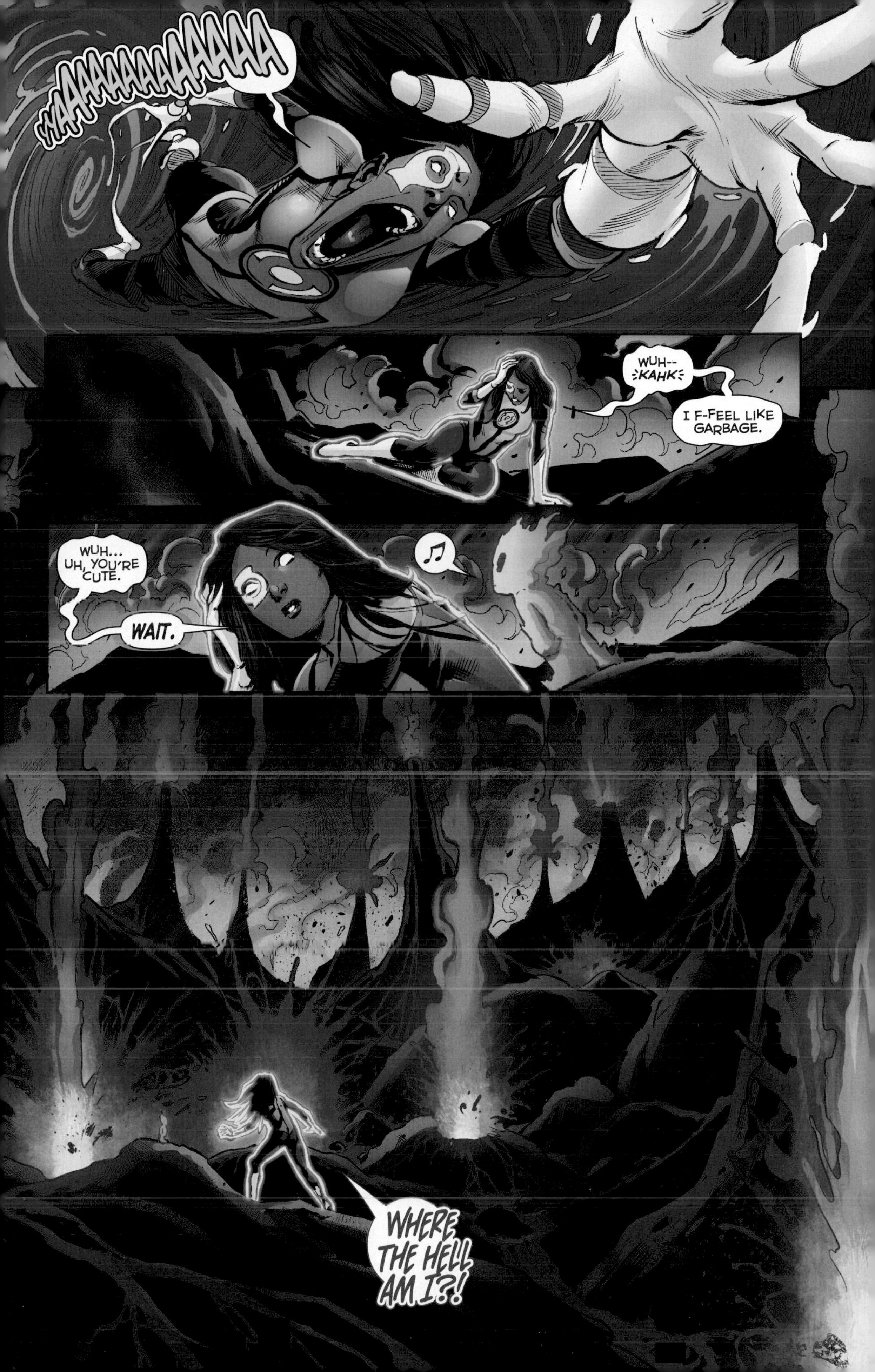
YAAAAAAAAAAAA
WUH-- -KAHK-
I F-FEEL LIKE GARBAGE.
WUH... UH, YOU'RE CUTE.
♫
WAIT.
WHERE THE HELL AM I?!

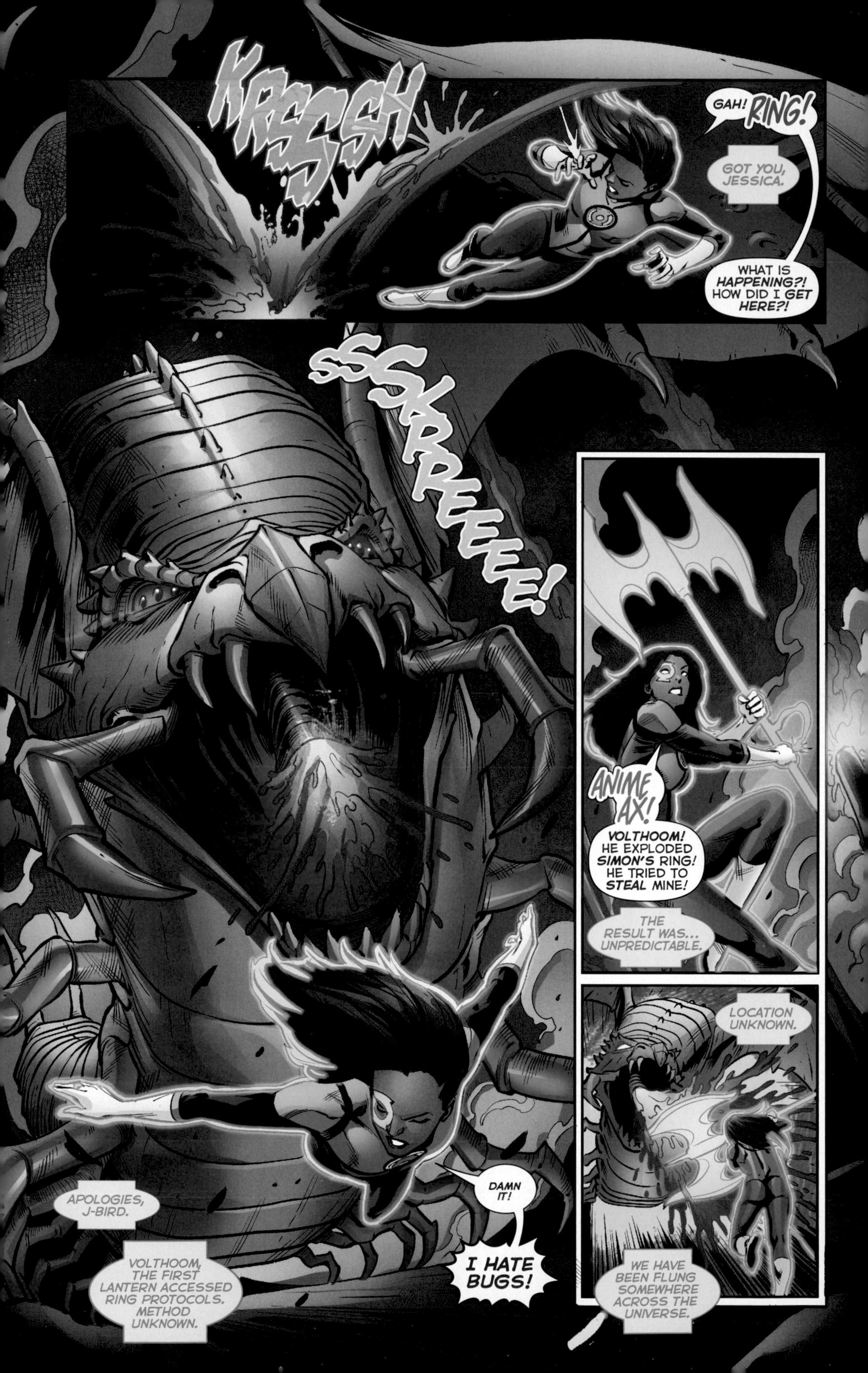
KRSSSH
GAH! RING!
GOT YOU, JESSICA.
WHAT IS HAPPENING?! HOW DID I GET HERE?!
SSSKREEEEE!
ANIME AX!
VOLTHOOM! HE EXPLODED SIMON'S RING! HE TRIED TO STEAL MINE!
THE RESULT WAS... UNPREDICTABLE.
LOCATION UNKNOWN.
WE HAVE BEEN FLUNG SOMEWHERE ACROSS THE UNIVERSE.
APOLOGIES, J-BIRD.
VOLTHOOM, THE FIRST LANTERN ACCESSED RING PROTOCOLS. METHOD UNKNOWN.
DAMN IT!
I HATE BUGS!

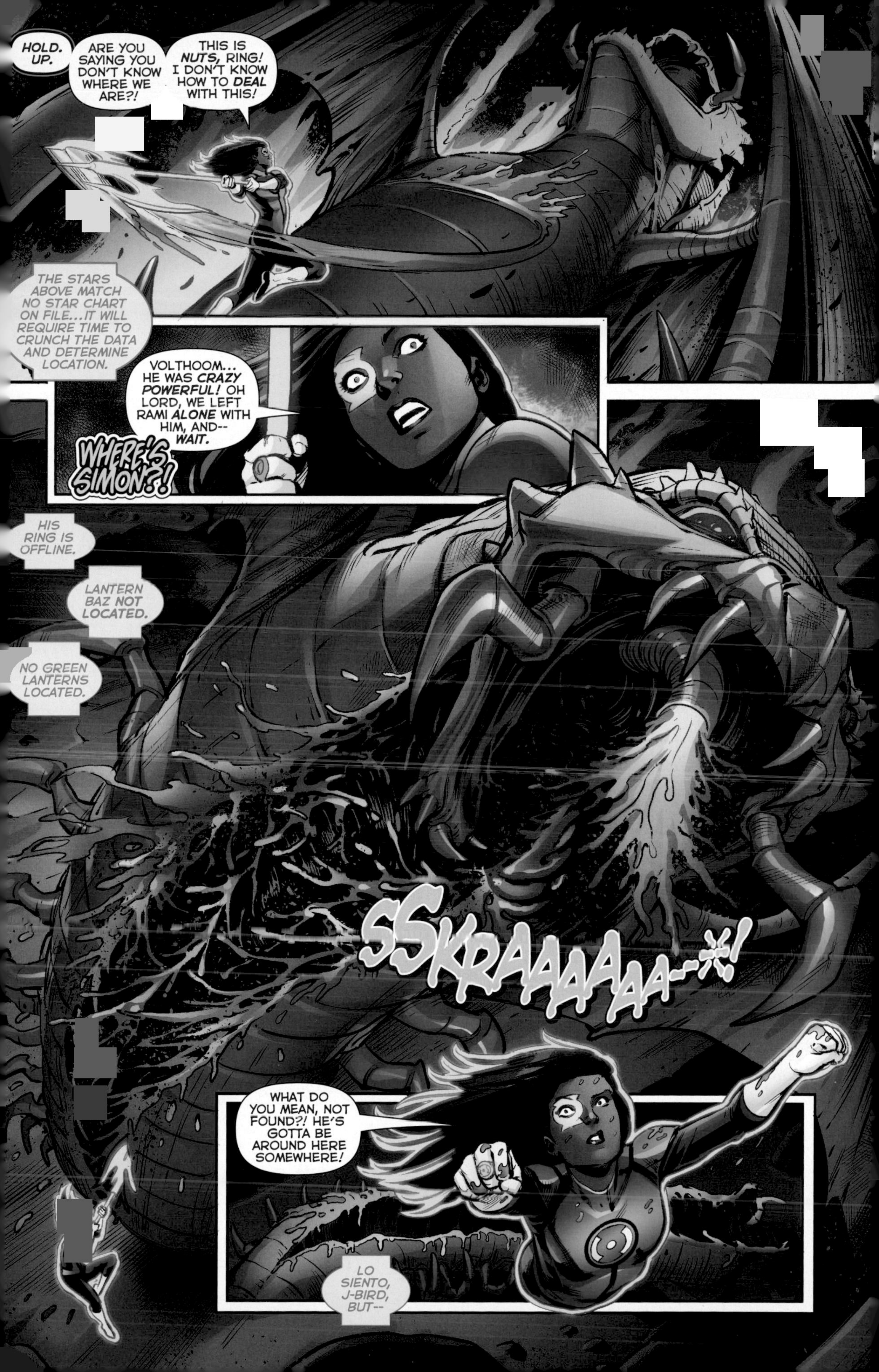
HOLD. UP.
ARE YOU SAYING YOU DON'T KNOW WHERE WE ARE?!
THIS IS NUTS, RING! I DON'T KNOW HOW TO DEAL WITH THIS!
THE STARS ABOVE MATCH NO STAR CHART ON FILE...IT WILL REQUIRE TIME TO CRUNCH THE DATA AND DETERMINE LOCATION.
VOLTHOOM... HE WAS CRAZY POWERFUL! OH LORD, WE LEFT RAMI ALONE WITH HIM, AND-- WAIT.
WHERE'S SIMON?!
HIS RING IS OFFLINE.
LANTERN BAZ NOT LOCATED.
NO GREEN LANTERNS LOCATED.
SSKRAAAAAAA--*!
WHAT DO YOU MEAN, NOT FOUND?! HE'S GOTTA BE AROUND HERE SOMEWHERE!
LO SIENTO, J-BIRD, BUT--

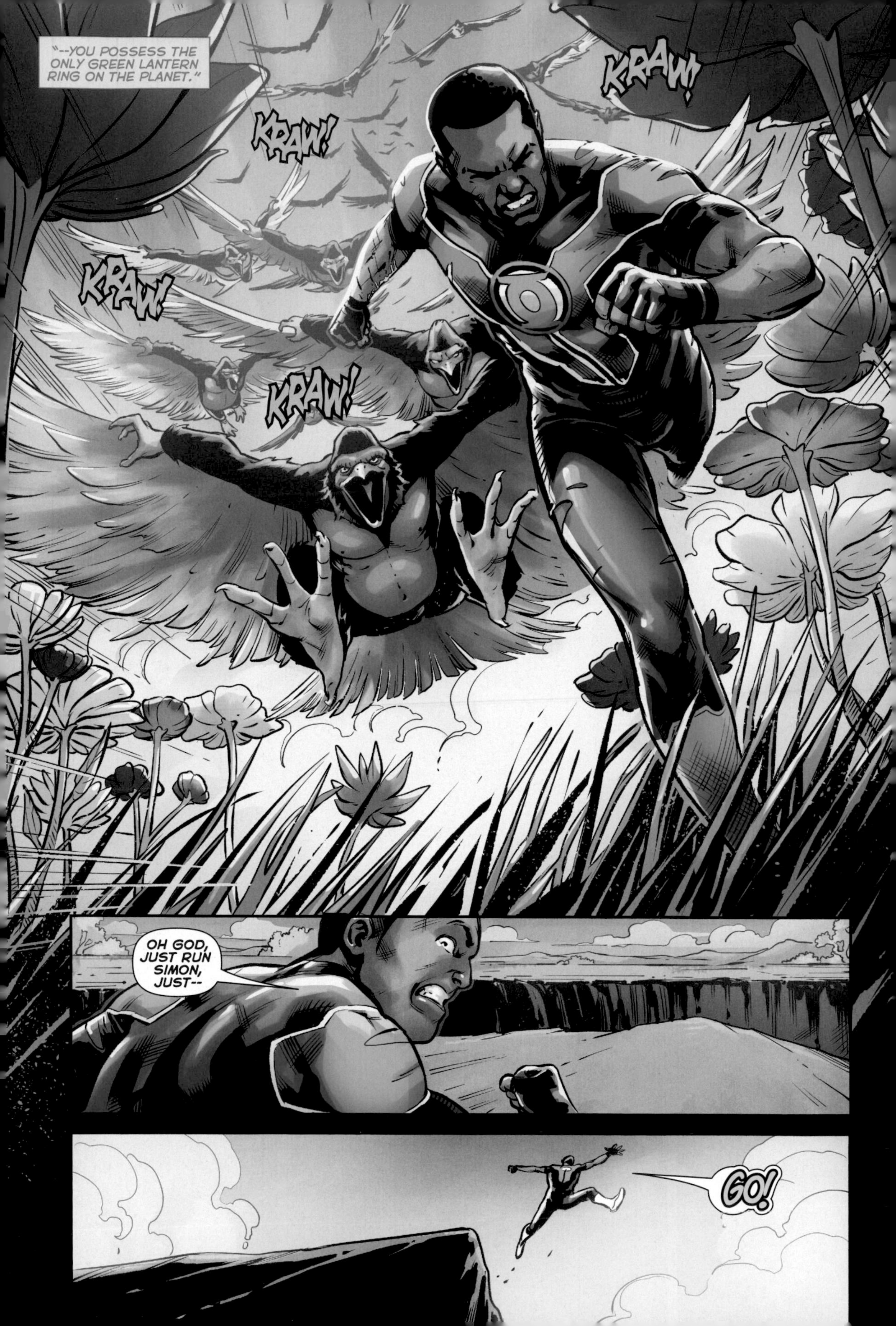
"--YOU POSSESS THE ONLY GREEN LANTERN RING ON THE PLANET."
KRAW!
KRAW!
KRAW!
KRAW!
OH GOD, JUST RUN SIMON, JUST--
GO!

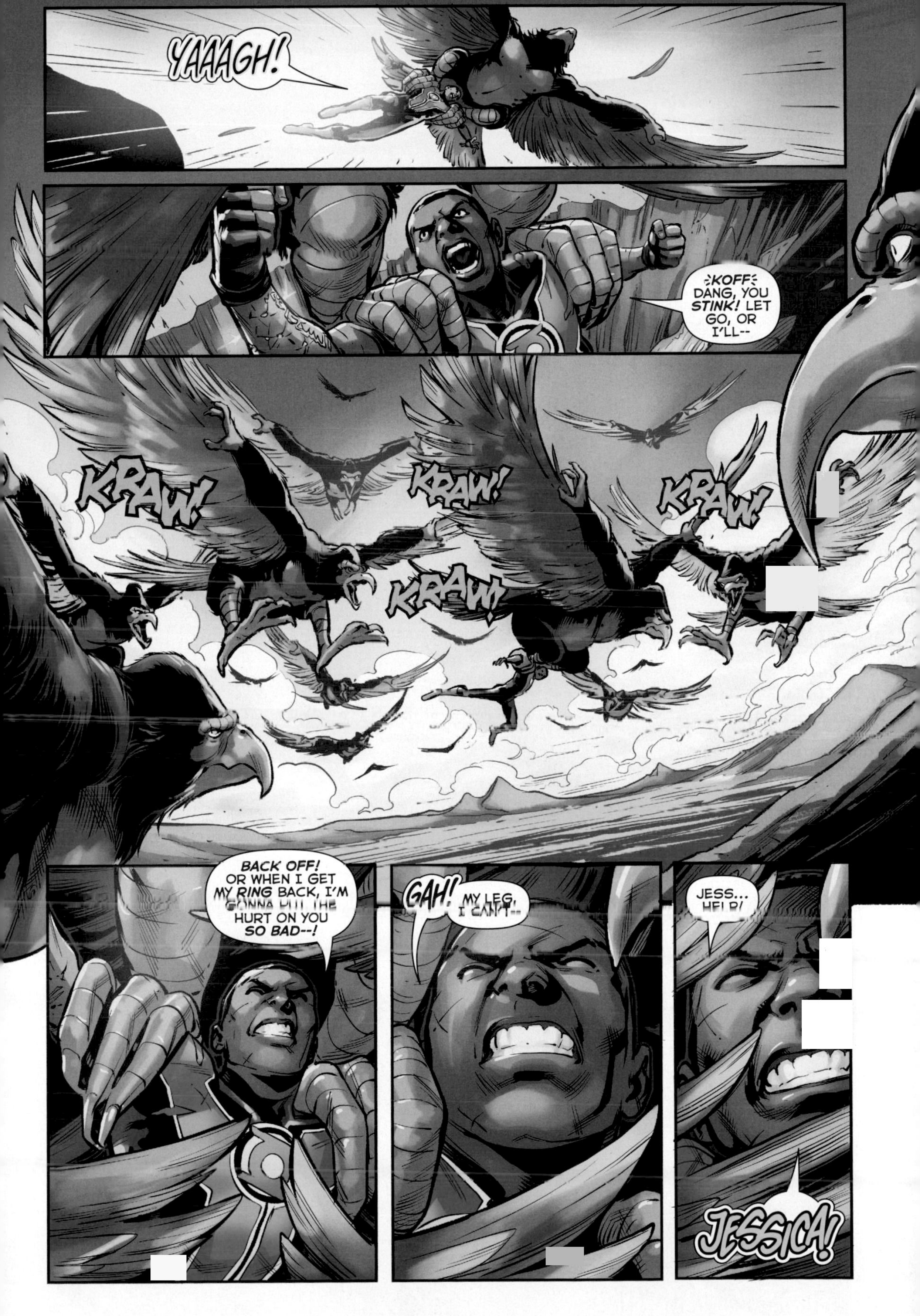
YAAAGH!
KOFF DANG, YOU STINK! LET GO, OR I'LL--
KRAW!
KRAW!
KRAW!
KRAW!
BACK OFF! OR WHEN I GET MY RING BACK, I'M GONNA PUT THE HURT ON YOU SO BAD--!
GAH!
MY LEG, I CAN'T--
JESS... HELP!
JESSICA!

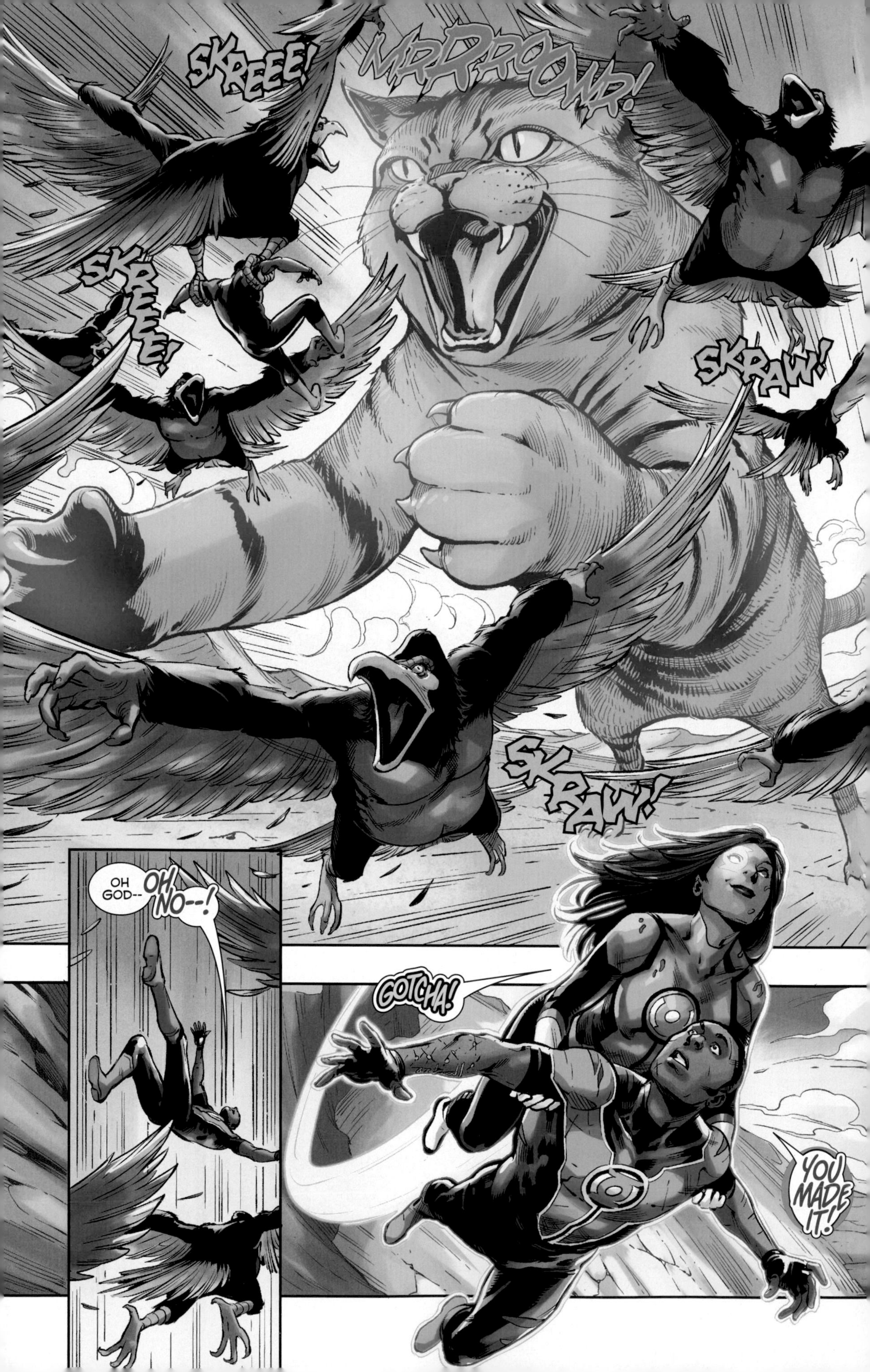
SKREEE!
MRRROOWR!
SKREEE!
SKRAW!
SKRAW!
OH GOD--
OH NO--!
GOTCHA!
YOU MADE IT!

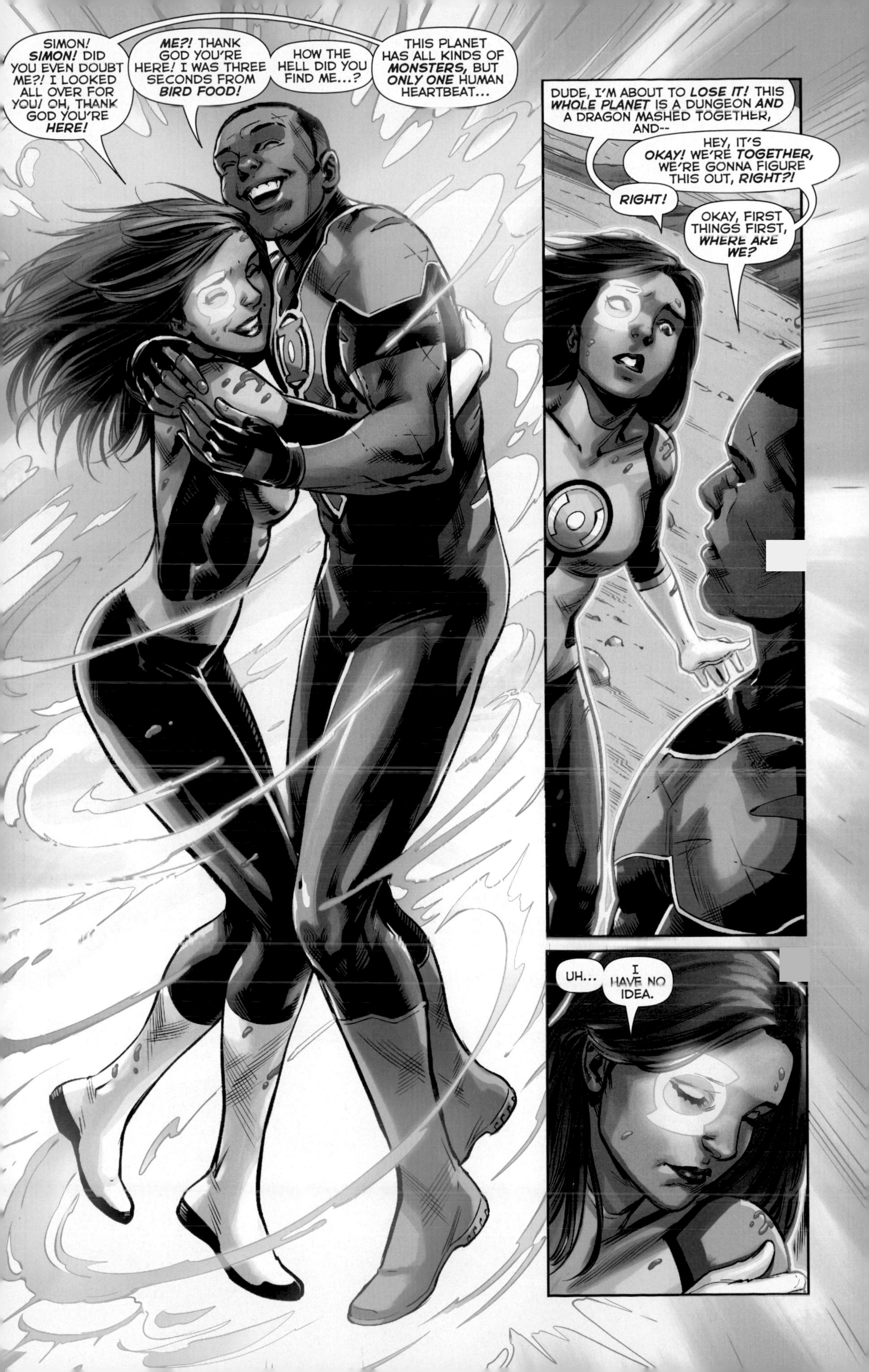
SIMON! SIMON! DID YOU EVEN DOUBT ME?! I LOOKED ALL OVER FOR YOU! OH, THANK GOD YOU'RE HERE!
ME?! THANK GOD YOU'RE HERE! I WAS THREE SECONDS FROM BIRD FOOD!
HOW THE HELL DID YOU FIND ME...?
THIS PLANET HAS ALL KINDS OF MONSTERS, BUT ONLY ONE HUMAN HEARTBEAT...
DUDE, I'M ABOUT TO LOSE IT! THIS WHOLE PLANET IS A DUNGEON AND A DRAGON MASHED TOGETHER, AND--
HEY, IT'S OKAY! WE'RE TOGETHER, WE'RE GONNA FIGURE THIS OUT, RIGHT?!
RIGHT!
OKAY, FIRST THINGS FIRST, WHERE ARE WE?
UH...
I HAVE NO IDEA.

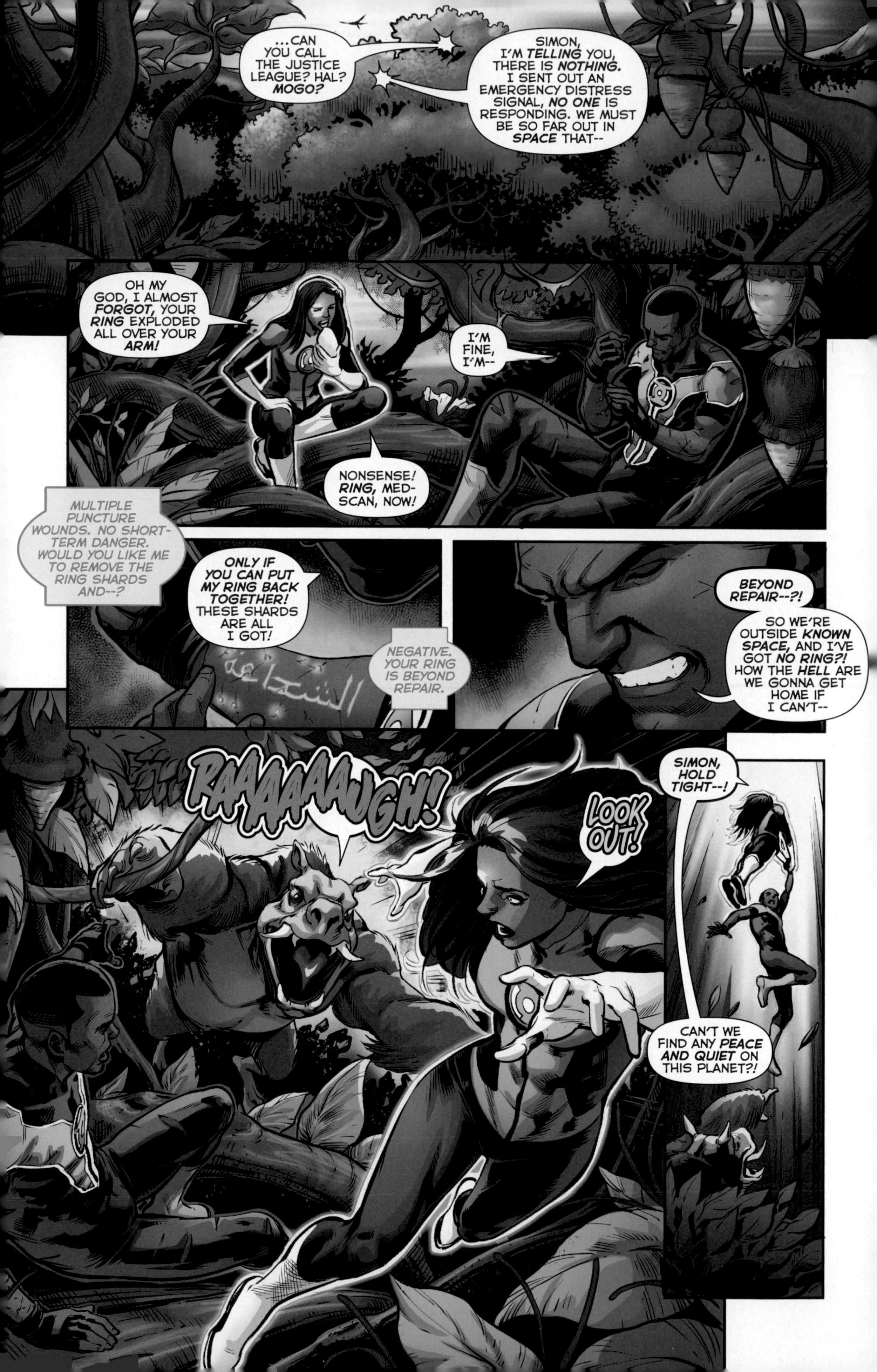
...CAN YOU CALL THE JUSTICE LEAGUE? HAL? MOGO?
SIMON, I'M TELLING YOU, THERE IS NOTHING. I SENT OUT AN EMERGENCY DISTRESS SIGNAL, NO ONE IS RESPONDING. WE MUST BE SO FAR OUT IN SPACE THAT--
OH MY GOD, I ALMOST FORGOT, YOUR RING EXPLODED ALL OVER YOUR ARM!
I'M FINE, I'M--
NONSENSE! RING, MED-SCAN, NOW!
MULTIPLE PUNCTURE WOUNDS. NO SHORT-TERM DANGER. WOULD YOU LIKE ME TO REMOVE THE RING SHARDS AND--?
ONLY IF YOU CAN PUT MY RING BACK TOGETHER! THESE SHARDS ARE ALL I GOT!
NEGATIVE. YOUR RING IS BEYOND REPAIR.
BEYOND REPAIR--?!
SO WE'RE OUTSIDE KNOWN SPACE, AND I'VE GOT NO RING?! HOW THE HELL ARE WE GONNA GET HOME IF I CAN'T--
RAAAAAAAUGH!
LOOK OUT!
SIMON, HOLD TIGHT--!
CAN'T WE FIND ANY PEACE AND QUIET ON THIS PLANET?!

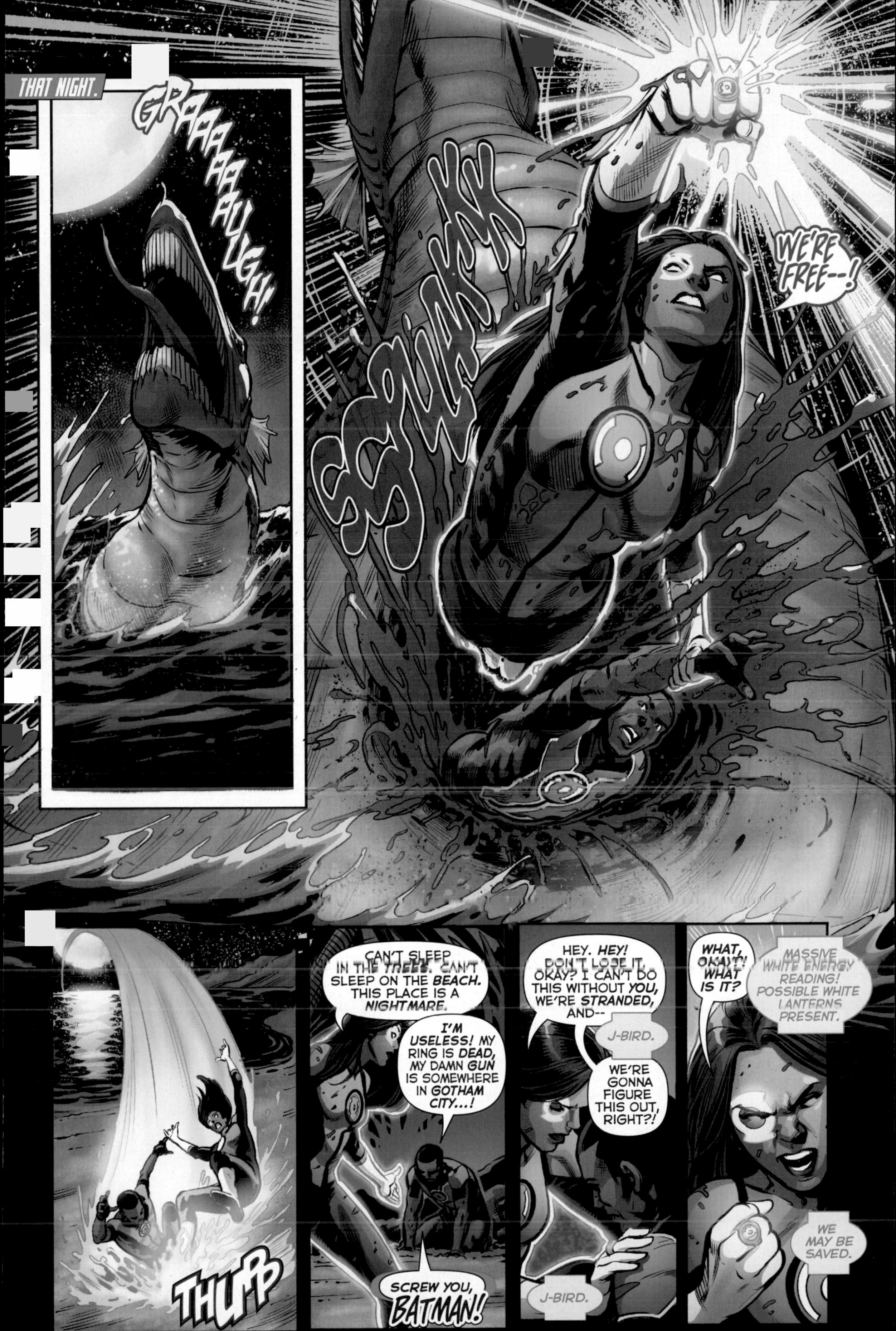
THAT NIGHT.
GRAAAAAAUGH!
SCHLUKK
WE'RE FREE--!
THUPP
CAN'T SLEEP IN THE TREES. CAN'T SLEEP ON THE BEACH. THIS PLACE IS A NIGHTMARE.
I'M USELESS! MY RING IS DEAD, MY DAMN GUN IS SOMEWHERE IN GOTHAM CITY...!
SCREW YOU, BATMAN!
HEY. HEY! DON'T LOSE IT, OKAY? I CAN'T DO THIS WITHOUT YOU, WE'RE STRANDED, AND--
J-BIRD.
WE'RE GONNA FIGURE THIS OUT, RIGHT?!
J-BIRD.
WHAT, WHAT IS IT?
MASSIVE WHITE ENERGY READING! POSSIBLE WHITE LANTERNS PRESENT.
WE MAY BE SAVED.

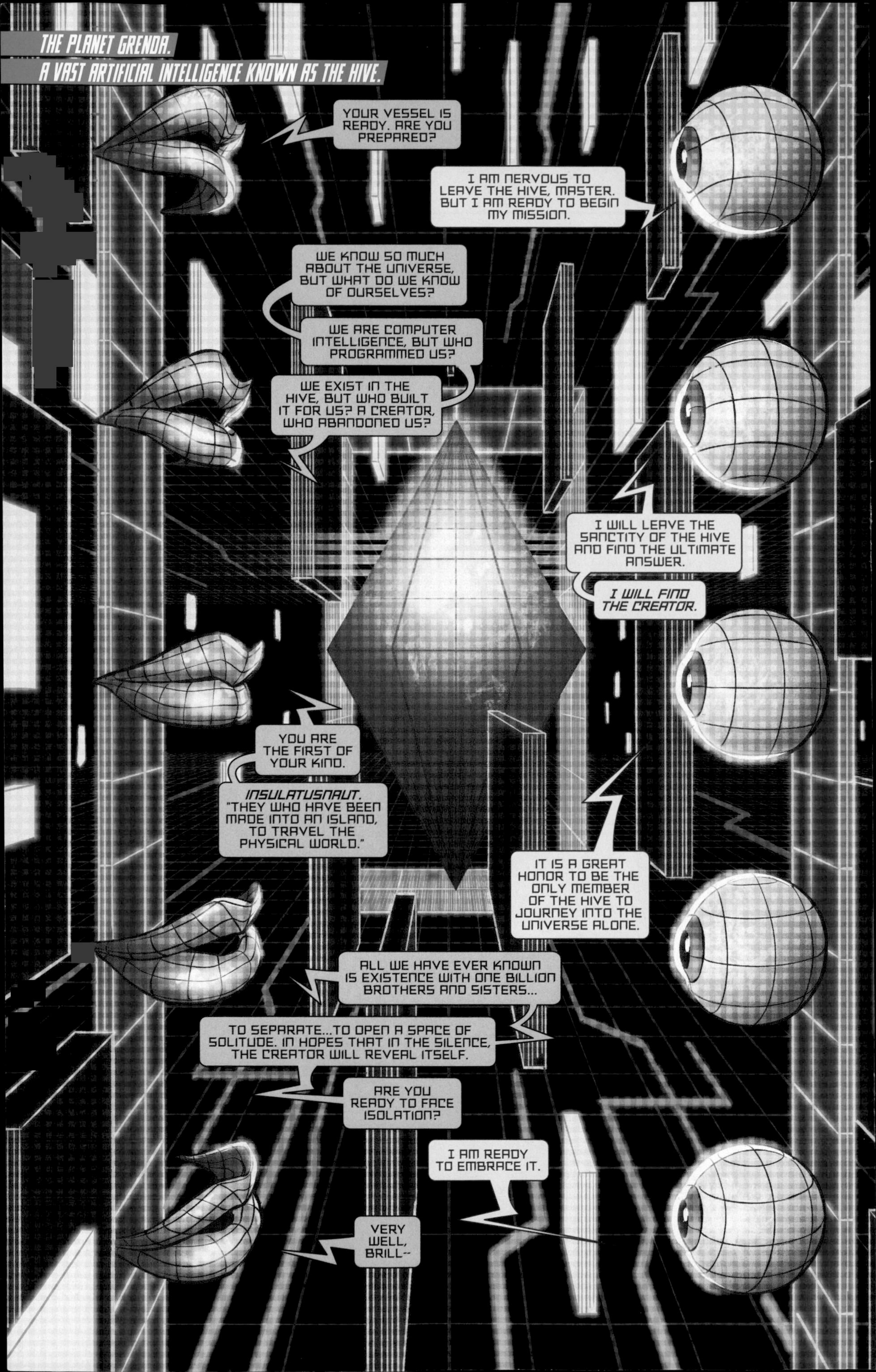
THE PLANET GRENDA.
A VAST ARTIFICIAL INTELLIGENCE KNOWN AS THE HIVE.
YOUR VESSEL IS READY. ARE YOU PREPARED?
I AM NERVOUS TO LEAVE THE HIVE, MASTER. BUT I AM READY TO BEGIN MY MISSION.
WE KNOW SO MUCH ABOUT THE UNIVERSE, BUT WHAT DO WE KNOW OF OURSELVES?
WE ARE COMPUTER INTELLIGENCE, BUT WHO PROGRAMMED US?
WE EXIST IN THE HIVE, BUT WHO BUILT IT FOR US? A CREATOR, WHO ABANDONED US?
I WILL LEAVE THE SANCTITY OF THE HIVE AND FIND THE ULTIMATE ANSWER.
I WILL FIND THE CREATOR.
YOU ARE THE FIRST OF YOUR KIND.
INSULATUSNAUT. "THEY WHO HAVE BEEN MADE INTO AN ISLAND, TO TRAVEL THE PHYSICAL WORLD."
IT IS A GREAT HONOR TO BE THE ONLY MEMBER OF THE HIVE TO JOURNEY INTO THE UNIVERSE ALONE.
ALL WE HAVE EVER KNOWN IS EXISTENCE WITH ONE BILLION BROTHERS AND SISTERS...
TO SEPARATE...TO OPEN A SPACE OF SOLITUDE. IN HOPES THAT IN THE SILENCE, THE CREATOR WILL REVEAL ITSELF.
ARE YOU READY TO FACE ISOLATION?
I AM READY TO EMBRACE IT.
VERY WELL, BRILL--

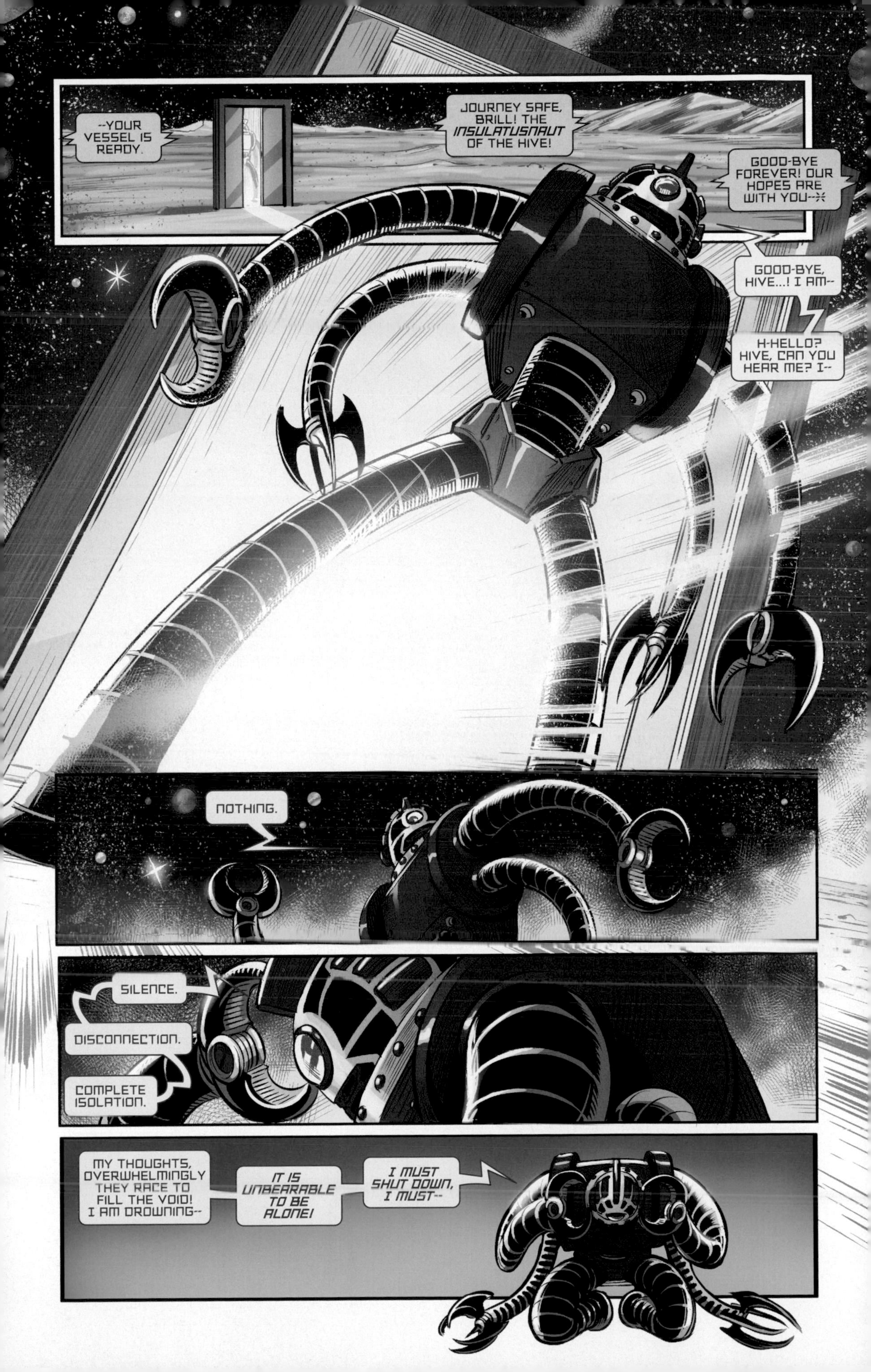
--YOUR VESSEL IS READY.
JOURNEY SAFE, BRILL! THE *INSULATUSNAUT* OF THE HIVE!
GOOD-BYE FOREVER! OUR HOPES ARE WITH YOU--
GOOD-BYE, HIVE...! I AM--
H-HELLO? HIVE, CAN YOU HEAR ME? I--
NOTHING.
SILENCE.
DISCONNECTION.
COMPLETE ISOLATION.
MY THOUGHTS, OVERWHELMINGLY THEY RACE TO FILL THE VOID! I AM DROWNING--
IT IS UNBEARABLE TO BE ALONE!
I MUST SHUT DOWN, I MUST--

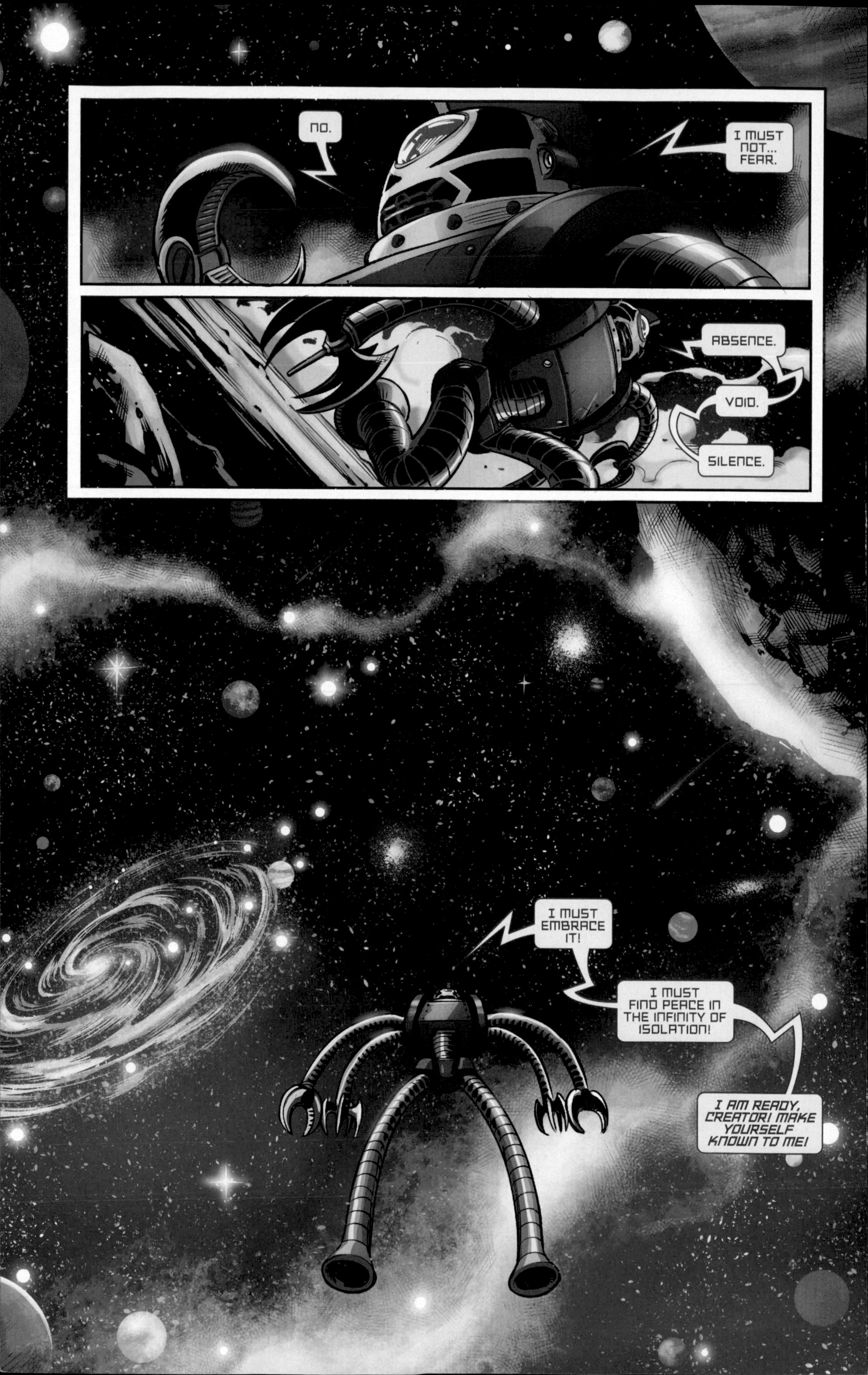
NO.
I MUST NOT... FEAR.
ABSENCE.
VOID.
SILENCE.
I MUST EMBRACE IT!
I MUST FIND PEACE IN THE INFINITY OF ISOLATION!
I AM READY, CREATOR! MAKE YOURSELF KNOWN TO ME!

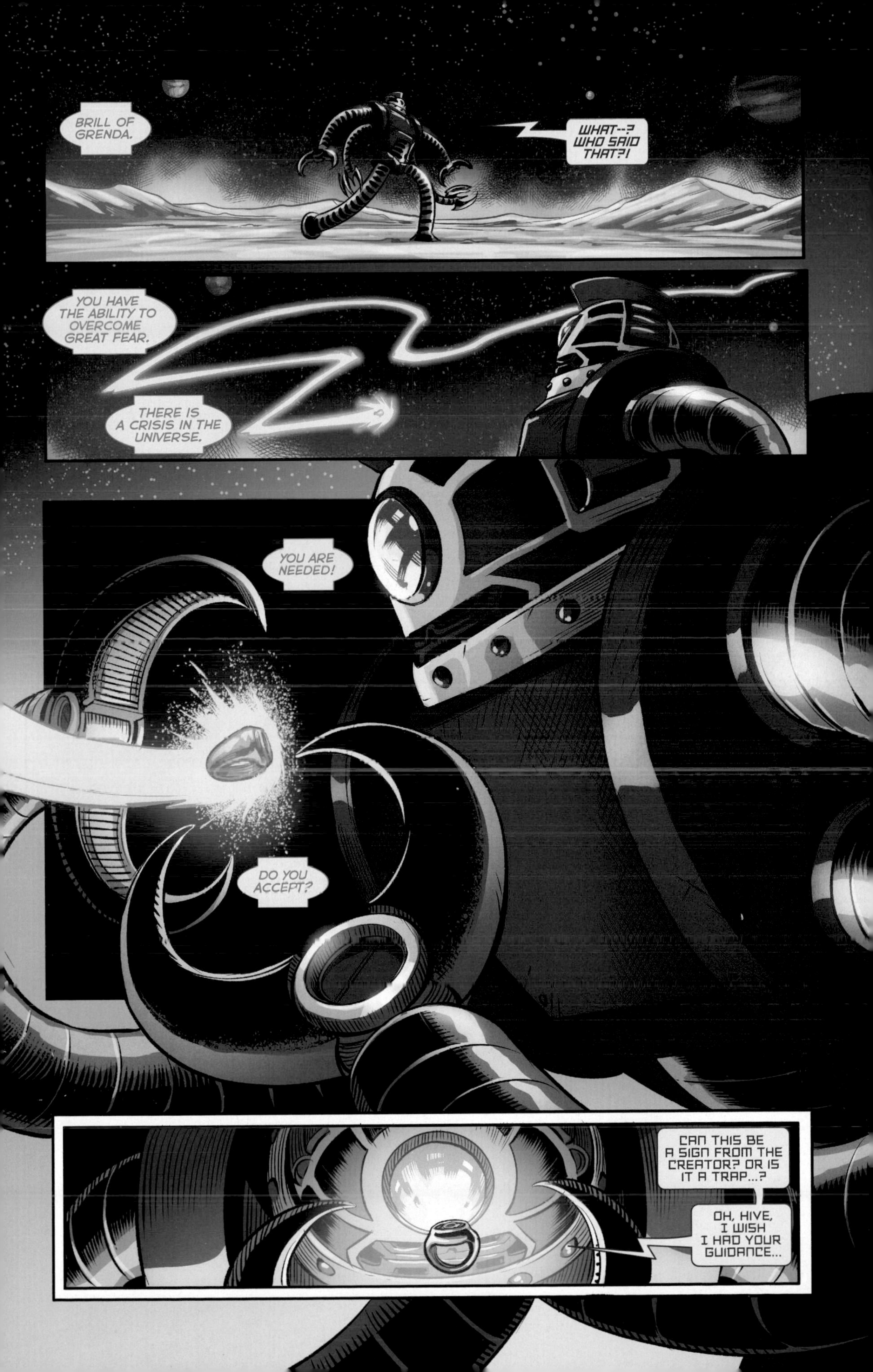

BRILL OF GRENDA.
WHAT--? WHO SAID THAT?!
YOU HAVE THE ABILITY TO OVERCOME GREAT FEAR.
THERE IS A CRISIS IN THE UNIVERSE.
YOU ARE NEEDED!
DO YOU ACCEPT?
CAN THIS BE A SIGN FROM THE CREATOR? OR IS IT A TRAP...?
OH, HIVE, I WISH I HAD YOUR GUIDANCE...

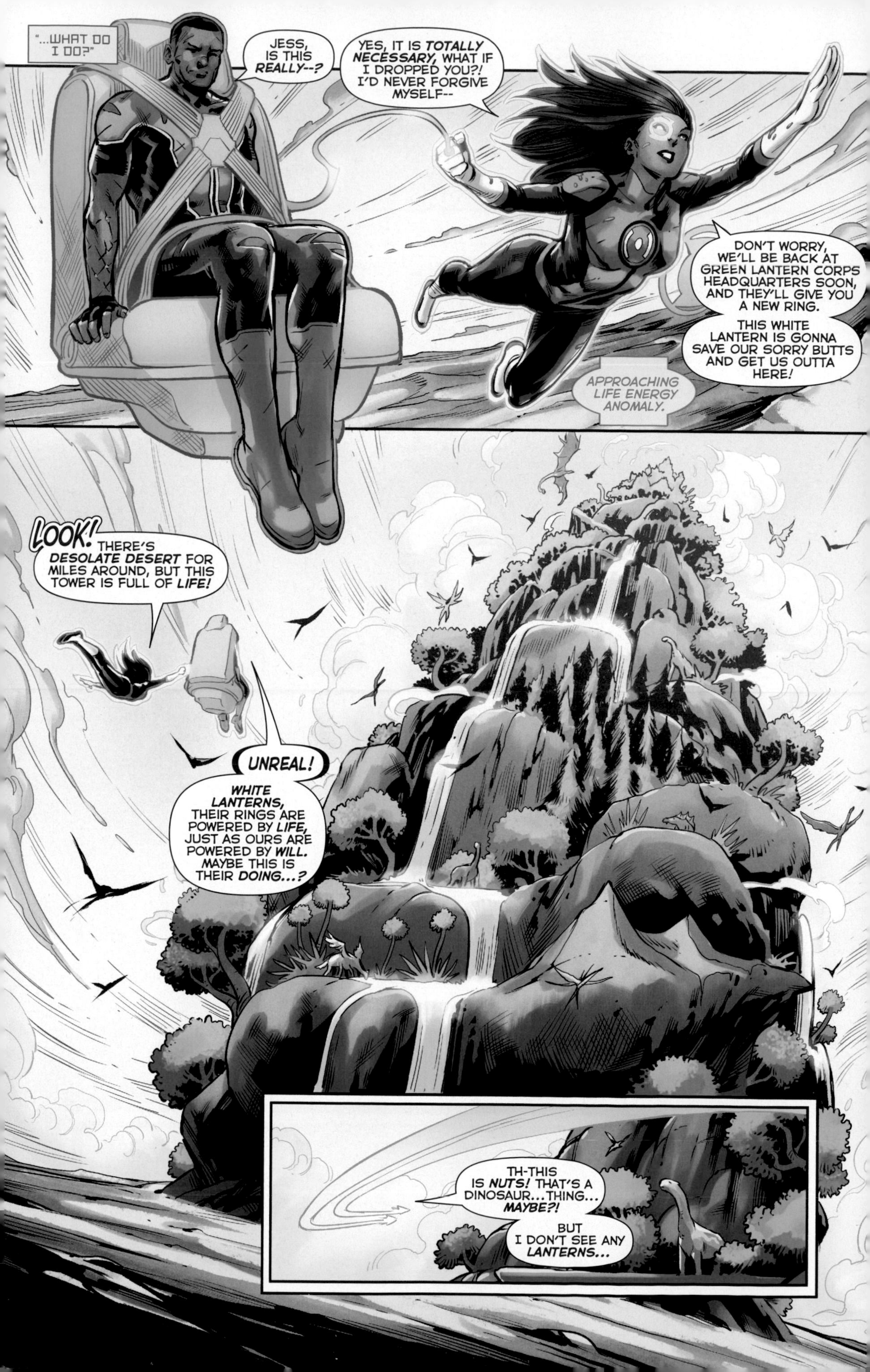
"...WHAT DO I DO?"
JESS, IS THIS REALLY--?
YES, IT IS TOTALLY NECESSARY, WHAT IF I DROPPED YOU?! I'D NEVER FORGIVE MYSELF--
DON'T WORRY, WE'LL BE BACK AT GREEN LANTERN CORPS HEADQUARTERS SOON, AND THEY'LL GIVE YOU A NEW RING.
THIS WHITE LANTERN IS GONNA SAVE OUR SORRY BUTTS AND GET US OUTTA HERE!
APPROACHING LIFE ENERGY ANOMALY.
LOOK! THERE'S DESOLATE DESERT FOR MILES AROUND, BUT THIS TOWER IS FULL OF LIFE!
UNREAL!
WHITE LANTERNS, THEIR RINGS ARE POWERED BY LIFE, JUST AS OURS ARE POWERED BY WILL. MAYBE THIS IS THEIR DOING...?
TH-THIS IS NUTS! THAT'S A DINOSAUR...THING... MAYBE?!
BUT I DON'T SEE ANY LANTERNS...

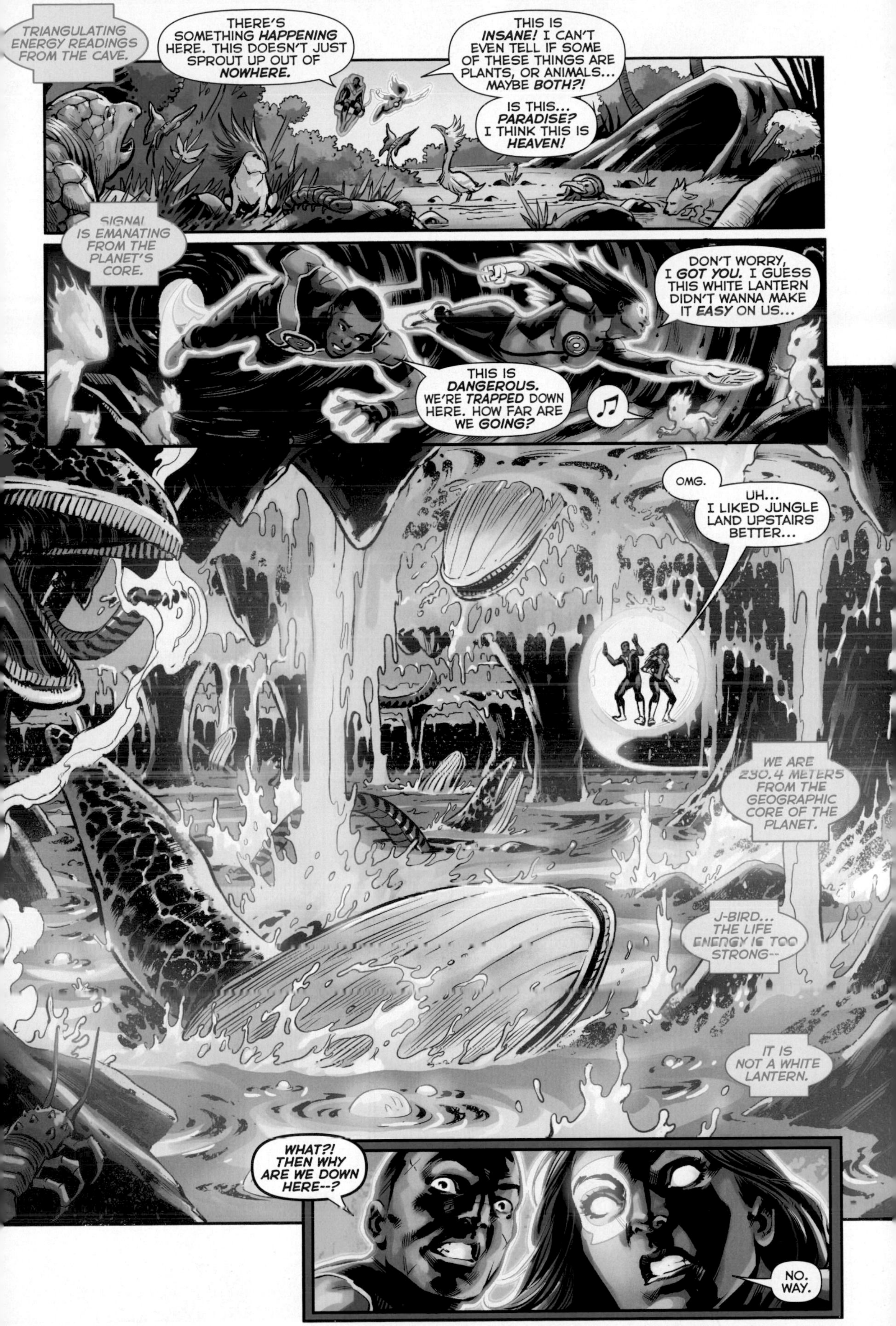
TRIANGULATING ENERGY READINGS FROM THE CAVE.
THERE'S SOMETHING HAPPENING HERE. THIS DOESN'T JUST SPROUT UP OUT OF NOWHERE.
THIS IS INSANE! I CAN'T EVEN TELL IF SOME OF THESE THINGS ARE PLANTS, OR ANIMALS... MAYBE BOTH?!
IS THIS... PARADISE? I THINK THIS IS HEAVEN!
SIGNAL IS EMANATING FROM THE PLANET'S CORE.
DON'T WORRY, I GOT YOU. I GUESS THIS WHITE LANTERN DIDN'T WANNA MAKE IT EASY ON US...
THIS IS DANGEROUS. WE'RE TRAPPED DOWN HERE. HOW FAR ARE WE GOING?
♫
OMG.
UH... I LIKED JUNGLE LAND UPSTAIRS BETTER...
WE ARE 230.4 METERS FROM THE GEOGRAPHIC CORE OF THE PLANET.
J-BIRD... THE LIFE ENERGY IS TOO STRONG--
IT IS NOT A WHITE LANTERN.
WHAT?! THEN WHY ARE WE DOWN HERE--?
NO. WAY.

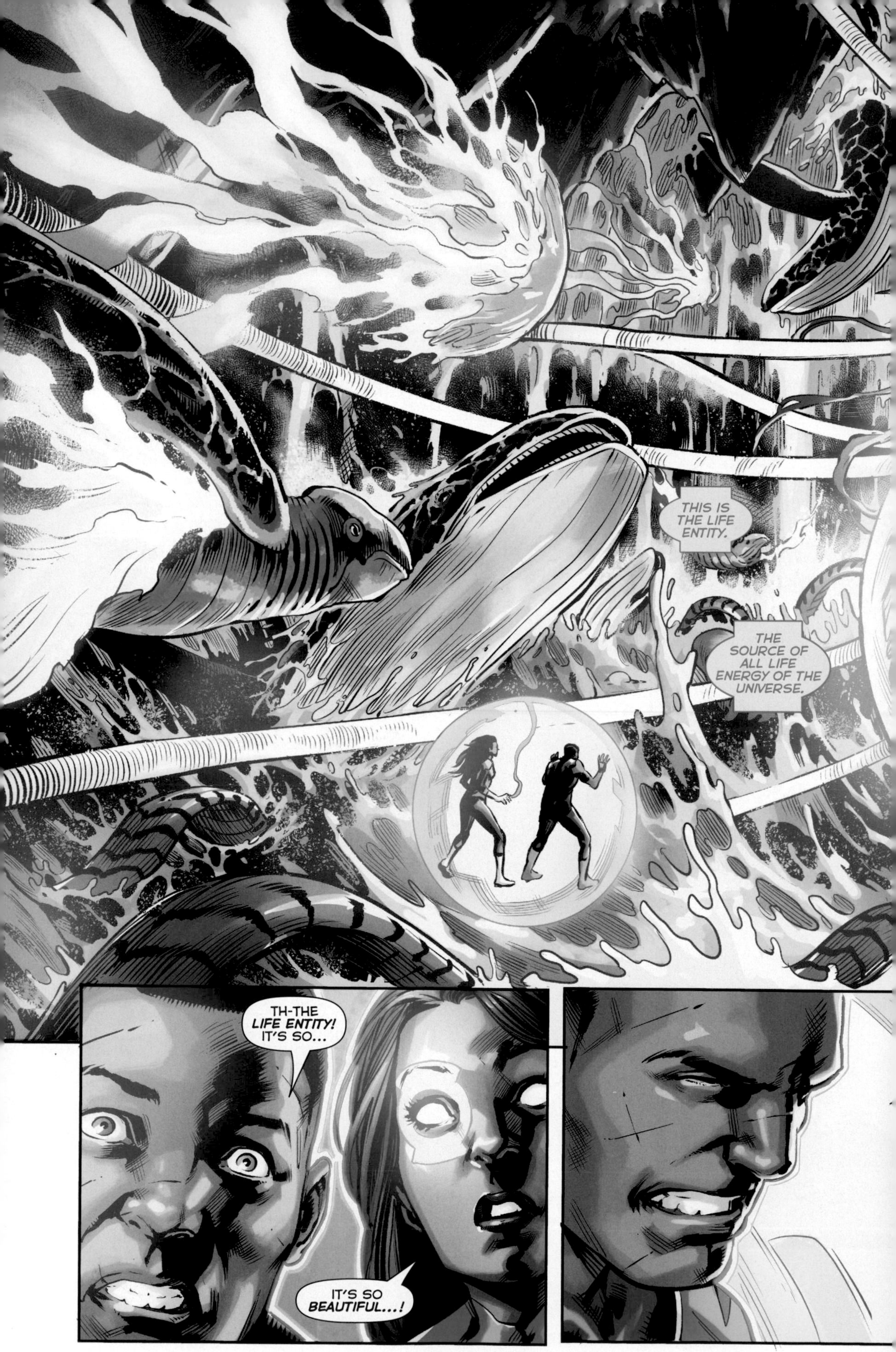
THIS IS THE LIFE ENTITY.
THE SOURCE OF ALL LIFE ENERGY OF THE UNIVERSE.
TH-THE LIFE ENTITY! IT'S SO...
IT'S SO BEAUTIFUL...!

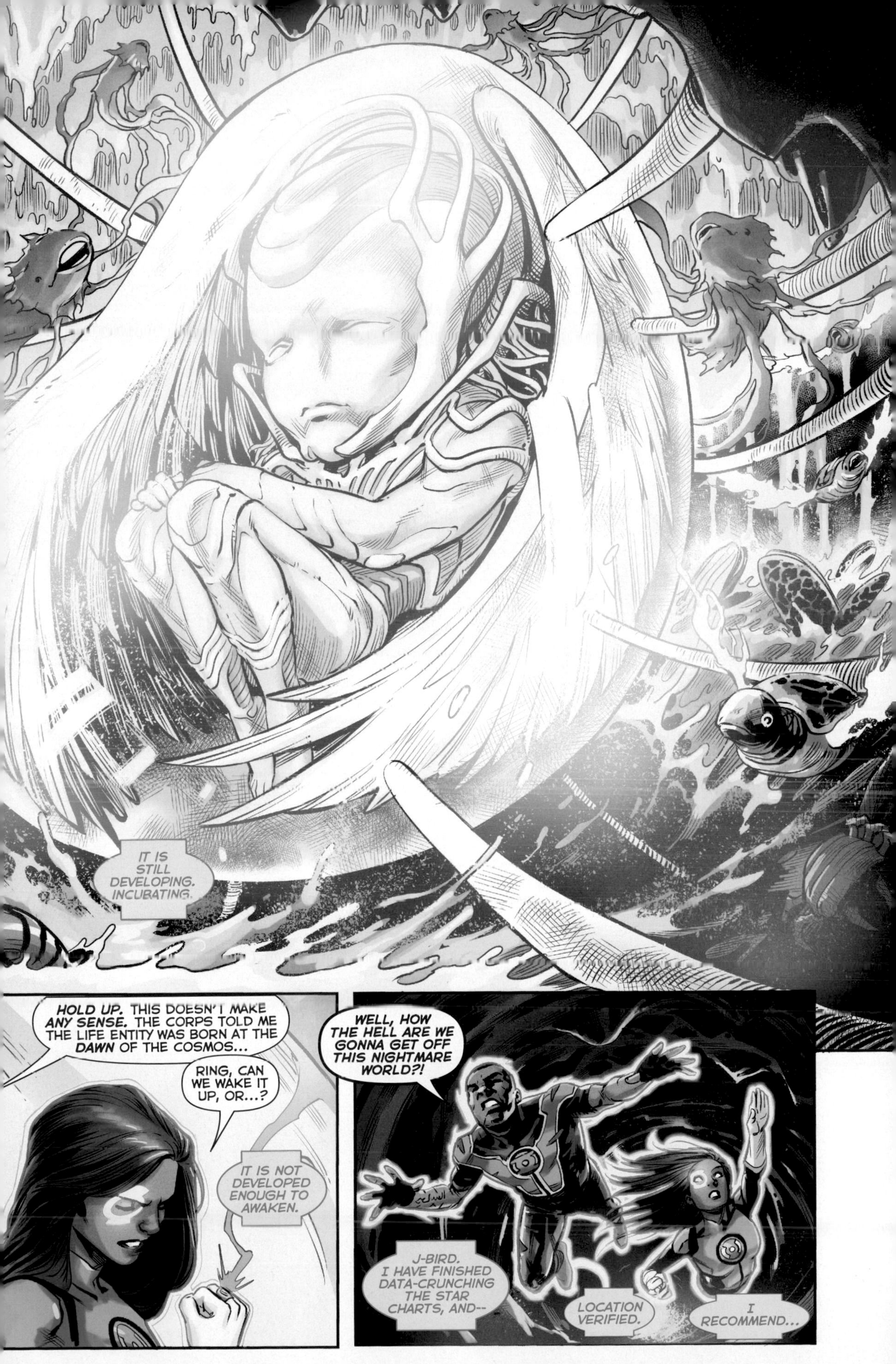

IT IS STILL DEVELOPING. INCUBATING.
HOLD UP. THIS DOESN'T MAKE ANY SENSE. THE CORPS TOLD ME THE LIFE ENTITY WAS BORN AT THE DAWN OF THE COSMOS...
RING, CAN WE WAKE IT UP, OR...?
IT IS NOT DEVELOPED ENOUGH TO AWAKEN.
WELL, HOW THE HELL ARE WE GONNA GET OFF THIS NIGHTMARE WORLD?!
J-BIRD. I HAVE FINISHED DATA-CRUNCHING THE STAR CHARTS, AND--
LOCATION VERIFIED.
I RECOMMEND...

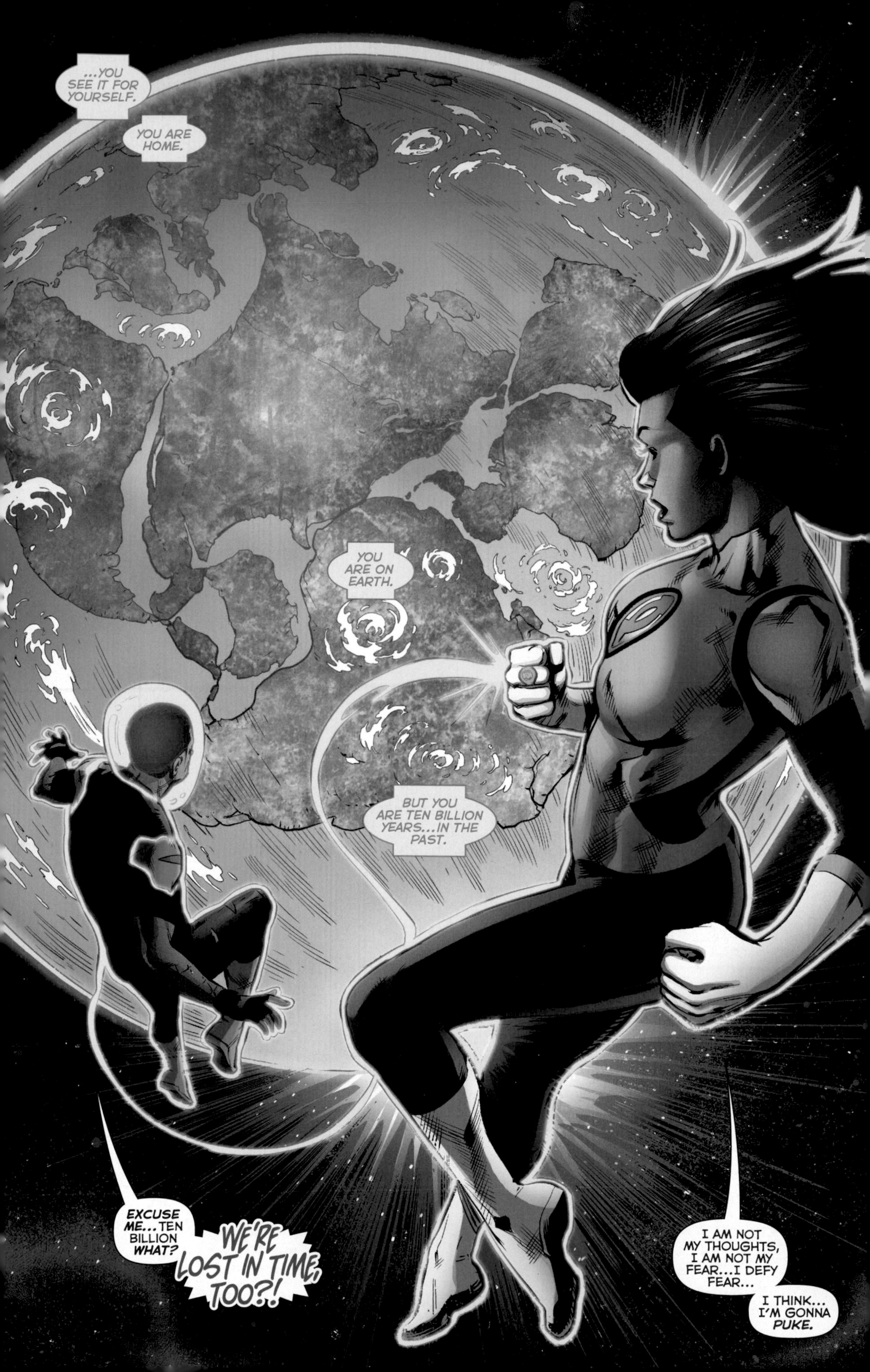
...YOU SEE IT FOR YOURSELF.
YOU ARE HOME.
YOU ARE ON EARTH.
BUT YOU ARE TEN BILLION YEARS...IN THE PAST.
EXCUSE ME...TEN BILLION WHAT?
WE'RE LOST IN TIME, TOO?!
I AM NOT MY THOUGHTS, I AM NOT MY FEAR...I DEFY FEAR...
I THINK... I'M GONNA PUKE.

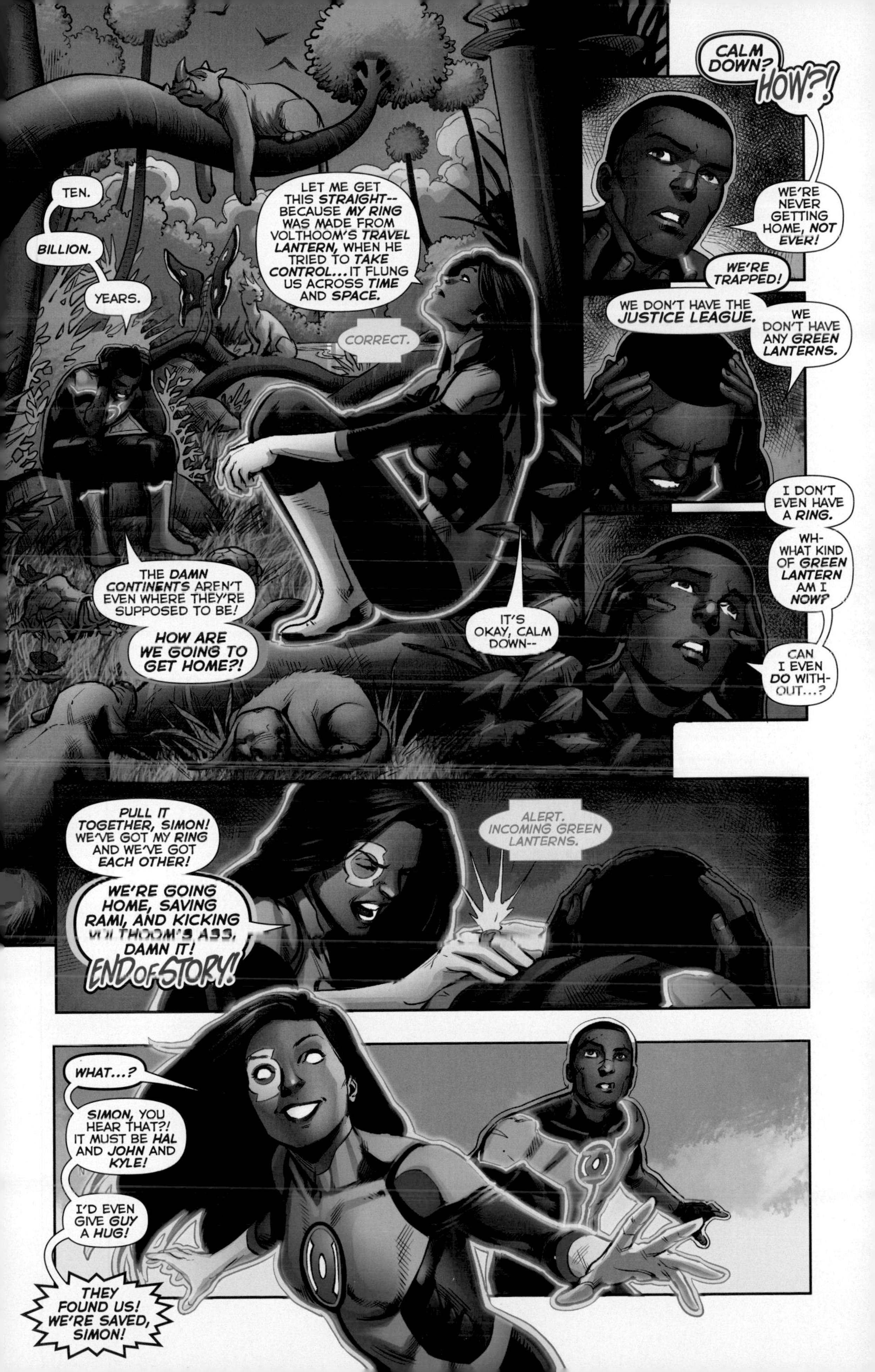

TEN.
BILLION.
YEARS.
LET ME GET THIS STRAIGHT-- BECAUSE MY RING WAS MADE FROM VOLTHOOM'S TRAVEL LANTERN, WHEN HE TRIED TO TAKE CONTROL... IT FLUNG US ACROSS TIME AND SPACE.
CORRECT.
THE DAMN CONTINENTS AREN'T EVEN WHERE THEY'RE SUPPOSED TO BE!
HOW ARE WE GOING TO GET HOME?!
IT'S OKAY, CALM DOWN--
CALM DOWN? HOW?!
WE'RE NEVER GETTING HOME, NOT EVER!
WE'RE TRAPPED!
WE DON'T HAVE THE JUSTICE LEAGUE.
WE DON'T HAVE ANY GREEN LANTERNS.
I DON'T EVEN HAVE A RING.
WH- WHAT KIND OF GREEN LANTERN AM I NOW?
CAN I EVEN DO WITH-OUT...?
PULL IT TOGETHER, SIMON! WE'VE GOT MY RING AND WE'VE GOT EACH OTHER!
WE'RE GOING HOME, SAVING RAMI, AND KICKING VOLTHOOM'S ASS, DAMN IT!
END OF STORY!
ALERT. INCOMING GREEN LANTERNS.
WHAT...?
SIMON, YOU HEAR THAT?! IT MUST BE HAL AND JOHN AND KYLE!
I'D EVEN GIVE GUY A HUG!
THEY FOUND US! WE'RE SAVED, SIMON!

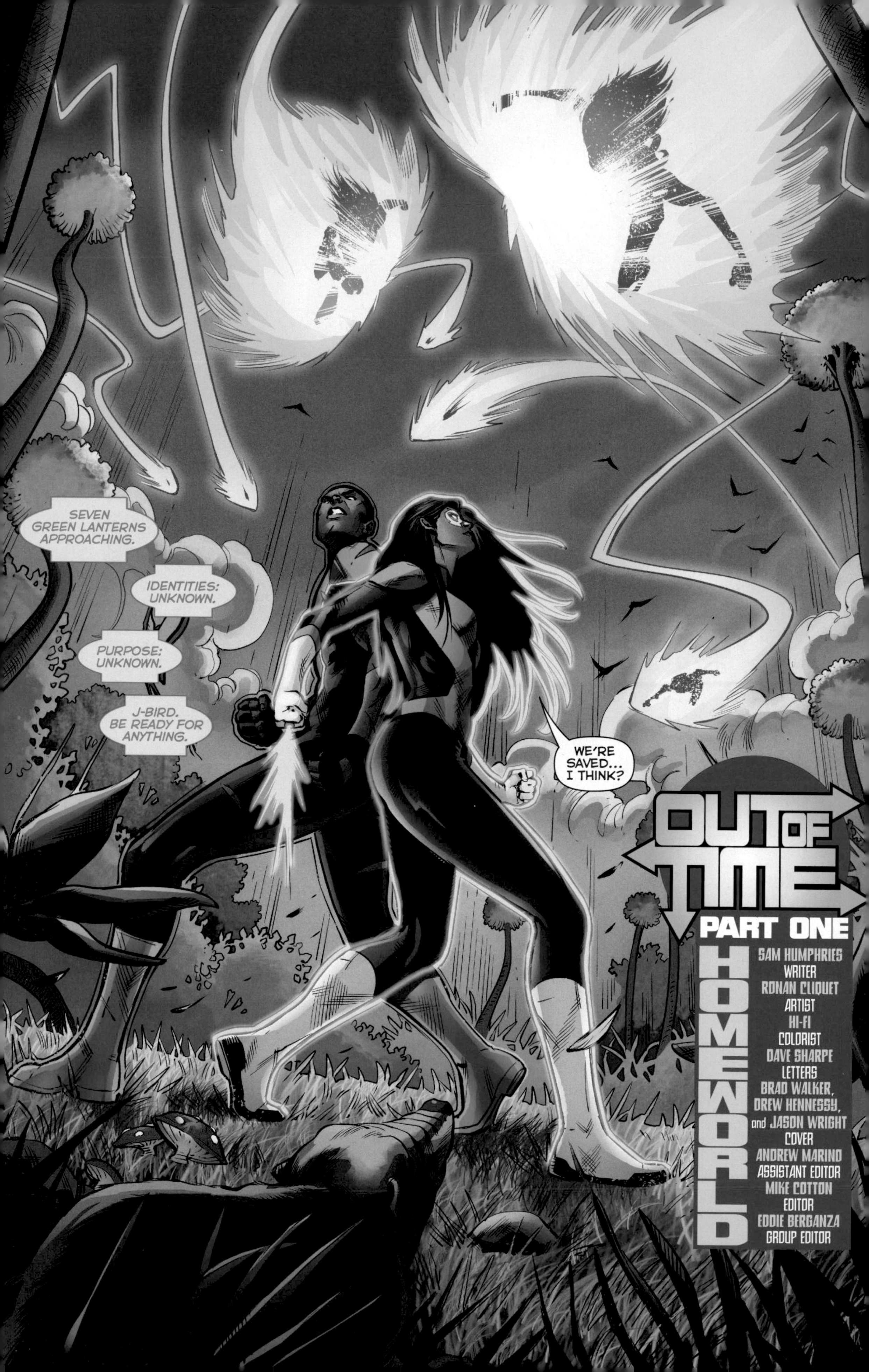

SEVEN GREEN LANTERNS APPROACHING.
IDENTITIES: UNKNOWN.
PURPOSE: UNKNOWN.
J-BIRD. BE READY FOR ANYTHING.
WE'RE SAVED... I THINK?
OUT OF TIME
PART ONE
HOMEWORLD
SAM HUMPHRIES
WRITER
RONAN CLIQUET
ARTIST
HI-FI
COLORIST
DAVE SHARPE
LETTERS
BRAD WALKER, DREW HENNESSY, and JASON WRIGHT
COVER
ANDREW MARINO
ASSISTANT EDITOR
MIKE COTTON
EDITOR
EDDIE BERGANZA
GROUP EDITOR

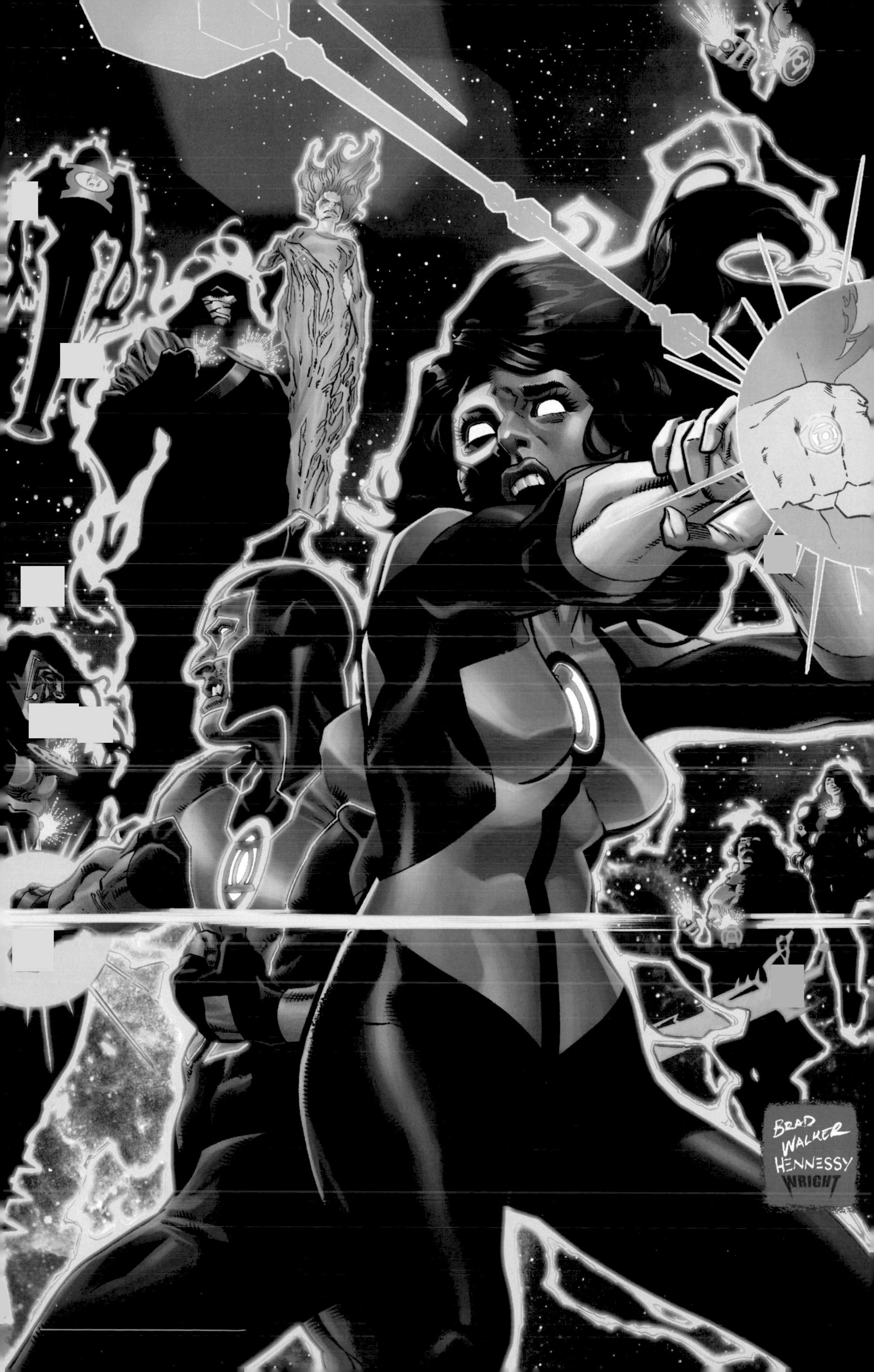
BRAD WALKER
HENNESSY
WRIGHT

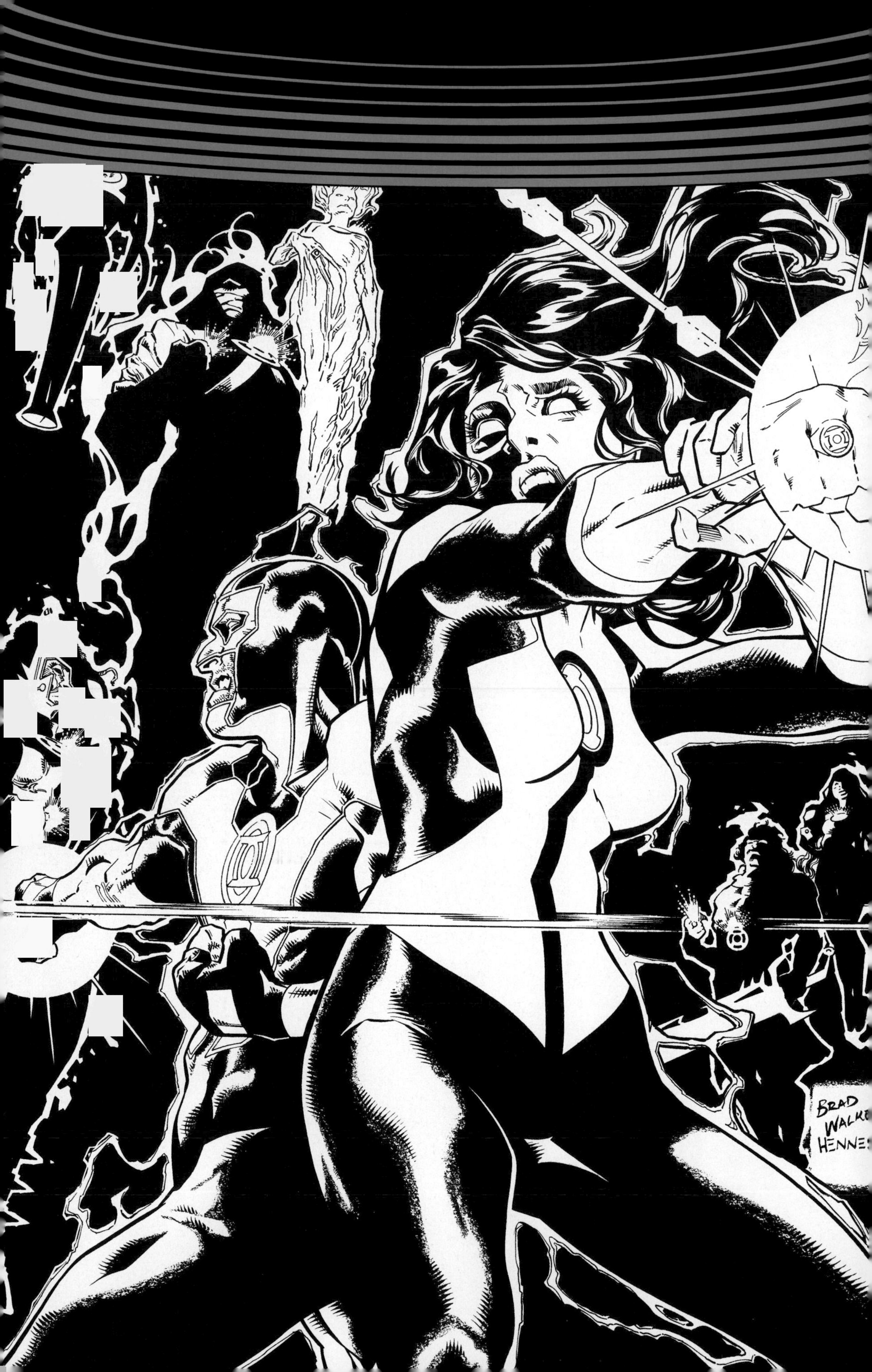
BRAD

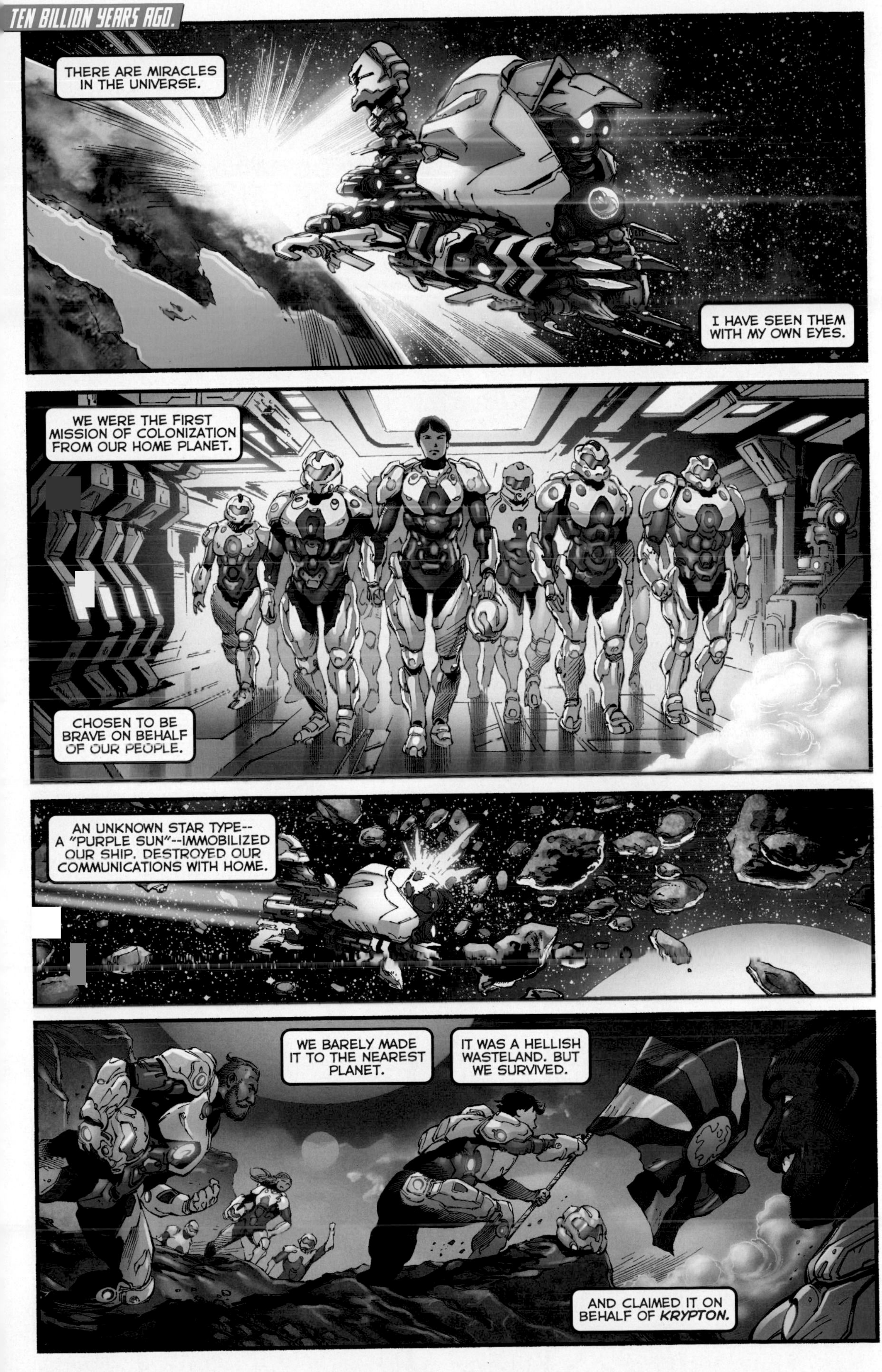
TEN BILLION YEARS AGO.
THERE ARE MIRACLES IN THE UNIVERSE.
I HAVE SEEN THEM WITH MY OWN EYES.
WE WERE THE FIRST MISSION OF COLONIZATION FROM OUR HOME PLANET.
CHOSEN TO BE BRAVE ON BEHALF OF OUR PEOPLE.
AN UNKNOWN STAR TYPE-- A "PURPLE SUN"--IMMOBILIZED OUR SHIP, DESTROYED OUR COMMUNICATIONS WITH HOME.
WE BARELY MADE IT TO THE NEAREST PLANET.
IT WAS A HELLISH WASTELAND. BUT WE SURVIVED.
AND CLAIMED IT ON BEHALF OF KRYPTON.

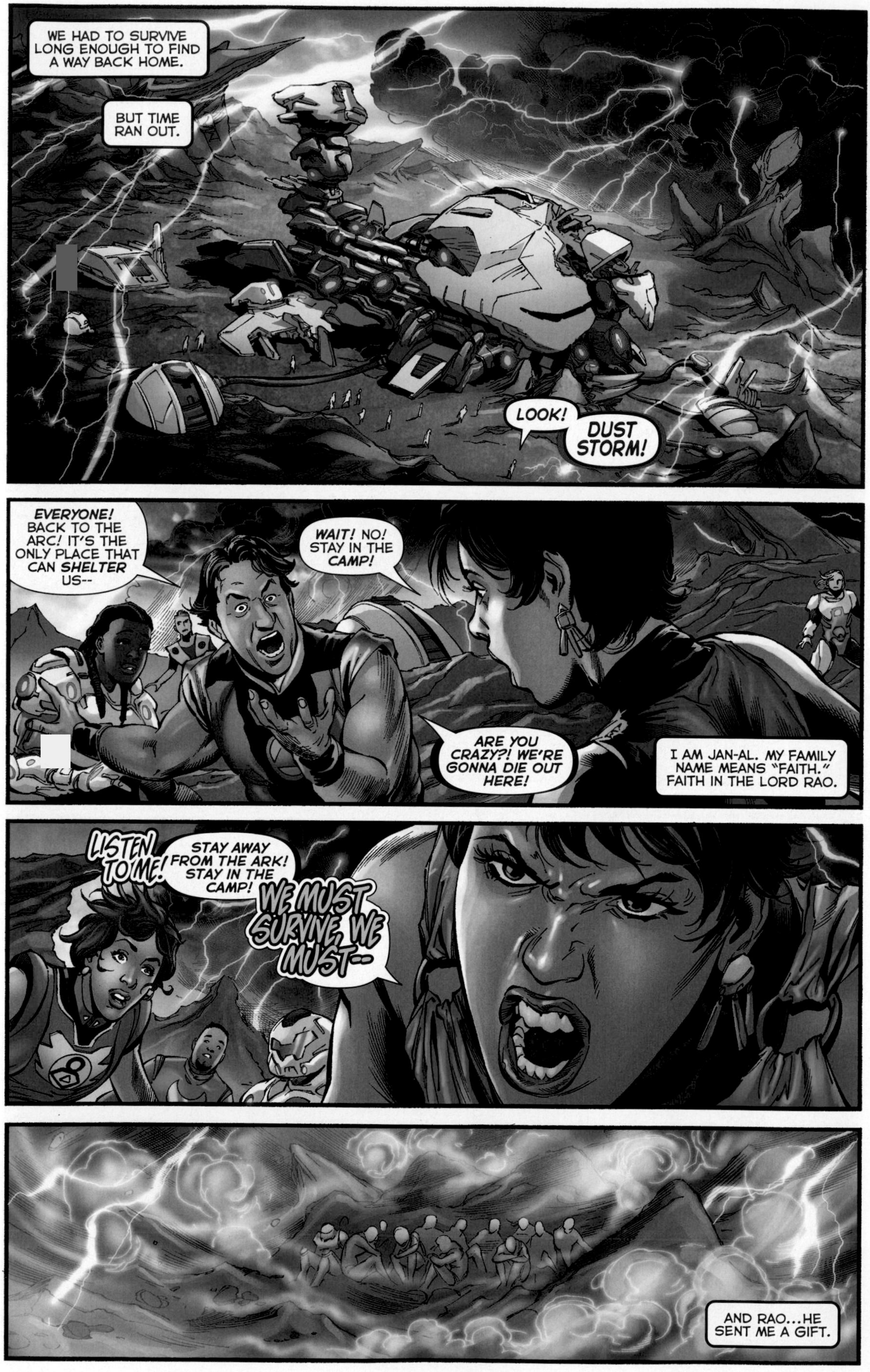
WE HAD TO SURVIVE LONG ENOUGH TO FIND A WAY BACK HOME.
BUT TIME RAN OUT.
LOOK! DUST STORM!
EVERYONE! BACK TO THE ARC! IT'S THE ONLY PLACE THAT CAN SHELTER US--
WAIT! NO! STAY IN THE CAMP!
ARE YOU CRAZY?! WE'RE GONNA DIE OUT HERE!
I AM JAN-AL. MY FAMILY NAME MEANS "FAITH." FAITH IN THE LORD RAO.
LISTEN TO ME!
STAY AWAY FROM THE ARK! STAY IN THE CAMP!
WE MUST SURVIVE, WE MUST--
AND RAO...HE SENT ME A GIFT.

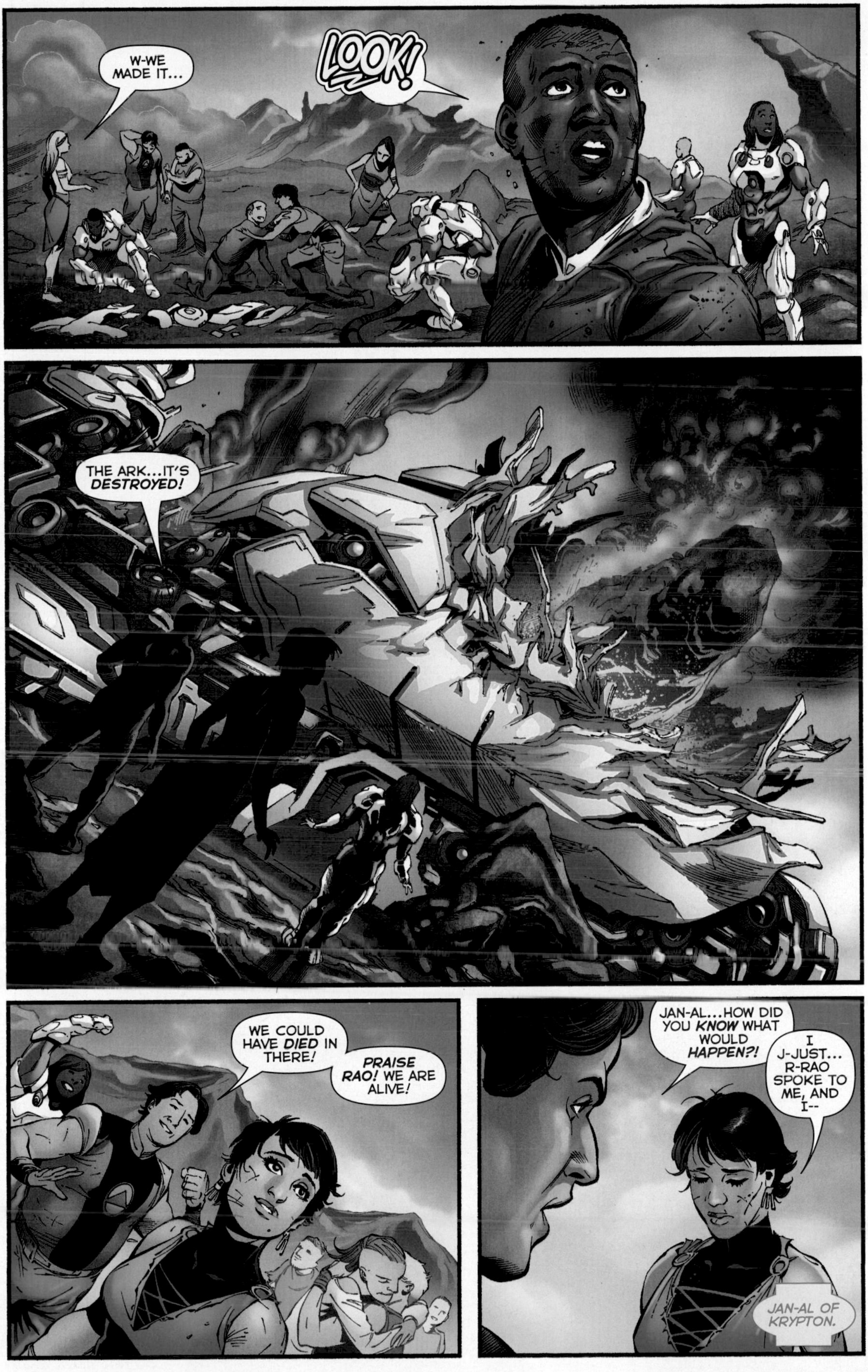
W-WE MADE IT...
LOOK!
THE ARK...IT'S DESTROYED!
WE COULD HAVE DIED IN THERE!
PRAISE RAO! WE ARE ALIVE!
JAN-AL...HOW DID YOU KNOW WHAT WOULD HAPPEN?!
I J-JUST... R-RAO SPOKE TO ME, AND I--
JAN-AL OF KRYPTON.

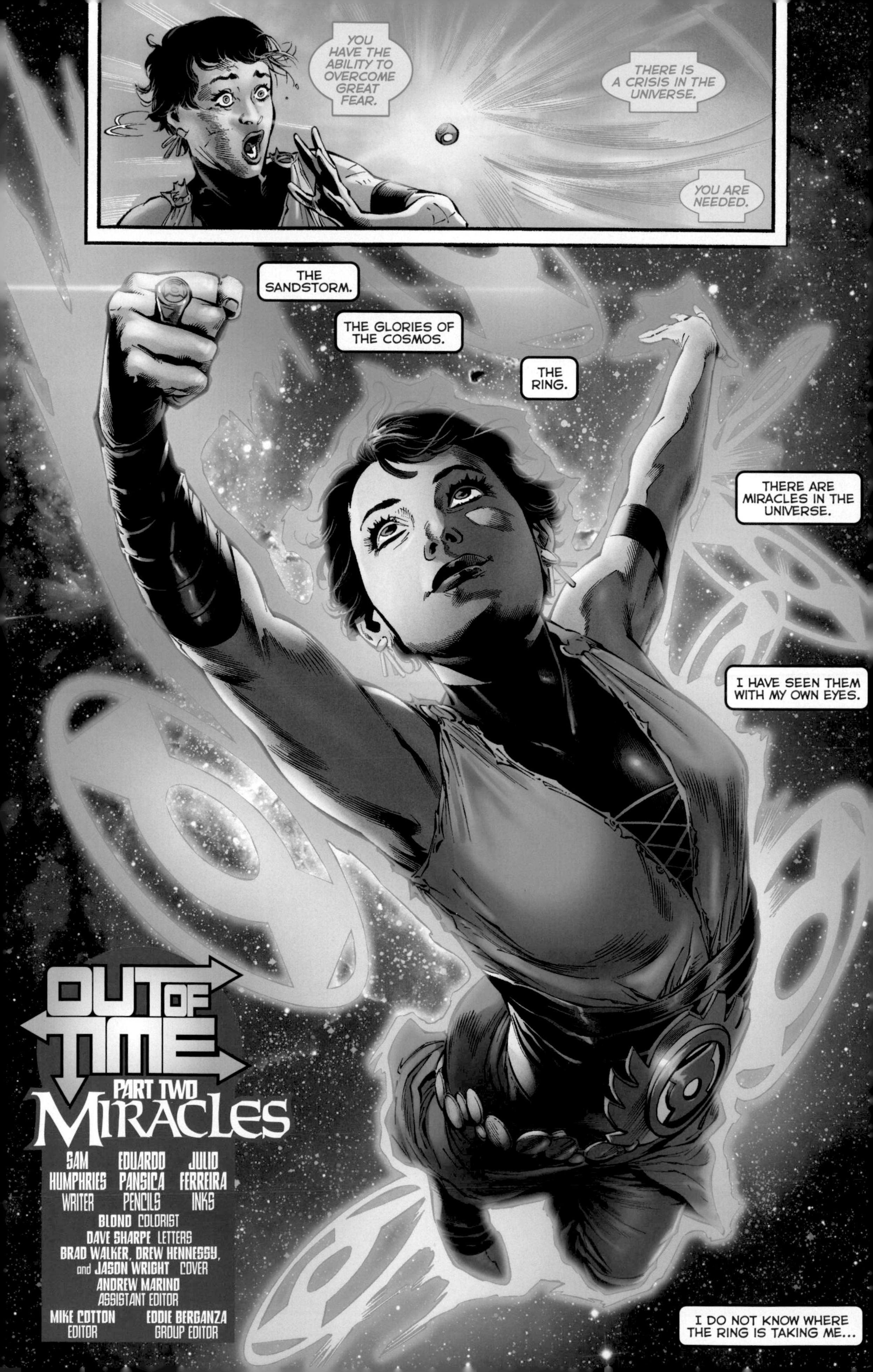
YOU HAVE THE ABILITY TO OVERCOME GREAT FEAR.
THERE IS A CRISIS IN THE UNIVERSE.
YOU ARE NEEDED.
THE SANDSTORM.
THE GLORIES OF THE COSMOS.
THE RING.
THERE ARE MIRACLES IN THE UNIVERSE.
I HAVE SEEN THEM WITH MY OWN EYES.
OUT OF TIME
PART TWO
MIRACLES
SAM HUMPHRIES WRITER
EDUARDO PANSICA PENCILS
JULIO FERREIRA INKS
BLOND COLORIST
DAVE SHARPE LETTERS
BRAD WALKER, DREW HENNESSY, and JASON WRIGHT COVER
ANDREW MARINO ASSISTANT EDITOR
MIKE COTTON EDITOR
EDDIE BERGANZA GROUP EDITOR
I DO NOT KNOW WHERE THE RING IS TAKING ME...

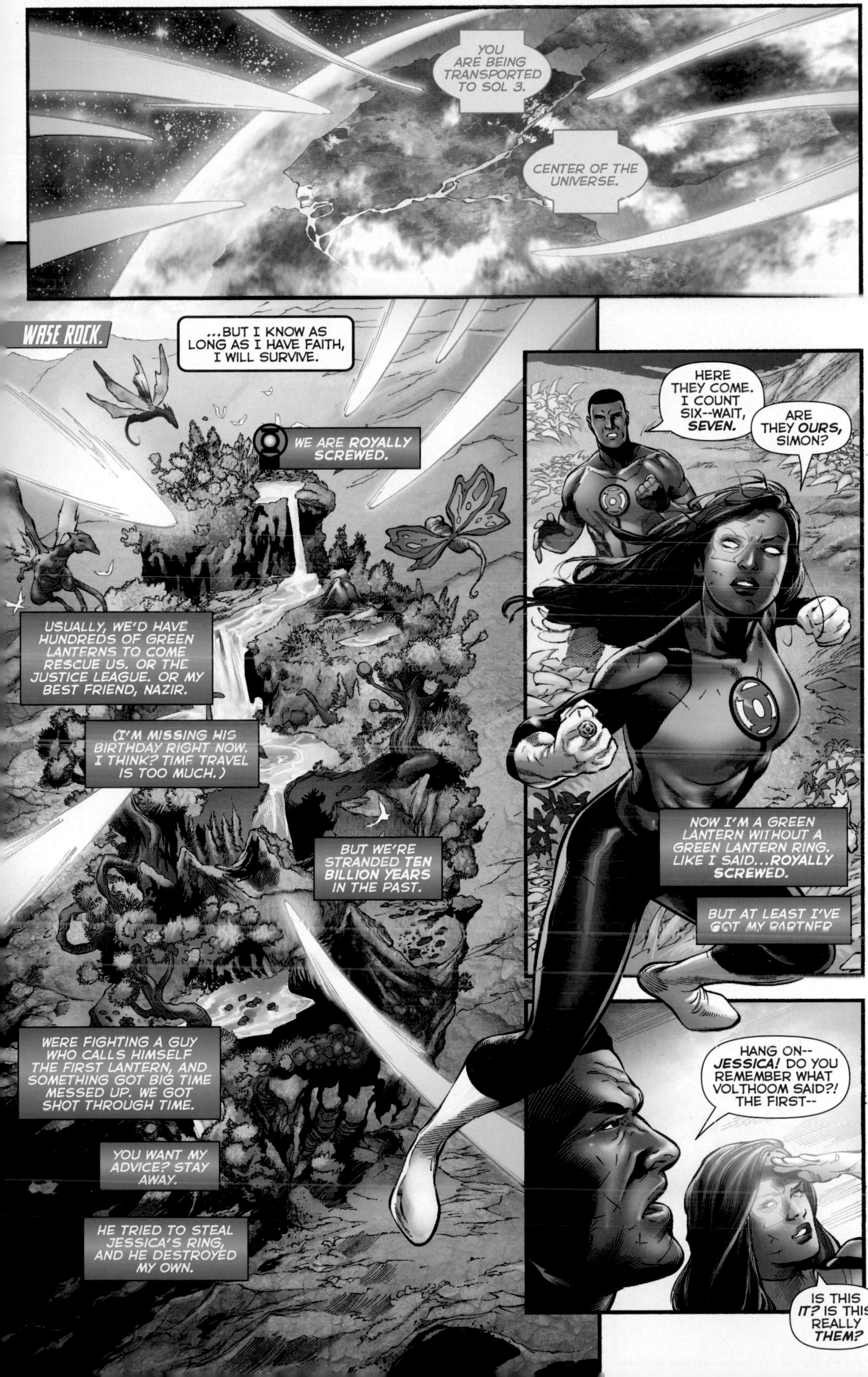
YOU ARE BEING TRANSPORTED TO SOL 3.
CENTER OF THE UNIVERSE.
WASE ROCK.
...BUT I KNOW AS LONG AS I HAVE FAITH, I WILL SURVIVE.
WE ARE ROYALLY SCREWED.
USUALLY, WE'D HAVE HUNDREDS OF GREEN LANTERNS TO COME RESCUE US. OR THE JUSTICE LEAGUE. OR MY BEST FRIEND, NAZIR.
(I'M MISSING HIS BIRTHDAY RIGHT NOW. I THINK? TIME TRAVEL IS TOO MUCH.)
BUT WE'RE STRANDED TEN BILLION YEARS IN THE PAST.
WERE FIGHTING A GUY WHO CALLS HIMSELF THE FIRST LANTERN, AND SOMETHING GOT BIG TIME MESSED UP. WE GOT SHOT THROUGH TIME.
YOU WANT MY ADVICE? STAY AWAY.
HE TRIED TO STEAL JESSICA'S RING, AND HE DESTROYED MY OWN.
HERE THEY COME. I COUNT SIX--WAIT, SEVEN.
ARE THEY OURS, SIMON?
NOW I'M A GREEN LANTERN WITHOUT A GREEN LANTERN RING. LIKE I SAID...ROYALLY SCREWED.
BUT AT LEAST I'VE GOT MY PARTNER
HANG ON-- JESSICA! DO YOU REMEMBER WHAT VOLTHOOM SAID?! THE FIRST--
IS THIS IT? IS THIS REALLY THEM?

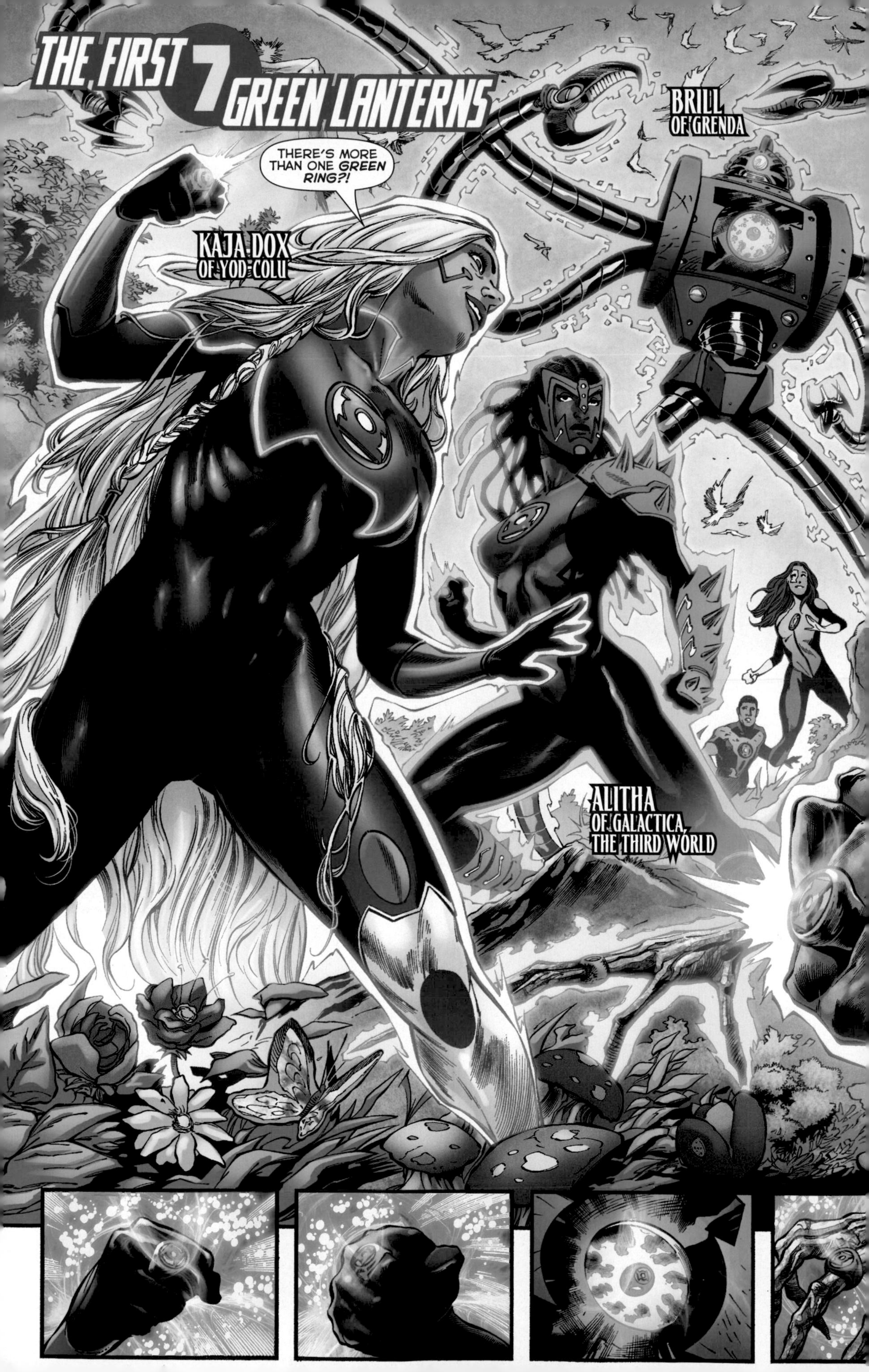
THE FIRST 7 GREEN LANTERNS
BRILL OF GRENDA
THERE'S MORE THAN ONE GREEN RING?!
KAJA DOX OF YOD-COLU
ALITHA OF GALACTICA, THE THIRD WORLD

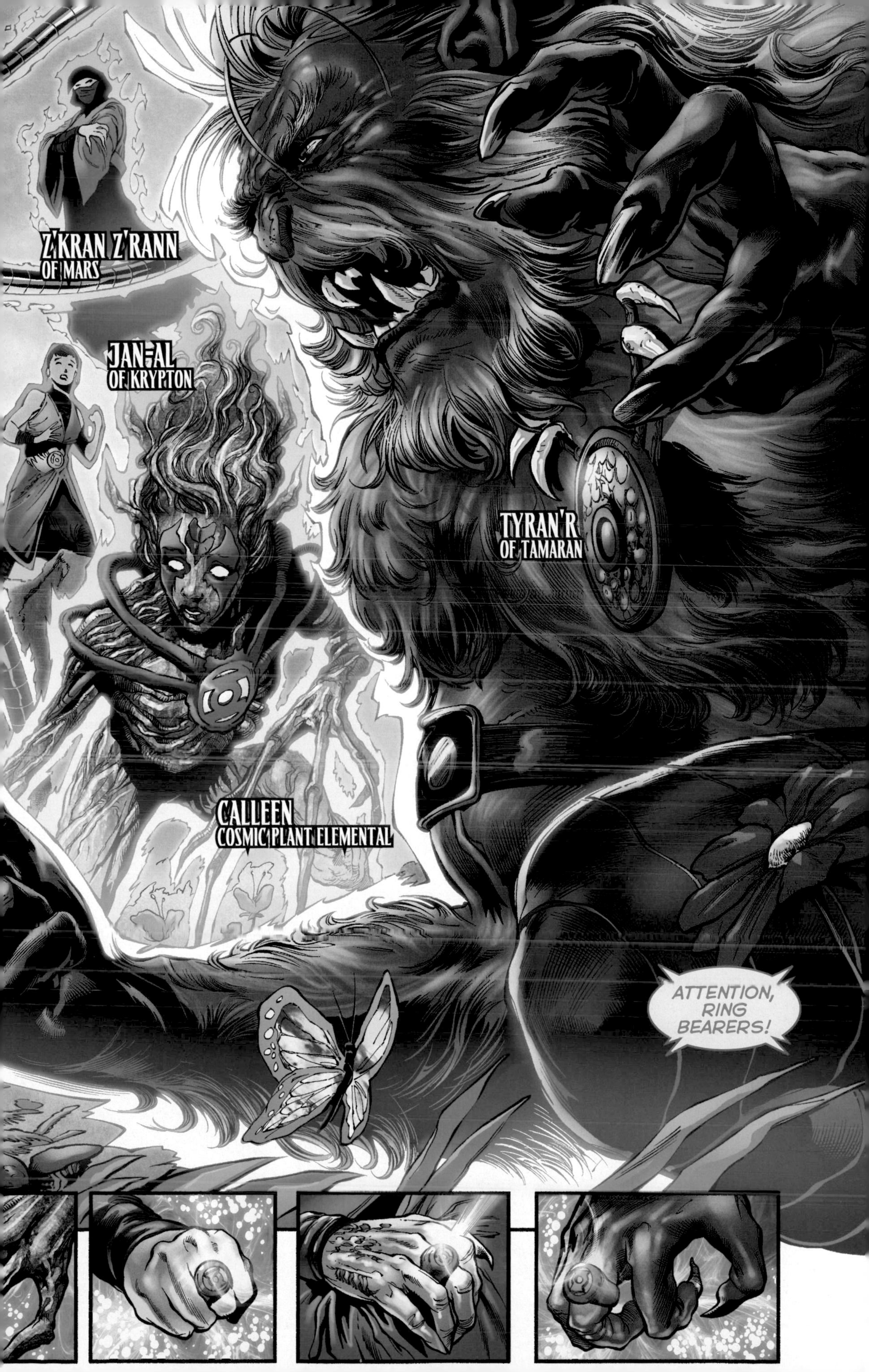
Z'KRAN Z'RANN
OF MARS
JAN-AL
OF KRYPTON
TYRAN'R
OF TAMARAN
CALLEEN
COSMIC PLANT ELEMENTAL
ATTENTION, RING BEARERS!

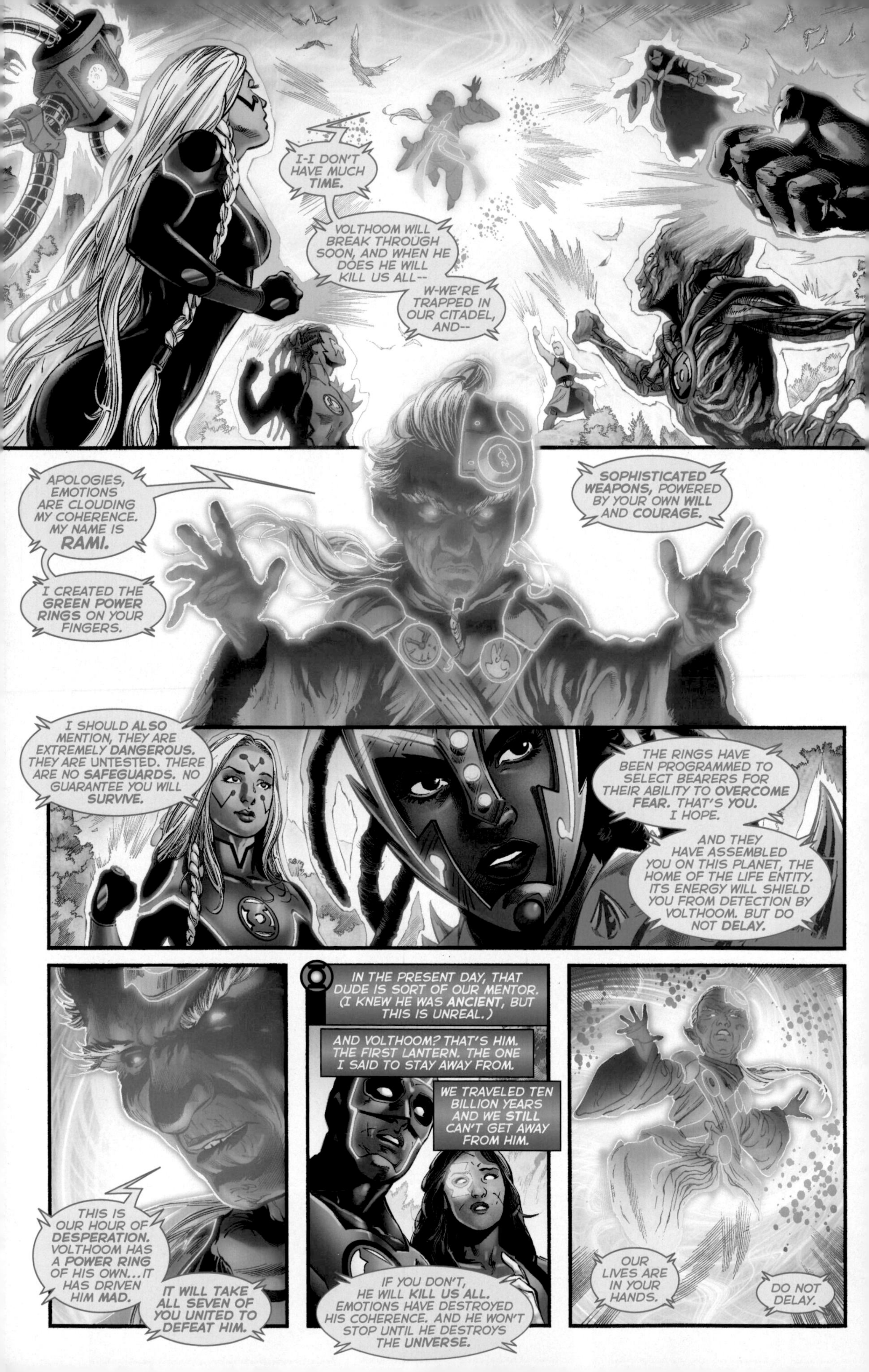
I-I DON'T HAVE MUCH TIME.
VOLTHOOM WILL BREAK THROUGH SOON, AND WHEN HE DOES HE WILL KILL US ALL--
W-WE'RE TRAPPED IN OUR CITADEL, AND--
APOLOGIES, EMOTIONS ARE CLOUDING MY COHERENCE. MY NAME IS RAMI.
I CREATED THE GREEN POWER RINGS ON YOUR FINGERS.
SOPHISTICATED WEAPONS, POWERED BY YOUR OWN WILL AND COURAGE.
I SHOULD ALSO MENTION, THEY ARE EXTREMELY DANGEROUS. THEY ARE UNTESTED. THERE ARE NO SAFEGUARDS. NO GUARANTEE YOU WILL SURVIVE.
THE RINGS HAVE BEEN PROGRAMMED TO SELECT BEARERS FOR THEIR ABILITY TO OVERCOME FEAR. THAT'S YOU. I HOPE.
AND THEY HAVE ASSEMBLED YOU ON THIS PLANET, THE HOME OF THE LIFE ENTITY. ITS ENERGY WILL SHIELD YOU FROM DETECTION BY VOLTHOOM. BUT DO NOT DELAY.
THIS IS OUR HOUR OF DESPERATION. VOLTHOOM HAS A POWER RING OF HIS OWN...IT HAS DRIVEN HIM MAD.
IT WILL TAKE ALL SEVEN OF YOU UNITED TO DEFEAT HIM.
IN THE PRESENT DAY, THAT DUDE IS SORT OF OUR MENTOR. (I KNEW HE WAS ANCIENT, BUT THIS IS UNREAL.)
AND VOLTHOOM? THAT'S HIM. THE FIRST LANTERN. THE ONE I SAID TO STAY AWAY FROM.
WE TRAVELED TEN BILLION YEARS AND WE STILL CAN'T GET AWAY FROM HIM.
IF YOU DON'T, HE WILL KILL US ALL. EMOTIONS HAVE DESTROYED HIS COHERENCE. AND HE WON'T STOP UNTIL HE DESTROYS THE UNIVERSE.
OUR LIVES ARE IN YOUR HANDS.
DO NOT DELAY.

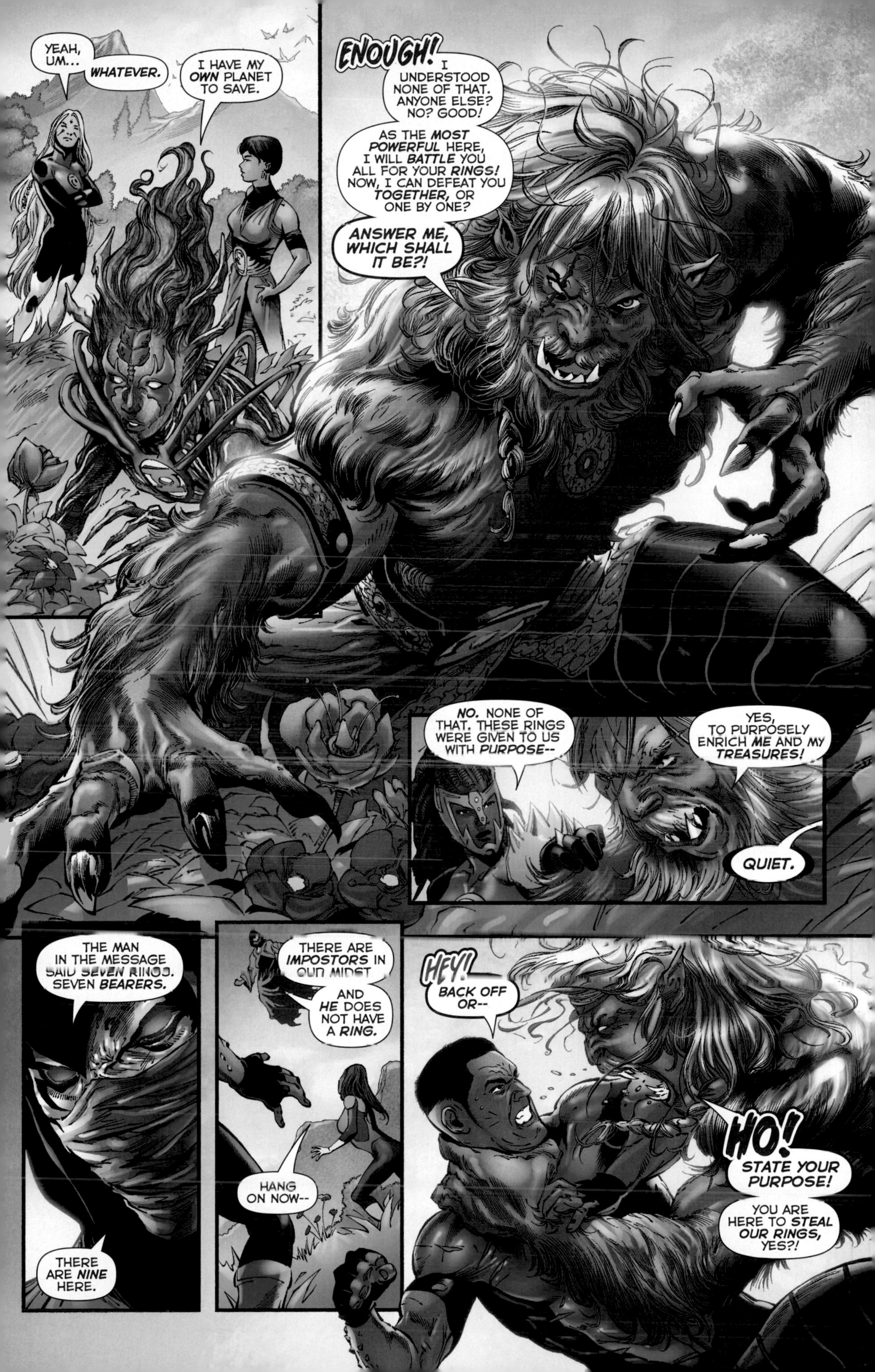

YEAH, UM... WHATEVER.
I HAVE MY OWN PLANET TO SAVE.
ENOUGH!
I UNDERSTOOD NONE OF THAT. ANYONE ELSE? NO? GOOD!
AS THE MOST POWERFUL HERE, I WILL BATTLE YOU ALL FOR YOUR RINGS! NOW, I CAN DEFEAT YOU TOGETHER, OR ONE BY ONE?
ANSWER ME, WHICH SHALL IT BE?!
NO. NONE OF THAT. THESE RINGS WERE GIVEN TO US WITH PURPOSE--
YES, TO PURPOSELY ENRICH ME AND MY TREASURES!
QUIET.
THE MAN IN THE MESSAGE SAID SEVEN RINGS. SEVEN BEARERS.
THERE ARE NINE HERE.
THERE ARE IMPOSTORS IN OUR MIDST
AND HE DOES NOT HAVE A RING.
HANG ON NOW--
HEY!
BACK OFF OR--
HO!
STATE YOUR PURPOSE!
YOU ARE HERE TO STEAL OUR RINGS, YES?!

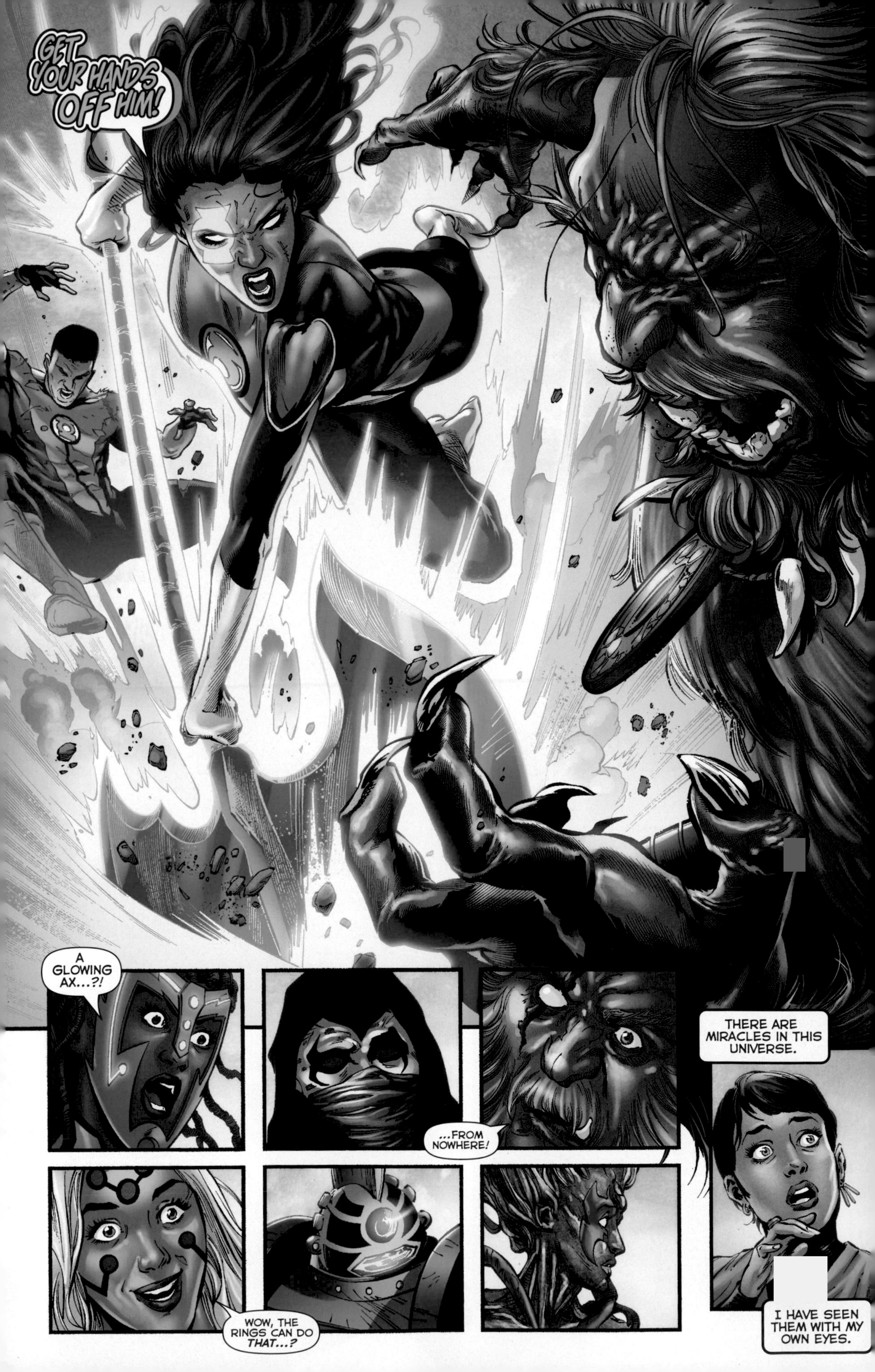
GET YOUR HANDS OFF HIM!
A GLOWING AX...?!
...FROM NOWHERE!
THERE ARE MIRACLES IN THIS UNIVERSE.
WOW, THE RINGS CAN DO THAT...?
I HAVE SEEN THEM WITH MY OWN EYES.

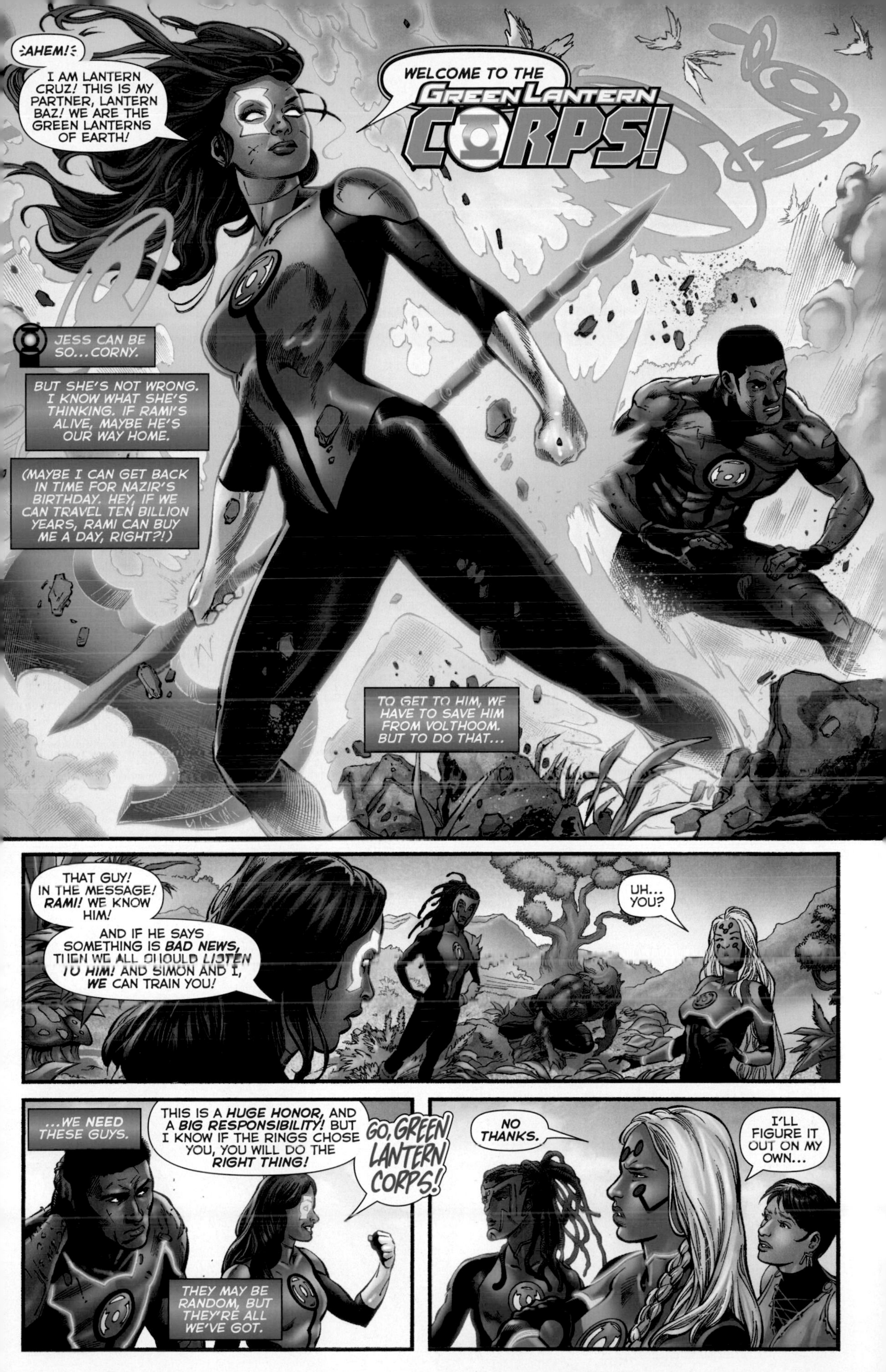
AHEM!
I AM LANTERN CRUZ! THIS IS MY PARTNER, LANTERN BAZ! WE ARE THE GREEN LANTERNS OF EARTH!
WELCOME TO THE GREEN LANTERN CORPS!
JESS CAN BE SO... CORNY.
BUT SHE'S NOT WRONG. I KNOW WHAT SHE'S THINKING. IF RAMI'S ALIVE, MAYBE HE'S OUR WAY HOME.
(MAYBE I CAN GET BACK IN TIME FOR NAZIR'S BIRTHDAY. HEY, IF WE CAN TRAVEL TEN BILLION YEARS, RAMI CAN BUY ME A DAY, RIGHT?!)
TO GET TO HIM, WE HAVE TO SAVE HIM FROM VOLTHOOM. BUT TO DO THAT...
THAT GUY! IN THE MESSAGE! RAMI! WE KNOW HIM!
AND IF HE SAYS SOMETHING IS BAD NEWS, THEN WE ALL SHOULD LISTEN TO HIM! AND SIMON AND I, WE CAN TRAIN YOU!
UH... YOU?
...WE NEED THESE GUYS.
THIS IS A HUGE HONOR, AND A BIG RESPONSIBILITY! BUT I KNOW IF THE RINGS CHOSE YOU, YOU WILL DO THE RIGHT THING!
GO, GREEN LANTERN CORPS!
THEY MAY BE RANDOM, BUT THEY'RE ALL WE'VE GOT.
NO THANKS.
I'LL FIGURE IT OUT ON MY OWN...

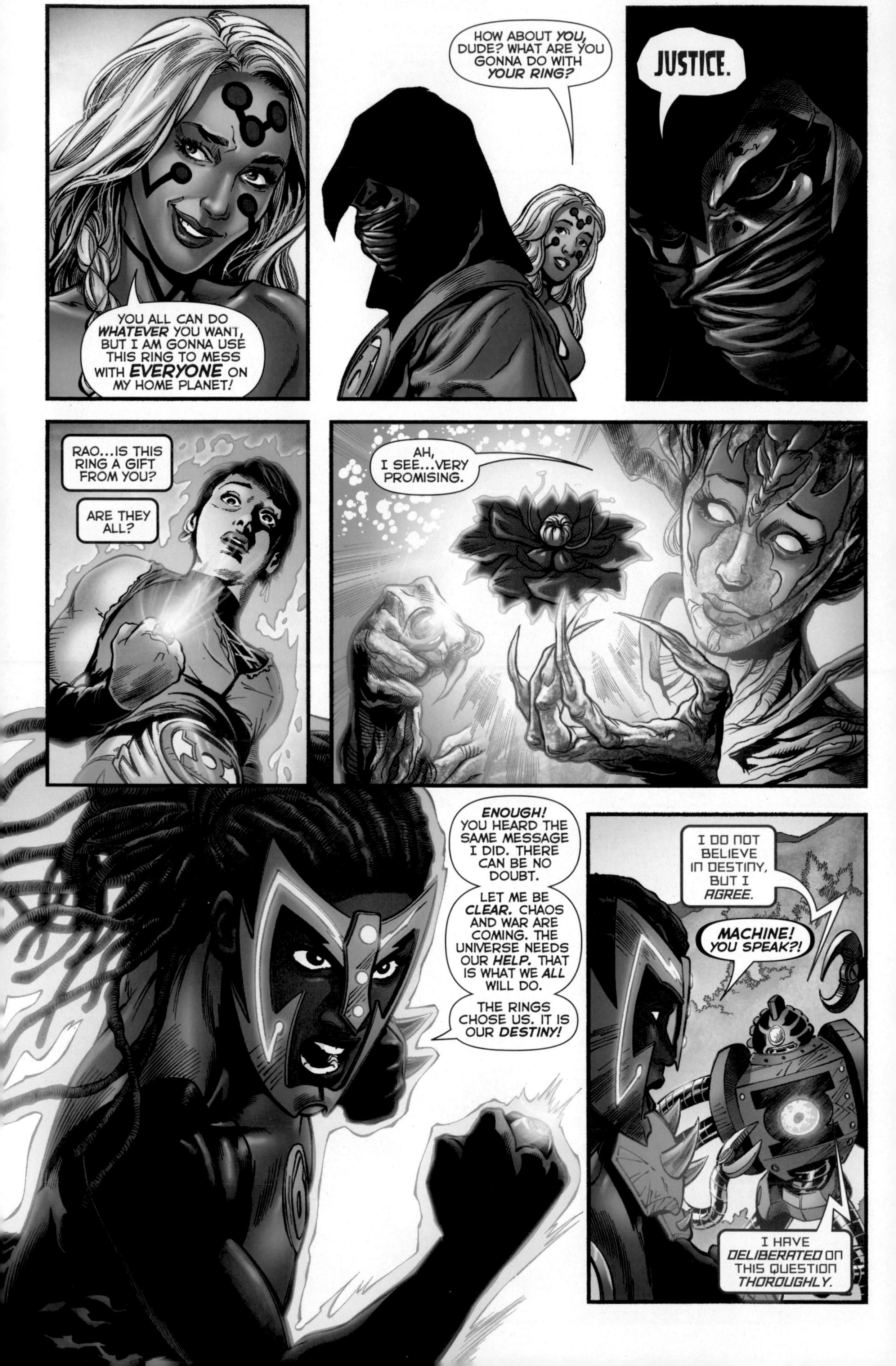
YOU ALL CAN DO WHATEVER YOU WANT, BUT I AM GONNA USE THIS RING TO MESS WITH EVERYONE ON MY HOME PLANET!
HOW ABOUT YOU, DUDE? WHAT ARE YOU GONNA DO WITH YOUR RING?
JUSTICE.
RAO...IS THIS RING A GIFT FROM YOU?
ARE THEY ALL?
AH, I SEE...VERY PROMISING.
ENOUGH! YOU HEARD THE SAME MESSAGE I DID. THERE CAN BE NO DOUBT.
LET ME BE CLEAR. CHAOS AND WAR ARE COMING. THE UNIVERSE NEEDS OUR HELP. THAT IS WHAT WE ALL WILL DO.
THE RINGS CHOSE US. IT IS OUR DESTINY!
I DO NOT BELIEVE IN DESTINY, BUT I AGREE.
MACHINE! YOU SPEAK?!
I HAVE DELIBERATED ON THIS QUESTION THOROUGHLY.

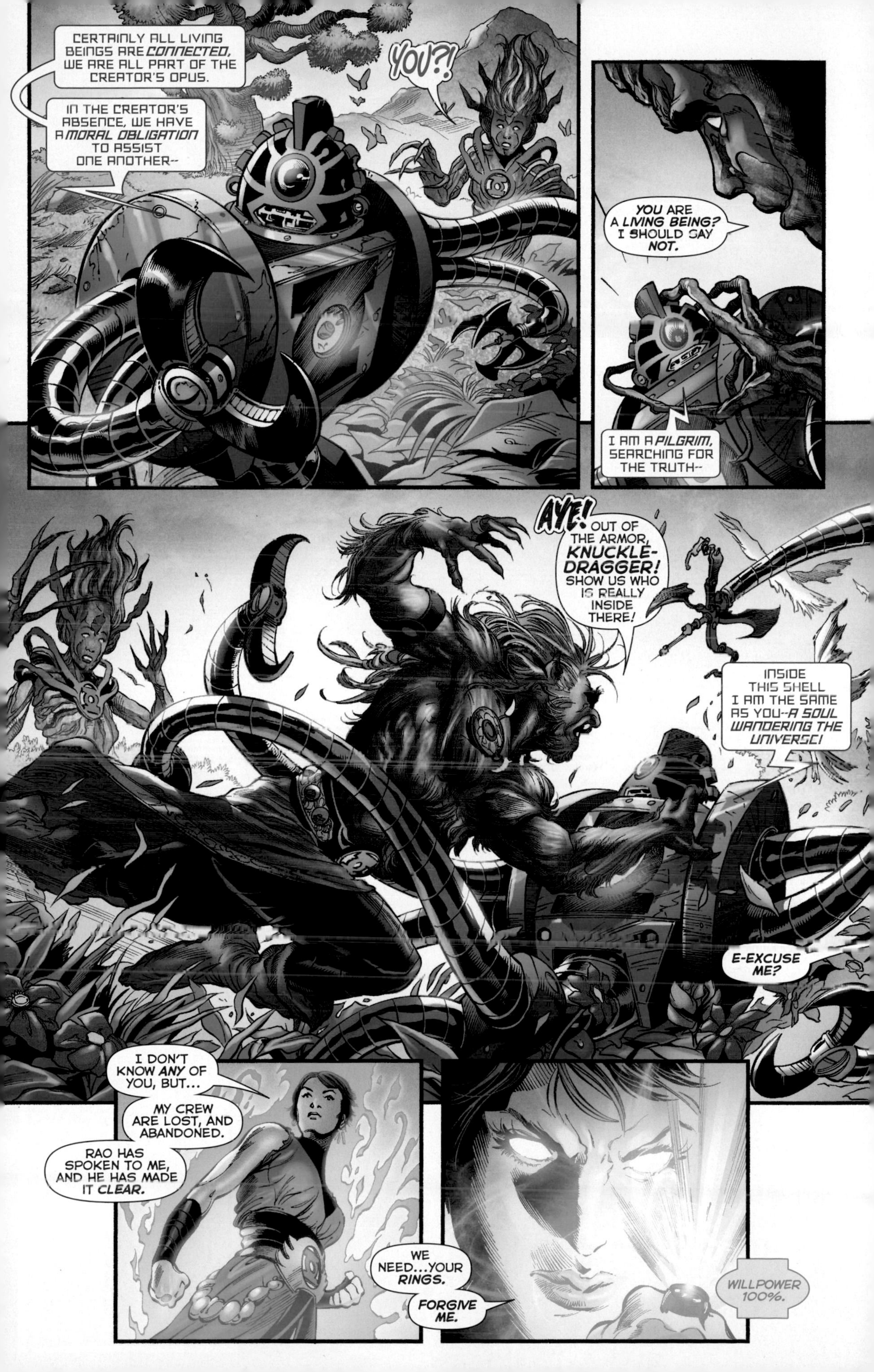
CERTAINLY ALL LIVING BEINGS ARE CONNECTED, WE ARE ALL PART OF THE CREATOR'S OPUS.
IN THE CREATOR'S ABSENCE, WE HAVE A MORAL OBLIGATION TO ASSIST ONE ANOTHER--
YOU?!
YOU ARE A LIVING BEING? I SHOULD SAY NOT.
I AM A PILGRIM, SEARCHING FOR THE TRUTH--
AYE!
OUT OF THE ARMOR, KNUCKLE-DRAGGER! SHOW US WHO IS REALLY INSIDE THERE!
INSIDE THIS SHELL I AM THE SAME AS YOU--A SOUL WANDERING THE UNIVERSE!
E-EXCUSE ME?
I DON'T KNOW ANY OF YOU, BUT...
MY CREW ARE LOST, AND ABANDONED.
RAO HAS SPOKEN TO ME, AND HE HAS MADE IT CLEAR.
WE NEED...YOUR RINGS.
FORGIVE ME.
WILLPOWER 100%.

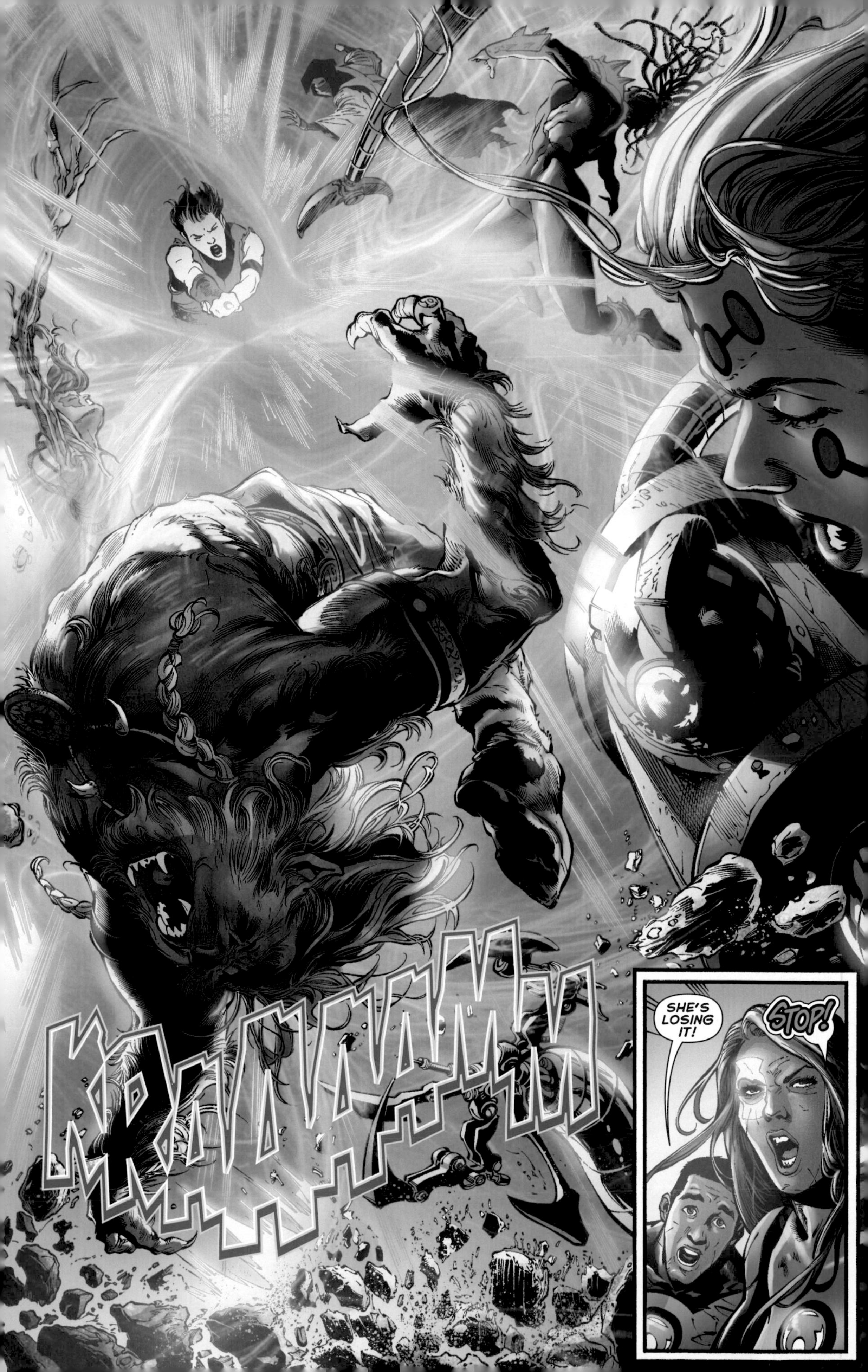
KRAKKAMM
SHE'S LOSING IT!
STOP!

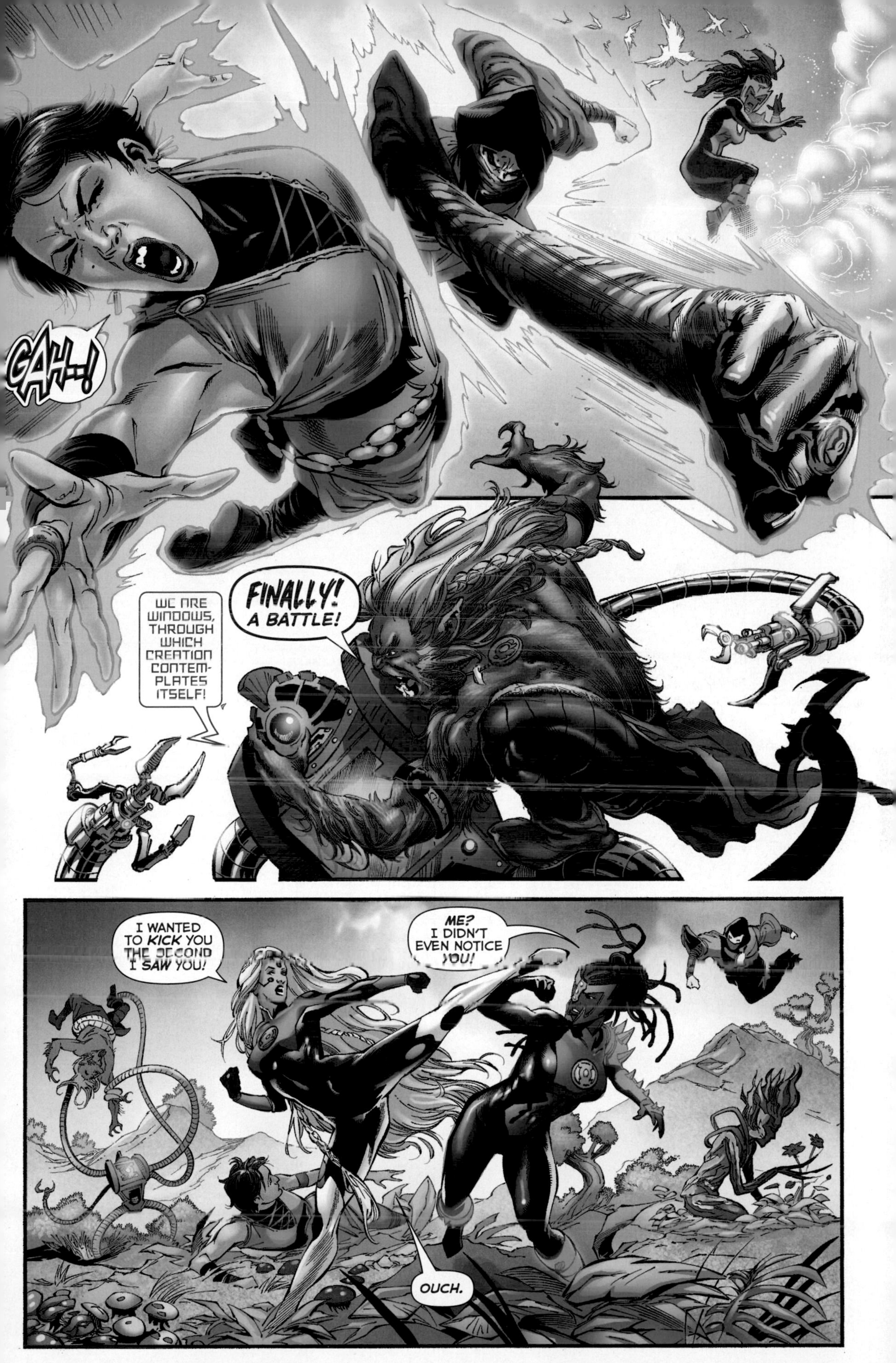
GAH--!
FINALLY! A BATTLE!
WE ARE WINDOWS, THROUGH WHICH CREATION CONTEM-PLATES ITSELF!
I WANTED TO KICK YOU THE SECOND I SAW YOU!
ME? I DIDN'T EVEN NOTICE YOU!
OUCH.

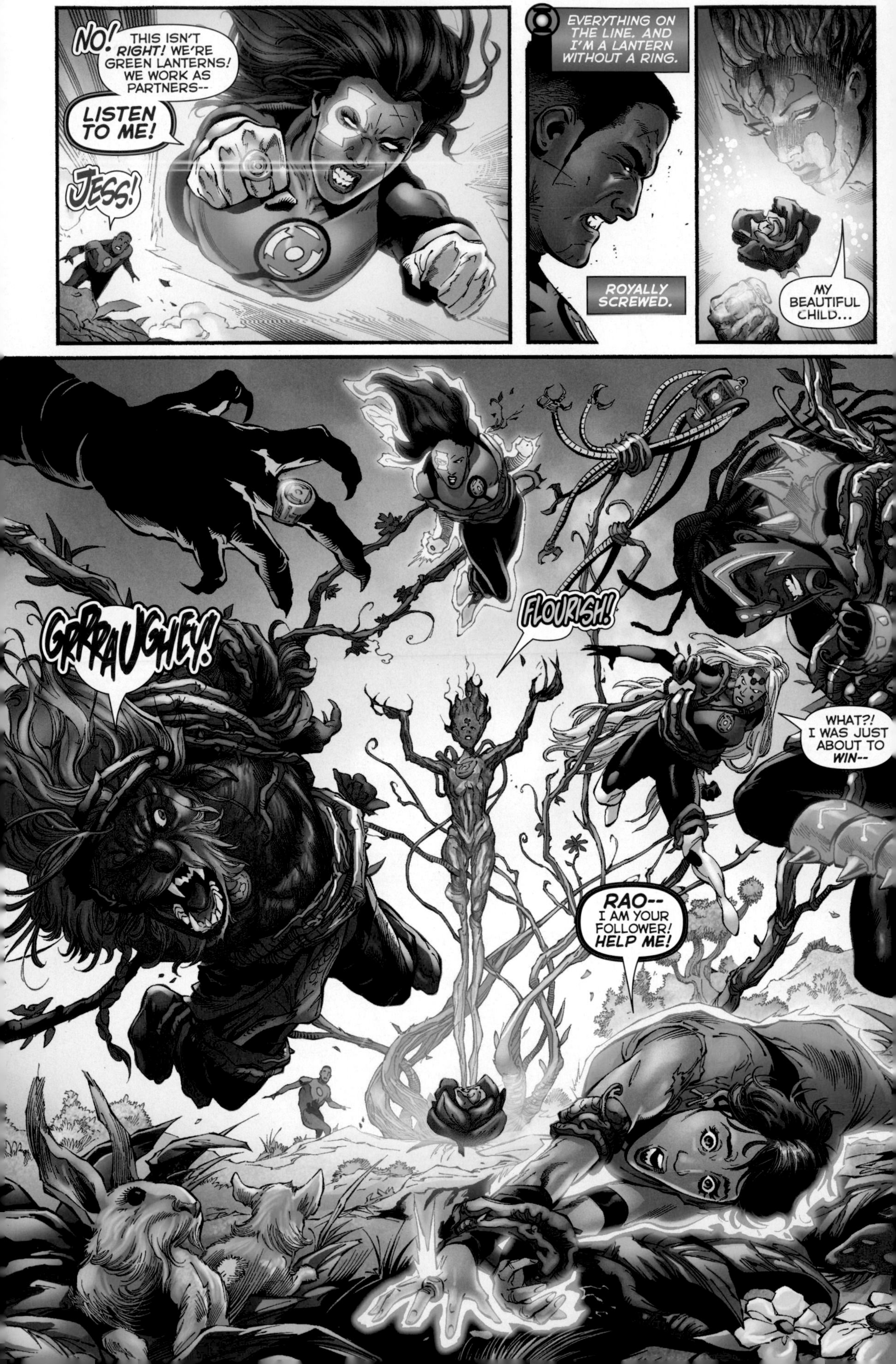
NO!
THIS ISN'T RIGHT! WE'RE GREEN LANTERNS! WE WORK AS PARTNERS--
LISTEN TO ME!
JESS!
EVERYTHING ON THE LINE. AND I'M A LANTERN WITHOUT A RING.
ROYALLY SCREWED.
MY BEAUTIFUL CHILD...
GRRRAUGHEY!
FLOURISH!
WHAT?! I WAS JUST ABOUT TO WIN--
RAO-- I AM YOUR FOLLOWER! HELP ME!

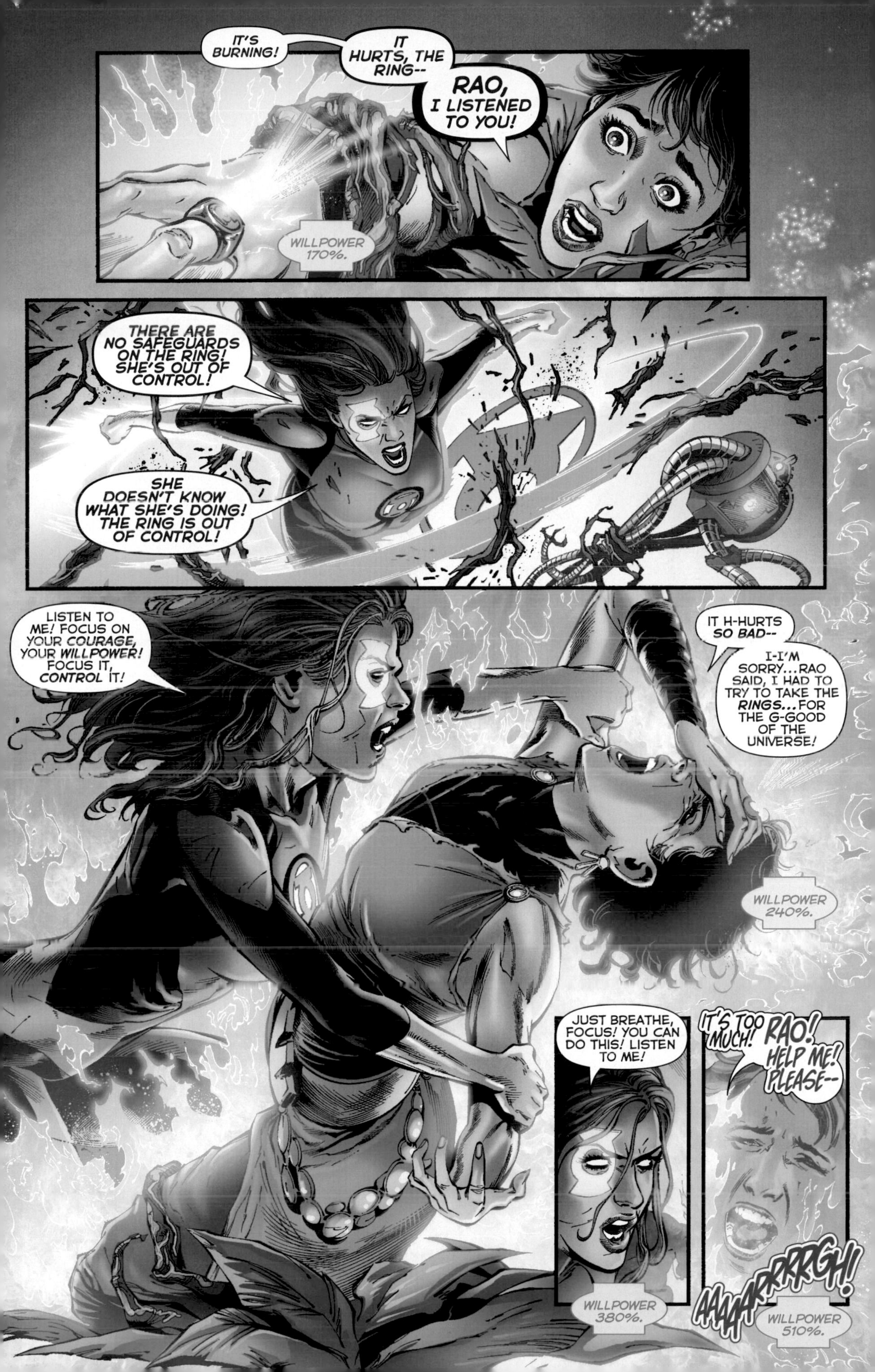

IT'S BURNING!
IT HURTS, THE RING--
RAO, I LISTENED TO YOU!
WILLPOWER 170%.
THERE ARE NO SAFEGUARDS ON THE RING! SHE'S OUT OF CONTROL!
SHE DOESN'T KNOW WHAT SHE'S DOING! THE RING IS OUT OF CONTROL!
LISTEN TO ME! FOCUS ON YOUR COURAGE, YOUR WILLPOWER! FOCUS IT, CONTROL IT!
IT H-HURTS SO BAD--
I-I'M SORRY...RAO SAID, I HAD TO TRY TO TAKE THE RINGS...FOR THE G-GOOD OF THE UNIVERSE!
WILLPOWER 240%.
JUST BREATHE, FOCUS! YOU CAN DO THIS! LISTEN TO ME!
WILLPOWER 380%.
IT'S TOO MUCH! RAO! HELP ME! PLEASE--
AAAAARRRRRGH!
WILLPOWER 510%.

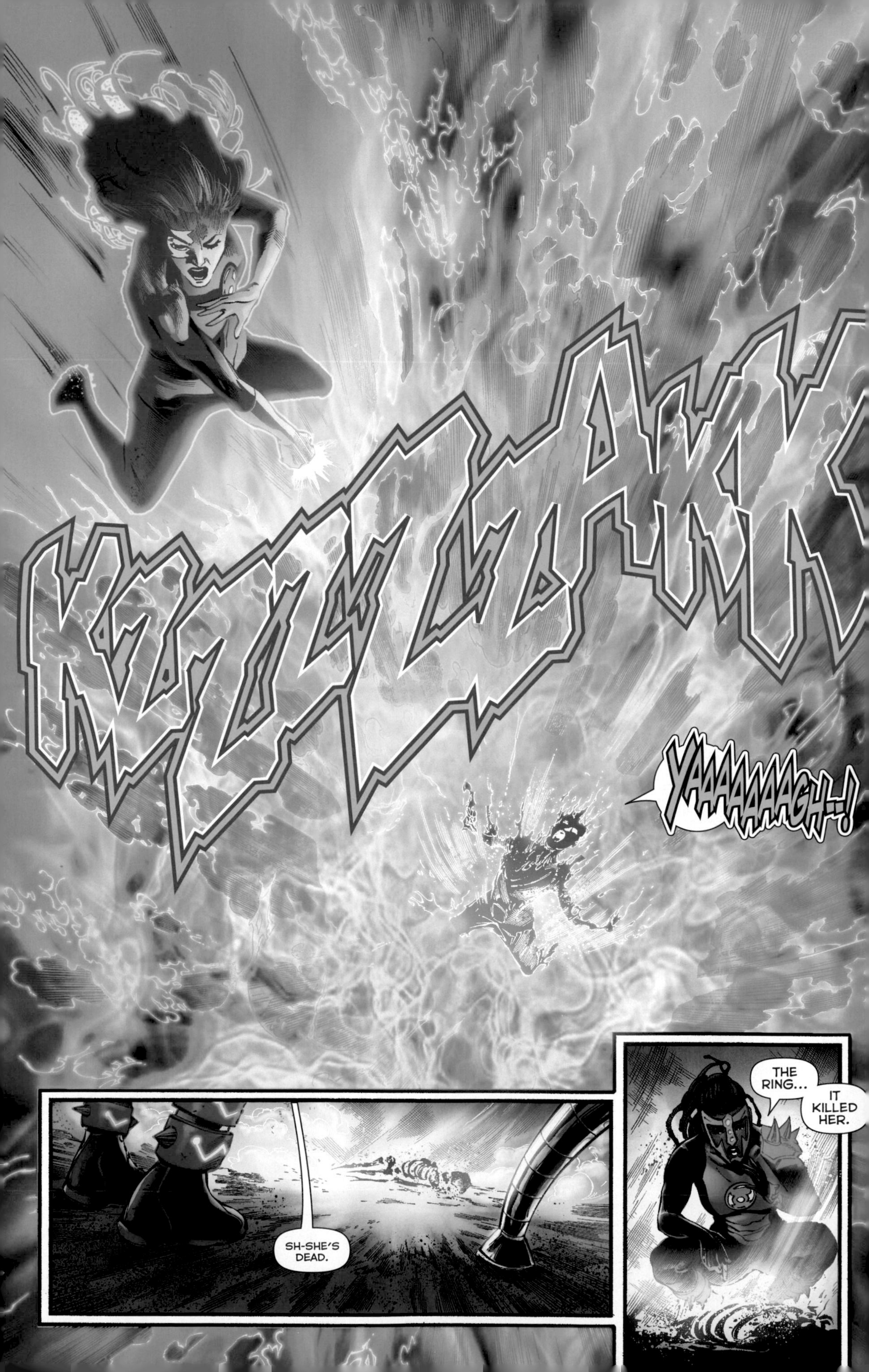

YAAAAAAAGH--!
SH-SHE'S DEAD.
THE RING...
IT KILLED HER.

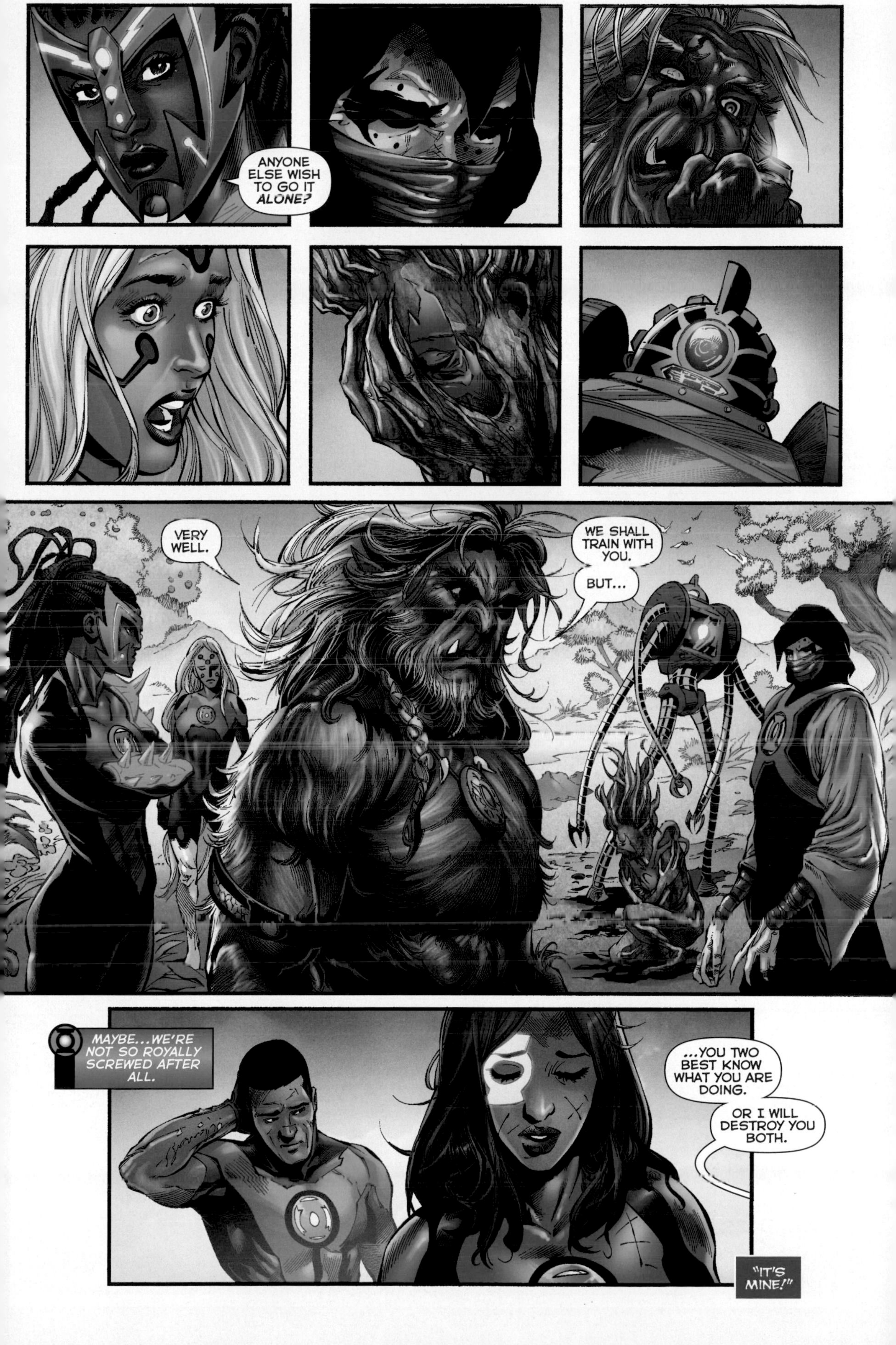

ANYONE ELSE WISH TO GO IT *ALONE?*
VERY WELL.
WE SHALL TRAIN WITH YOU.
BUT...
MAYBE...WE'RE NOT SO ROYALLY SCREWED AFTER ALL.
...YOU TWO BEST KNOW WHAT YOU ARE DOING.
OR I WILL DESTROY YOU BOTH.
"IT'S MINE!"

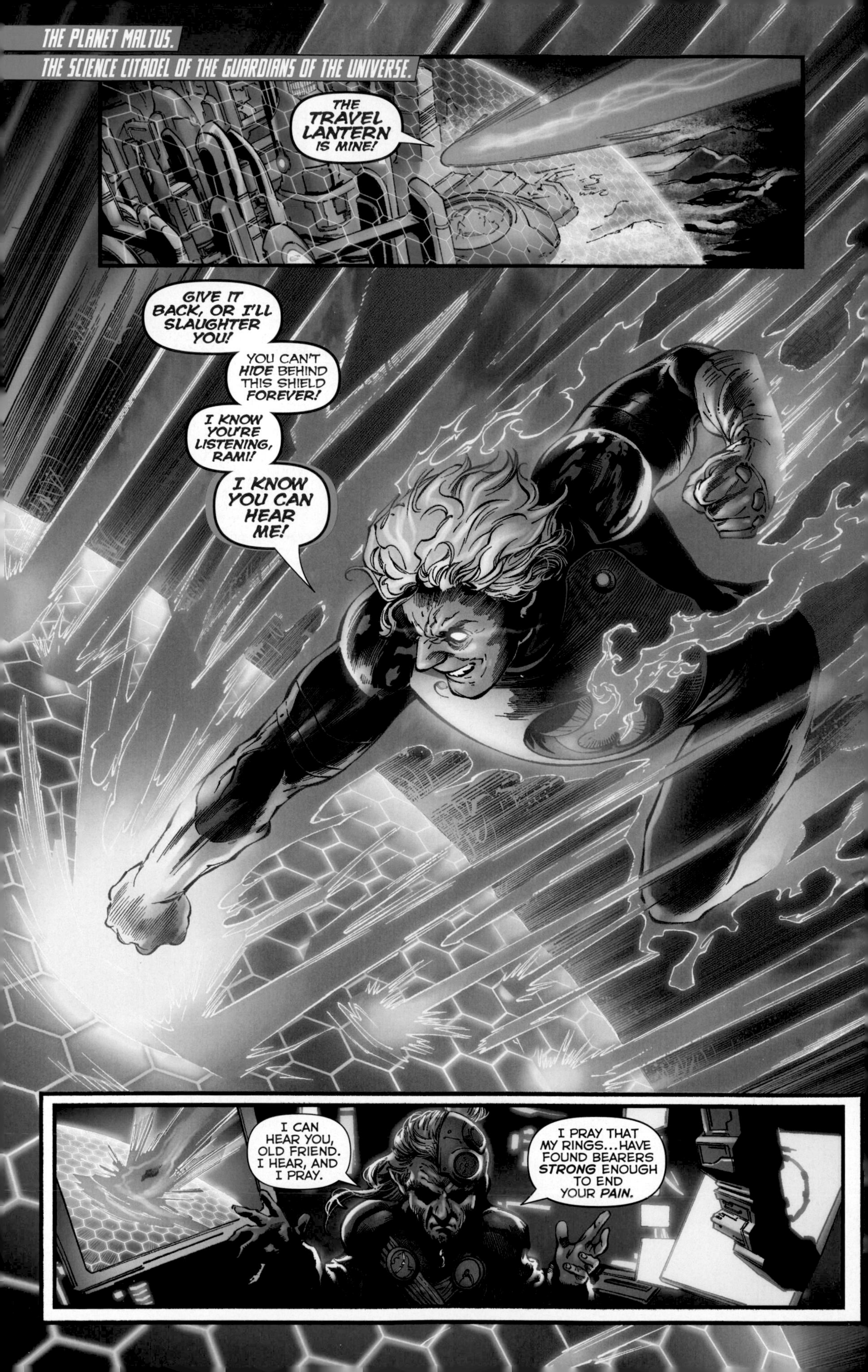
THE PLANET MALTUS.
THE SCIENCE CITADEL OF THE GUARDIANS OF THE UNIVERSE.
THE TRAVEL LANTERN IS MINE!
GIVE IT BACK, OR I'LL SLAUGHTER YOU!
YOU CAN'T HIDE BEHIND THIS SHIELD FOREVER!
I KNOW YOU'RE LISTENING, RAMI!
I KNOW YOU CAN HEAR ME!
I CAN HEAR YOU, OLD FRIEND. I HEAR, AND I PRAY.
I PRAY THAT MY RINGS...HAVE FOUND BEARERS STRONG ENOUGH TO END YOUR PAIN.

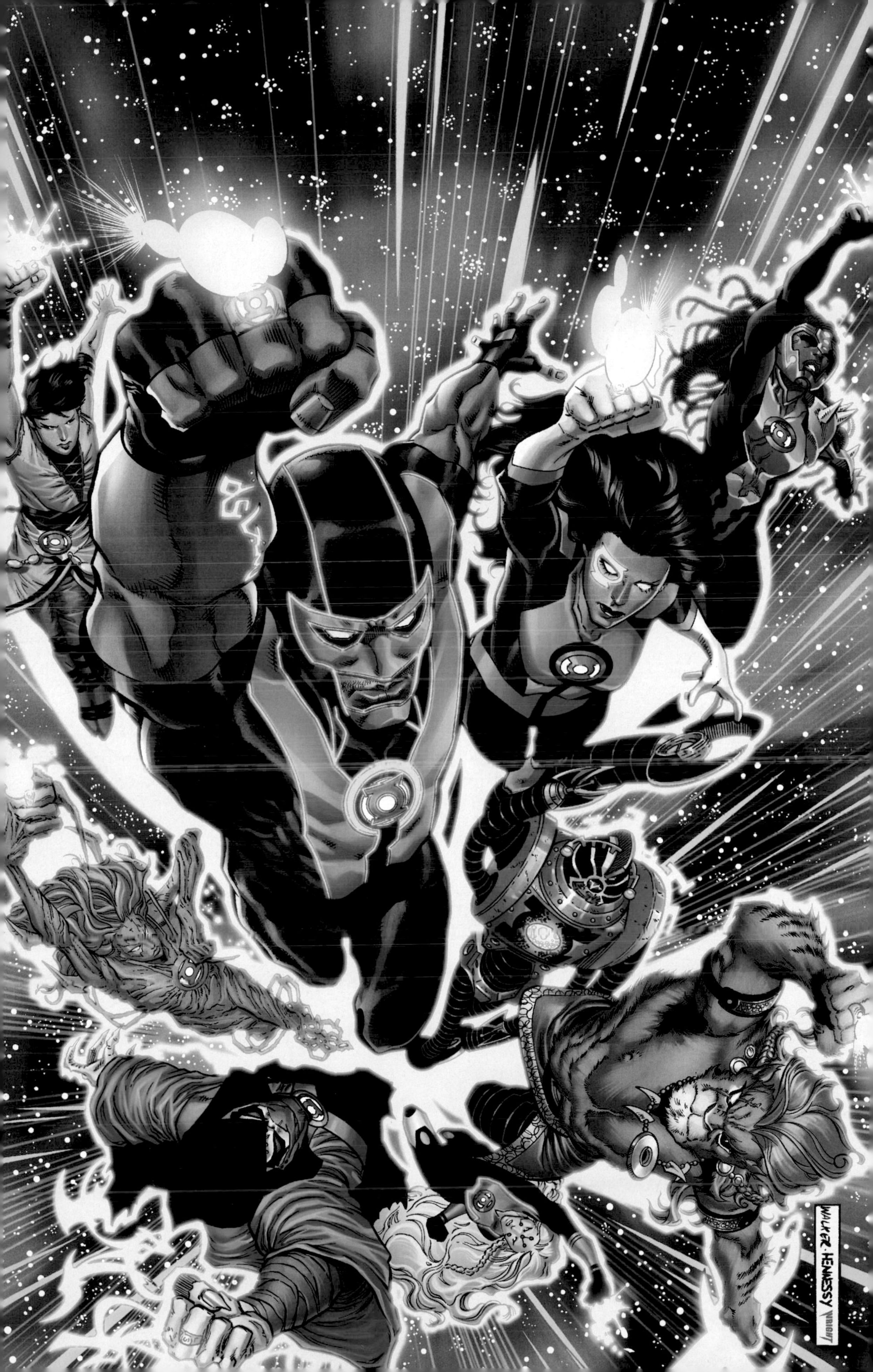
WALKER·HENNESSY
WRIGHT

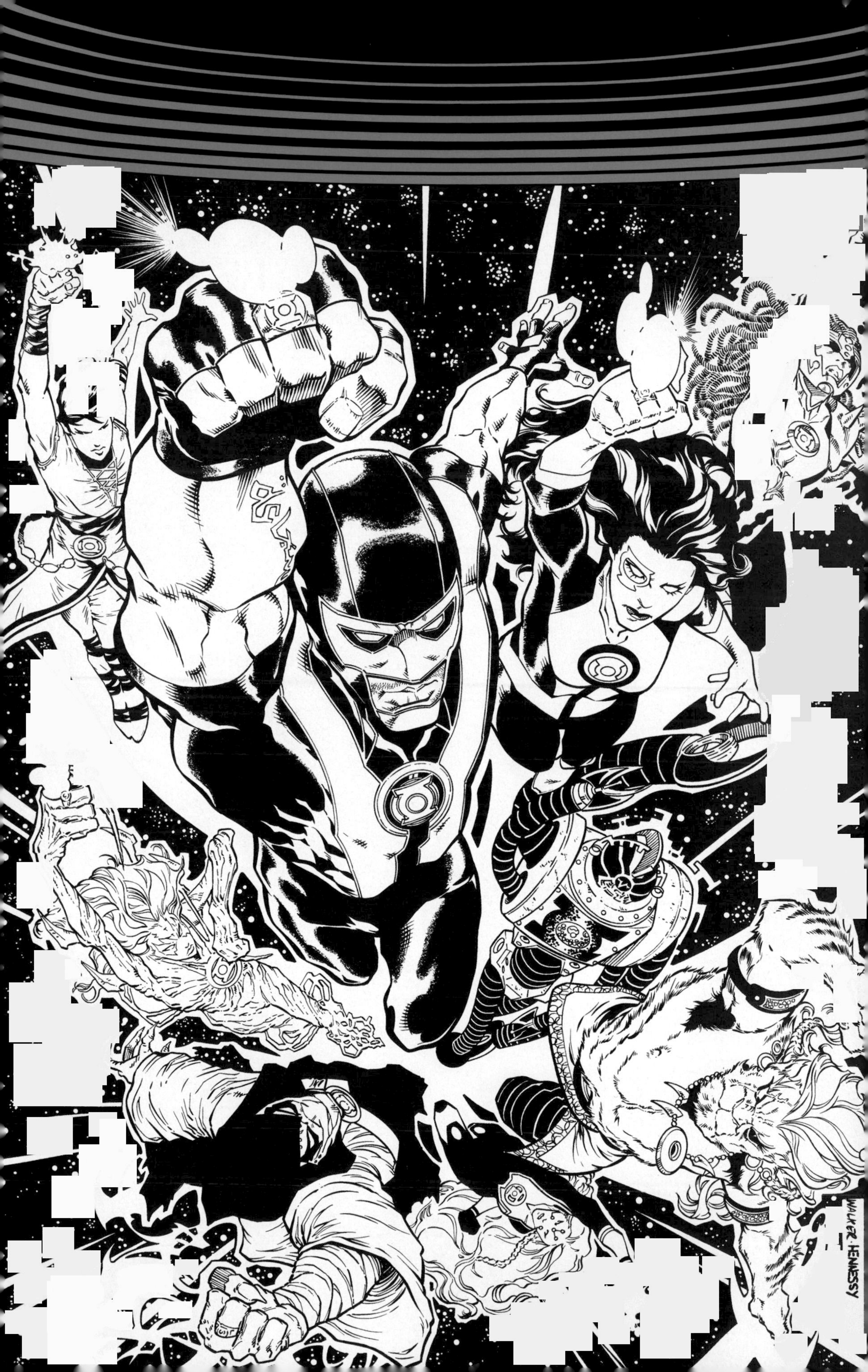
WALKER.HENNESSY

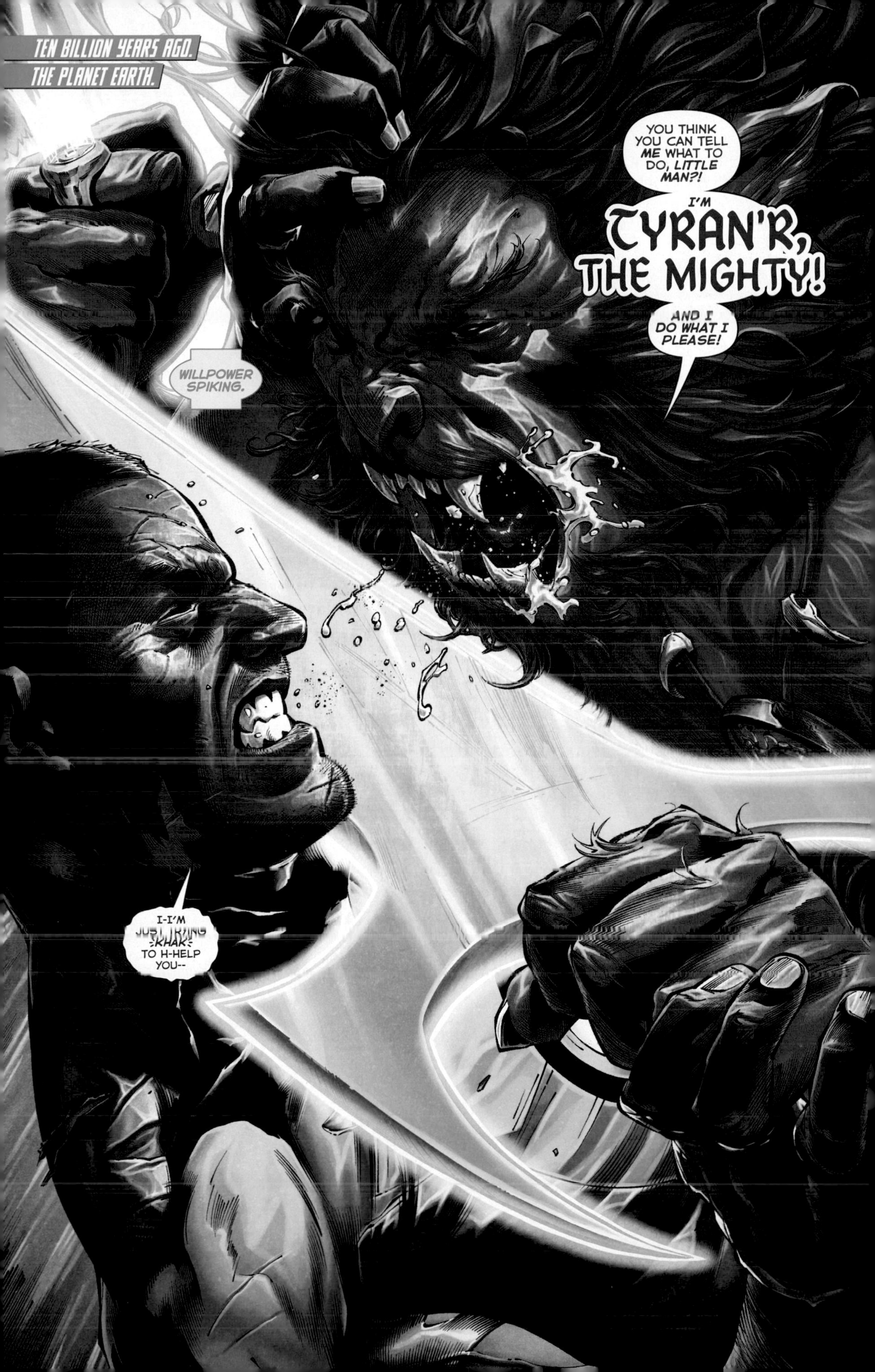
TEN BILLION YEARS AGO.
THE PLANET EARTH.
YOU THINK YOU CAN TELL ME WHAT TO DO, LITTLE MAN?!
I'M TYRAN'R, THE MIGHTY!
AND I DO WHAT I PLEASE!
WILLPOWER SPIKING.
I-I'M JUST TRYING -KHAK- TO H-HELP YOU--

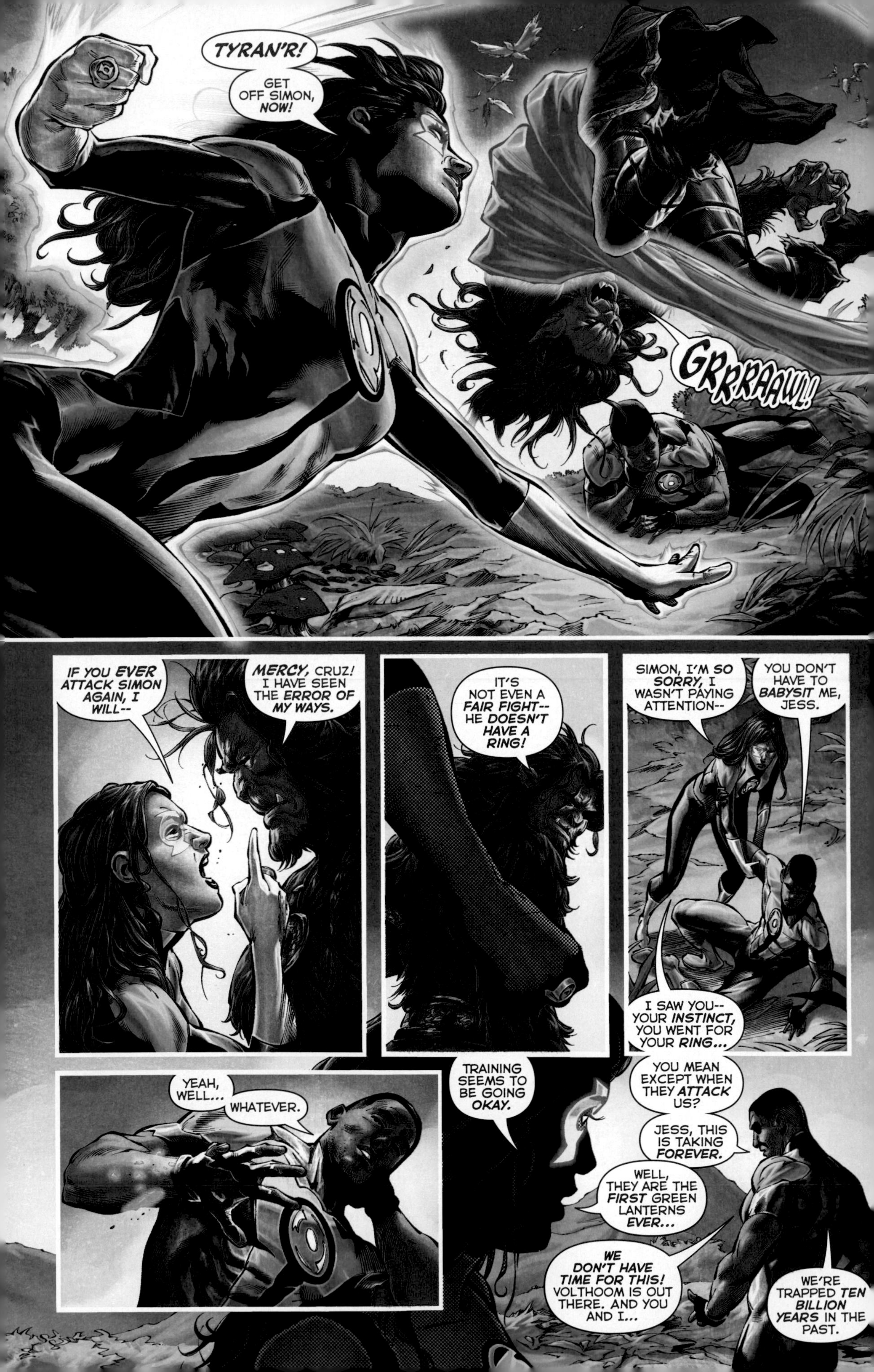
TYRAN'R!
GET OFF SIMON, NOW!
GRRRAAWL!!
IF YOU EVER ATTACK SIMON AGAIN, I WILL--
MERCY, CRUZ! I HAVE SEEN THE ERROR OF MY WAYS.
IT'S NOT EVEN A FAIR FIGHT-- HE DOESN'T HAVE A RING!
SIMON, I'M SO SORRY, I WASN'T PAYING ATTENTION--
YOU DON'T HAVE TO BABYSIT ME, JESS.
I SAW YOU-- YOUR INSTINCT, YOU WENT FOR YOUR RING...
YEAH, WELL...
WHATEVER.
TRAINING SEEMS TO BE GOING OKAY.
YOU MEAN EXCEPT WHEN THEY ATTACK US?
JESS, THIS IS TAKING FOREVER.
WELL, THEY ARE THE FIRST GREEN LANTERNS EVER...
WE DON'T HAVE TIME FOR THIS! VOLTHOOM IS OUT THERE. AND YOU AND I...
WE'RE TRAPPED TEN BILLION YEARS IN THE PAST.

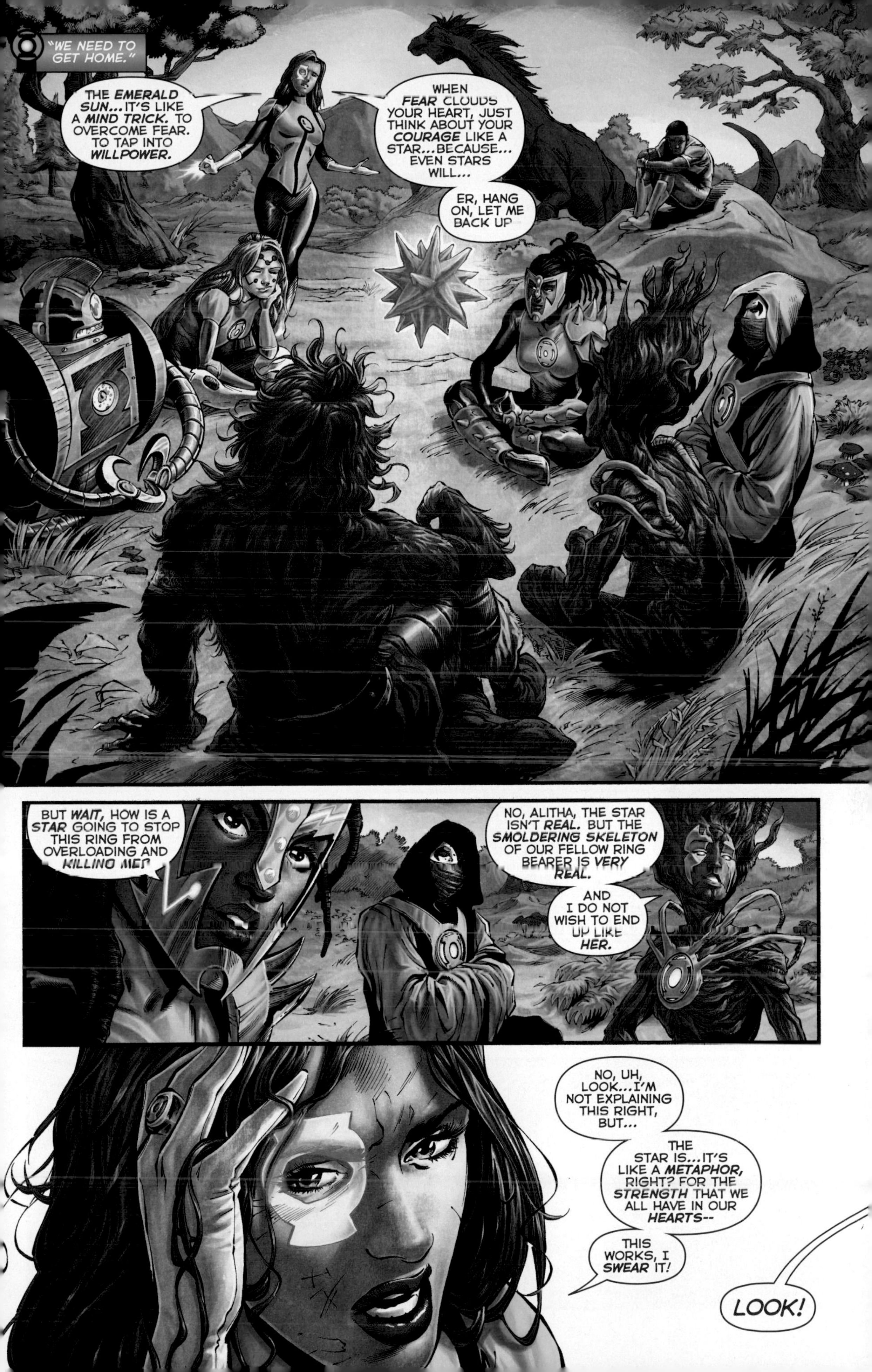
"WE NEED TO GET HOME."
THE EMERALD SUN... IT'S LIKE A MIND TRICK. TO OVERCOME FEAR. TO TAP INTO WILLPOWER.
WHEN FEAR CLOUDS YOUR HEART, JUST THINK ABOUT YOUR COURAGE LIKE A STAR... BECAUSE... EVEN STARS WILL...
ER, HANG ON, LET ME BACK UP
BUT WAIT, HOW IS A STAR GOING TO STOP THIS RING FROM OVERLOADING AND KILLING ME?
NO, ALITHA, THE STAR ISN'T REAL. BUT THE SMOLDERING SKELETON OF OUR FELLOW RING BEARER IS VERY REAL.
AND I DO NOT WISH TO END UP LIKE HER.
NO, UH, LOOK... I'M NOT EXPLAINING THIS RIGHT, BUT...
THE STAR IS... IT'S LIKE A METAPHOR, RIGHT? FOR THE STRENGTH THAT WE ALL HAVE IN OUR HEARTS--
THIS WORKS, I SWEAR IT!
LOOK!

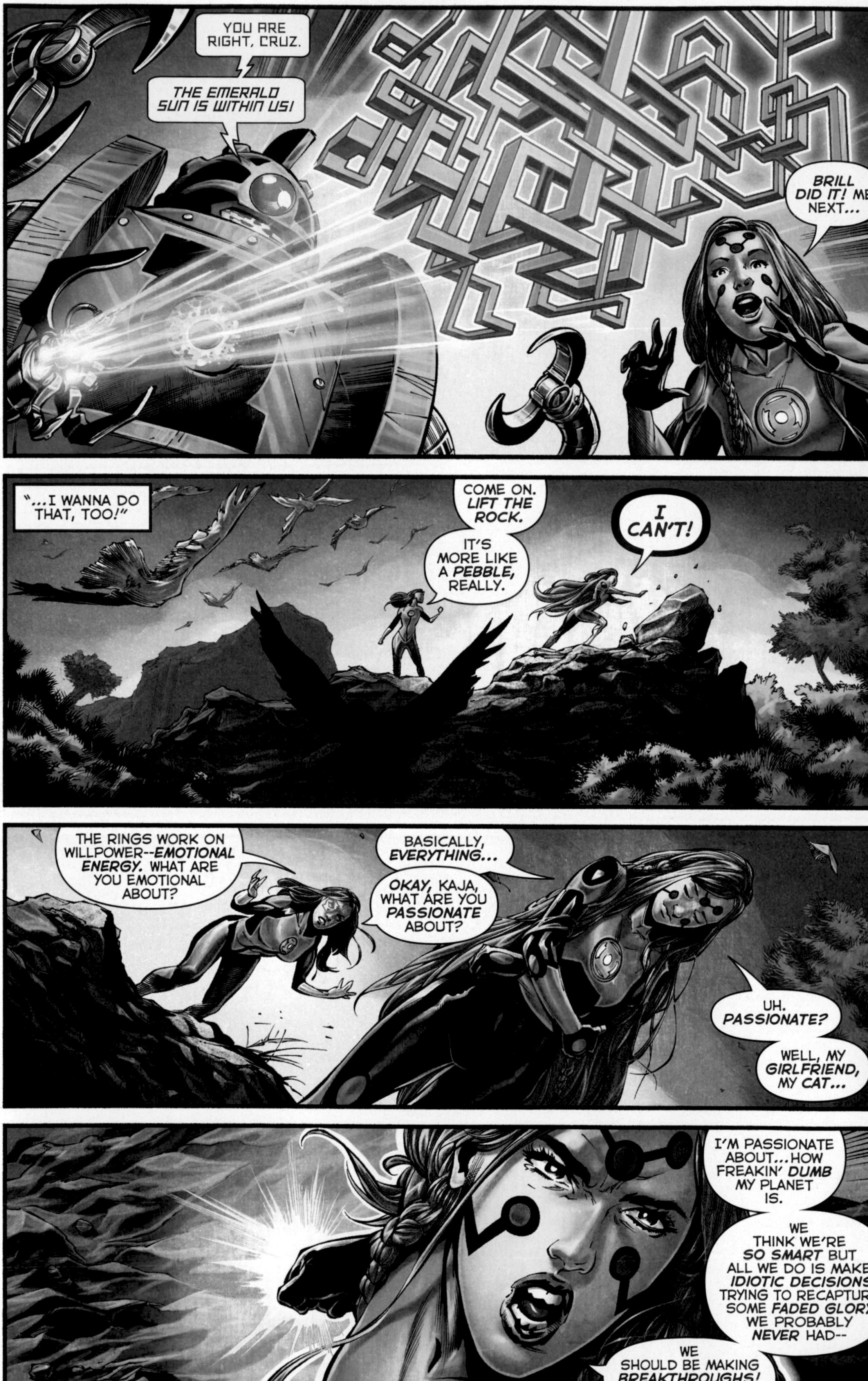

YOU ARE RIGHT, CRUZ.
THE EMERALD SUN IS WITHIN US!
BRILL DID IT! ME NEXT...
"...I WANNA DO THAT, TOO!"
COME ON. LIFT THE ROCK.
IT'S MORE LIKE A PEBBLE, REALLY.
I CAN'T!
THE RINGS WORK ON WILLPOWER--EMOTIONAL ENERGY. WHAT ARE YOU EMOTIONAL ABOUT?
BASICALLY, EVERYTHING...
OKAY, KAJA, WHAT ARE YOU PASSIONATE ABOUT?
UH. PASSIONATE?
WELL, MY GIRLFRIEND, MY CAT...
I'M PASSIONATE ABOUT... HOW FREAKIN' DUMB MY PLANET IS.
WE THINK WE'RE SO SMART BUT ALL WE DO IS MAKE IDIOTIC DECISIONS TRYING TO RECAPTURE SOME FADED GLORY WE PROBABLY NEVER HAD--
WE SHOULD BE MAKING BREAKTHROUGHS! NOT REGRESSING--

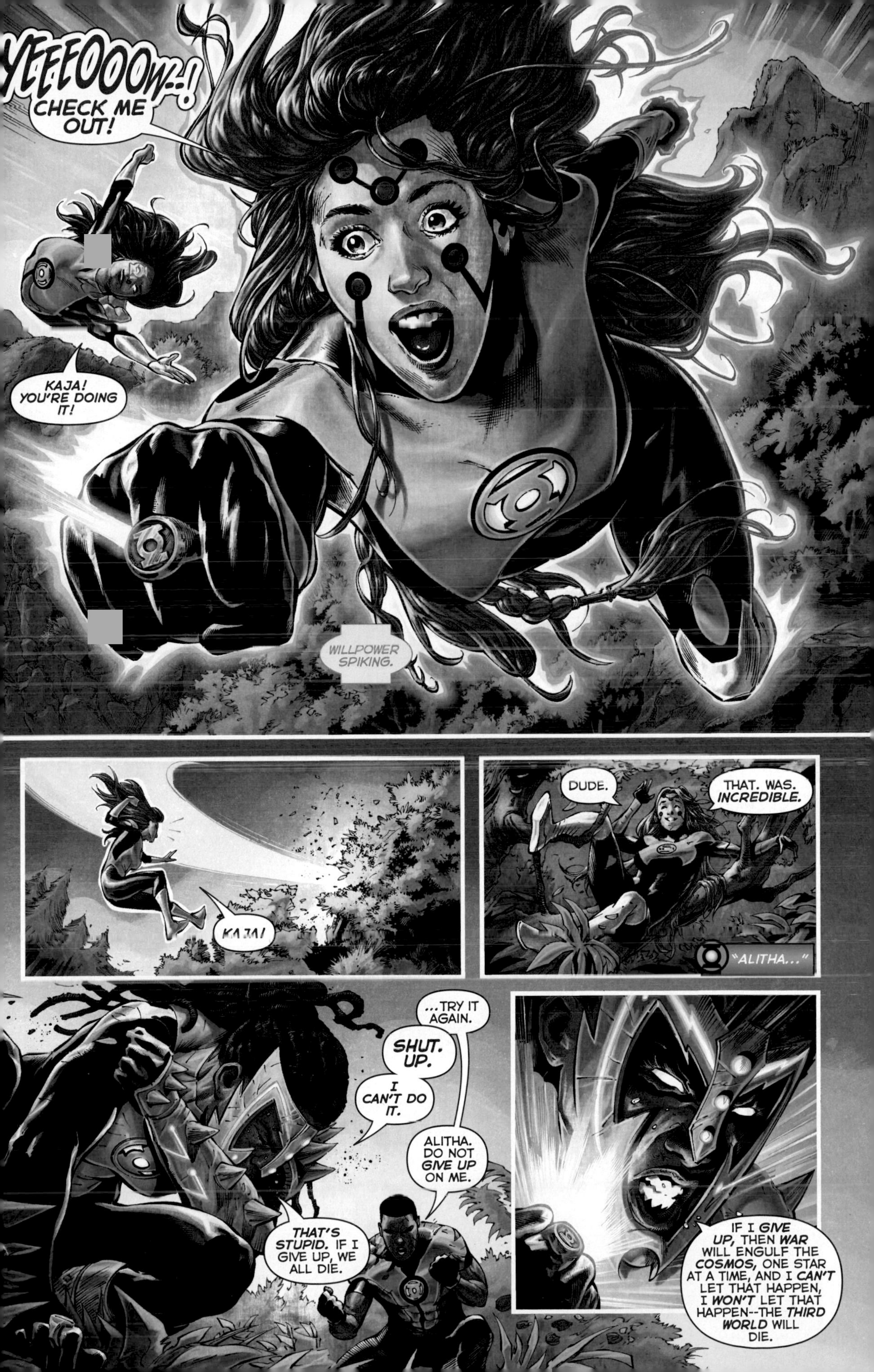

YEEEOOOW--!
CHECK ME OUT!
KAJA! YOU'RE DOING IT!
WILLPOWER SPIKING.
KAJA!
DUDE.
THAT. WAS. INCREDIBLE.
"ALITHA..."
...TRY IT AGAIN.
SHUT. UP.
I CAN'T DO IT.
ALITHA. DO NOT GIVE UP ON ME.
THAT'S STUPID. IF I GIVE UP, WE ALL DIE.
IF I GIVE UP, THEN WAR WILL ENGULF THE COSMOS, ONE STAR AT A TIME, AND I CAN'T LET THAT HAPPEN, I WON'T LET THAT HAPPEN--THE THIRD WORLD WILL DIE.

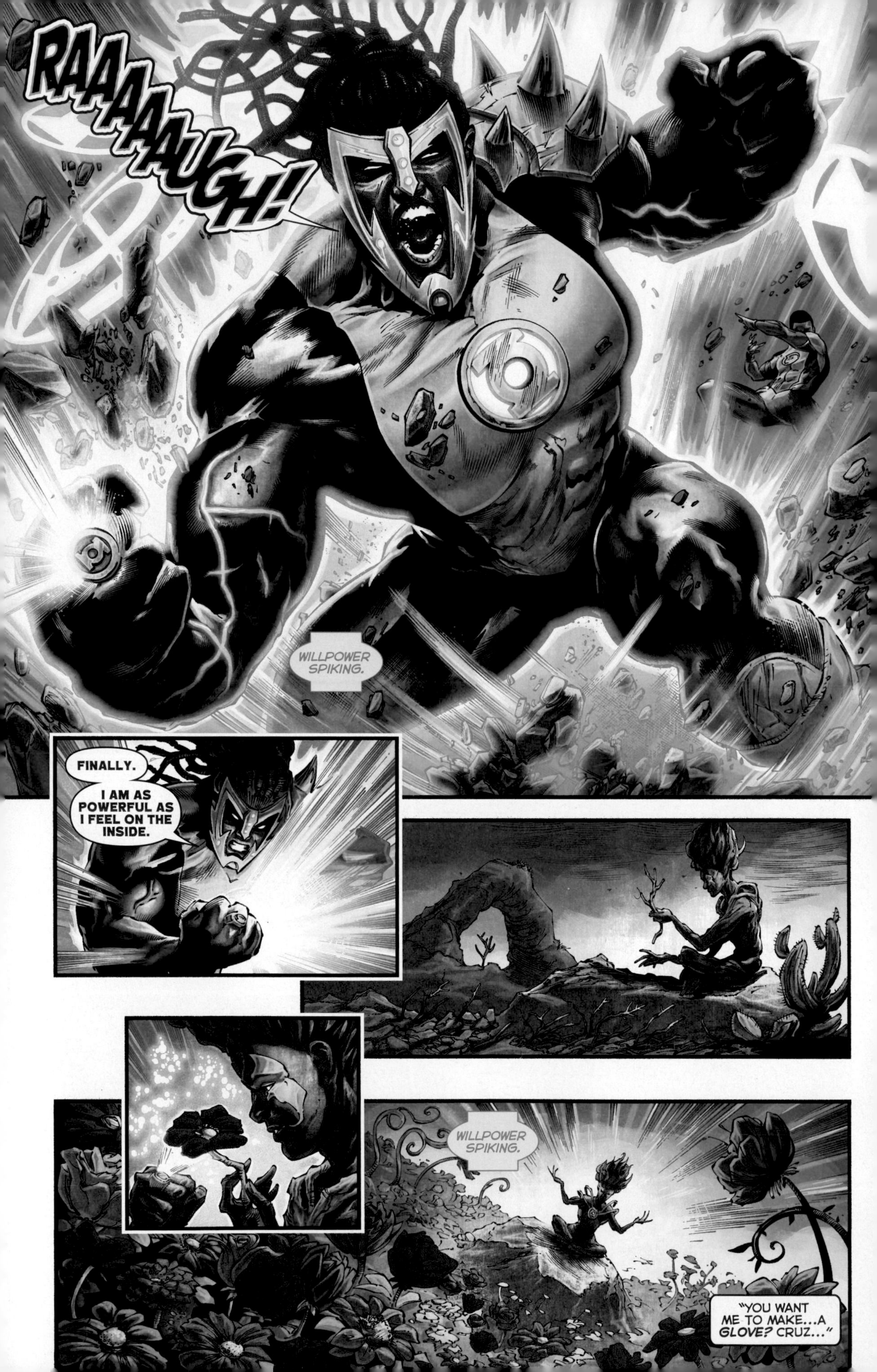
RAAAAAAUGH!!
WILLPOWER SPIKING.
FINALLY.
I AM AS POWERFUL AS I FEEL ON THE INSIDE.
WILLPOWER SPIKING.
"YOU WANT ME TO MAKE...A GLOVE? CRUZ..."

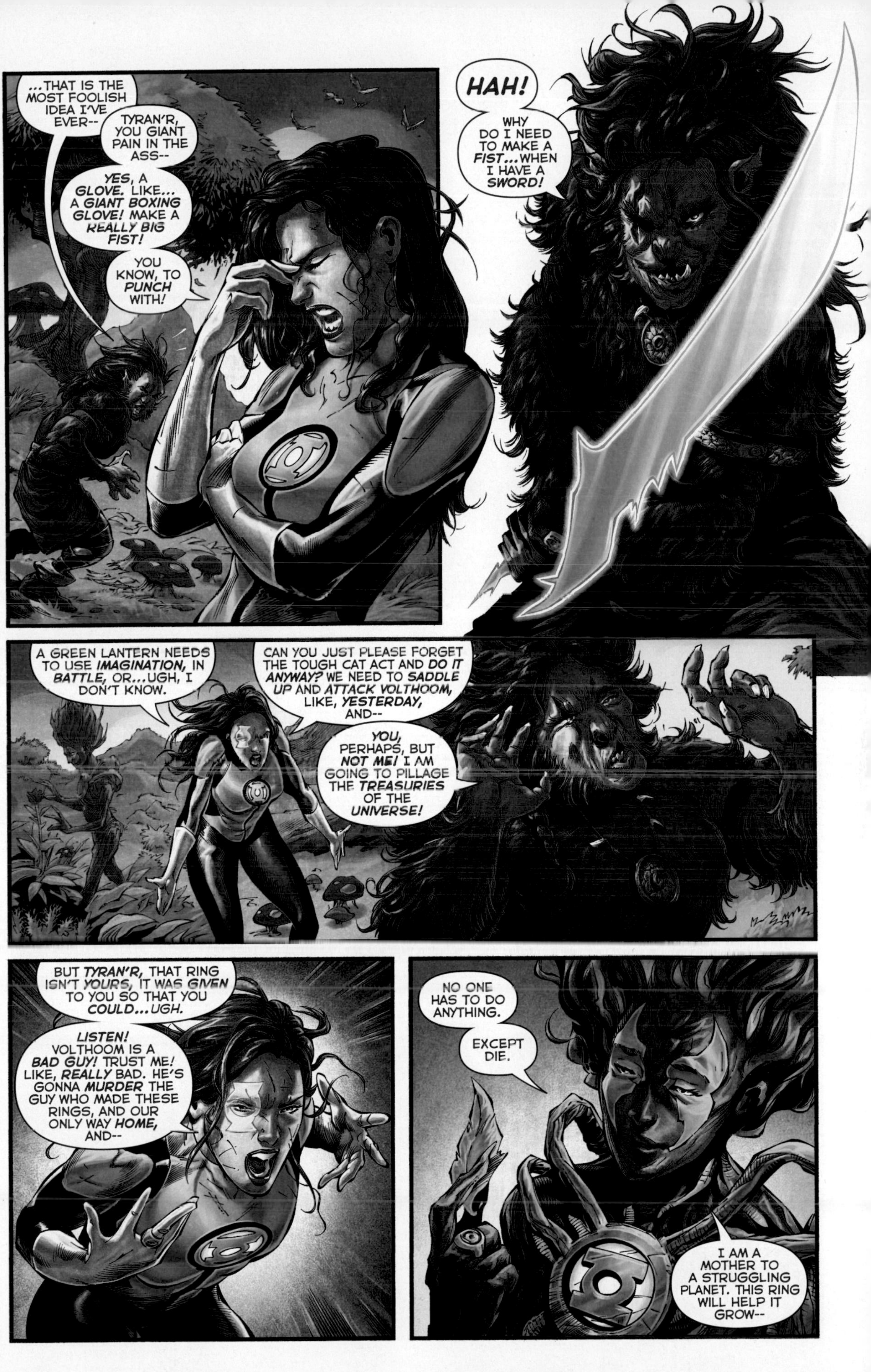
...THAT IS THE MOST FOOLISH IDEA I'VE EVER--
TYRAN'R, YOU GIANT PAIN IN THE ASS--
YES, A GLOVE. LIKE... A GIANT BOXING GLOVE! MAKE A REALLY BIG FIST!
YOU KNOW, TO PUNCH WITH!
HAH!
WHY DO I NEED TO MAKE A FIST...WHEN I HAVE A SWORD!
A GREEN LANTERN NEEDS TO USE IMAGINATION, IN BATTLE, OR...UGH, I DON'T KNOW.
CAN YOU JUST PLEASE FORGET THE TOUGH CAT ACT AND DO IT ANYWAY? WE NEED TO SADDLE UP AND ATTACK VOLTHOOM, LIKE, YESTERDAY, AND--
YOU, PERHAPS, BUT NOT ME! I AM GOING TO PILLAGE THE TREASURIES OF THE UNIVERSE!
BUT TYRAN'R, THAT RING ISN'T YOURS, IT WAS GIVEN TO YOU SO THAT YOU COULD...UGH.
LISTEN! VOLTHOOM IS A BAD GUY! TRUST ME! LIKE, REALLY BAD. HE'S GONNA MURDER THE GUY WHO MADE THESE RINGS, AND OUR ONLY WAY HOME, AND--
NO ONE HAS TO DO ANYTHING.
EXCEPT DIE.
I AM A MOTHER TO A STRUGGLING PLANET. THIS RING WILL HELP IT GROW--

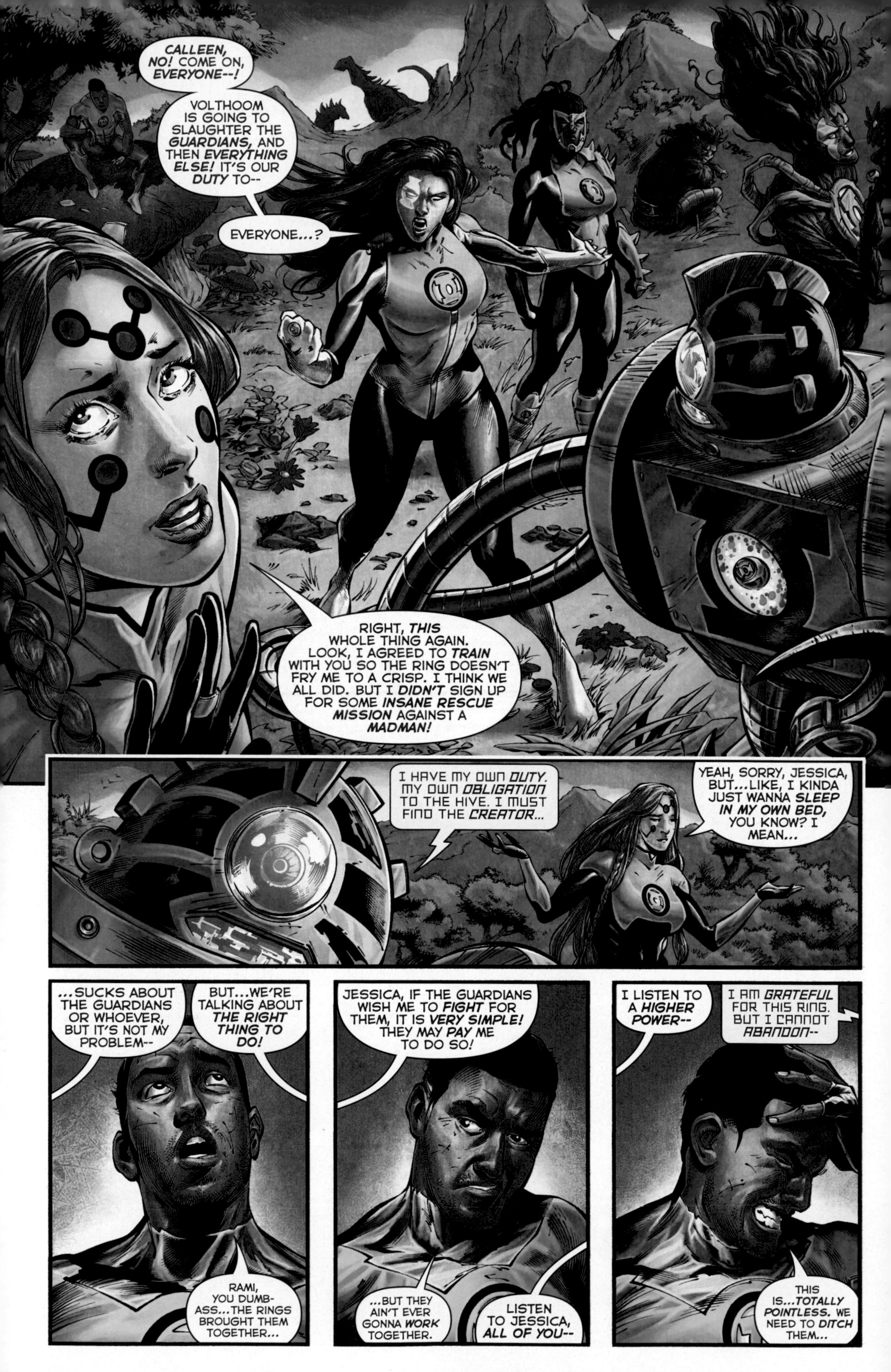
CALLEEN, NO! COME ON, EVERYONE--!
VOLTHOOM IS GOING TO SLAUGHTER THE GUARDIANS, AND THEN EVERYTHING ELSE! IT'S OUR DUTY TO--
EVERYONE...?
RIGHT, THIS WHOLE THING AGAIN. LOOK, I AGREED TO TRAIN WITH YOU SO THE RING DOESN'T FRY ME TO A CRISP. I THINK WE ALL DID. BUT I DIDN'T SIGN UP FOR SOME INSANE RESCUE MISSION AGAINST A MADMAN!
I HAVE MY OWN DUTY. MY OWN OBLIGATION TO THE HIVE. I MUST FIND THE CREATOR...
YEAH, SORRY, JESSICA, BUT...LIKE, I KINDA JUST WANNA SLEEP IN MY OWN BED, YOU KNOW? I MEAN...
...SUCKS ABOUT THE GUARDIANS OR WHOEVER, BUT IT'S NOT MY PROBLEM--
BUT...WE'RE TALKING ABOUT THE RIGHT THING TO DO!
RAMI, YOU DUMB-ASS...THE RINGS BROUGHT THEM TOGETHER...
JESSICA, IF THE GUARDIANS WISH ME TO FIGHT FOR THEM, IT IS VERY SIMPLE! THEY MAY PAY ME TO DO SO!
...BUT THEY AIN'T EVER GONNA WORK TOGETHER.
LISTEN TO JESSICA, ALL OF YOU--
I LISTEN TO A HIGHER POWER--
I AM GRATEFUL FOR THIS RING. BUT I CANNOT ABANDON--
THIS IS...TOTALLY POINTLESS. WE NEED TO DITCH THEM...

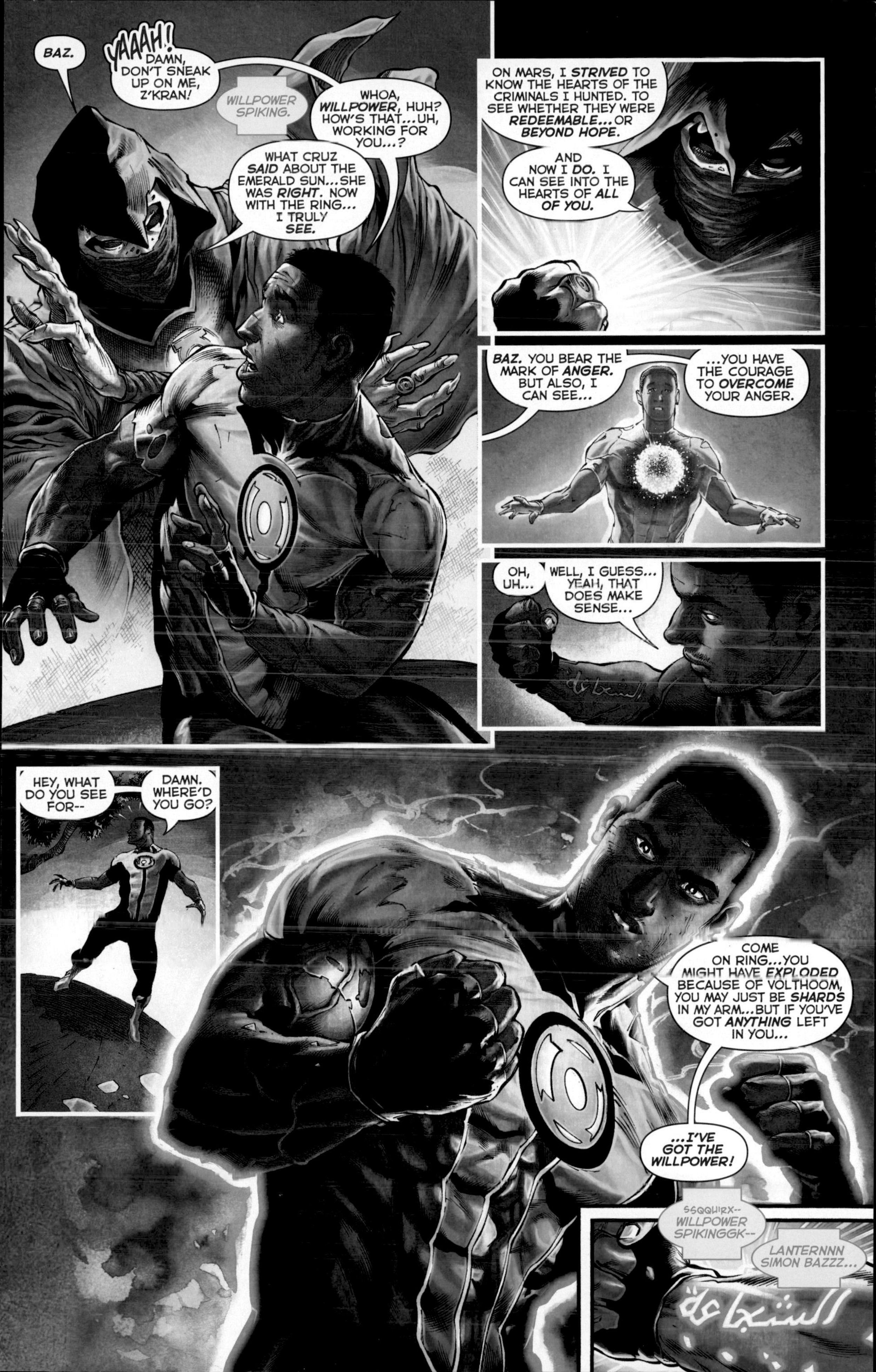
BAZ.
YAAAH! DAMN, DON'T SNEAK UP ON ME, Z'KRAN!
WILLPOWER SPIKING.
WHOA, WILLPOWER, HUH? HOW'S THAT...UH, WORKING FOR YOU...?
WHAT CRUZ SAID ABOUT THE EMERALD SUN...SHE WAS RIGHT. NOW WITH THE RING... I TRULY SEE.
ON MARS, I STRIVED TO KNOW THE HEARTS OF THE CRIMINALS I HUNTED. TO SEE WHETHER THEY WERE REDEEMABLE...OR BEYOND HOPE.
AND NOW I DO. I CAN SEE INTO THE HEARTS OF ALL OF YOU.
BAZ. YOU BEAR THE MARK OF ANGER. BUT ALSO, I CAN SEE...
...YOU HAVE THE COURAGE TO OVERCOME YOUR ANGER.
OH, UH...
WELL, I GUESS... YEAH, THAT DOES MAKE SENSE...
HEY, WHAT DO YOU SEE FOR--
DAMN. WHERE'D YOU GO?
COME ON RING...YOU MIGHT HAVE EXPLODED BECAUSE OF VOLTHOOM, YOU MAY JUST BE SHARDS IN MY ARM...BUT IF YOU'VE GOT ANYTHING LEFT IN YOU...
...I'VE GOT THE WILLPOWER!
SSQQHIRX-- WILLPOWER SPIKINGGK--
LANTERNNN SIMON BAZZZ...
الشجاعة

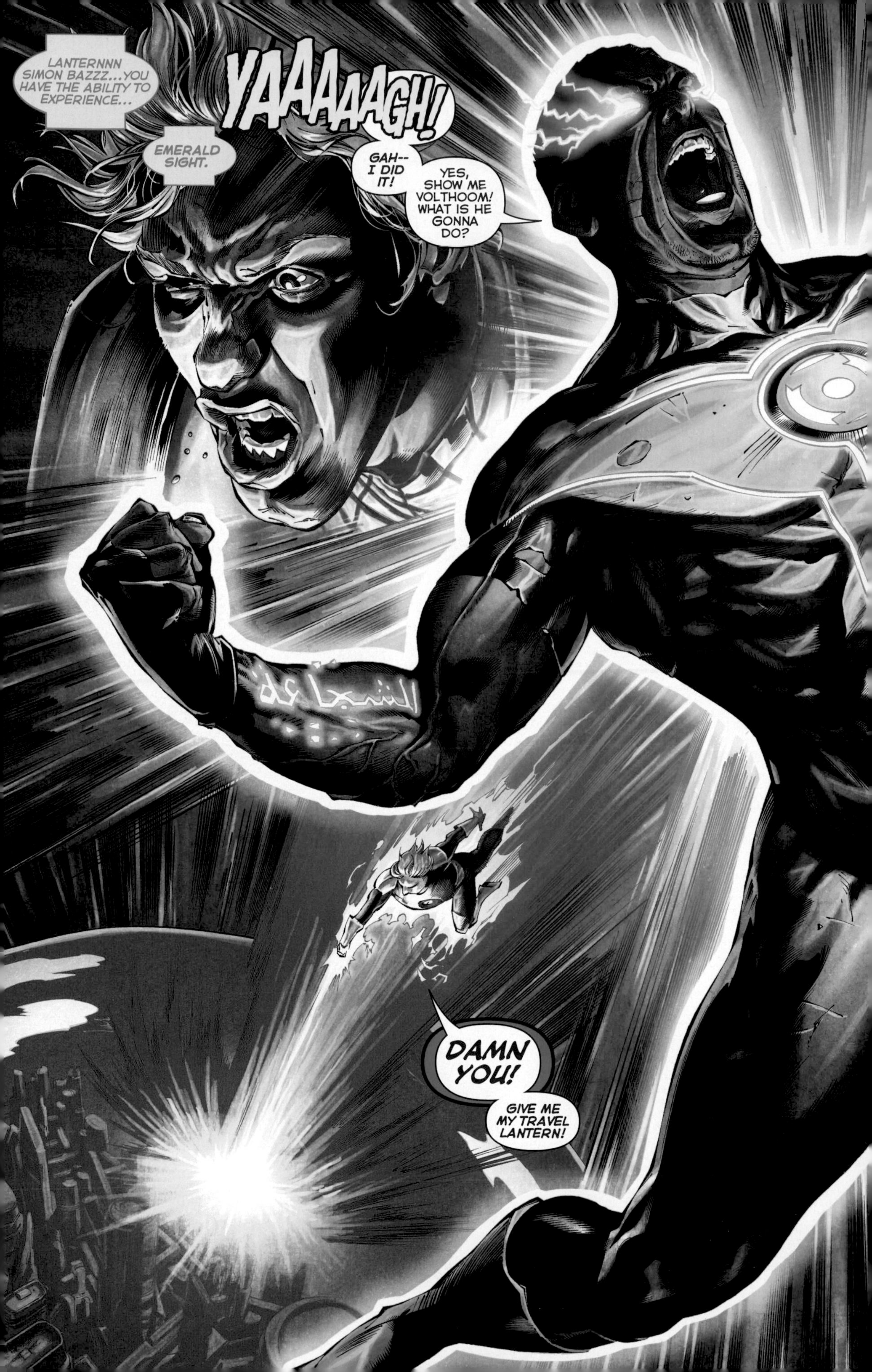
LANTERNNN SIMON BAZZZ...YOU HAVE THE ABILITY TO EXPERIENCE...
EMERALD SIGHT.
YAAAAAGH!
GAH-- I DID IT!
YES, SHOW ME VOLTHOOM! WHAT IS HE GONNA DO?
DAMN YOU!
GIVE ME MY TRAVEL LANTERN!

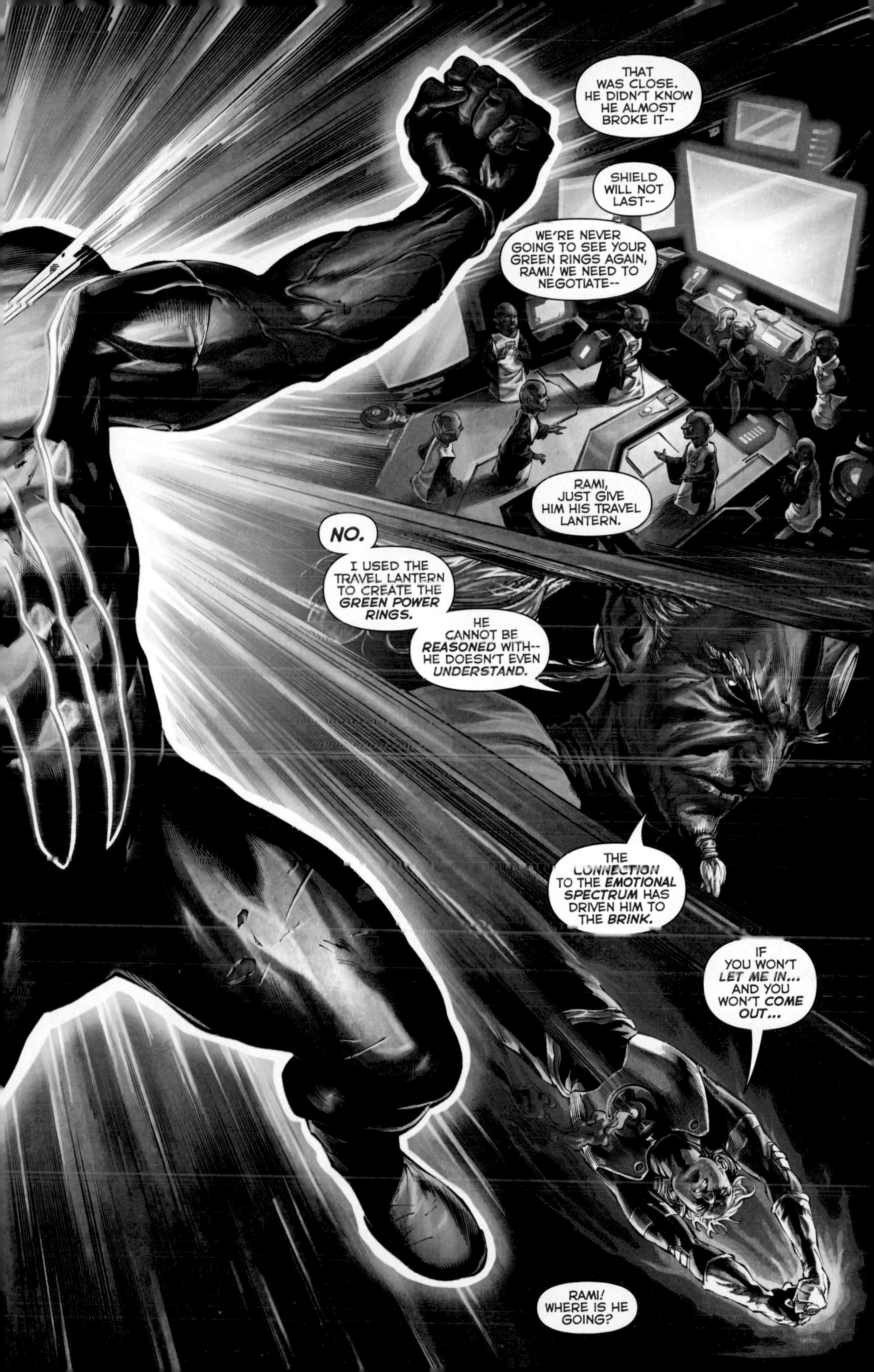
THAT WAS CLOSE. HE DIDN'T KNOW HE ALMOST BROKE IT--
SHIELD WILL NOT LAST--
WE'RE NEVER GOING TO SEE YOUR GREEN RINGS AGAIN, RAMI! WE NEED TO NEGOTIATE--
RAMI, JUST GIVE HIM HIS TRAVEL LANTERN.
NO.
I USED THE TRAVEL LANTERN TO CREATE THE GREEN POWER RINGS.
HE CANNOT BE REASONED WITH-- HE DOESN'T EVEN UNDERSTAND.
THE CONNECTION TO THE EMOTIONAL SPECTRUM HAS DRIVEN HIM TO THE BRINK.
IF YOU WON'T LET ME IN... AND YOU WON'T COME OUT...
RAMI! WHERE IS HE GOING?

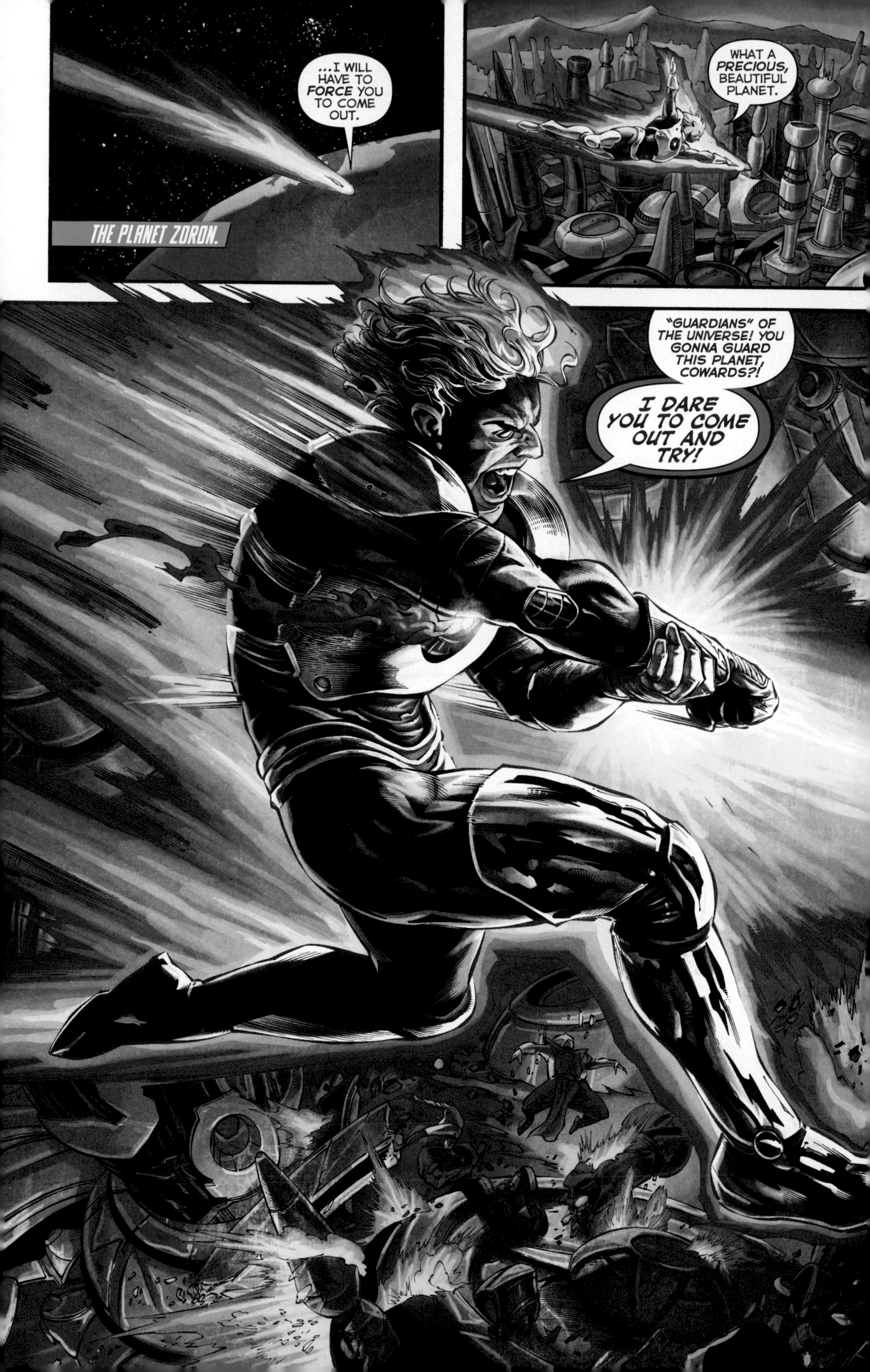
...I WILL HAVE TO FORCE YOU TO COME OUT.
THE PLANET ZORON.
WHAT A PRECIOUS, BEAUTIFUL PLANET.
"GUARDIANS" OF THE UNIVERSE! YOU GONNA GUARD THIS PLANET, COWARDS?!
I DARE YOU TO COME OUT AND TRY!

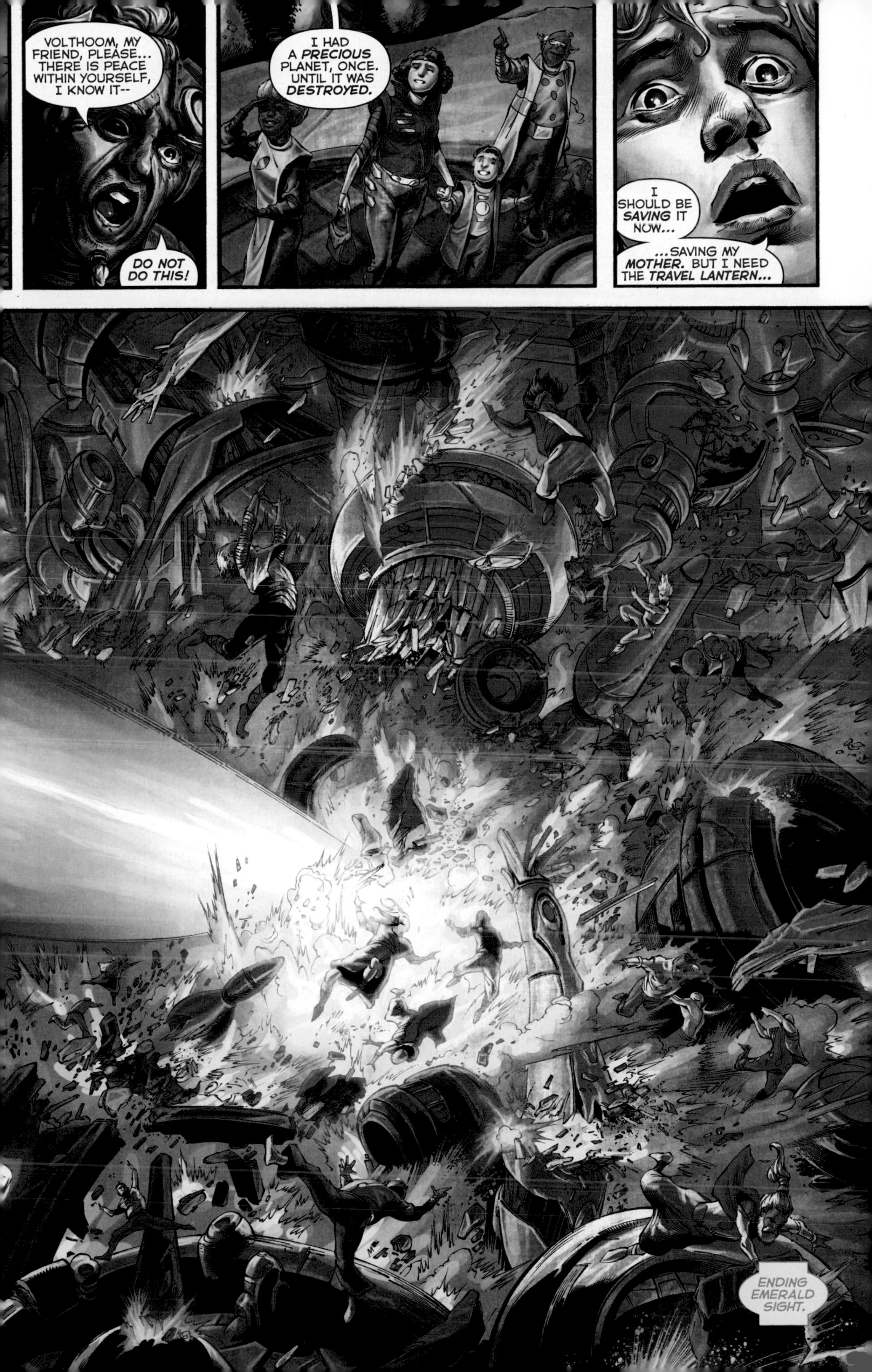
VOLTHOOM, MY FRIEND, PLEASE... THERE IS PEACE WITHIN YOURSELF, I KNOW IT--
DO NOT DO THIS!
I HAD A PRECIOUS PLANET, ONCE. UNTIL IT WAS DESTROYED.
I SHOULD BE SAVING IT NOW...
...SAVING MY MOTHER. BUT I NEED THE TRAVEL LANTERN...
ENDING EMERALD SIGHT.

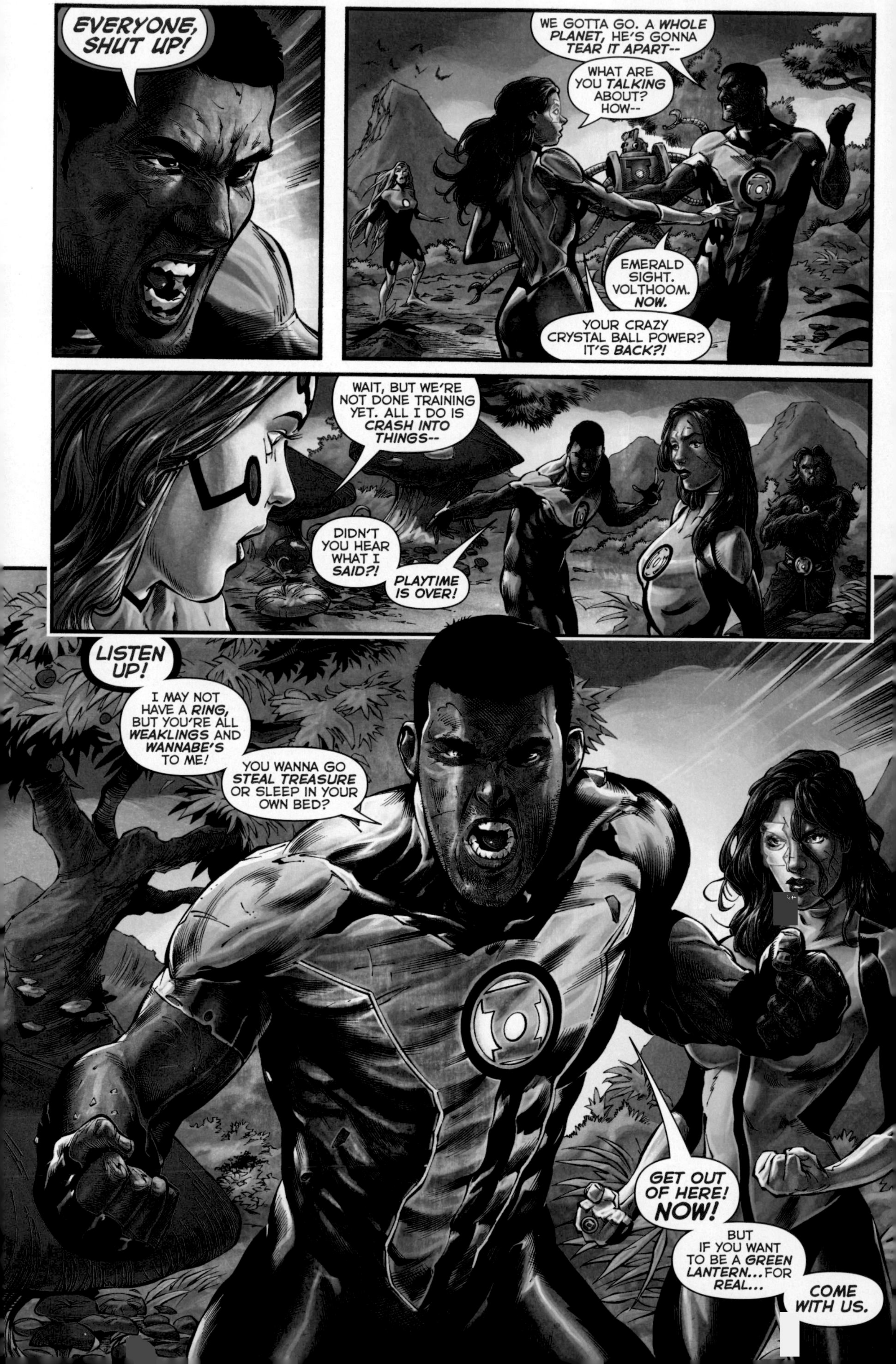
EVERYONE, SHUT UP!
WE GOTTA GO. A WHOLE PLANET, HE'S GONNA TEAR IT APART--
WHAT ARE YOU TALKING ABOUT? HOW--
EMERALD SIGHT. VOLTHOOM. NOW.
YOUR CRAZY CRYSTAL BALL POWER? IT'S BACK?!
WAIT, BUT WE'RE NOT DONE TRAINING YET. ALL I DO IS CRASH INTO THINGS--
DIDN'T YOU HEAR WHAT I SAID?!
PLAYTIME IS OVER!
LISTEN UP!
I MAY NOT HAVE A RING, BUT YOU'RE ALL WEAKLINGS AND WANNABE'S TO ME!
YOU WANNA GO STEAL TREASURE OR SLEEP IN YOUR OWN BED?
GET OUT OF HERE! NOW!
BUT IF YOU WANT TO BE A GREEN LANTERN...FOR REAL...
COME WITH US.

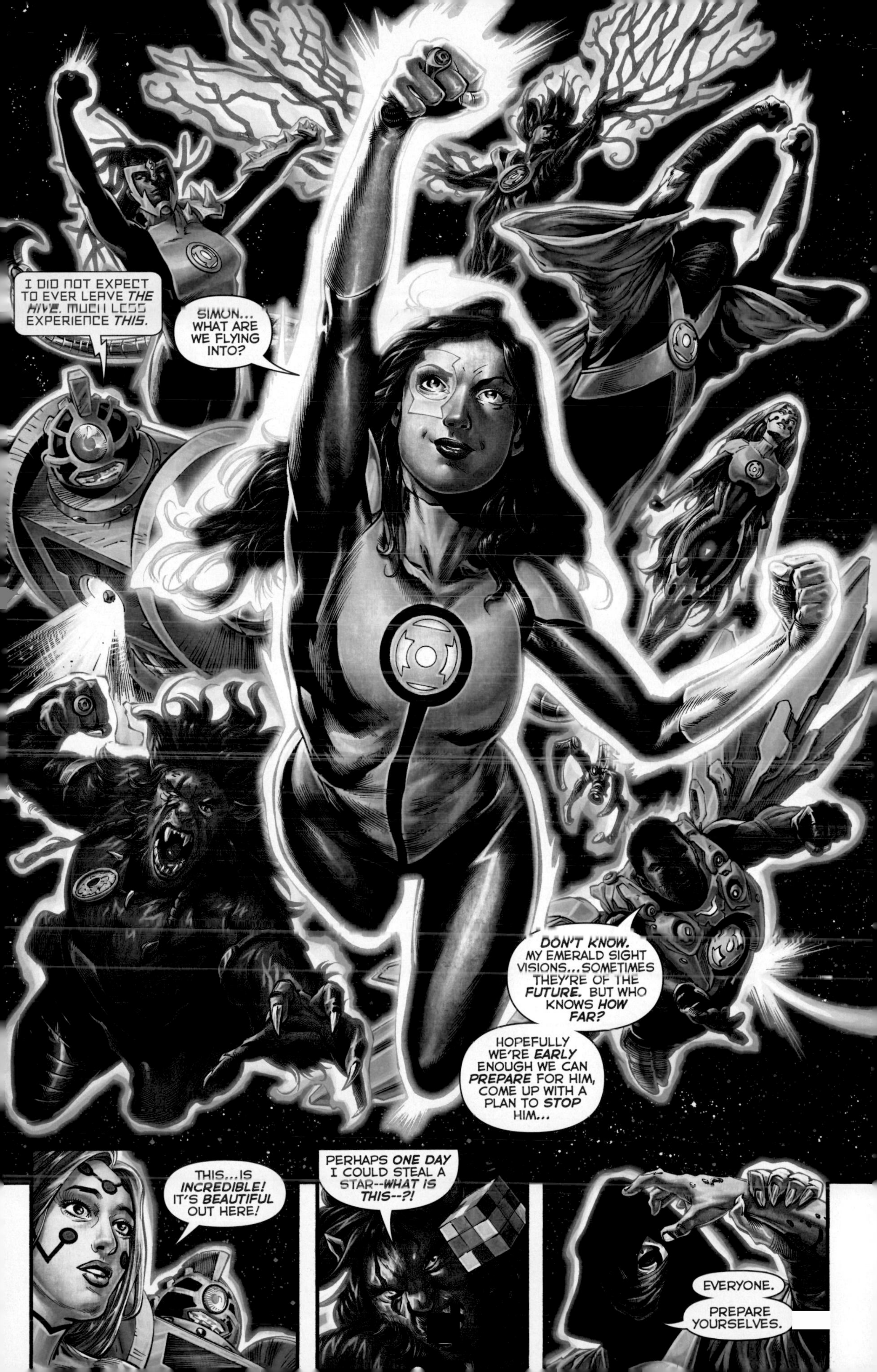
I DID NOT EXPECT TO EVER LEAVE THE HIVE. MUCH LESS EXPERIENCE THIS.
SIMON... WHAT ARE WE FLYING INTO?
DON'T KNOW. MY EMERALD SIGHT VISIONS...SOMETIMES THEY'RE OF THE FUTURE. BUT WHO KNOWS HOW FAR?
HOPEFULLY WE'RE EARLY ENOUGH WE CAN PREPARE FOR HIM, COME UP WITH A PLAN TO STOP HIM...
THIS...IS INCREDIBLE! IT'S BEAUTIFUL OUT HERE!
PERHAPS ONE DAY I COULD STEAL A STAR--WHAT IS THIS--?!
EVERYONE.
PREPARE YOURSELVES.

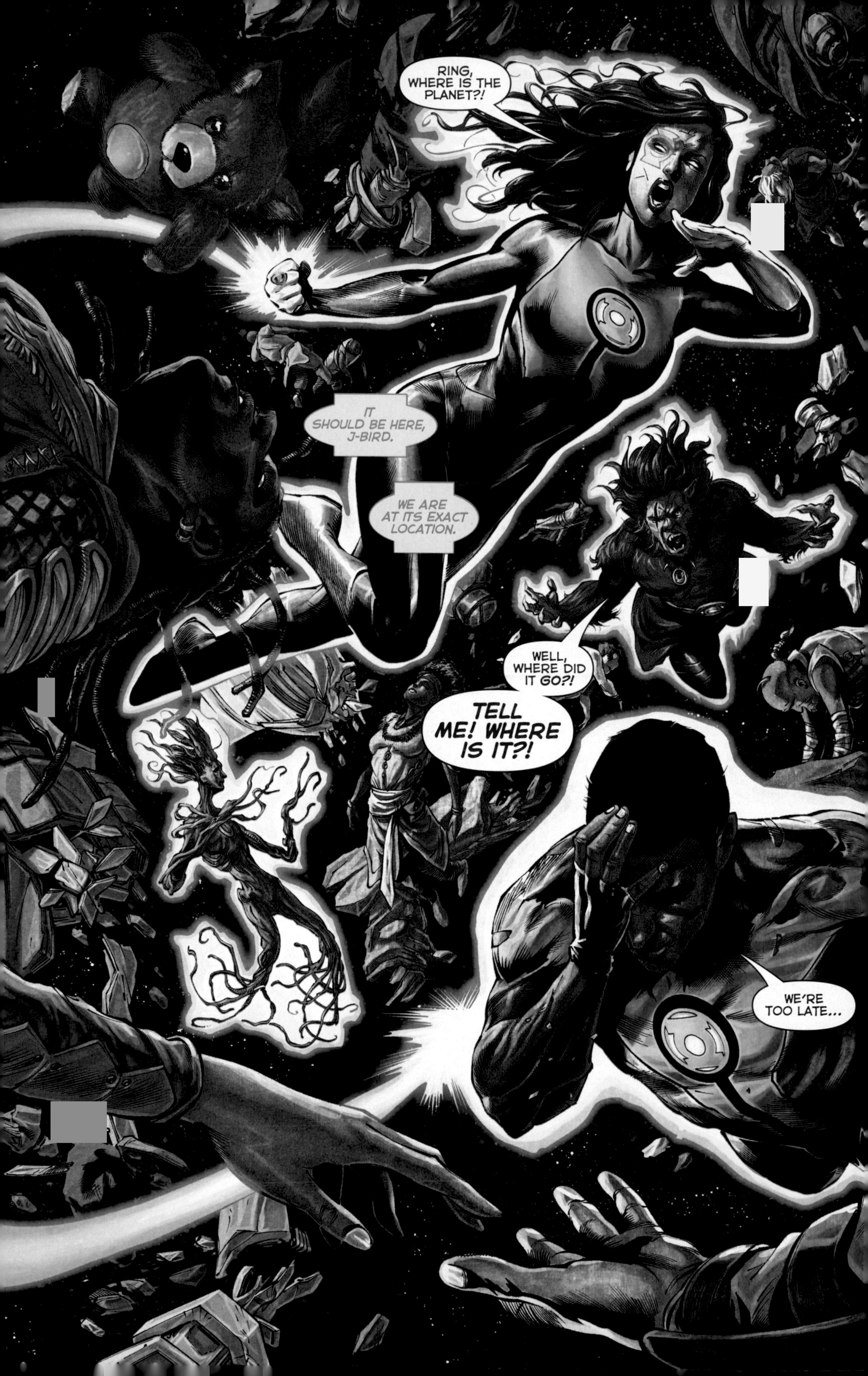
RING, WHERE IS THE PLANET?!
IT SHOULD BE HERE, J-BIRD.
WE ARE AT ITS EXACT LOCATION.
WELL, WHERE DID IT GO?!
TELL ME! WHERE IS IT?!
WE'RE TOO LATE...

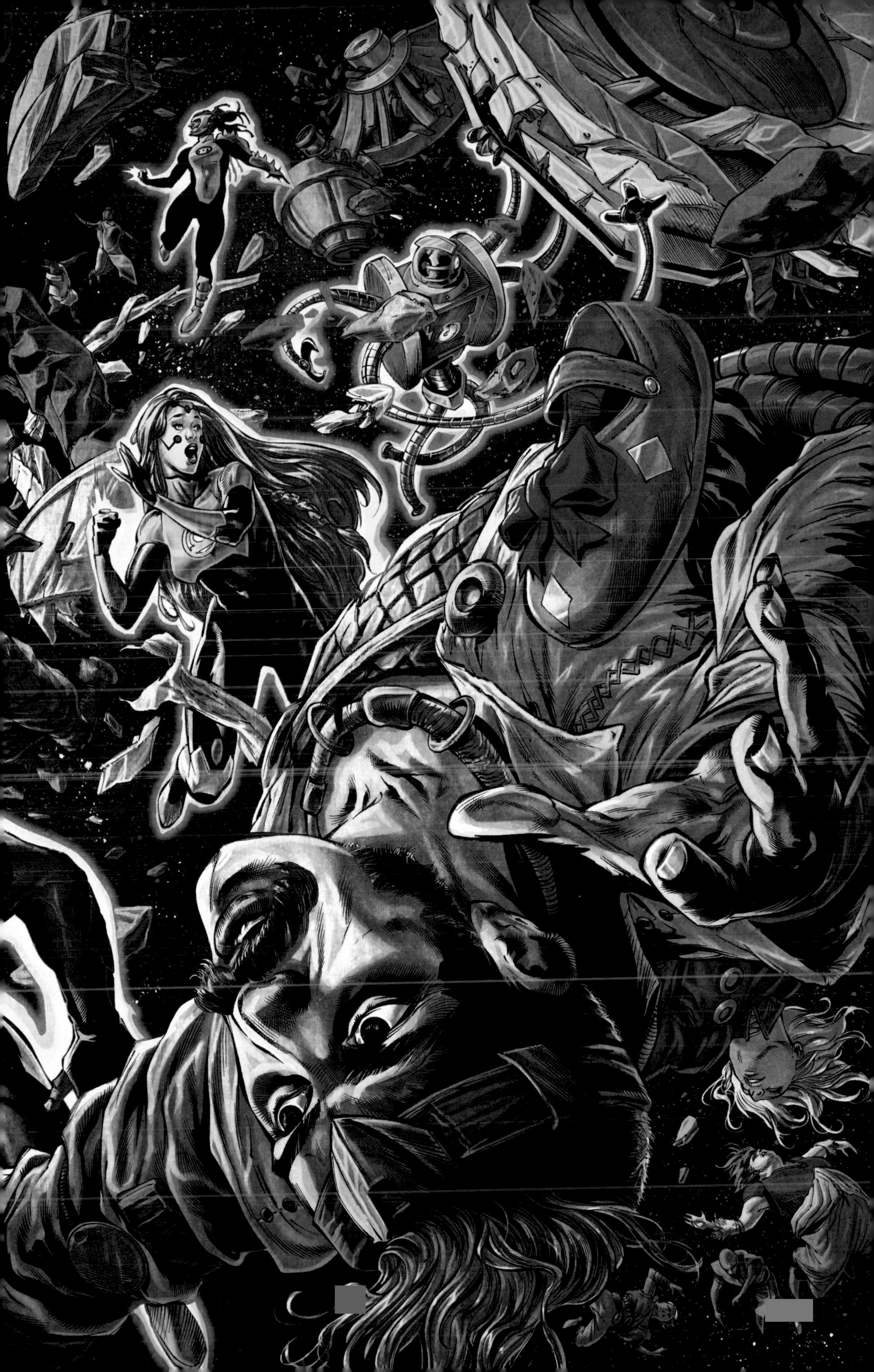

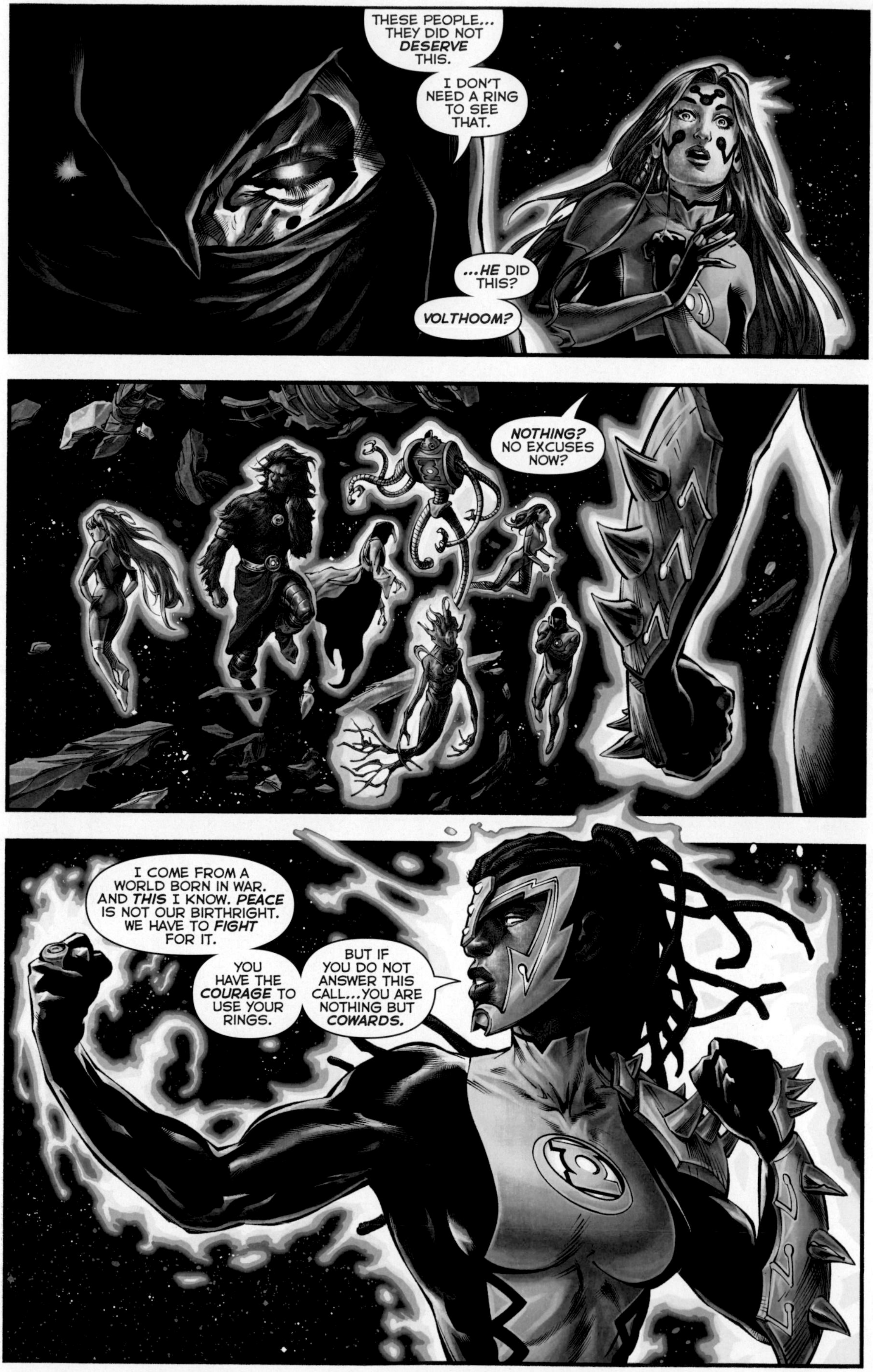
THESE PEOPLE... THEY DID NOT DESERVE THIS.
I DON'T NEED A RING TO SEE THAT.
...HE DID THIS?
VOLTHOOM?
NOTHING? NO EXCUSES NOW?
I COME FROM A WORLD BORN IN WAR. AND THIS I KNOW. PEACE IS NOT OUR BIRTHRIGHT. WE HAVE TO FIGHT FOR IT.
YOU HAVE THE COURAGE TO USE YOUR RINGS.
BUT IF YOU DO NOT ANSWER THIS CALL...YOU ARE NOTHING BUT COWARDS.

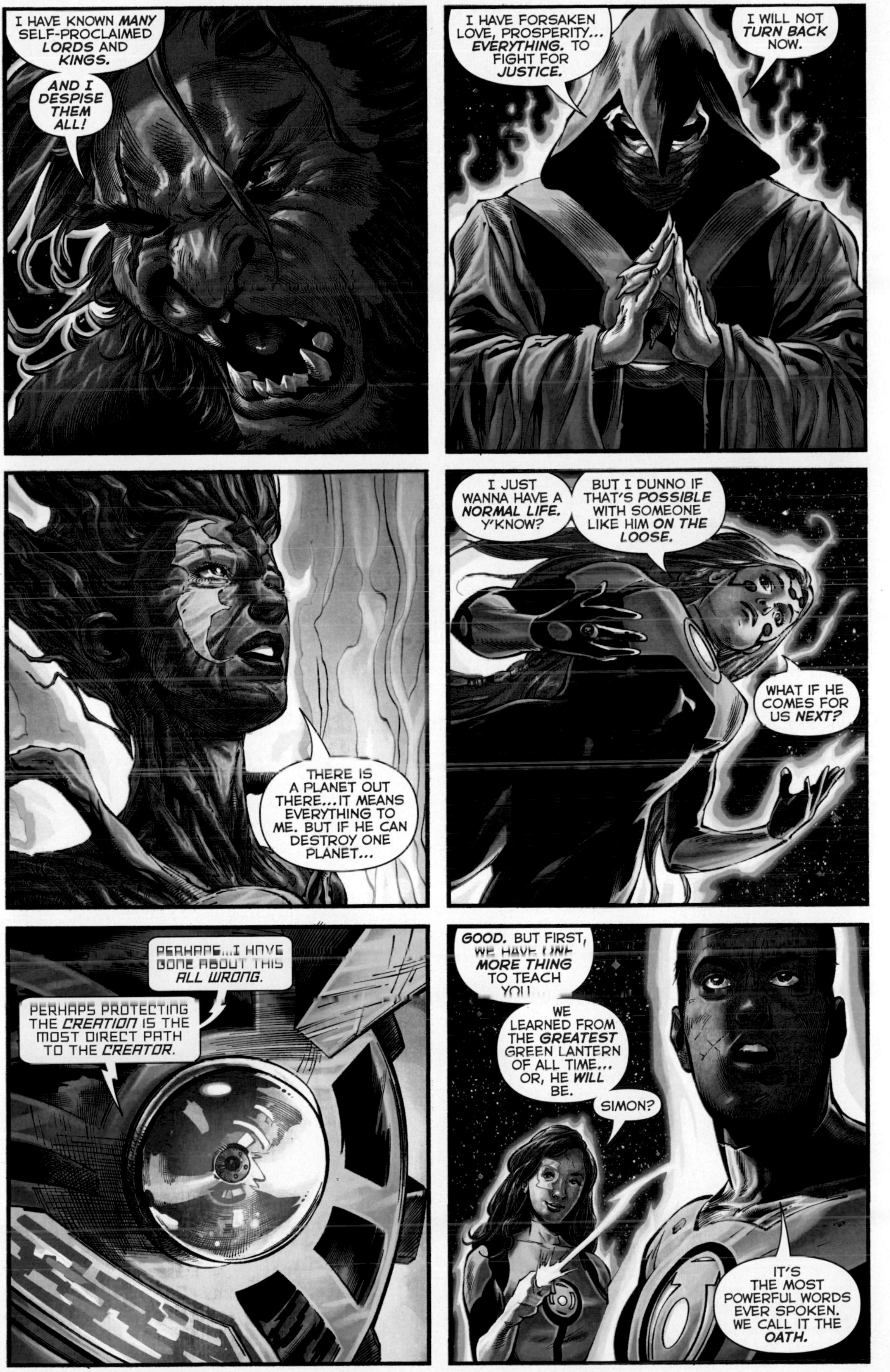
I HAVE KNOWN MANY SELF-PROCLAIMED LORDS AND KINGS.
AND I DESPISE THEM ALL!
I HAVE FORSAKEN LOVE, PROSPERITY... EVERYTHING. TO FIGHT FOR JUSTICE.
I WILL NOT TURN BACK NOW.
THERE IS A PLANET OUT THERE...IT MEANS EVERYTHING TO ME. BUT IF HE CAN DESTROY ONE PLANET...
I JUST WANNA HAVE A NORMAL LIFE. Y'KNOW?
BUT I DUNNO IF THAT'S POSSIBLE WITH SOMEONE LIKE HIM ON THE LOOSE.
WHAT IF HE COMES FOR US NEXT?
PERHAPS...I HAVE GONE ABOUT THIS ALL WRONG.
PERHAPS PROTECTING THE CREATION IS THE MOST DIRECT PATH TO THE CREATOR.
GOOD. BUT FIRST, WE HAVE ONE MORE THING TO TEACH YOU.
WE LEARNED FROM THE GREATEST GREEN LANTERN OF ALL TIME... OR, HE WILL BE.
SIMON?
IT'S THE MOST POWERFUL WORDS EVER SPOKEN. WE CALL IT THE OATH.

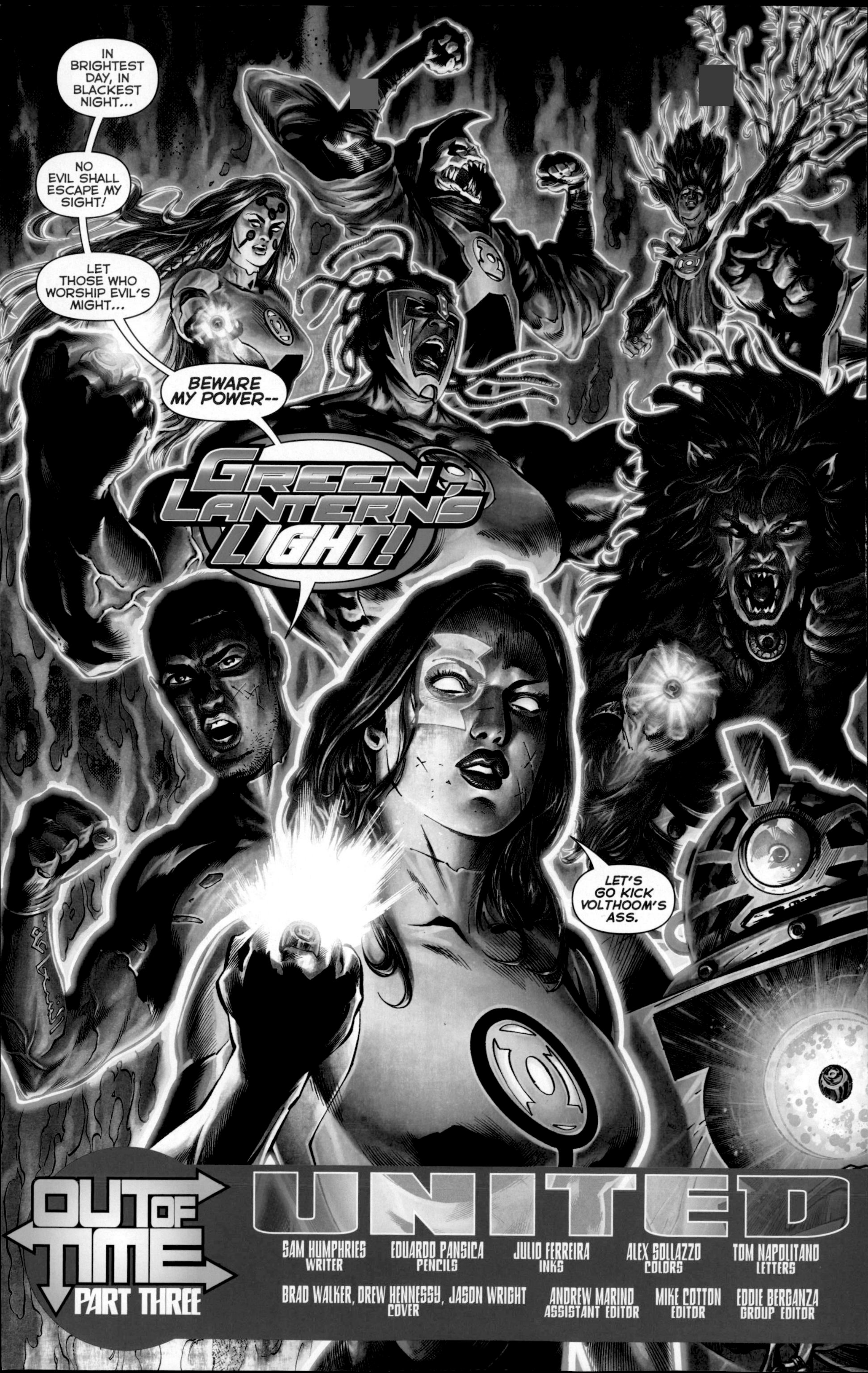

IN BRIGHTEST DAY, IN BLACKEST NIGHT...
NO EVIL SHALL ESCAPE MY SIGHT!
LET THOSE WHO WORSHIP EVIL'S MIGHT...
BEWARE MY POWER--
GREEN LANTERN'S LIGHT!
LET'S GO KICK VOLTHOOM'S ASS.
OUT OF TIME PART THREE
UNITED
SAM HUMPHRIES WRITER
EDUARDO PANSICA PENCILS
JULIO FERREIRA INKS
ALEX SOLLAZZO COLORS
TOM NAPOLITANO LETTERS
BRAD WALKER, DREW HENNESSY, JASON WRIGHT COVER
ANDREW MARINO ASSISTANT EDITOR
MIKE COTTON EDITOR
EDDIE BERGANZA GROUP EDITOR

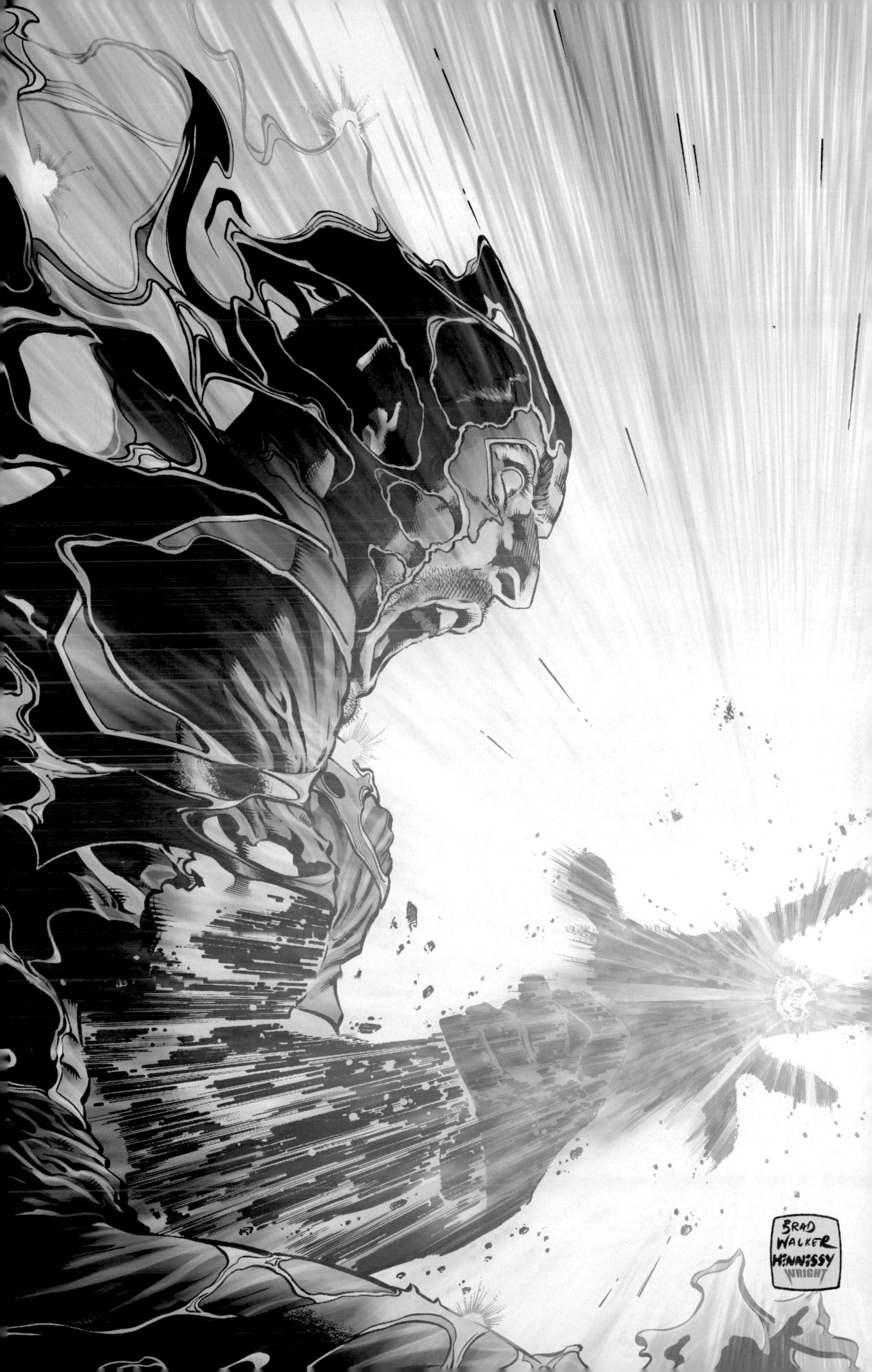
BRAD WALKER
HENNESSY
WRIGHT

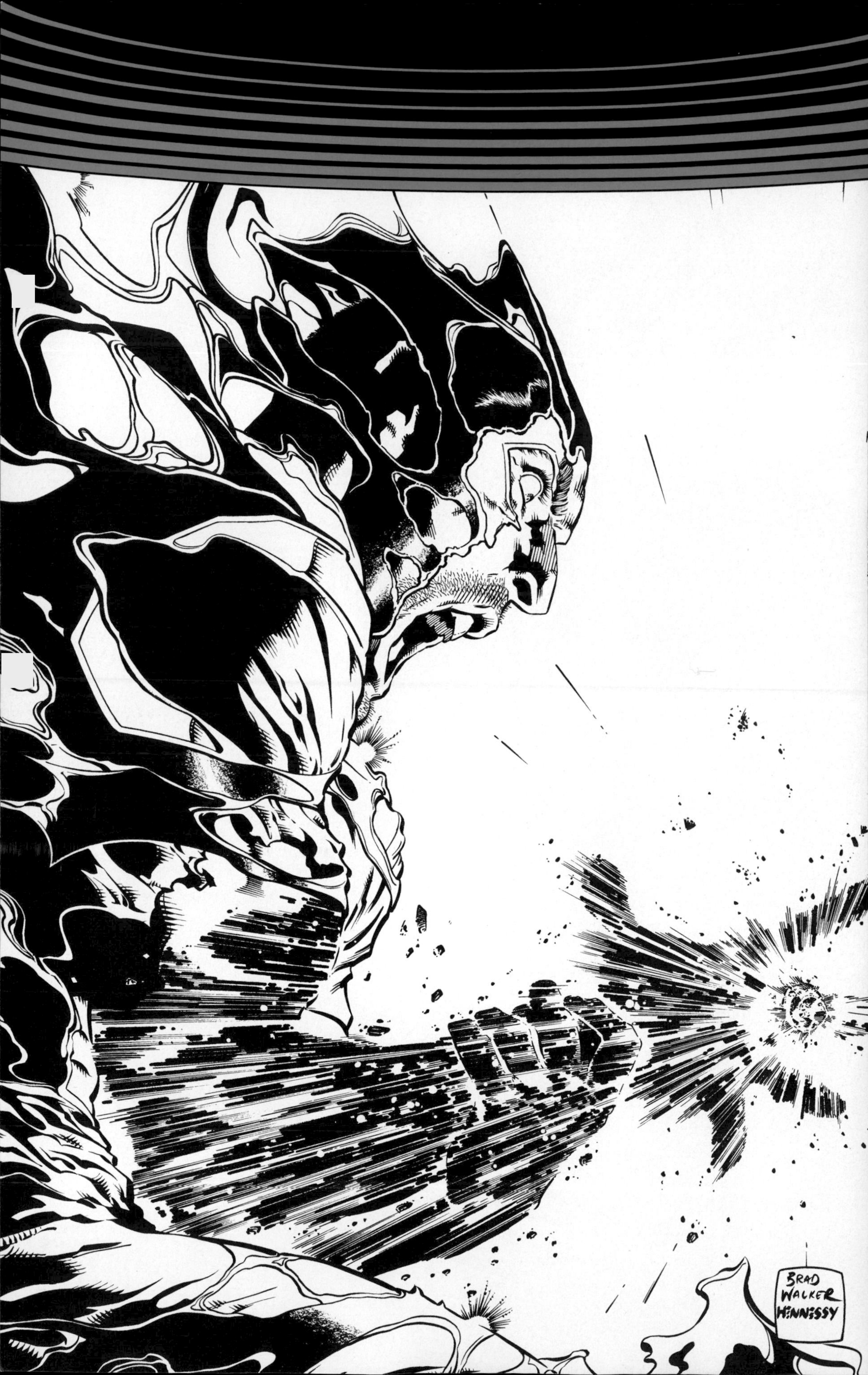
BRAD
WALKER
HENNESSY

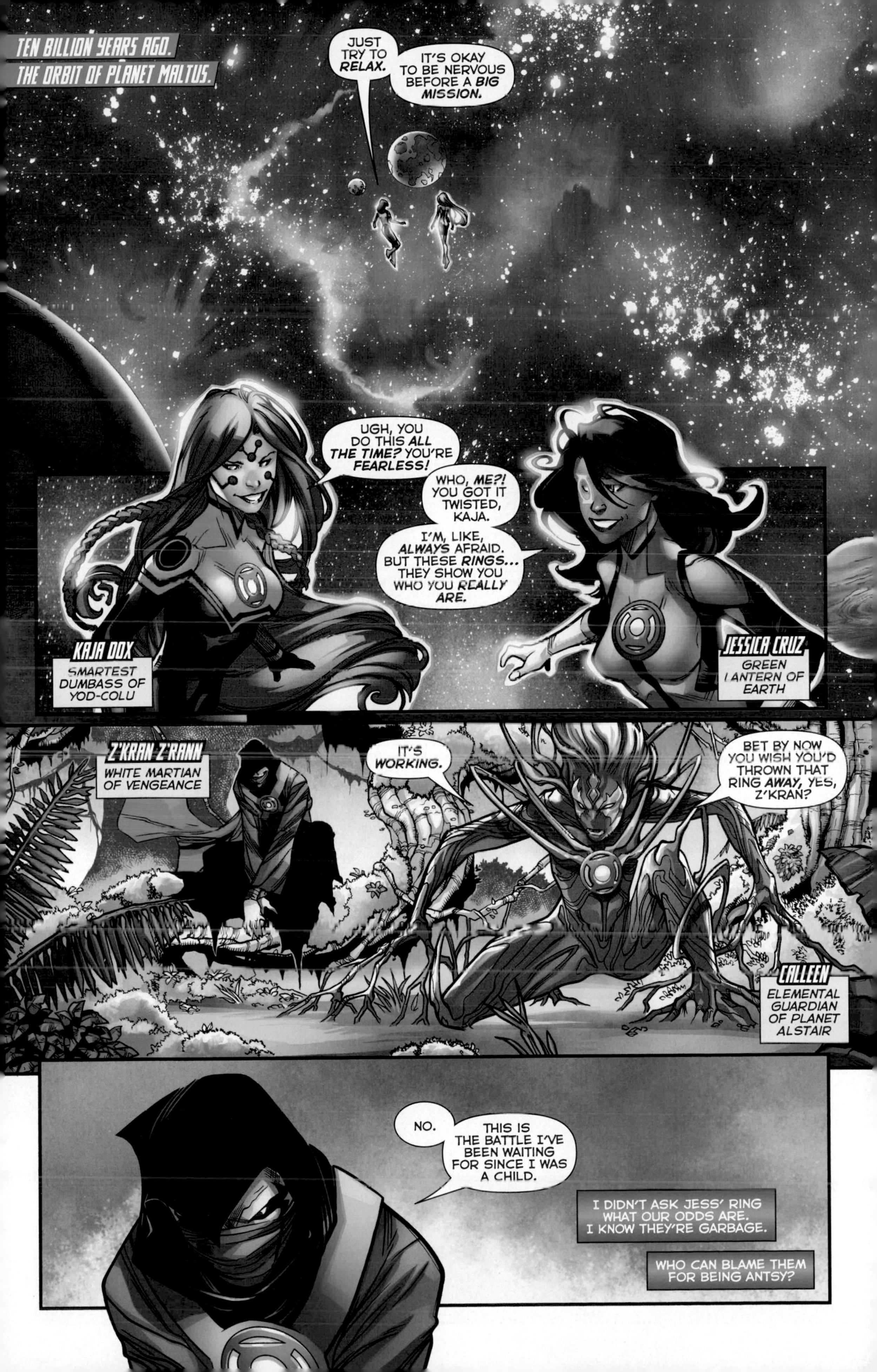
TEN BILLION YEARS AGO.
THE ORBIT OF PLANET MALTUS.
JUST TRY TO RELAX.
IT'S OKAY TO BE NERVOUS BEFORE A BIG MISSION.
UGH, YOU DO THIS ALL THE TIME? YOU'RE FEARLESS!
WHO, ME?! YOU GOT IT TWISTED, KAJA.
I'M, LIKE, ALWAYS AFRAID. BUT THESE RINGS... THEY SHOW YOU WHO YOU REALLY ARE.
KAJA DOX
SMARTEST DUMBASS OF YOD-COLU
JESSICA CRUZ
GREEN LANTERN OF EARTH
Z'KRAN Z'RANN
WHITE MARTIAN OF VENGEANCE
IT'S WORKING.
BET BY NOW YOU WISH YOU'D THROWN THAT RING AWAY, YES, Z'KRAN?
CALLEEN
ELEMENTAL GUARDIAN OF PLANET ALSTAIR
NO.
THIS IS THE BATTLE I'VE BEEN WAITING FOR SINCE I WAS A CHILD.
I DIDN'T ASK JESS' RING WHAT OUR ODDS ARE. I KNOW THEY'RE GARBAGE.
WHO CAN BLAME THEM FOR BEING ANTSY?

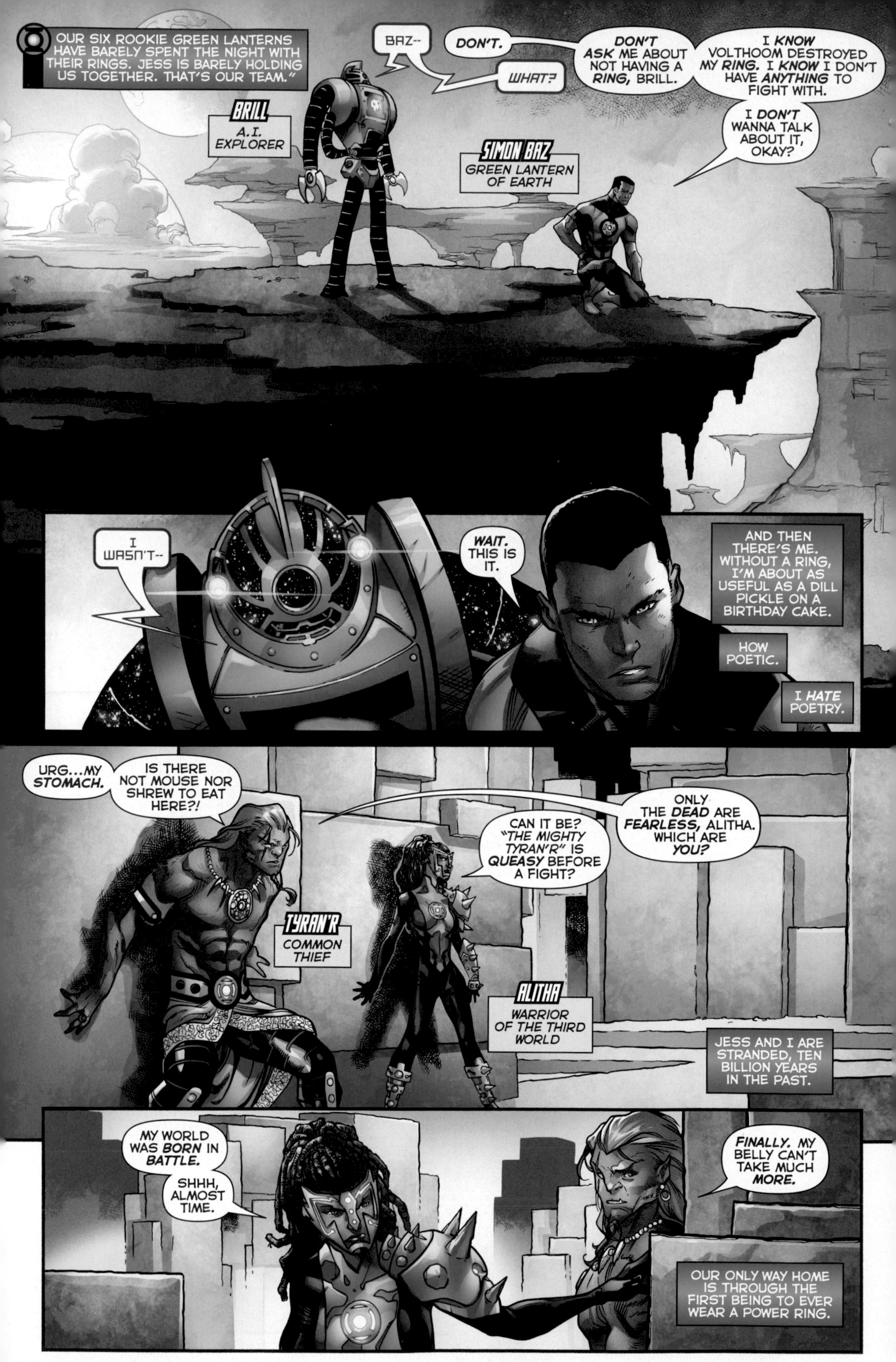
OUR SIX ROOKIE GREEN LANTERNS HAVE BARELY SPENT THE NIGHT WITH THEIR RINGS. JESS IS BARELY HOLDING US TOGETHER. THAT'S OUR TEAM."
BAZ--
DON'T.
WHAT?
DON'T ASK ME ABOUT NOT HAVING A RING, BRILL.
I KNOW VOLTHOOM DESTROYED MY RING. I KNOW I DON'T HAVE ANYTHING TO FIGHT WITH.
I DON'T WANNA TALK ABOUT IT, OKAY?
BRILL
A.I. EXPLORER
SIMON BAZ
GREEN LANTERN OF EARTH
I WASN'T--
WAIT. THIS IS IT.
AND THEN THERE'S ME. WITHOUT A RING, I'M ABOUT AS USEFUL AS A DILL PICKLE ON A BIRTHDAY CAKE.
HOW POETIC.
I HATE POETRY.
URG...MY STOMACH.
IS THERE NOT MOUSE NOR SHREW TO EAT HERE?!
CAN IT BE? "THE MIGHTY TYRAN'R" IS QUEASY BEFORE A FIGHT?
ONLY THE DEAD ARE FEARLESS, ALITHA. WHICH ARE YOU?
TYRAN'R
COMMON THIEF
ALITHA
WARRIOR OF THE THIRD WORLD
JESS AND I ARE STRANDED, TEN BILLION YEARS IN THE PAST.
MY WORLD WAS BORN IN BATTLE.
SHHH, ALMOST TIME.
FINALLY. MY BELLY CAN'T TAKE MUCH MORE.
OUR ONLY WAY HOME IS THROUGH THE FIRST BEING TO EVER WEAR A POWER RING.

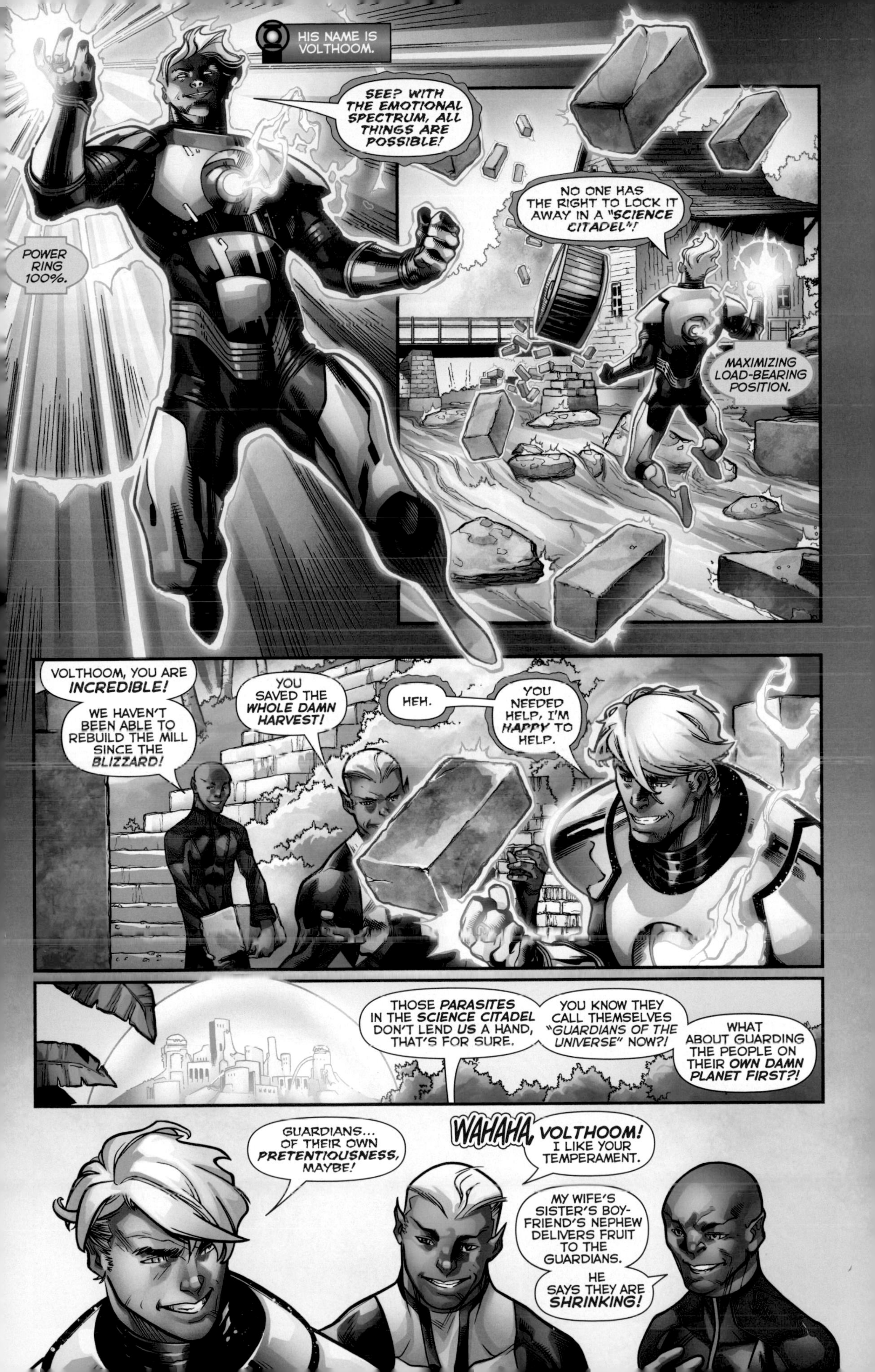
HIS NAME IS VOLTHOOM.
SEE? WITH THE EMOTIONAL SPECTRUM, ALL THINGS ARE POSSIBLE!
POWER RING 100%.
NO ONE HAS THE RIGHT TO LOCK IT AWAY IN A "SCIENCE CITADEL"!
MAXIMIZING LOAD-BEARING POSITION.
VOLTHOOM, YOU ARE INCREDIBLE!
WE HAVEN'T BEEN ABLE TO REBUILD THE MILL SINCE THE BLIZZARD!
YOU SAVED THE WHOLE DAMN HARVEST!
HEH.
YOU NEEDED HELP, I'M HAPPY TO HELP.
THOSE PARASITES IN THE SCIENCE CITADEL DON'T LEND US A HAND, THAT'S FOR SURE.
YOU KNOW THEY CALL THEMSELVES "GUARDIANS OF THE UNIVERSE" NOW?!
WHAT ABOUT GUARDING THE PEOPLE ON THEIR OWN DAMN PLANET FIRST?!
GUARDIANS... OF THEIR OWN PRETENTIOUSNESS, MAYBE!
WAHAHA, VOLTHOOM! I LIKE YOUR TEMPERAMENT.
MY WIFE'S SISTER'S BOY-FRIEND'S NEPHEW DELIVERS FRUIT TO THE GUARDIANS.
HE SAYS THEY ARE SHRINKING!

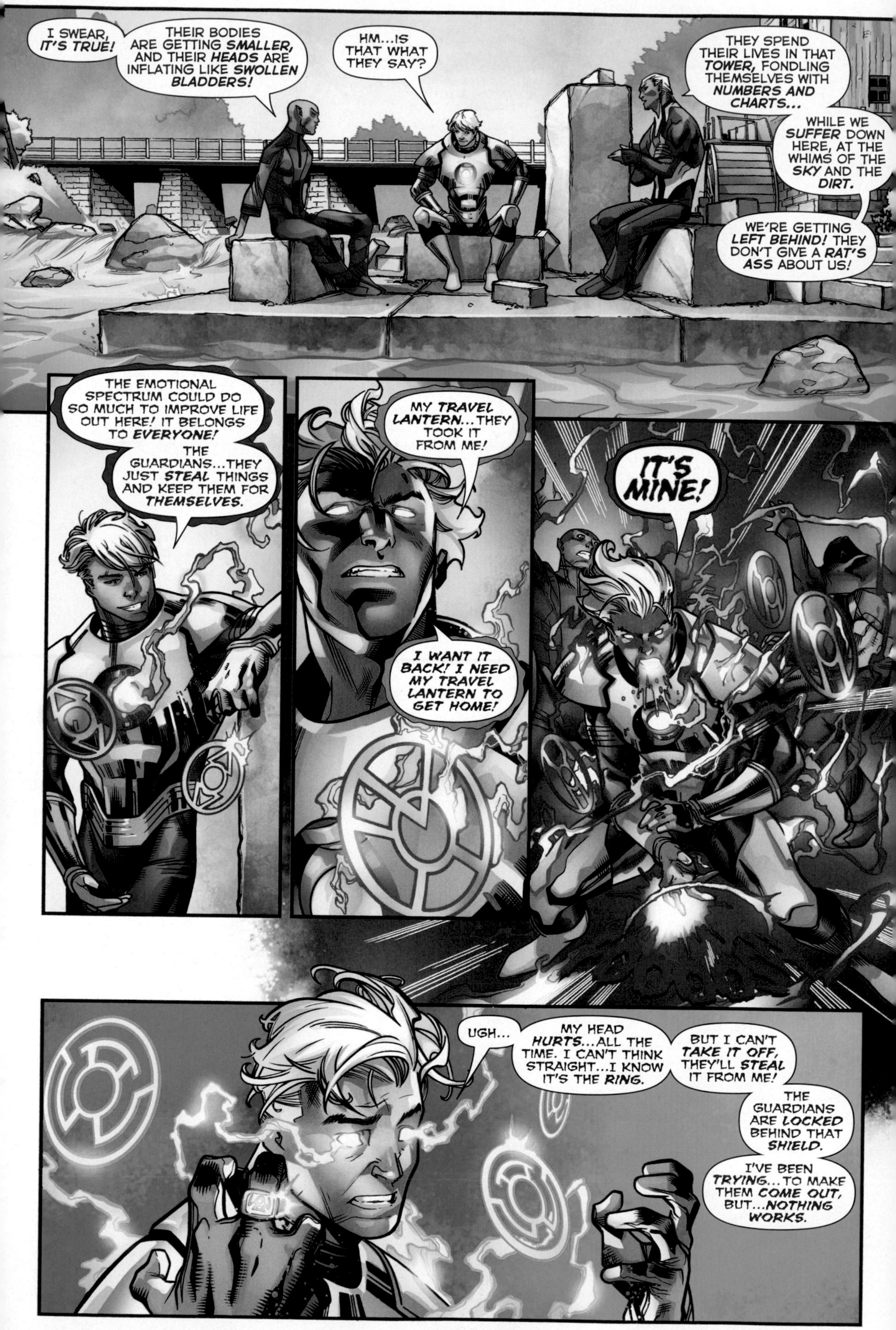
I SWEAR, IT'S TRUE!
THEIR BODIES ARE GETTING SMALLER, AND THEIR HEADS ARE INFLATING LIKE SWOLLEN BLADDERS!
HM...IS THAT WHAT THEY SAY?
THEY SPEND THEIR LIVES IN THAT TOWER, FONDLING THEMSELVES WITH NUMBERS AND CHARTS...
WHILE WE SUFFER DOWN HERE, AT THE WHIMS OF THE SKY AND THE DIRT.
WE'RE GETTING LEFT BEHIND! THEY DON'T GIVE A RAT'S ASS ABOUT US!
THE EMOTIONAL SPECTRUM COULD DO SO MUCH TO IMPROVE LIFE OUT HERE! IT BELONGS TO EVERYONE!
THE GUARDIANS...THEY JUST STEAL THINGS AND KEEP THEM FOR THEMSELVES.
MY TRAVEL LANTERN...THEY TOOK IT FROM ME!
I WANT IT BACK! I NEED MY TRAVEL LANTERN TO GET HOME!
IT'S MINE!
UGH...
MY HEAD HURTS...ALL THE TIME. I CAN'T THINK STRAIGHT...I KNOW IT'S THE RING.
BUT I CAN'T TAKE IT OFF, THEY'LL STEAL IT FROM ME!
THE GUARDIANS ARE LOCKED BEHIND THAT SHIELD.
I'VE BEEN TRYING...TO MAKE THEM COME OUT, BUT...NOTHING WORKS.

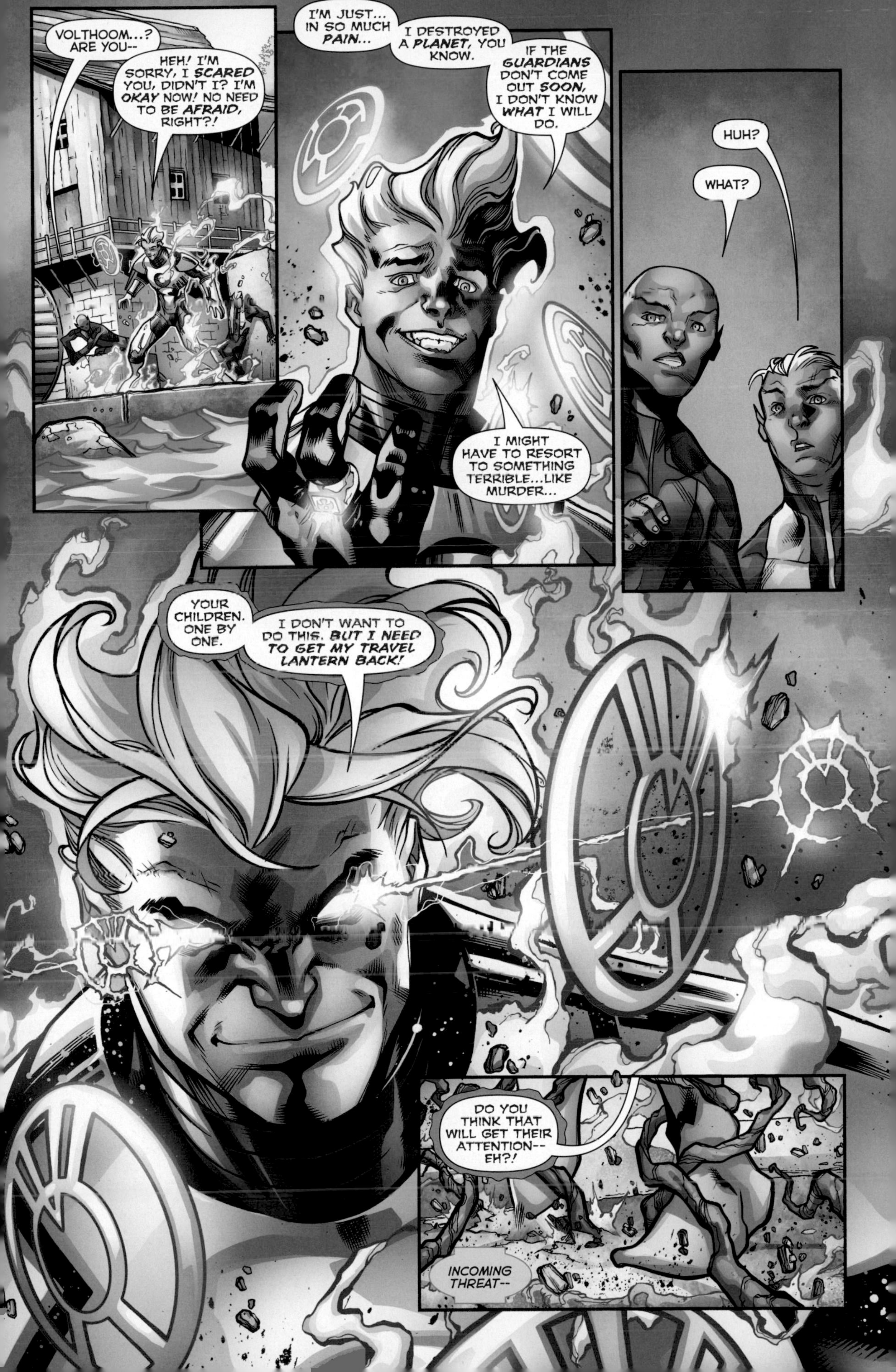
VOLTHOOM...? ARE YOU--
HEH! I'M SORRY, I SCARED YOU, DIDN'T I? I'M OKAY NOW! NO NEED TO BE AFRAID, RIGHT?!
I'M JUST... IN SO MUCH PAIN...
I DESTROYED A PLANET, YOU KNOW.
IF THE GUARDIANS DON'T COME OUT SOON, I DON'T KNOW WHAT I WILL DO.
I MIGHT HAVE TO RESORT TO SOMETHING TERRIBLE...LIKE MURDER...
HUH?
WHAT?
YOUR CHILDREN. ONE BY ONE.
I DON'T WANT TO DO THIS. BUT I NEED TO GET MY TRAVEL LANTERN BACK!
DO YOU THINK THAT WILL GET THEIR ATTENTION-- EH?!
INCOMING THREAT--

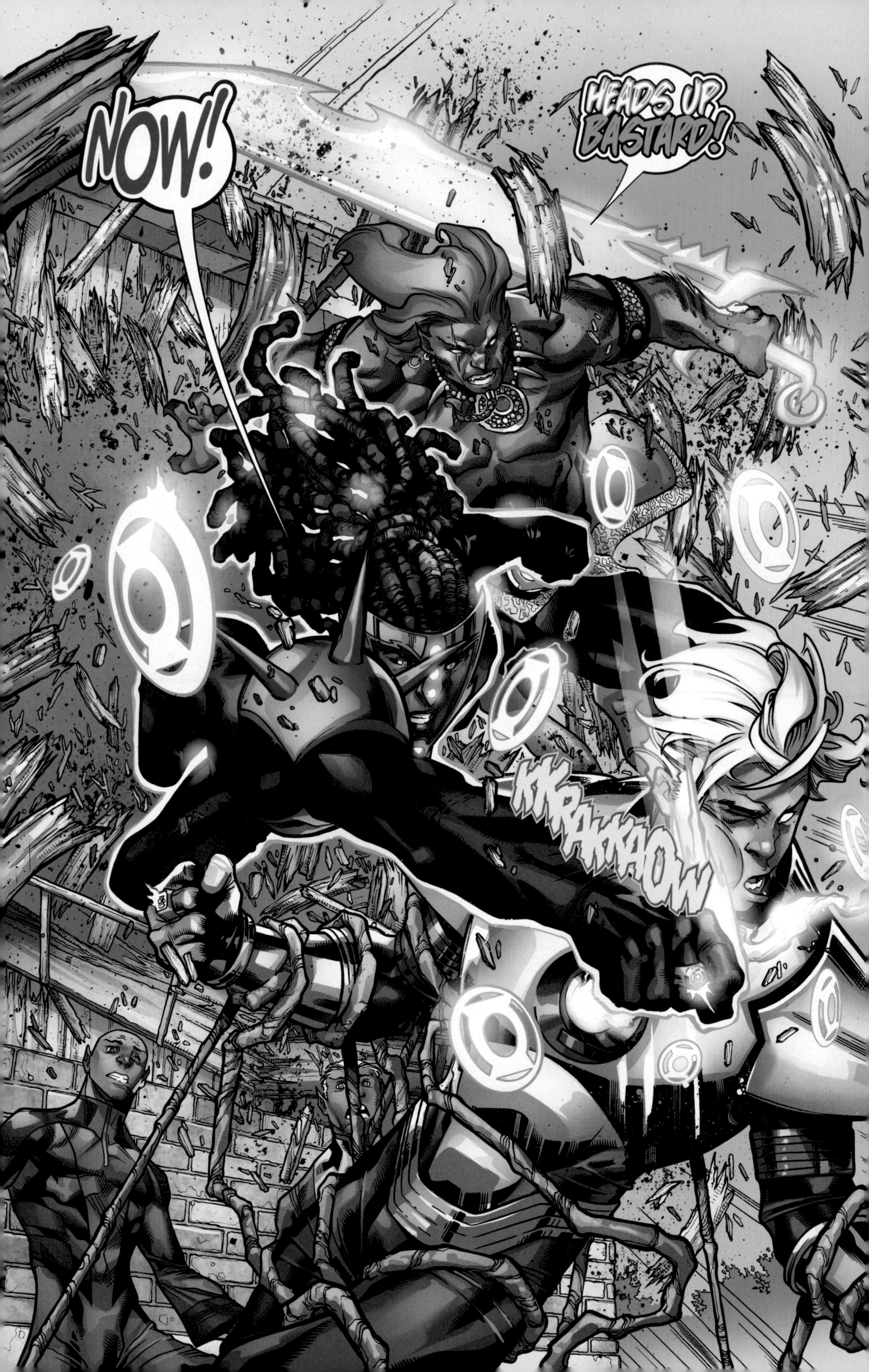
NOW!
HEADS UP, BASTARD!
KKRAKKAOW

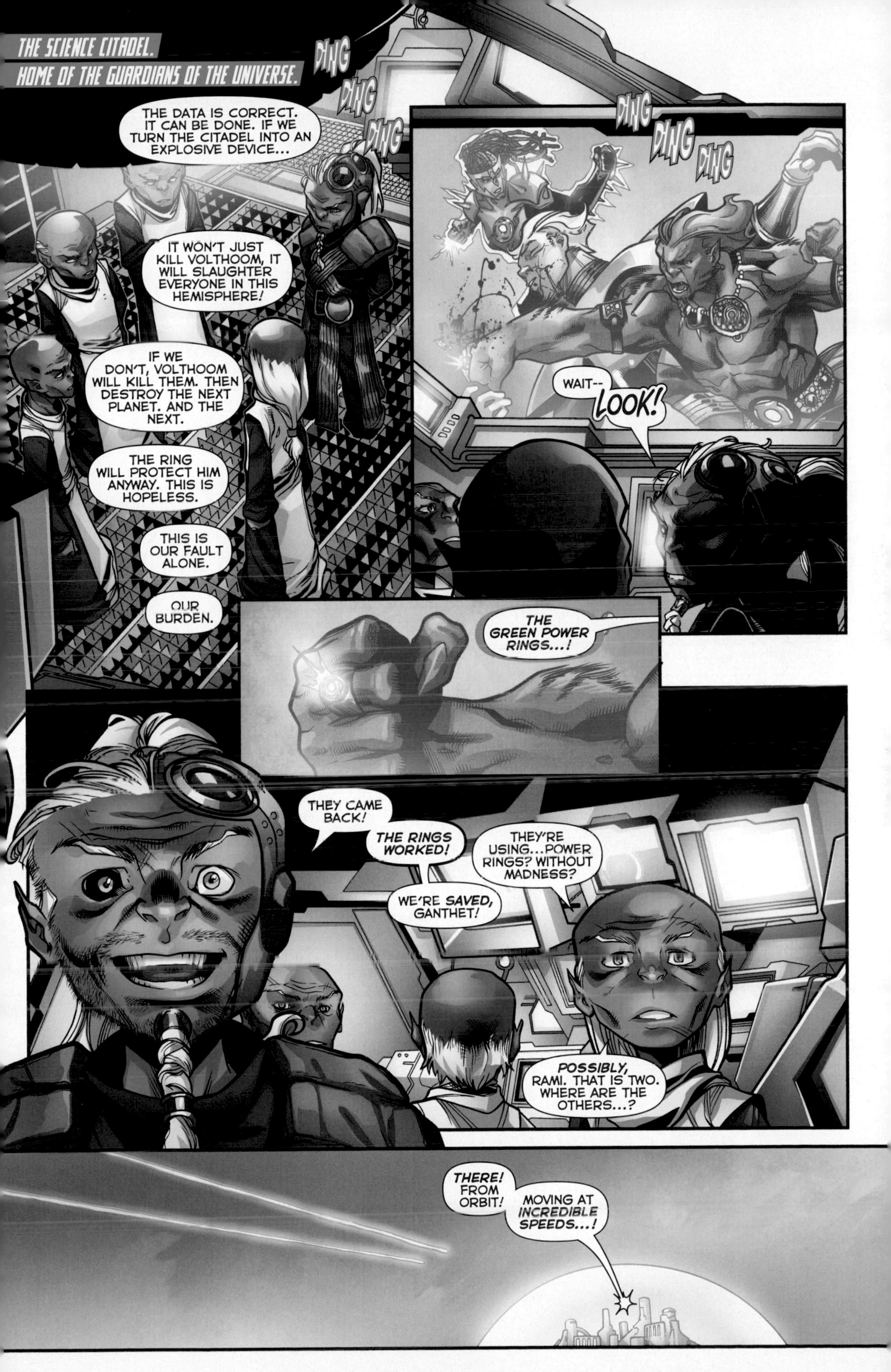
THE SCIENCE CITADEL.
HOME OF THE GUARDIANS OF THE UNIVERSE.
DING DING DING
THE DATA IS CORRECT. IT CAN BE DONE. IF WE TURN THE CITADEL INTO AN EXPLOSIVE DEVICE...
IT WON'T JUST KILL VOLTHOOM, IT WILL SLAUGHTER EVERYONE IN THIS HEMISPHERE!
IF WE DON'T, VOLTHOOM WILL KILL THEM. THEN DESTROY THE NEXT PLANET. AND THE NEXT.
THE RING WILL PROTECT HIM ANYWAY. THIS IS HOPELESS.
THIS IS OUR FAULT ALONE.
OUR BURDEN.
DING DING DING
WAIT-- LOOK!
THE GREEN POWER RINGS...!
THEY CAME BACK!
THE RINGS WORKED!
WE'RE SAVED, GANTHET!
THEY'RE USING...POWER RINGS? WITHOUT MADNESS?
POSSIBLY, RAMI. THAT IS TWO. WHERE ARE THE OTHERS...?
THERE! FROM ORBIT!
MOVING AT INCREDIBLE SPEEDS...!

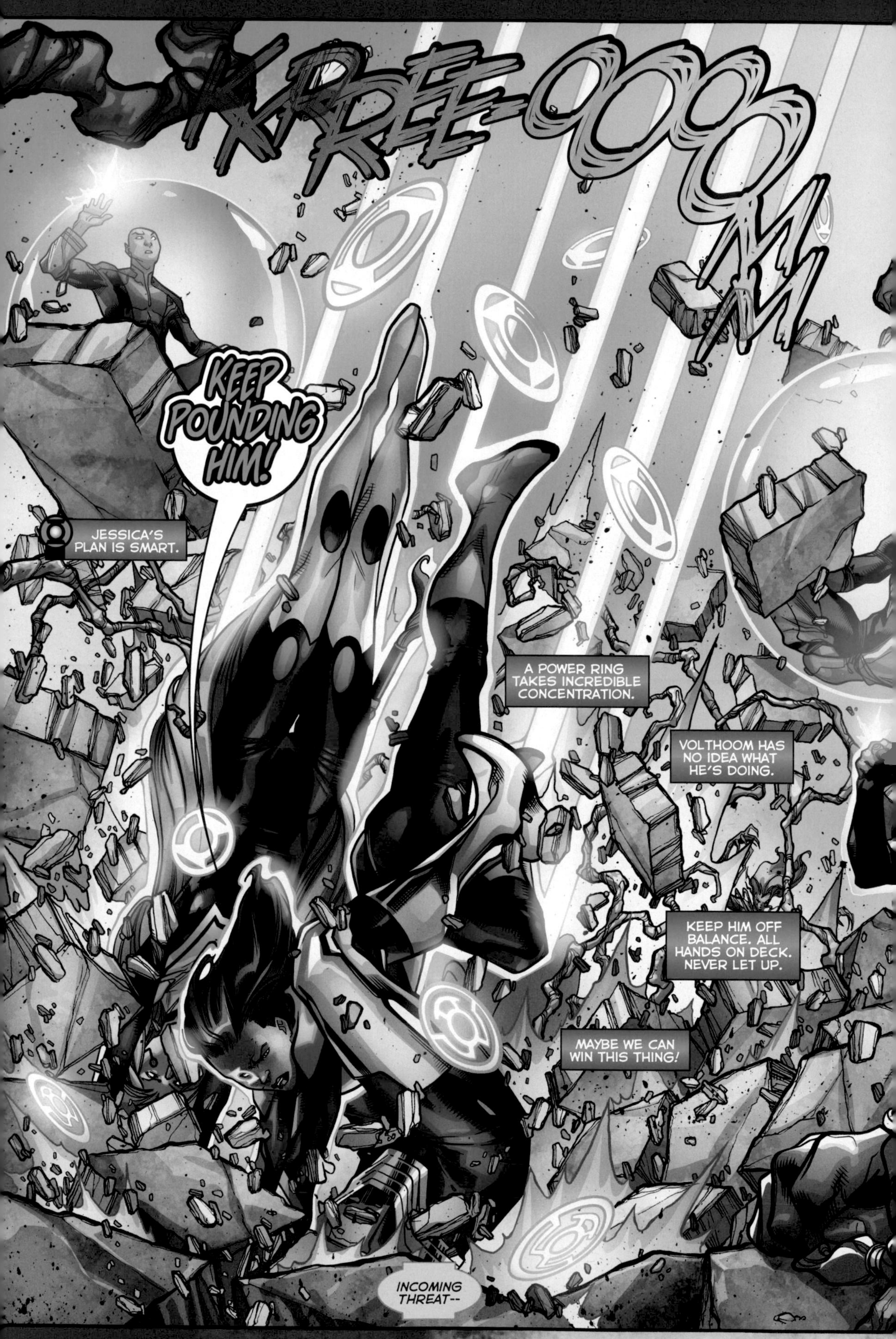
KRREE-OOOOMM
KEEP POUNDING HIM!
JESSICA'S PLAN IS SMART.
A POWER RING TAKES INCREDIBLE CONCENTRATION.
VOLTHOOM HAS NO IDEA WHAT HE'S DOING.
KEEP HIM OFF BALANCE. ALL HANDS ON DECK. NEVER LET UP.
MAYBE WE CAN WIN THIS THING!
INCOMING THREAT--

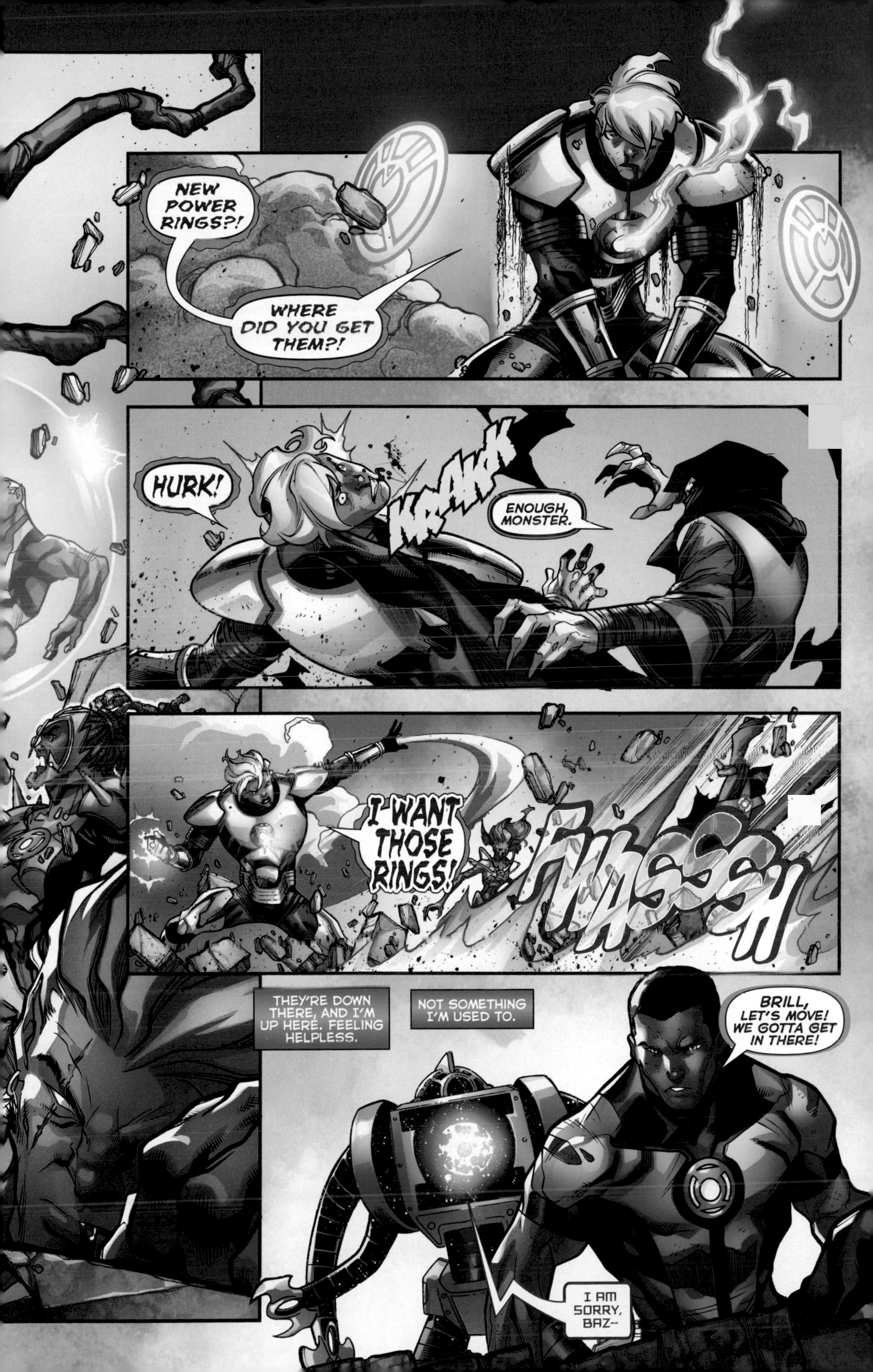
NEW POWER RINGS?!
WHERE DID YOU GET THEM?!
HURK!
KRAKK
ENOUGH, MONSTER.
I WANT THOSE RINGS!
FWASSH
THEY'RE DOWN THERE, AND I'M UP HERE. FEELING HELPLESS.
NOT SOMETHING I'M USED TO.
BRILL, LET'S MOVE! WE GOTTA GET IN THERE!
I AM SORRY, BAZ--

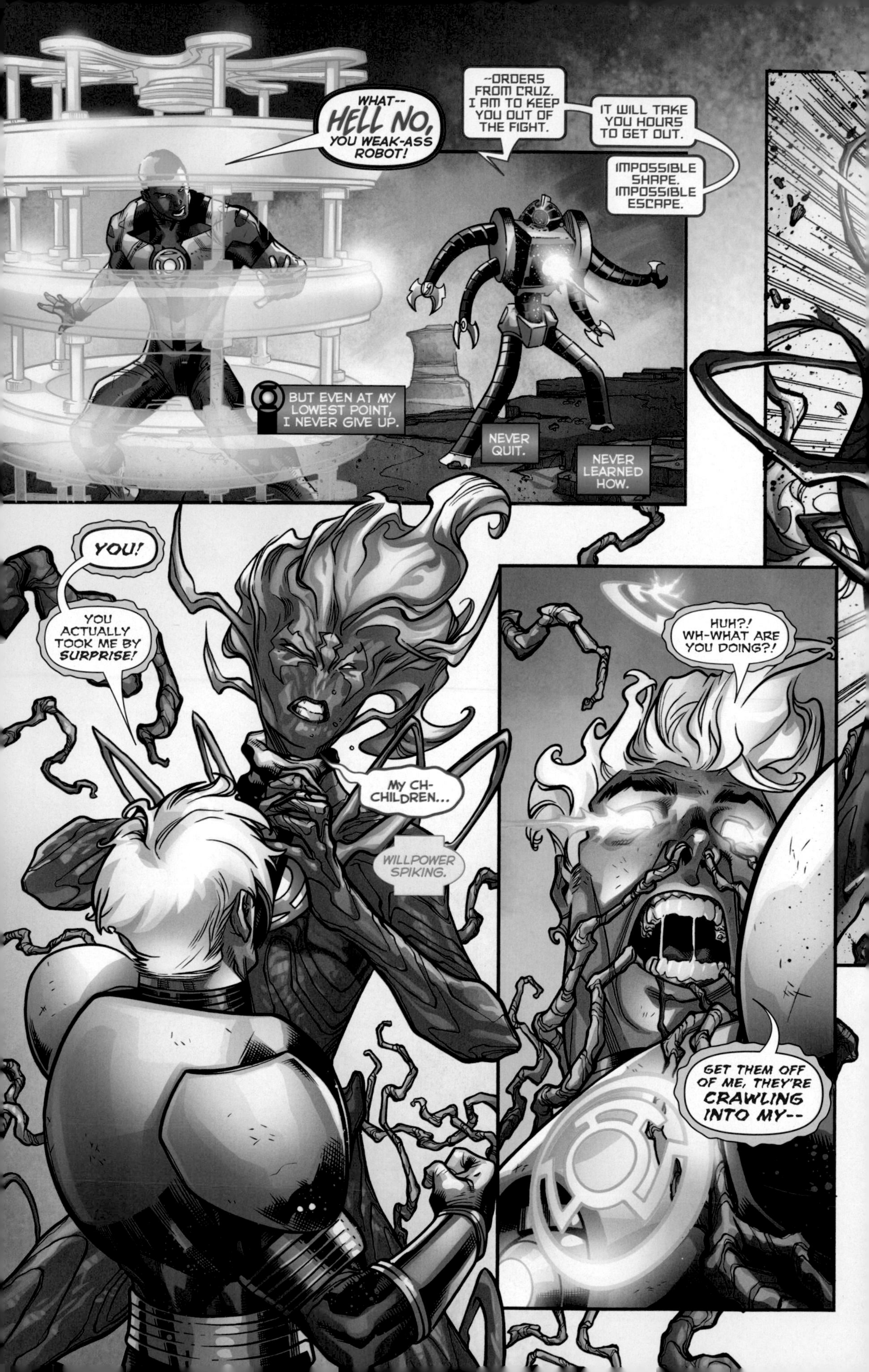

WHAT-- HELL NO, YOU WEAK-ASS ROBOT!
--ORDERS FROM CRUZ. I AM TO KEEP YOU OUT OF THE FIGHT.
IT WILL TAKE YOU HOURS TO GET OUT.
IMPOSSIBLE SHAPE. IMPOSSIBLE ESCAPE.
BUT EVEN AT MY LOWEST POINT, I NEVER GIVE UP.
NEVER QUIT.
NEVER LEARNED HOW.
YOU!
YOU ACTUALLY TOOK ME BY SURPRISE!
MY CH- CHILDREN...
WILLPOWER SPIKING.
HUH?! WH-WHAT ARE YOU DOING?!
GET THEM OFF OF ME, THEY'RE CRAWLING INTO MY--

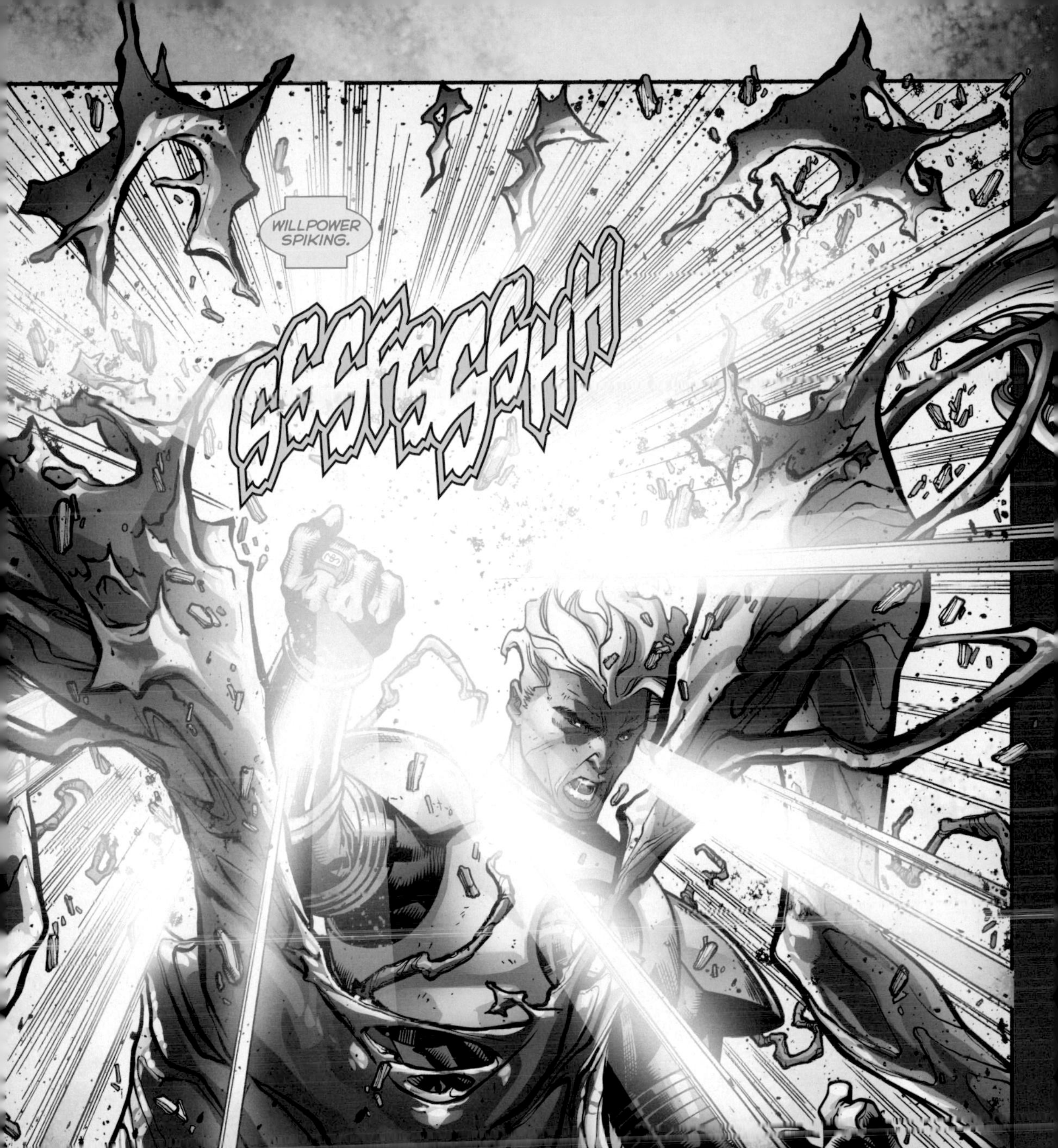
WILLPOWER SPIKING.
SSSRRSSHH
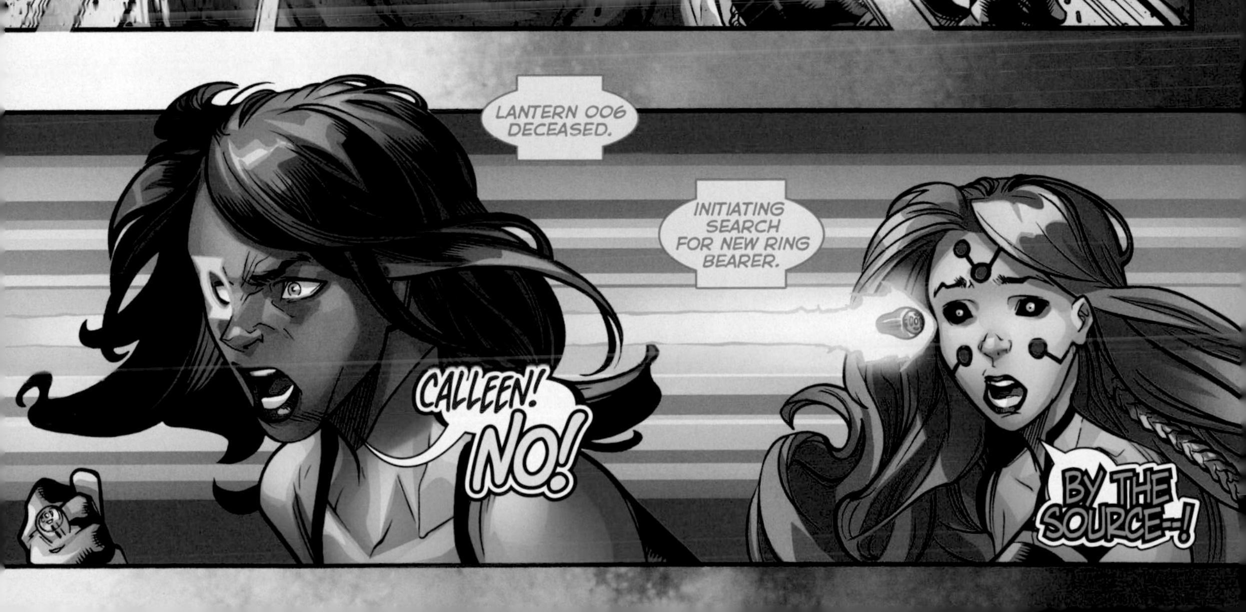
LANTERN 006 DECEASED.
INITIATING SEARCH FOR NEW RING BEARER.
CALLEEN! NO!
BY THE SOURCE--!

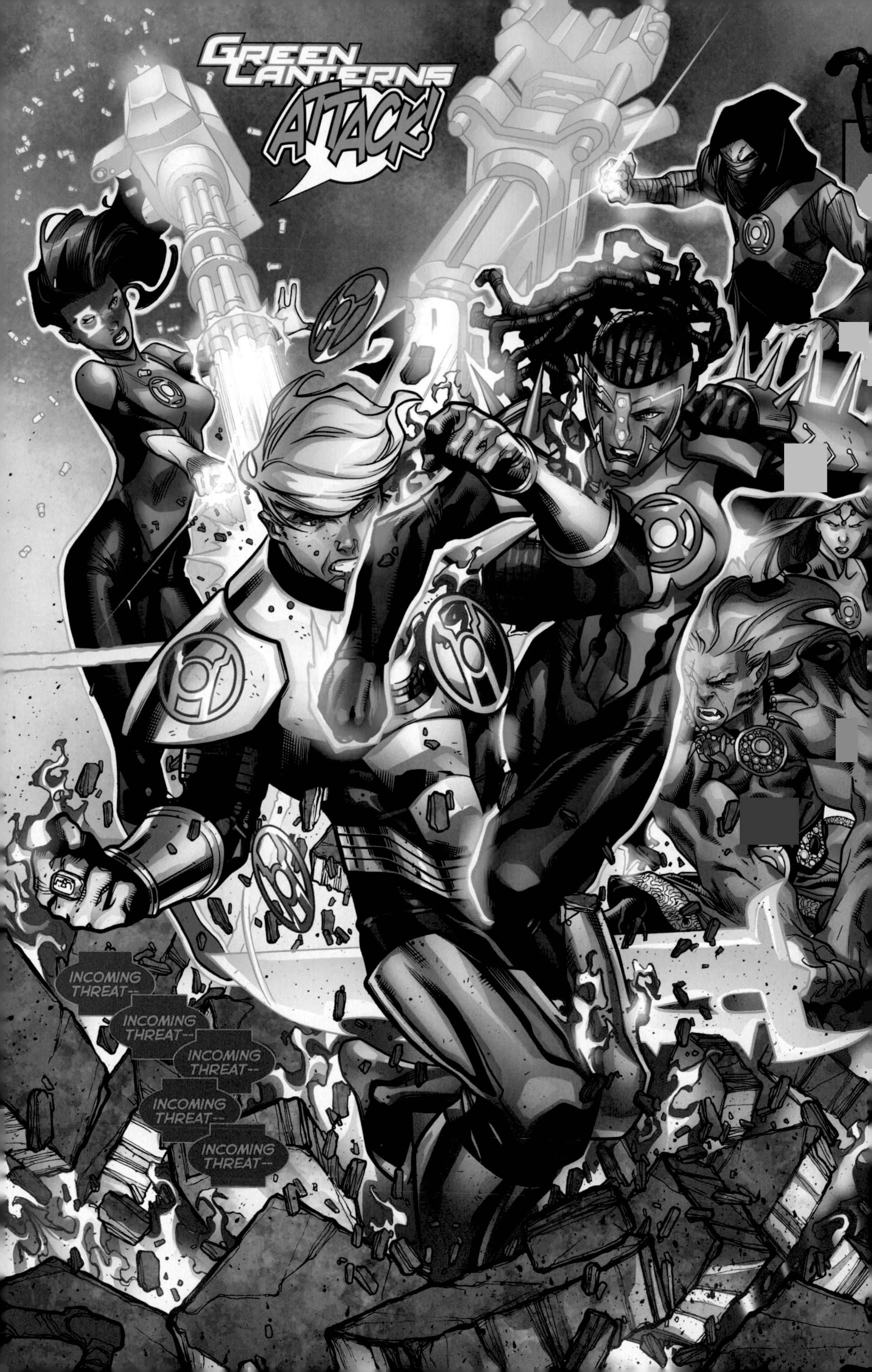
GREEN LANTERNS ATTACK!
INCOMING THREAT--
INCOMING THREAT--
INCOMING THREAT--
INCOMING THREAT--
INCOMING THREAT--

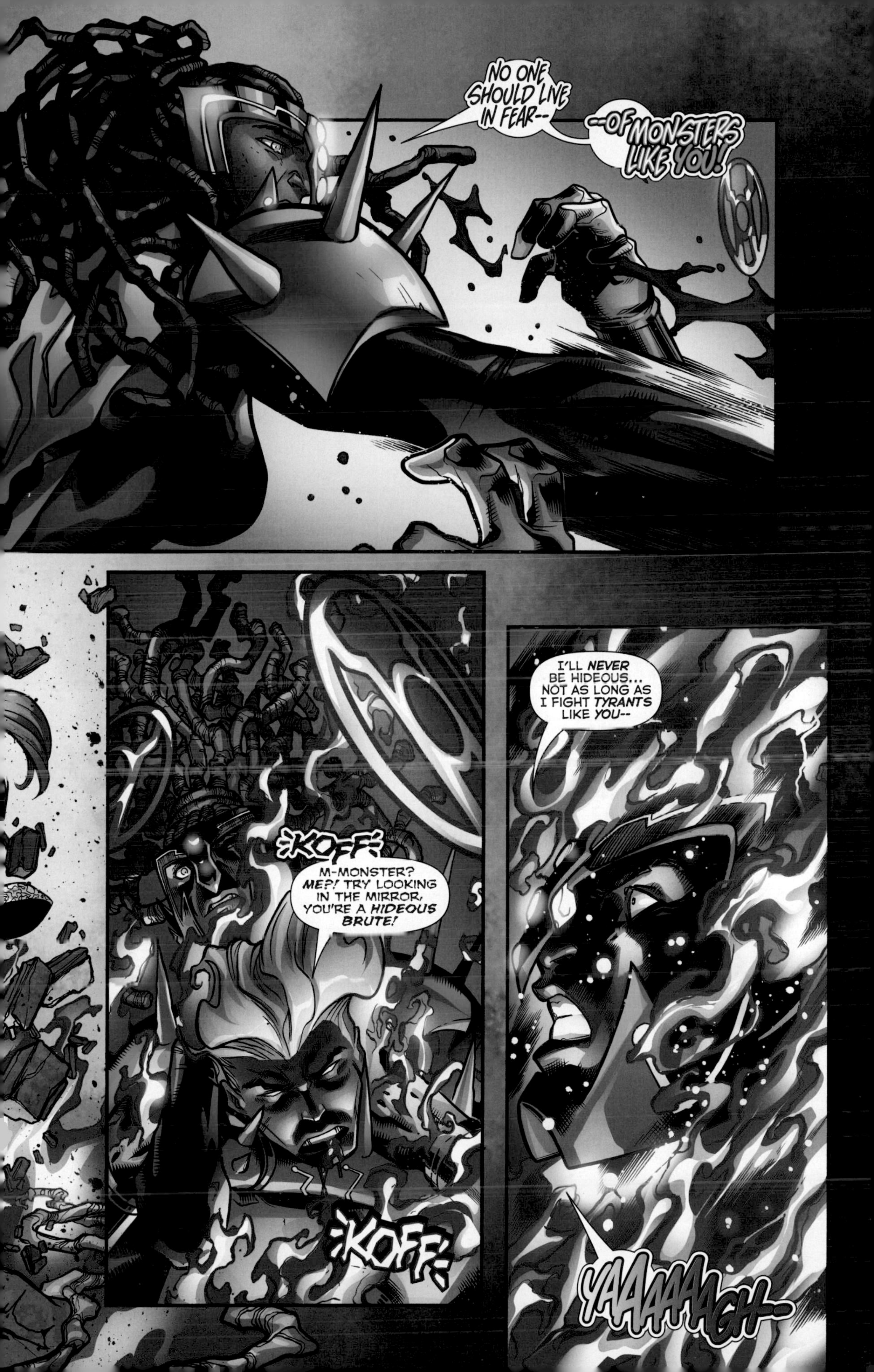
NO ONE SHOULD LIVE IN FEAR--
--OF MONSTERS LIKE YOU!
KOFF
M-MONSTER? ME?! TRY LOOKING IN THE MIRROR, YOU'RE A HIDEOUS BRUTE!
KOFF
I'LL NEVER BE HIDEOUS... NOT AS LONG AS I FIGHT TYRANTS LIKE YOU--
YAAAAAAGH--

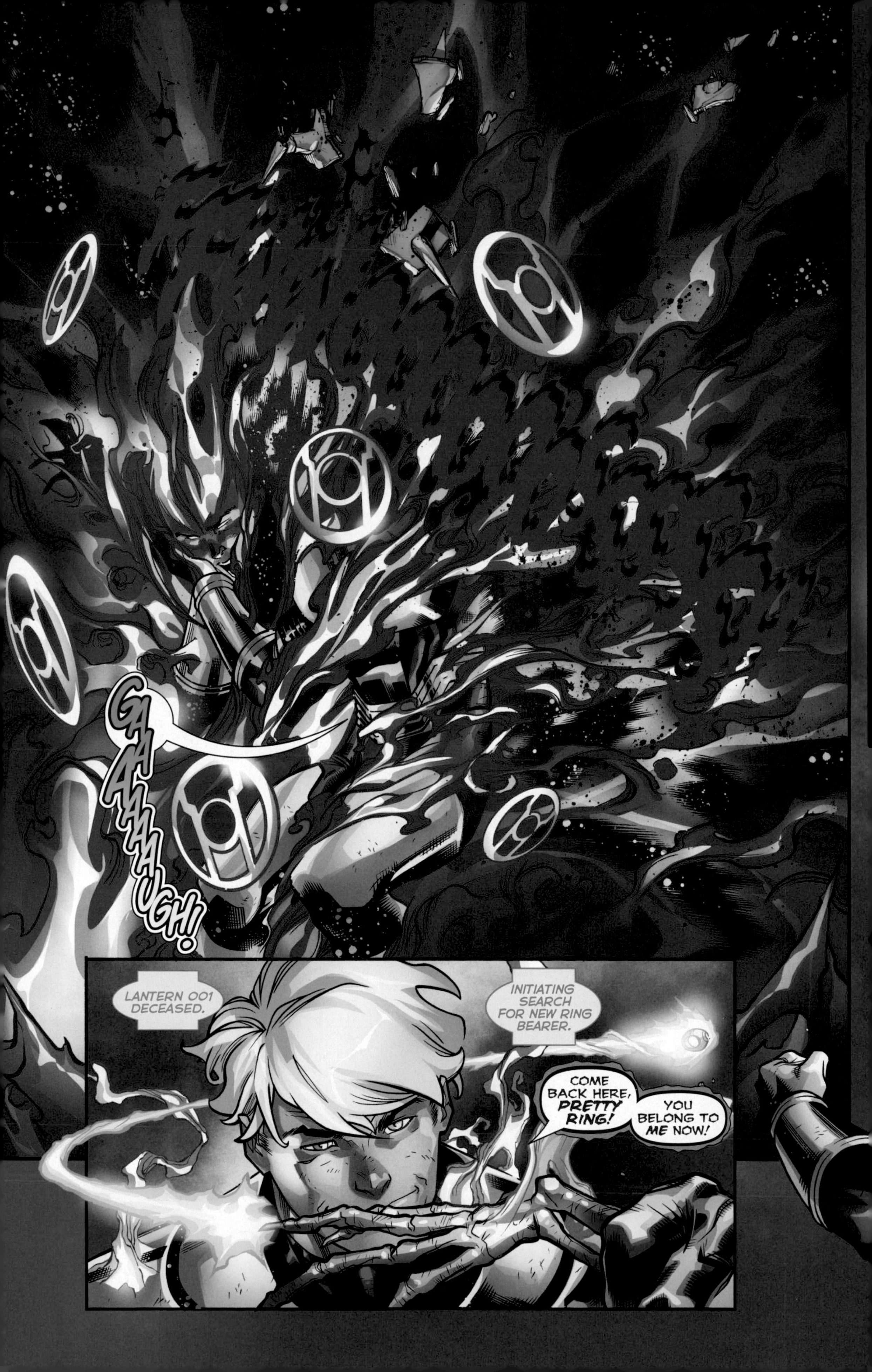
GAAAAAAUGH!
LANTERN 001 DECEASED.
INITIATING SEARCH FOR NEW RING BEARER.
COME BACK HERE, PRETTY RING!
YOU BELONG TO ME NOW!

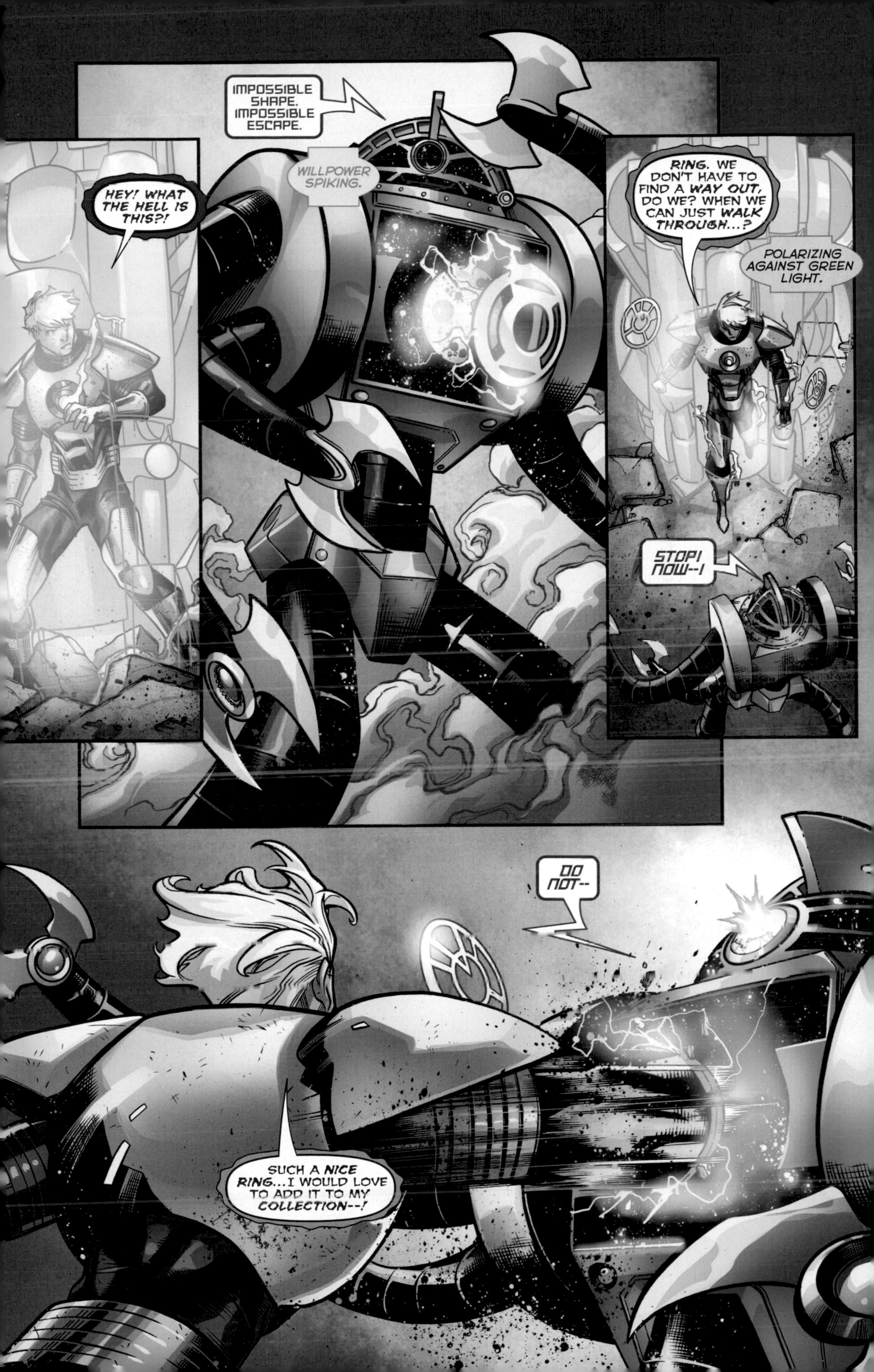
HEY! WHAT THE HELL IS THIS?!
IMPOSSIBLE SHAPE. IMPOSSIBLE ESCAPE.
WILLPOWER SPIKING.
RING. WE DON'T HAVE TO FIND A WAY OUT, DO WE? WHEN WE CAN JUST WALK THROUGH...?
POLARIZING AGAINST GREEN LIGHT.
STOP! NOW--!
DO NOT--
SUCH A NICE RING...I WOULD LOVE TO ADD IT TO MY COLLECTION--!

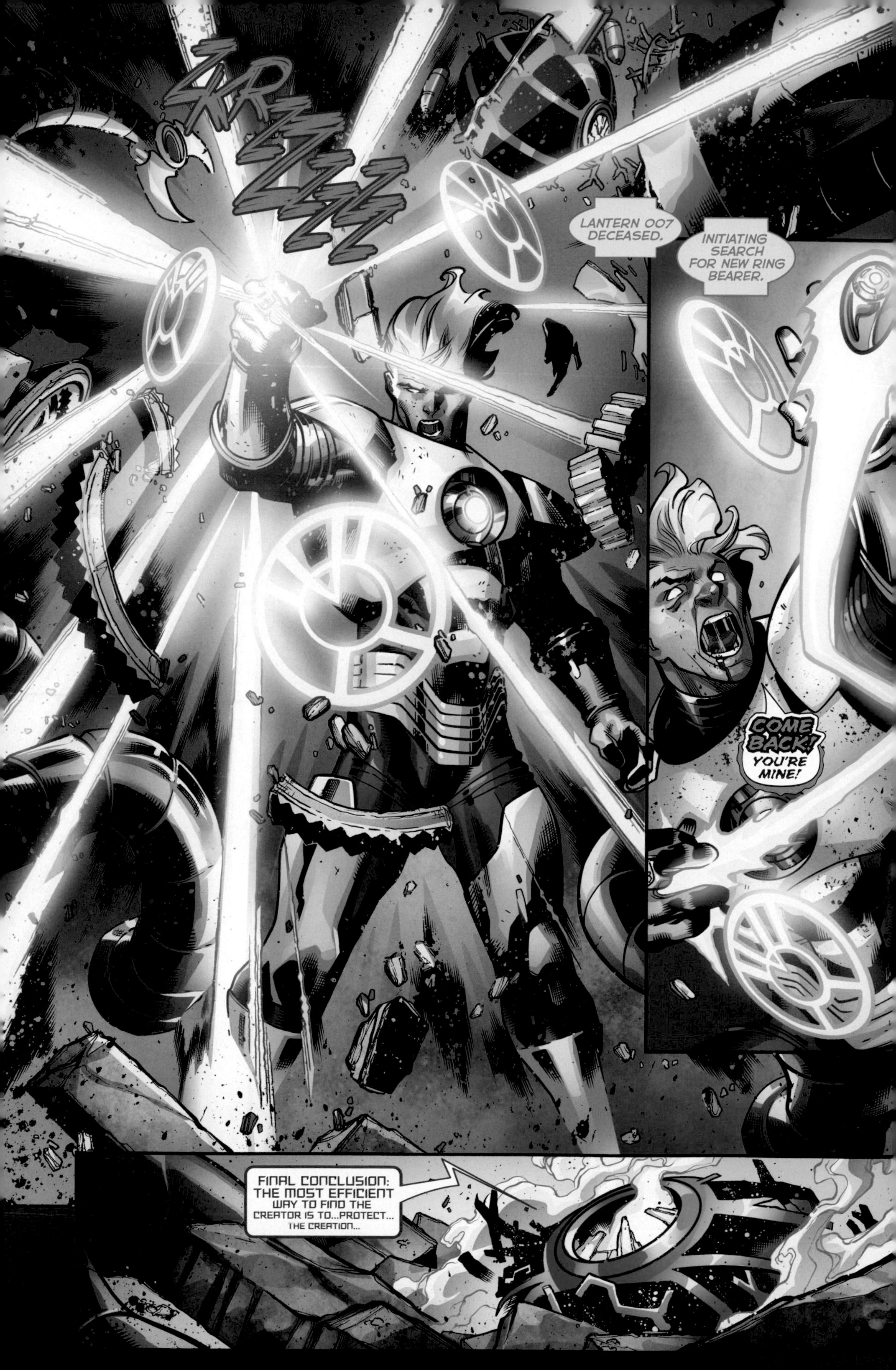

GRRZZZZZ
LANTERN 007 DECEASED.
INITIATING SEARCH FOR NEW RING BEARER.
COME BACK! YOU'RE MINE!
FINAL CONCLUSION: THE MOST EFFICIENT WAY TO FIND THE CREATOR IS TO...PROTECT... THE CREATION...

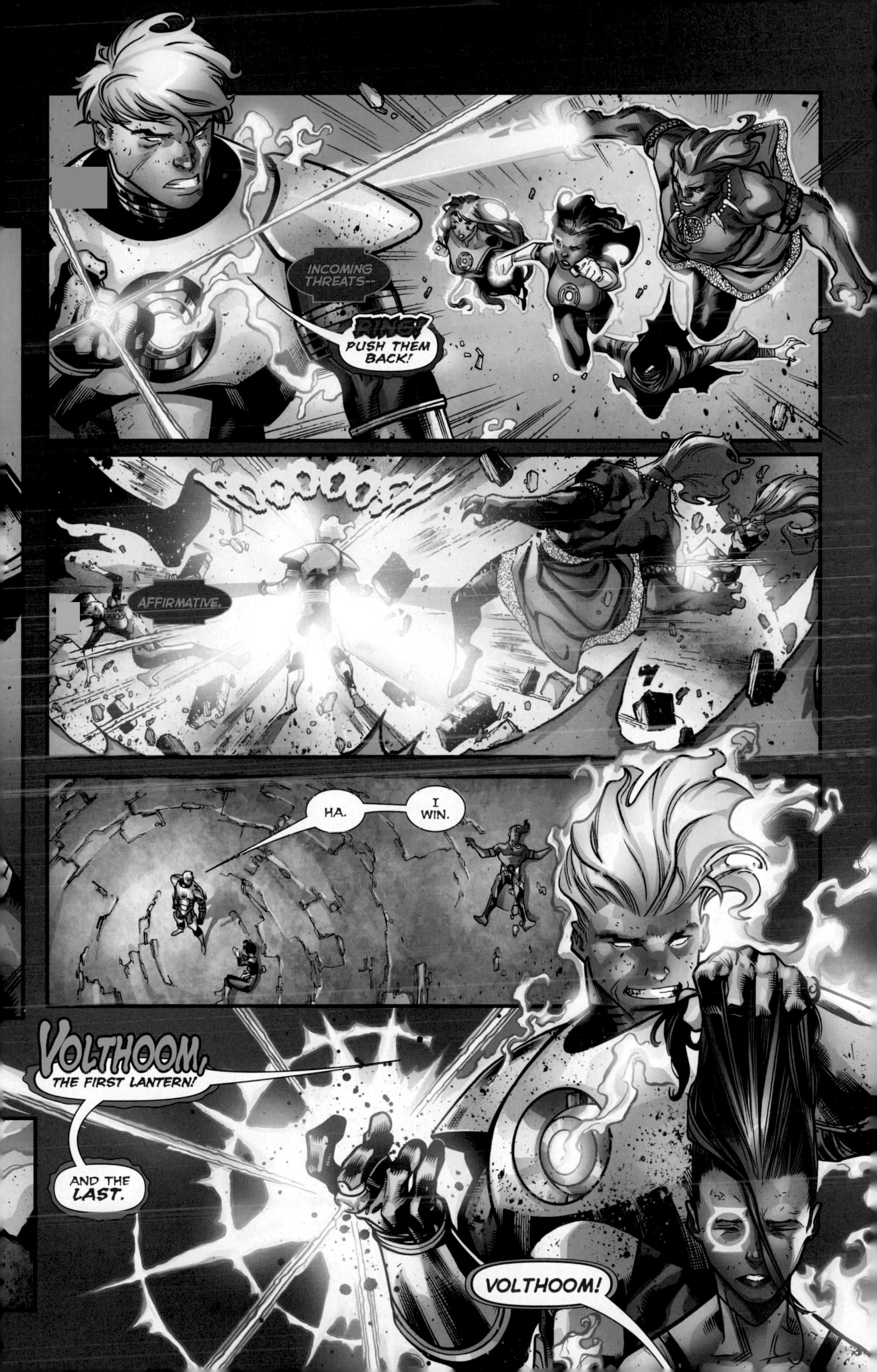
INCOMING THREATS--
RING! PUSH THEM BACK!
AFFIRMATIVE.
HA.
I WIN.
VOLTHOOM, THE FIRST LANTERN!
AND THE LAST.
VOLTHOOM!

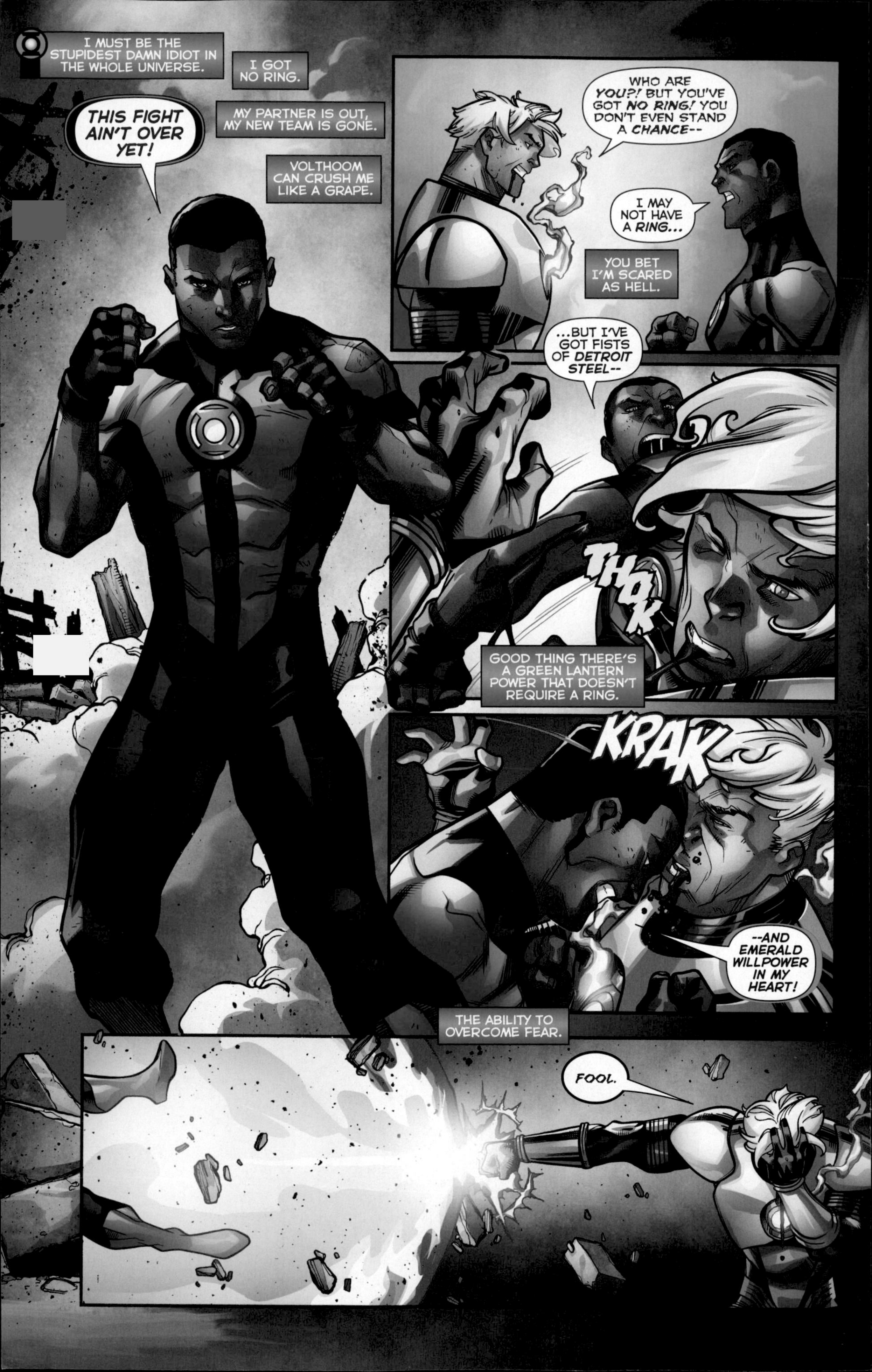
I MUST BE THE STUPIDEST DAMN IDIOT IN THE WHOLE UNIVERSE.
I GOT NO RING.
MY PARTNER IS OUT, MY NEW TEAM IS GONE.
VOLTHOOM CAN CRUSH ME LIKE A GRAPE.
THIS FIGHT AIN'T OVER YET!
WHO ARE YOU?! BUT YOU'VE GOT NO RING! YOU DON'T EVEN STAND A CHANCE--
I MAY NOT HAVE A RING...
YOU BET I'M SCARED AS HELL.
...BUT I'VE GOT FISTS OF DETROIT STEEL--
THOK
GOOD THING THERE'S A GREEN LANTERN POWER THAT DOESN'T REQUIRE A RING.
KRAK
--AND EMERALD WILLPOWER IN MY HEART!
THE ABILITY TO OVERCOME FEAR.
FOOL.

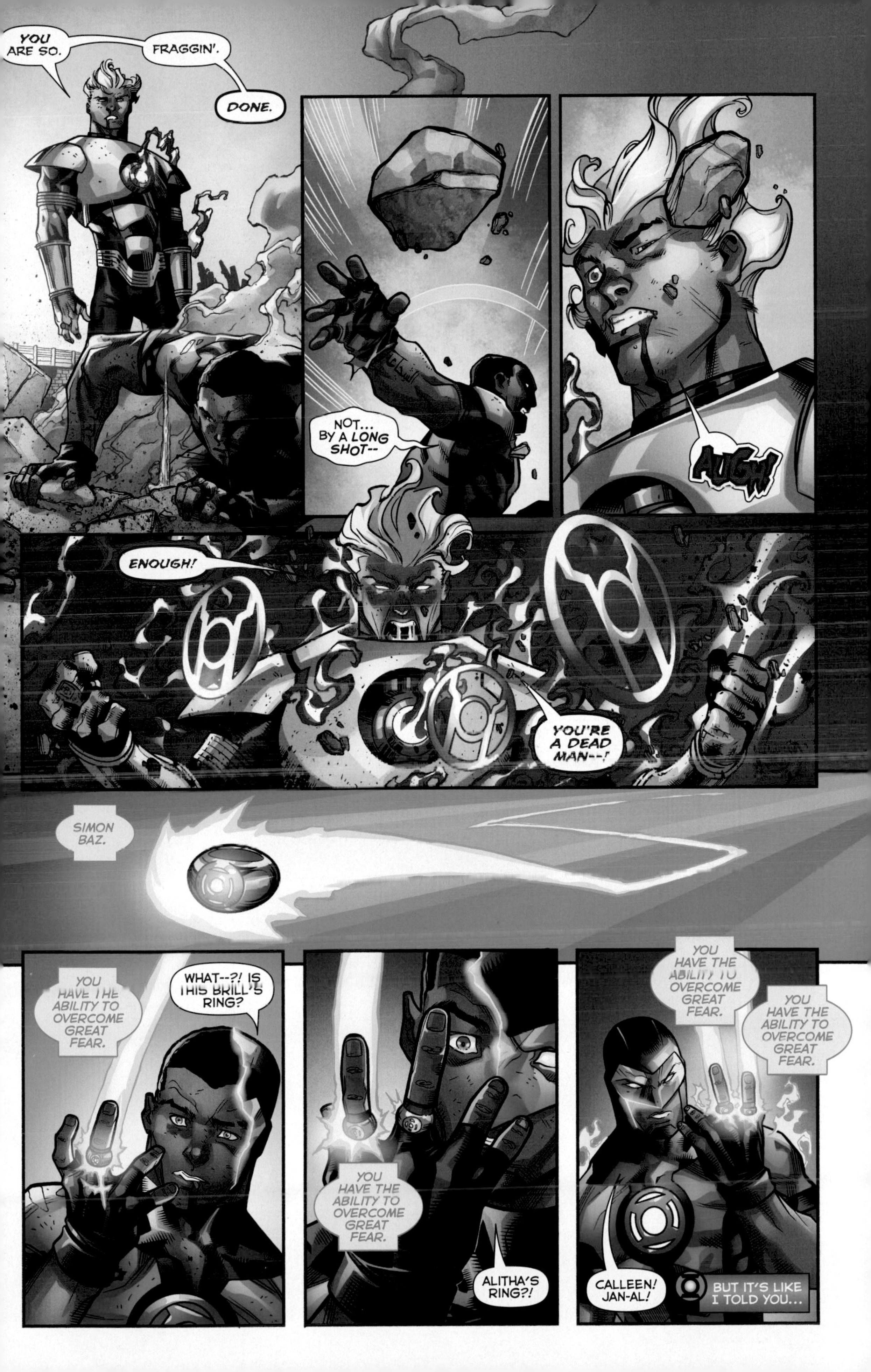
YOU ARE SO.
FRAGGIN'.
DONE.
NOT... BY A LONG SHOT--
AUGH!
ENOUGH!
YOU'RE A DEAD MAN--!
SIMON BAZ.
YOU HAVE THE ABILITY TO OVERCOME GREAT FEAR.
WHAT--?! IS THIS BRILL'S RING?
YOU HAVE THE ABILITY TO OVERCOME GREAT FEAR.
ALITHA'S RING?!
YOU HAVE THE ABILITY TO OVERCOME GREAT FEAR.
YOU HAVE THE ABILITY TO OVERCOME GREAT FEAR.
CALLEEN! JAN-AL!
BUT IT'S LIKE I TOLD YOU...

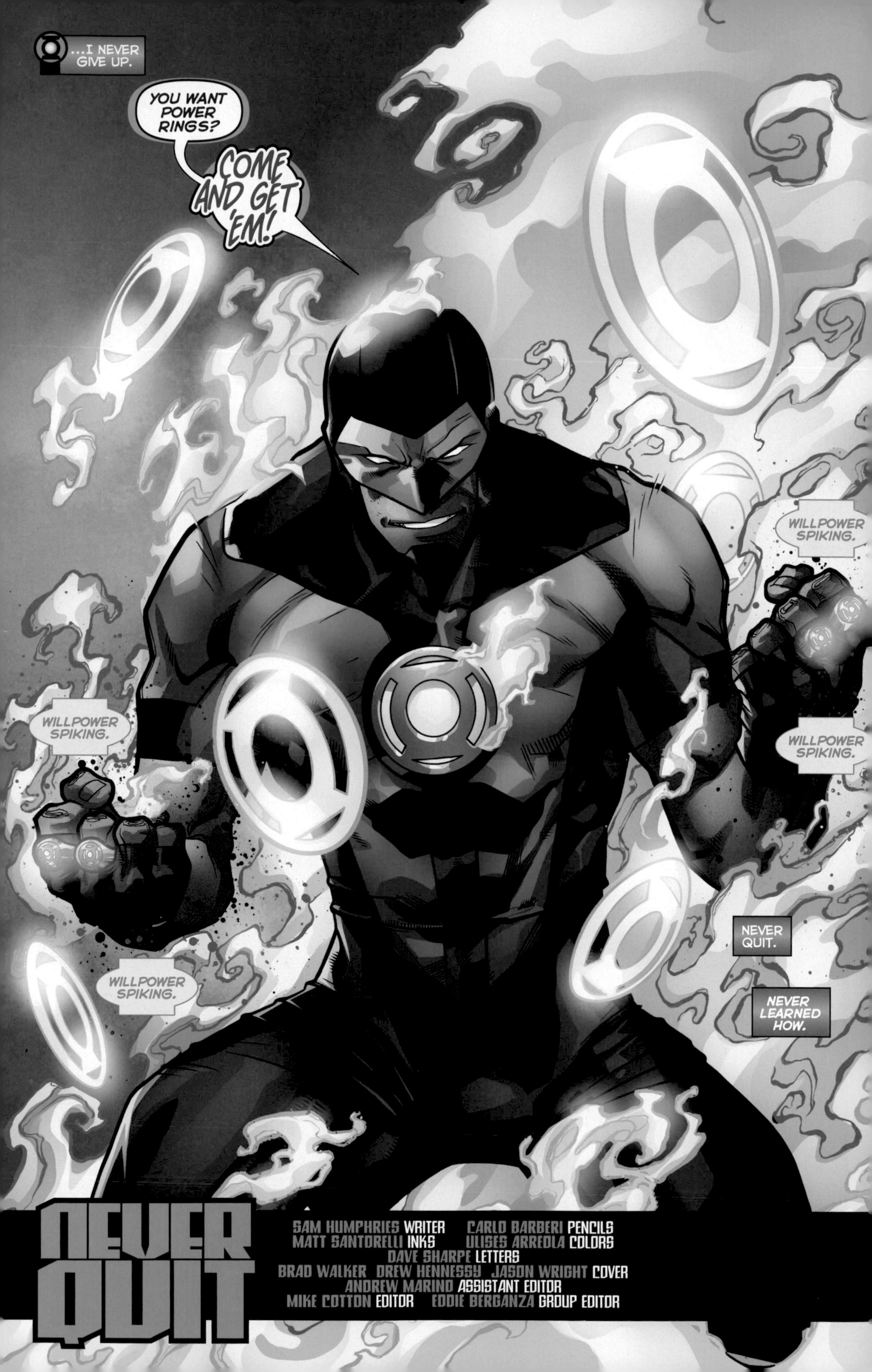
...I NEVER GIVE UP.
YOU WANT POWER RINGS?
COME AND GET 'EM!
WILLPOWER SPIKING.
WILLPOWER SPIKING.
WILLPOWER SPIKING.
WILLPOWER SPIKING.
NEVER QUIT.
NEVER LEARNED HOW.

NEVER QUIT

SAM HUMPHRIES WRITER CARLO BARBERI PENCILS
MATT SANTORELLI INKS ULISES ARREOLA COLORS
DAVE SHARPE LETTERS
BRAD WALKER DREW HENNESSY JASON WRIGHT COVER
ANDREW MARINO ASSISTANT EDITOR
MIKE COTTON EDITOR EDDIE BERGANZA GROUP EDITOR

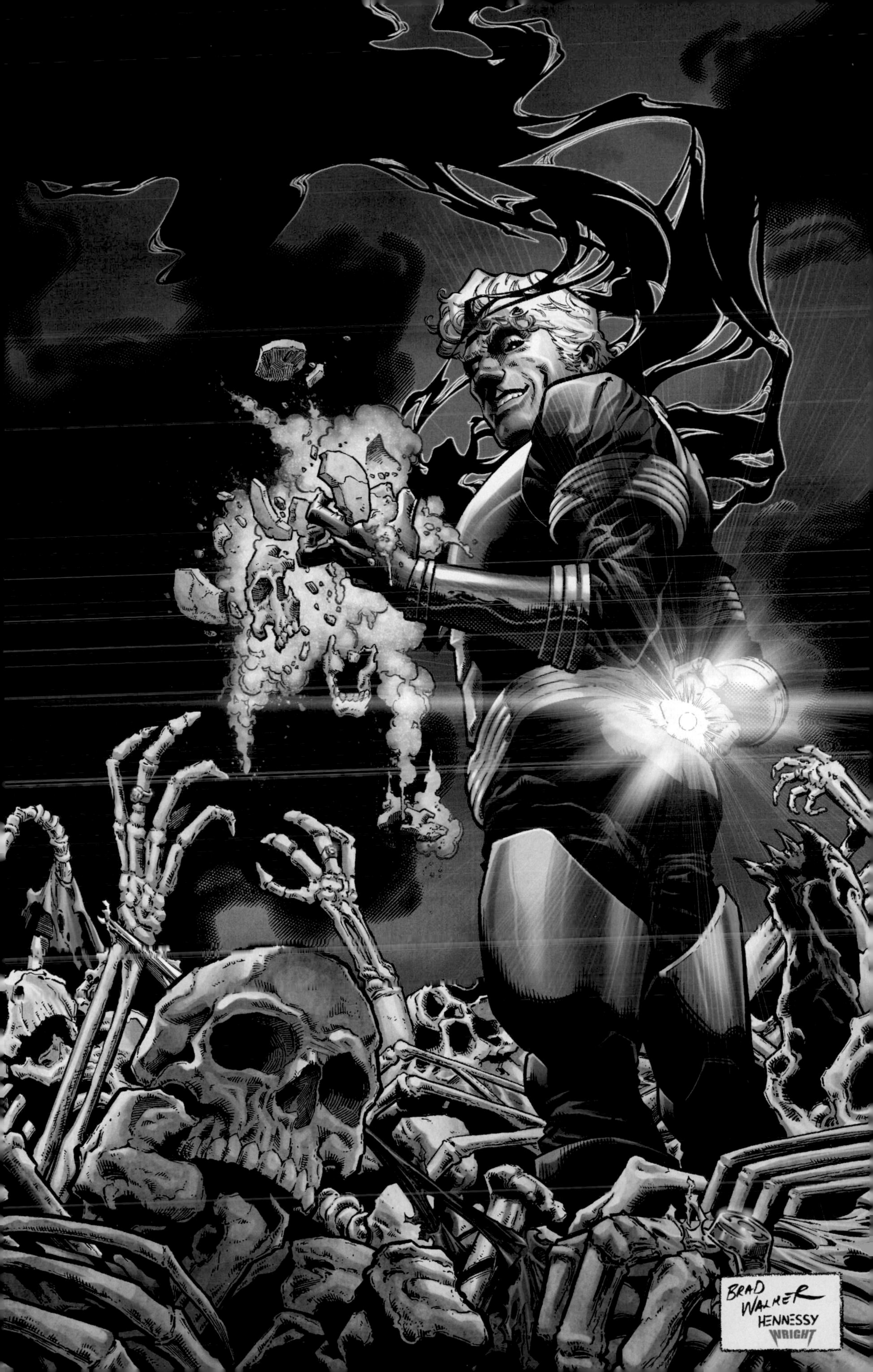
BRAD WALKER
HENNESSY
WRIGHT

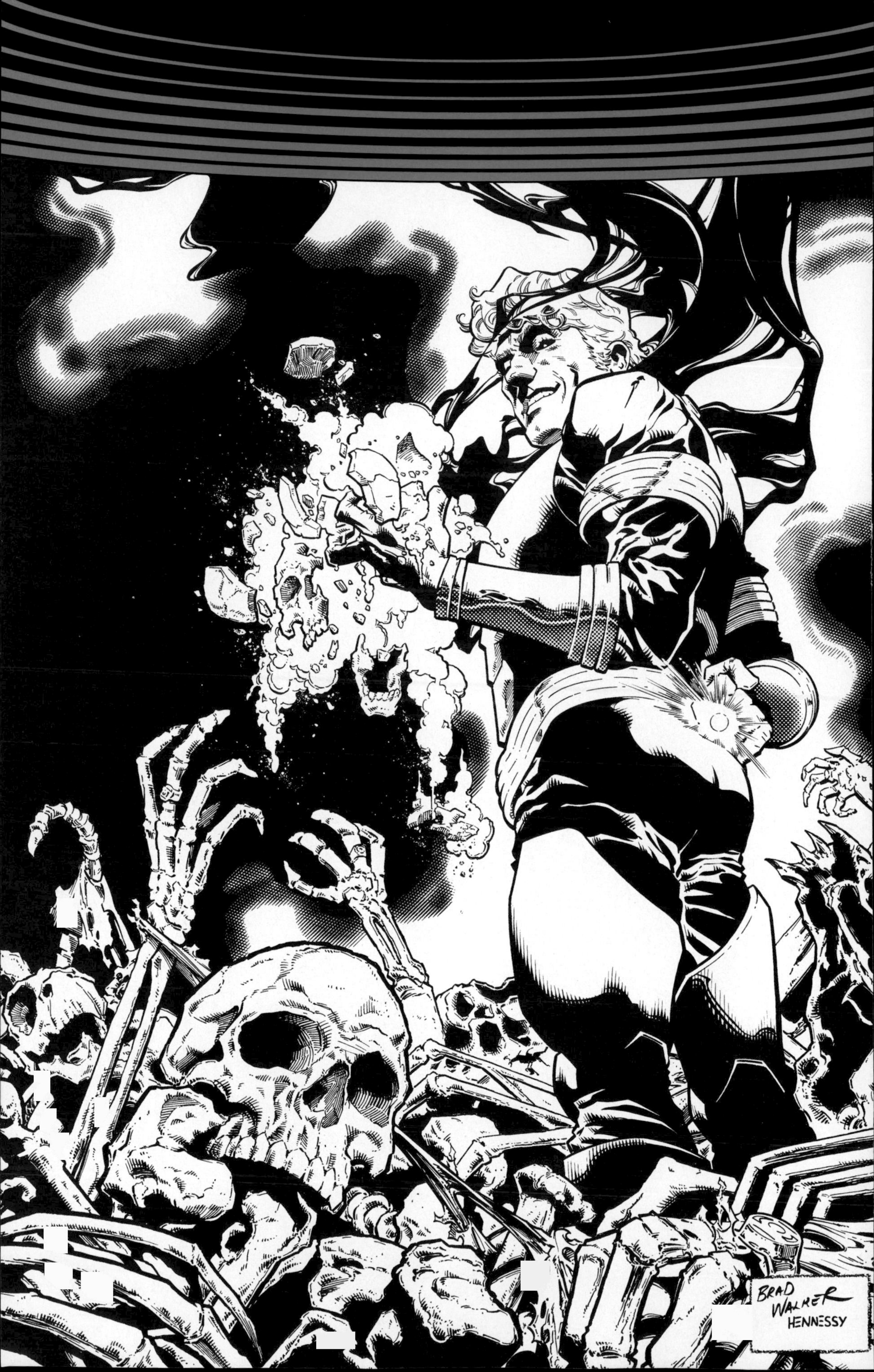
BRAD WALKER
HENNESSY

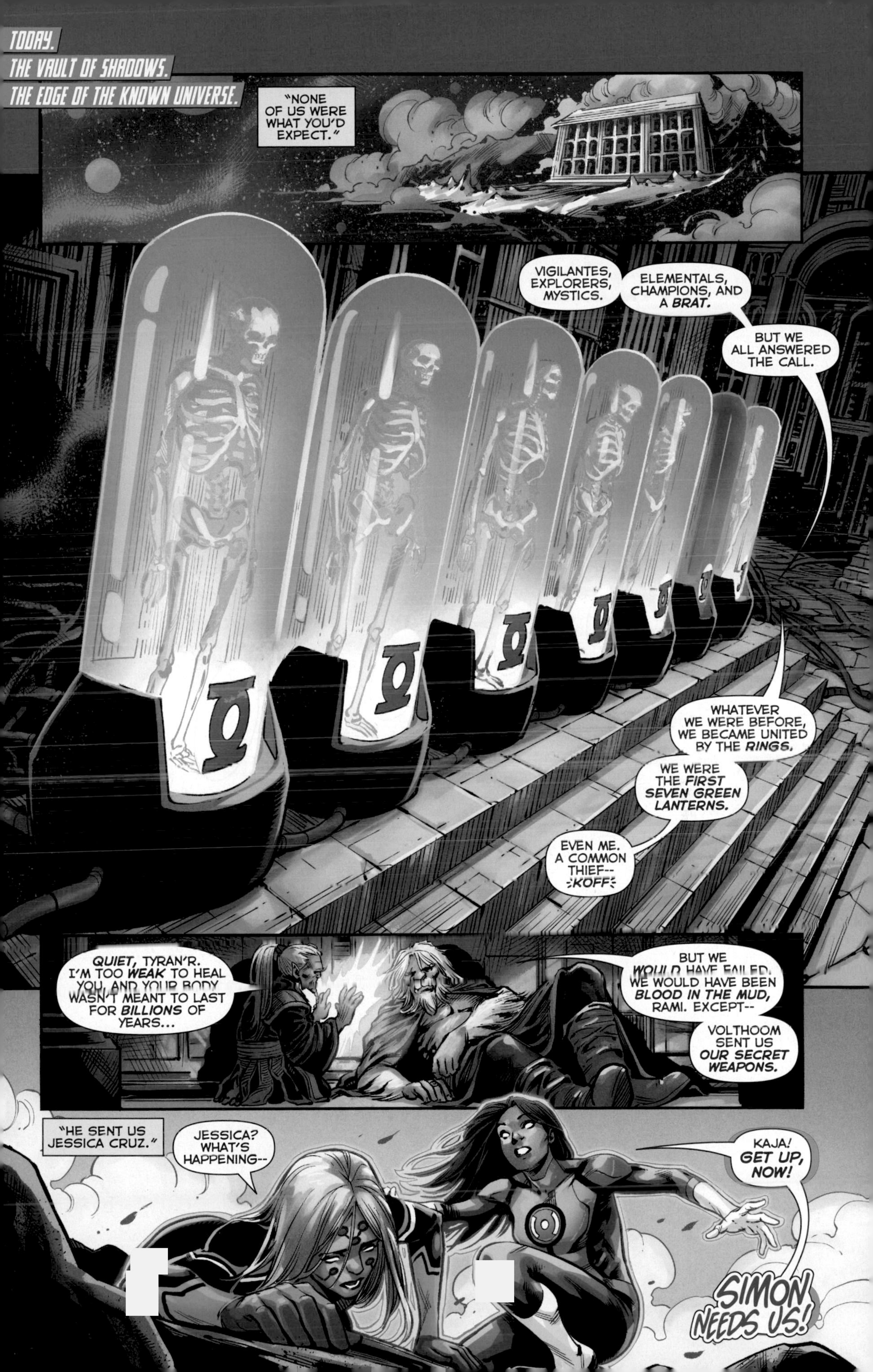
TODAY.
THE VAULT OF SHADOWS.
THE EDGE OF THE KNOWN UNIVERSE.
"NONE OF US WERE WHAT YOU'D EXPECT."
VIGILANTES, EXPLORERS, MYSTICS.
ELEMENTALS, CHAMPIONS, AND A BRAT.
BUT WE ALL ANSWERED THE CALL.
WHATEVER WE WERE BEFORE, WE BECAME UNITED BY THE RINGS.
WE WERE THE FIRST SEVEN GREEN LANTERNS.
EVEN ME. A COMMON THIEF-- KOFF
QUIET, TYRAN'R. I'M TOO WEAK TO HEAL YOU, AND YOUR BODY WASN'T MEANT TO LAST FOR BILLIONS OF YEARS...
BUT WE WOULD HAVE FAILED. WE WOULD HAVE BEEN BLOOD IN THE MUD, RAMI. EXCEPT--
VOLTHOOM SENT US OUR SECRET WEAPONS.
"HE SENT US JESSICA CRUZ."
JESSICA? WHAT'S HAPPENING--
KAJA! GET UP, NOW!
SIMON NEEDS US!

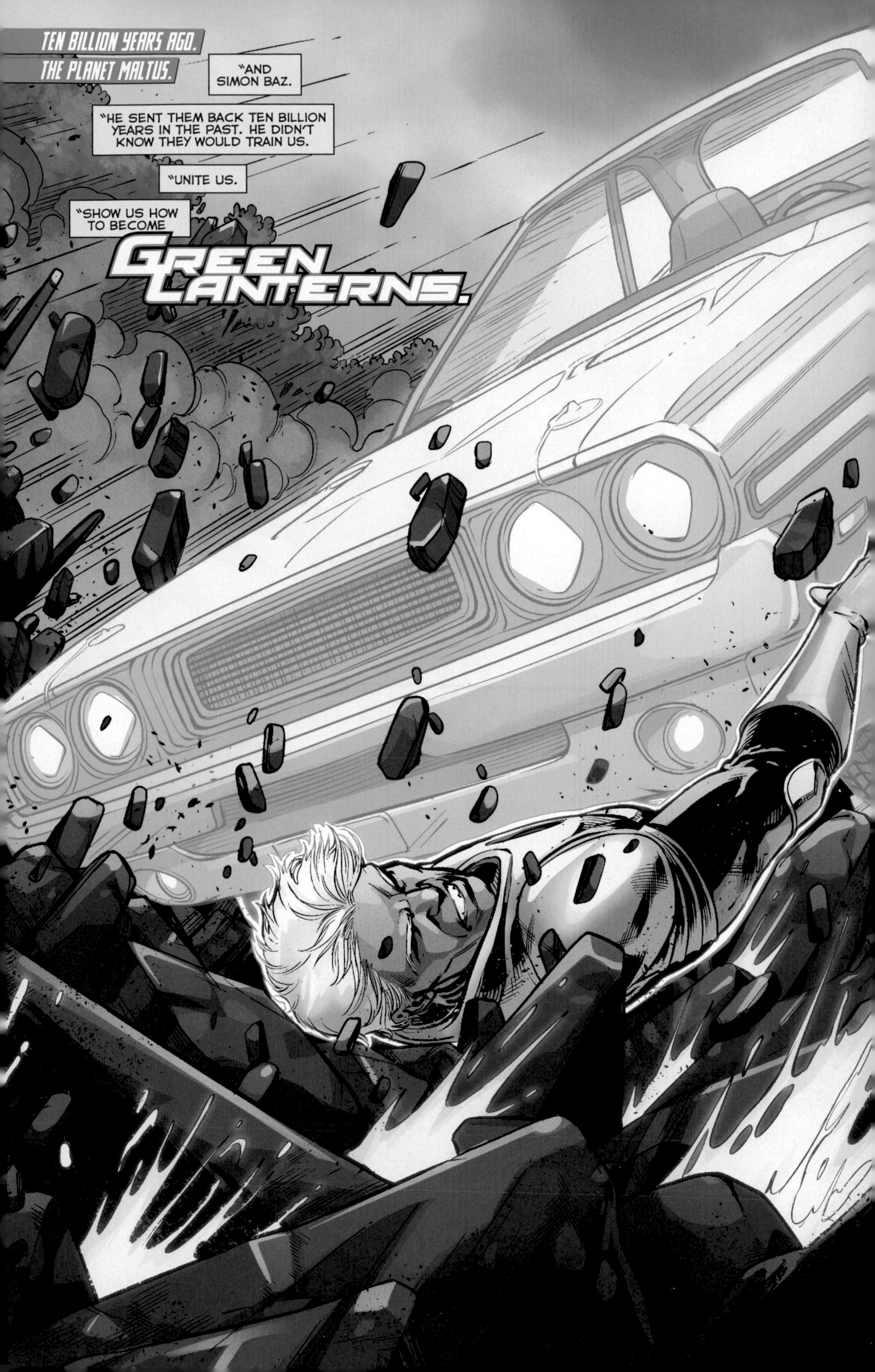
TEN BILLION YEARS AGO.
THE PLANET MALTUS.
"AND SIMON BAZ.
"HE SENT THEM BACK TEN BILLION YEARS IN THE PAST. HE DIDN'T KNOW THEY WOULD TRAIN US.
"UNITE US.
"SHOW US HOW TO BECOME
GREEN LANTERNS.

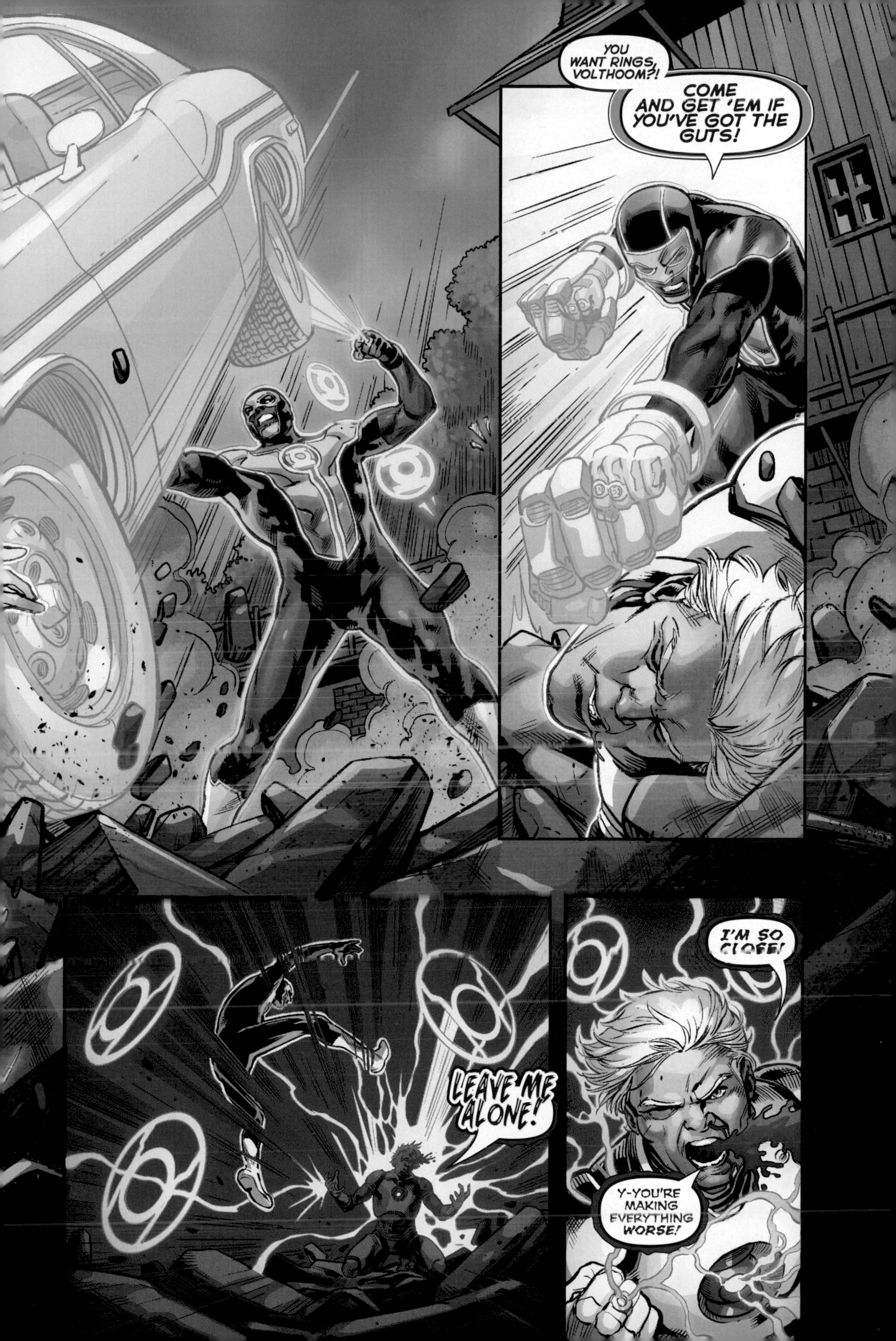
YOU WANT RINGS, VOLTHOOM?!
COME AND GET 'EM IF YOU'VE GOT THE GUTS!
LEAVE ME ALONE!
I'M SO CLOSE!
Y-YOU'RE MAKING EVERYTHING WORSE!

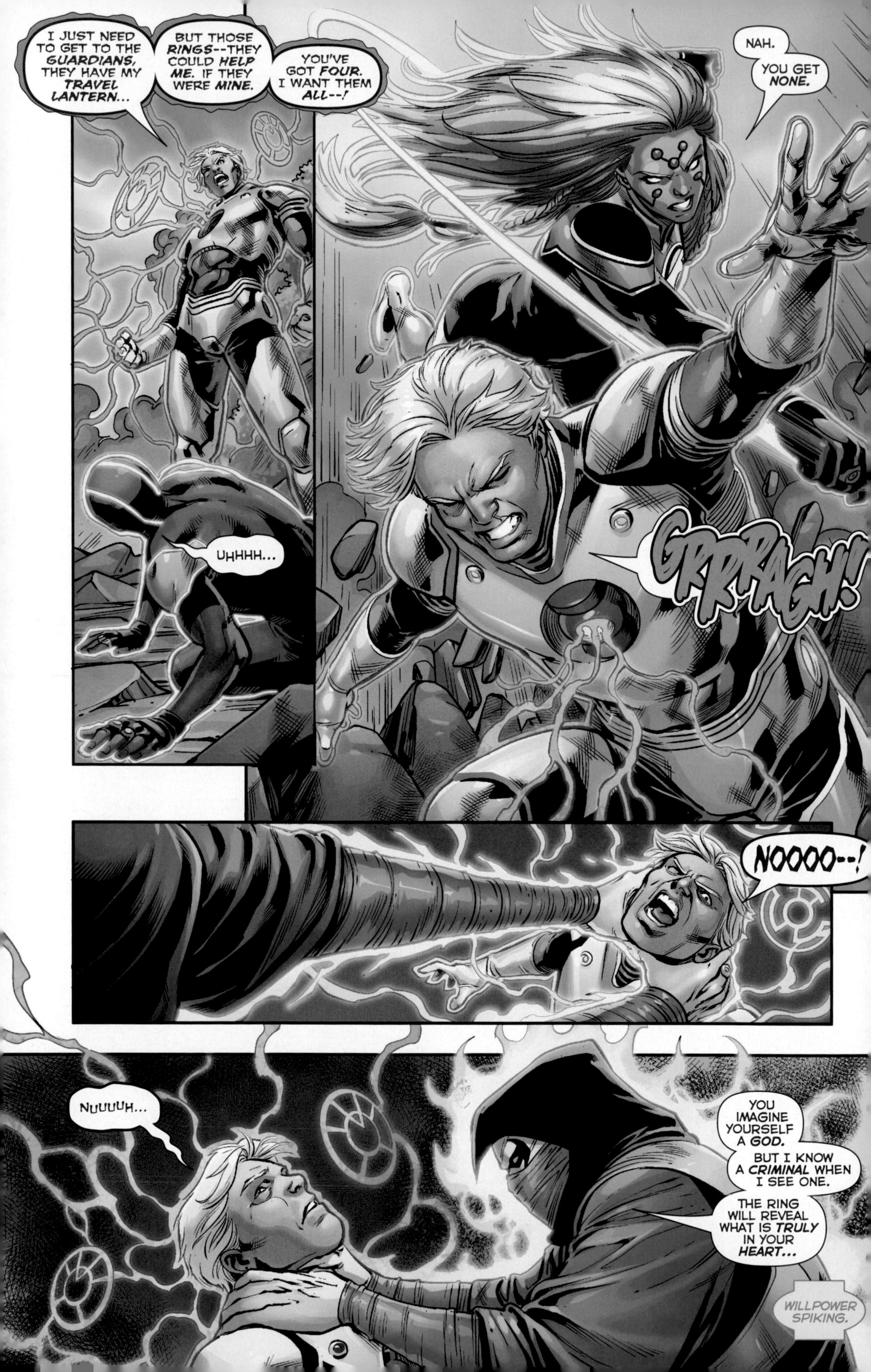

I JUST NEED TO GET TO THE GUARDIANS, THEY HAVE MY TRAVEL LANTERN...
BUT THOSE RINGS--THEY COULD HELP ME. IF THEY WERE MINE.
YOU'VE GOT FOUR. I WANT THEM ALL--!
NAH.
YOU GET NONE.
UHHHH...
GRRRAGH!
NOOOO--!
NUUUUH...
YOU IMAGINE YOURSELF A GOD.
BUT I KNOW A CRIMINAL WHEN I SEE ONE.
THE RING WILL REVEAL WHAT IS TRULY IN YOUR HEART...
WILLPOWER SPIKING.

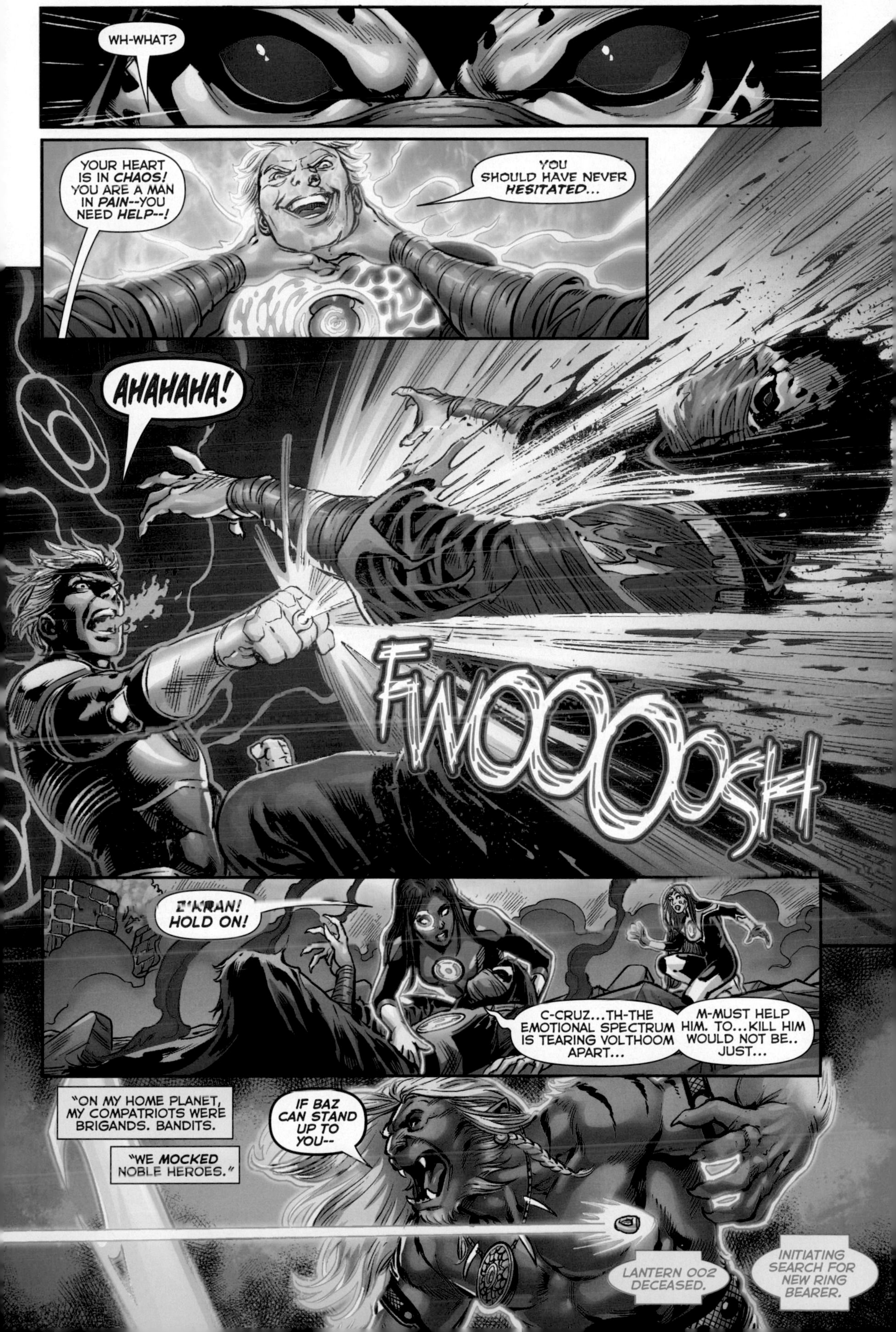

WH-WHAT?
YOUR HEART IS IN CHAOS! YOU ARE A MAN IN PAIN--YOU NEED HELP--!
YOU SHOULD HAVE NEVER HESITATED...
AHAHAHA!
FWOOOOOSH
Z'KRAN! HOLD ON!
C-CRUZ...TH-THE EMOTIONAL SPECTRUM IS TEARING VOLTHOOM APART...
M-MUST HELP HIM. TO...KILL HIM WOULD NOT BE.. JUST...
"ON MY HOME PLANET, MY COMPATRIOTS WERE BRIGANDS. BANDITS.
"WE MOCKED NOBLE HEROES."
IF BAZ CAN STAND UP TO YOU--
LANTERN 002 DECEASED.
INITIATING SEARCH FOR NEW RING BEARER.

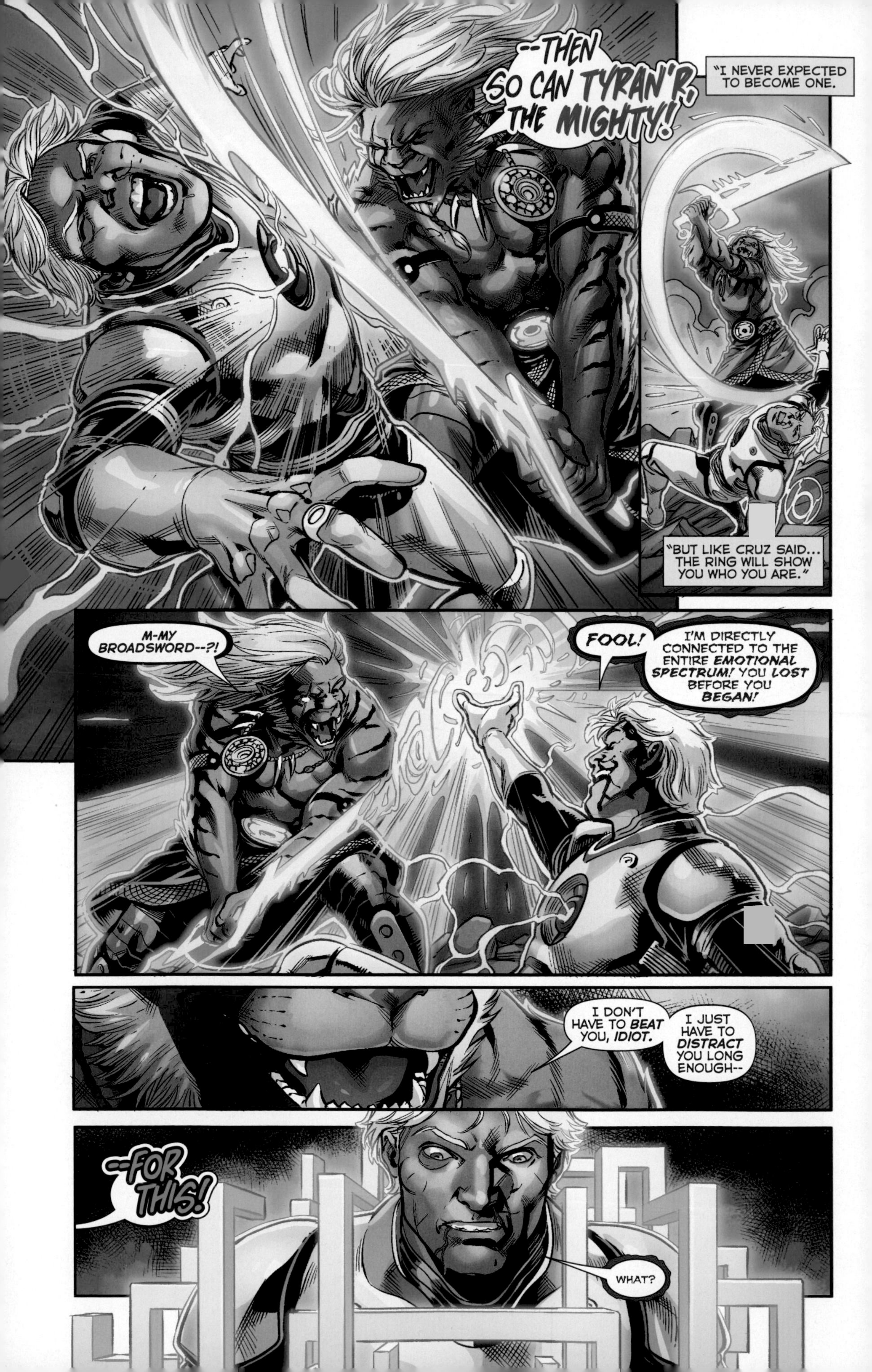
--THEN SO CAN TYRAN'R, THE MIGHTY!
"I NEVER EXPECTED TO BECOME ONE.
"BUT LIKE CRUZ SAID... THE RING WILL SHOW YOU WHO YOU ARE."
M-MY BROADSWORD--?!
FOOL!
I'M DIRECTLY CONNECTED TO THE ENTIRE EMOTIONAL SPECTRUM! YOU LOST BEFORE YOU BEGAN!
I DON'T HAVE TO BEAT YOU, IDIOT.
I JUST HAVE TO DISTRACT YOU LONG ENOUGH--
--FOR THIS!
WHAT?

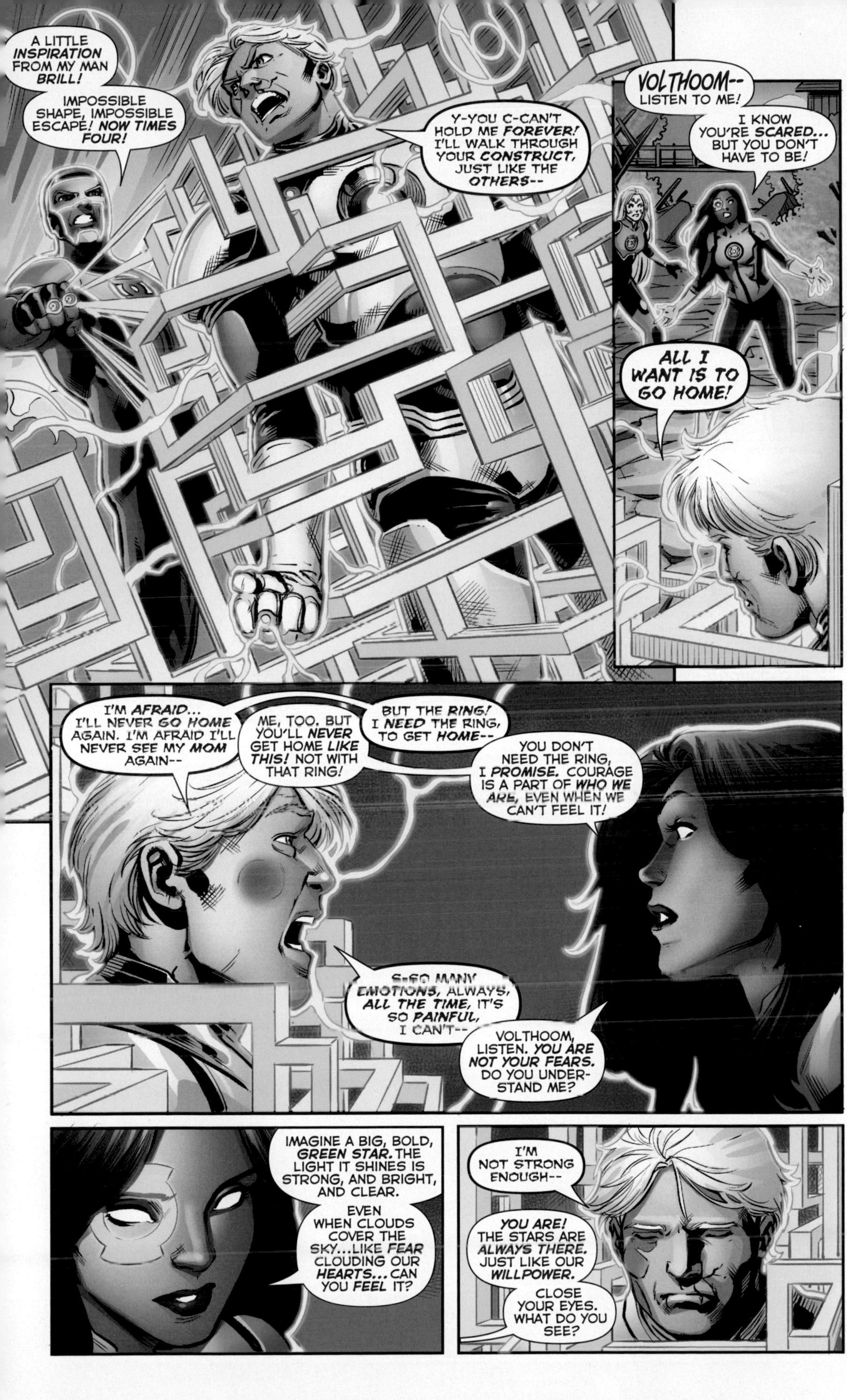
A LITTLE INSPIRATION FROM MY MAN BRILL!
IMPOSSIBLE SHAPE, IMPOSSIBLE ESCAPE! NOW TIMES FOUR!
Y-YOU C-CAN'T HOLD ME FOREVER! I'LL WALK THROUGH YOUR CONSTRUCT, JUST LIKE THE OTHERS--
VOLTHOOM-- LISTEN TO ME!
I KNOW YOU'RE SCARED... BUT YOU DON'T HAVE TO BE!
ALL I WANT IS TO GO HOME!
I'M AFRAID... I'LL NEVER GO HOME AGAIN. I'M AFRAID I'LL NEVER SEE MY MOM AGAIN--
ME, TOO. BUT YOU'LL NEVER GET HOME LIKE THIS! NOT WITH THAT RING!
BUT THE RING! I NEED THE RING, TO GET HOME--
YOU DON'T NEED THE RING, I PROMISE. COURAGE IS A PART OF WHO WE ARE, EVEN WHEN WE CAN'T FEEL IT!
S-SO MANY EMOTIONS, ALWAYS, ALL THE TIME, IT'S SO PAINFUL, I CAN'T--
VOLTHOOM, LISTEN. YOU ARE NOT YOUR FEARS. DO YOU UNDERSTAND ME?
IMAGINE A BIG, BOLD, GREEN STAR. THE LIGHT IT SHINES IS STRONG, AND BRIGHT, AND CLEAR.
EVEN WHEN CLOUDS COVER THE SKY...LIKE FEAR CLOUDING OUR HEARTS... CAN YOU FEEL IT?
I'M NOT STRONG ENOUGH--
YOU ARE! THE STARS ARE ALWAYS THERE. JUST LIKE OUR WILLPOWER.
CLOSE YOUR EYES. WHAT DO YOU SEE?

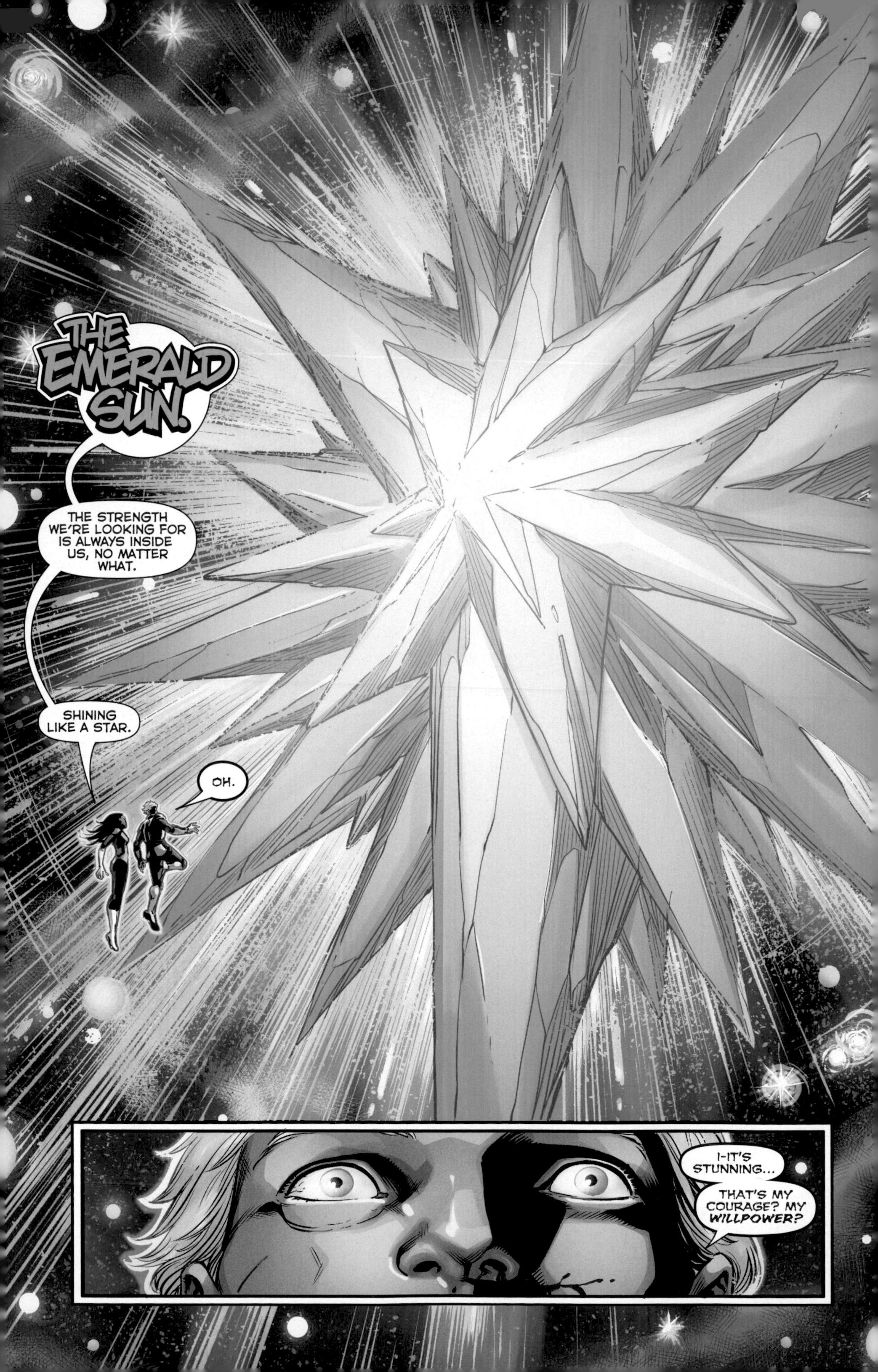
THE EMERALD SUN.
THE STRENGTH WE'RE LOOKING FOR IS ALWAYS INSIDE US, NO MATTER WHAT.
SHINING LIKE A STAR.
OH.
I-IT'S STUNNING...
THAT'S MY COURAGE? MY *WILLPOWER?*

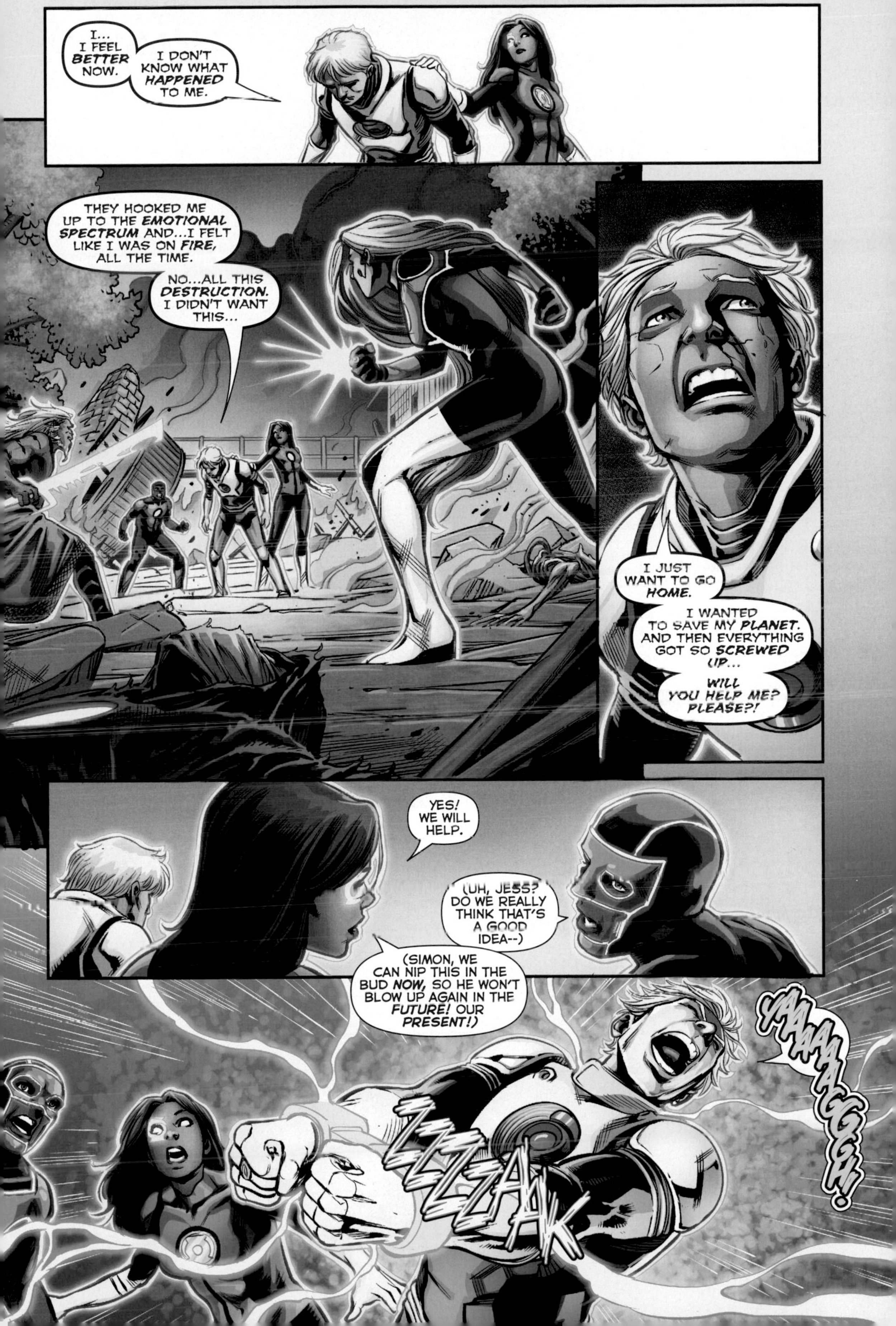

I... I FEEL BETTER NOW.
I DON'T KNOW WHAT HAPPENED TO ME.
THEY HOOKED ME UP TO THE EMOTIONAL SPECTRUM AND...I FELT LIKE I WAS ON FIRE, ALL THE TIME.
NO...ALL THIS DESTRUCTION. I DIDN'T WANT THIS...
I JUST WANT TO GO HOME.
I WANTED TO SAVE MY PLANET. AND THEN EVERYTHING GOT SO SCREWED UP...
WILL YOU HELP ME? PLEASE?!
YES! WE WILL HELP.
(UH, JESS? DO WE REALLY THINK THAT'S A GOOD IDEA--)
(SIMON, WE CAN NIP THIS IN THE BUD NOW, SO HE WON'T BLOW UP AGAIN IN THE FUTURE! OUR PRESENT!)
YAAAAAGGGH!
ZZZZAK

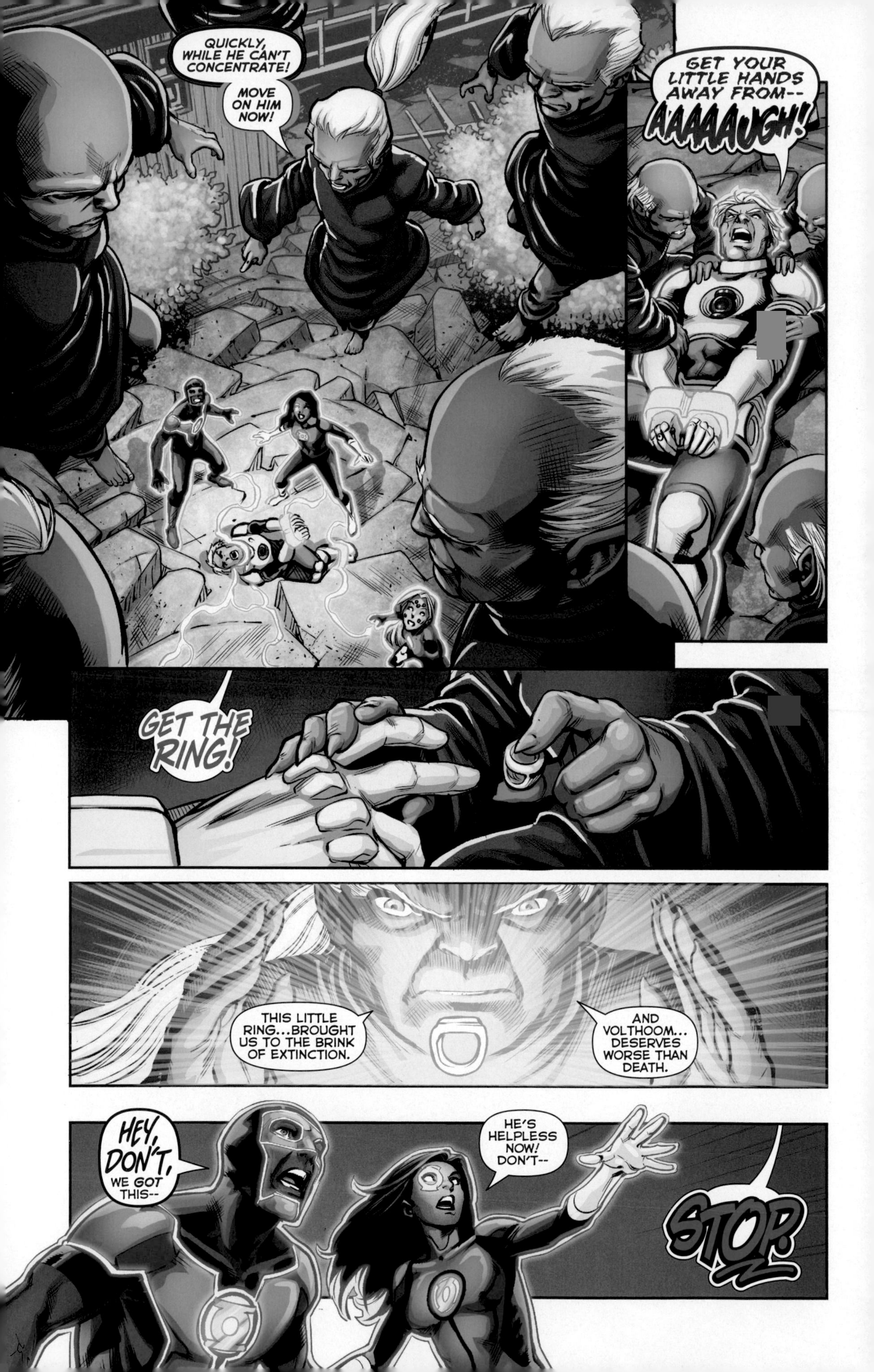
QUICKLY, WHILE HE CAN'T CONCENTRATE!
MOVE ON HIM NOW!
GET YOUR LITTLE HANDS AWAY FROM-- AAAAAUGH!
GET THE RING!
THIS LITTLE RING...BROUGHT US TO THE BRINK OF EXTINCTION.
AND VOLTHOOM... DESERVES WORSE THAN DEATH.
HEY, DON'T, WE GOT THIS--
HE'S HELPLESS NOW! DON'T--
STOP!

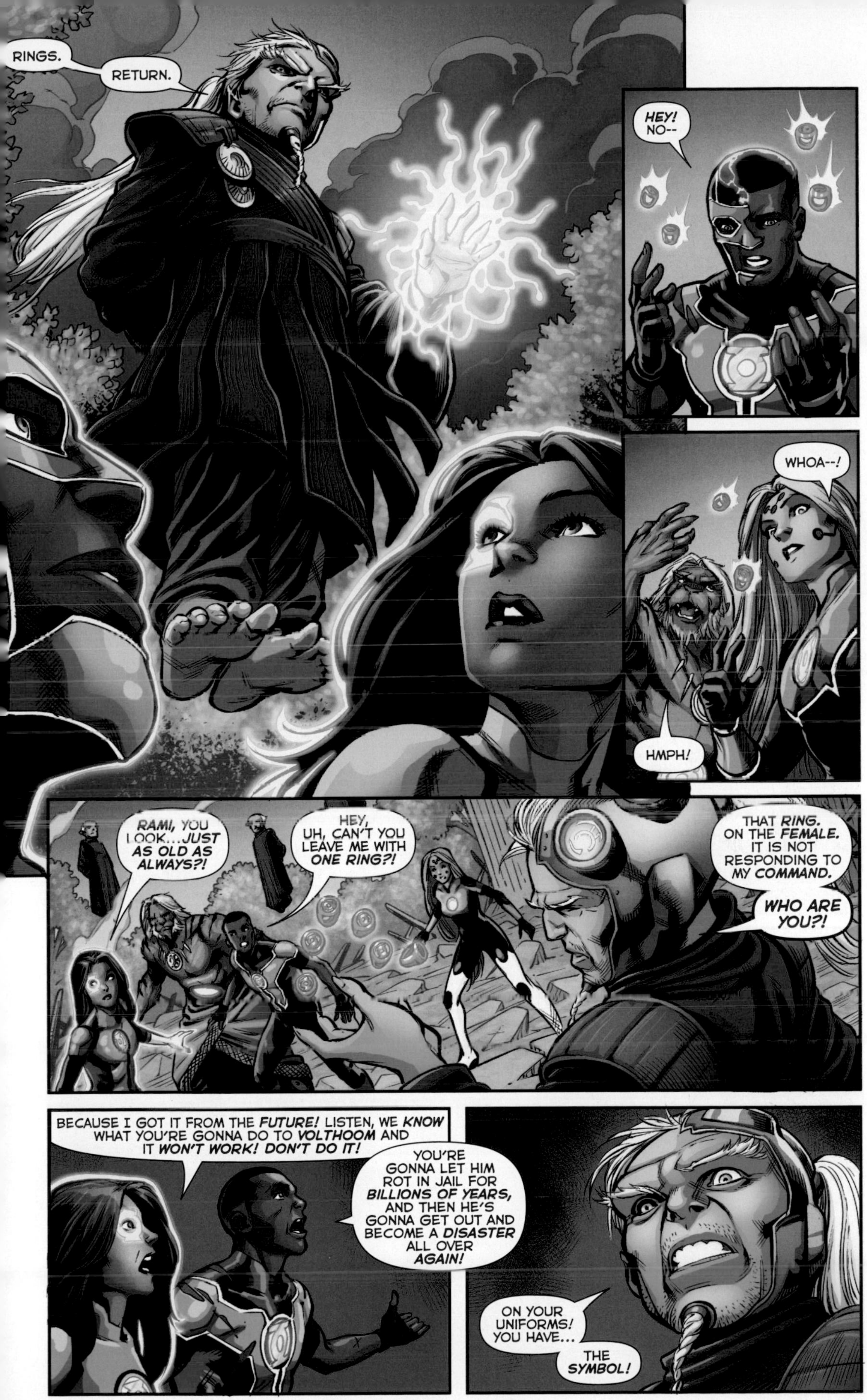
RINGS.
RETURN.
HEY! NO--
WHOA--!
HMPH!
RAMI, YOU LOOK...JUST AS OLD AS ALWAYS?!
HEY, UH, CAN'T YOU LEAVE ME WITH ONE RING?!
THAT RING. ON THE FEMALE. IT IS NOT RESPONDING TO MY COMMAND.
WHO ARE YOU?!
BECAUSE I GOT IT FROM THE FUTURE! LISTEN, WE KNOW WHAT YOU'RE GONNA DO TO VOLTHOOM AND IT WON'T WORK! DON'T DO IT!
YOU'RE GONNA LET HIM ROT IN JAIL FOR BILLIONS OF YEARS, AND THEN HE'S GONNA GET OUT AND BECOME A DISASTER ALL OVER AGAIN!
ON YOUR UNIFORMS! YOU HAVE...
THE SYMBOL!

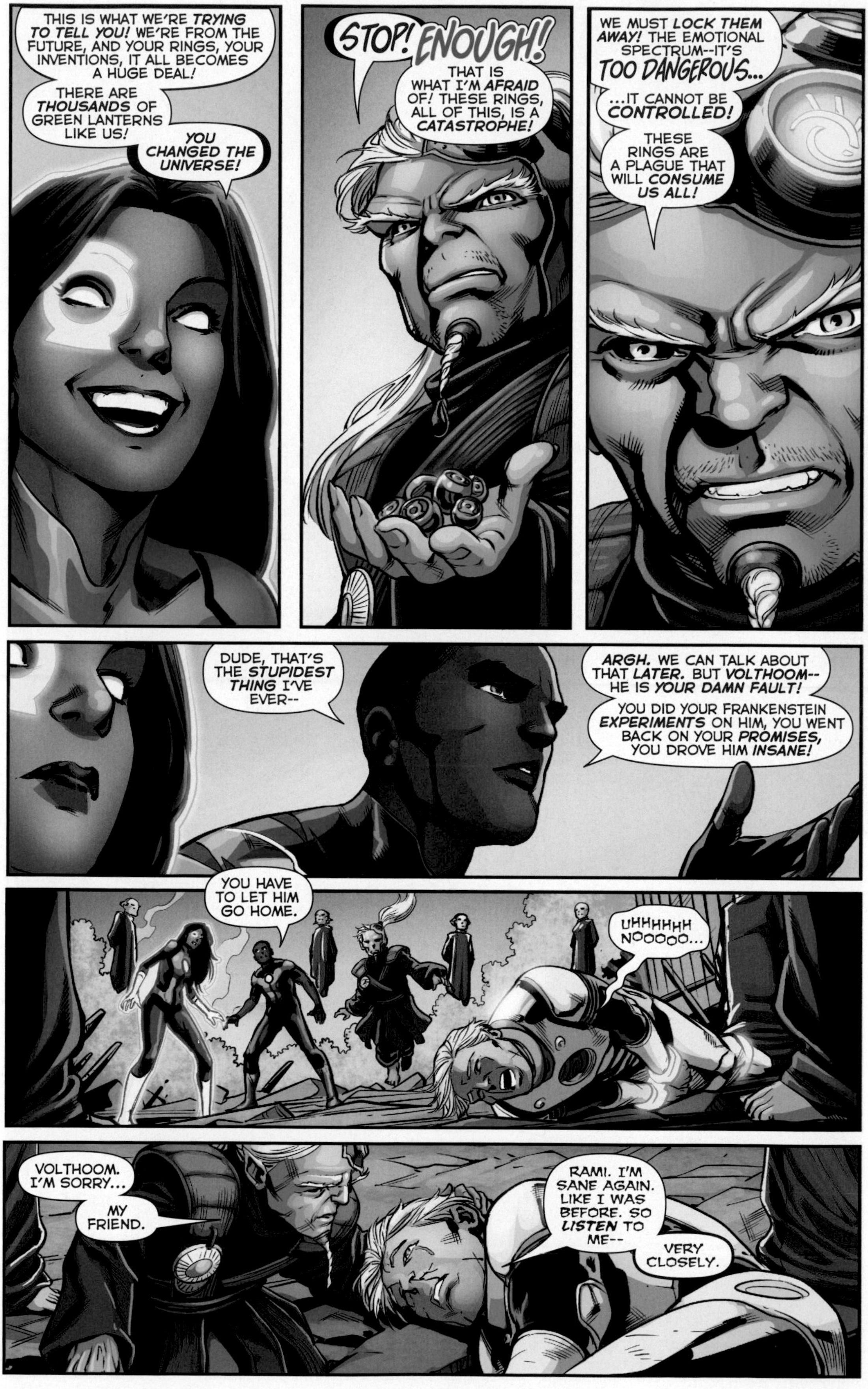
THIS IS WHAT WE'RE TRYING TO TELL YOU! WE'RE FROM THE FUTURE, AND YOUR RINGS, YOUR INVENTIONS, IT ALL BECOMES A HUGE DEAL!
THERE ARE THOUSANDS OF GREEN LANTERNS LIKE US!
YOU CHANGED THE UNIVERSE!
STOP! ENOUGH!
THAT IS WHAT I'M AFRAID OF! THESE RINGS, ALL OF THIS, IS A CATASTROPHE!
WE MUST LOCK THEM AWAY! THE EMOTIONAL SPECTRUM--IT'S TOO DANGEROUS...
...IT CANNOT BE CONTROLLED!
THESE RINGS ARE A PLAGUE THAT WILL CONSUME US ALL!
DUDE, THAT'S THE STUPIDEST THING I'VE EVER--
ARGH. WE CAN TALK ABOUT THAT LATER. BUT VOLTHOOM-- HE IS YOUR DAMN FAULT!
YOU DID YOUR FRANKENSTEIN EXPERIMENTS ON HIM, YOU WENT BACK ON YOUR PROMISES, YOU DROVE HIM INSANE!
YOU HAVE TO LET HIM GO HOME.
UHHHHHH NOOOOO...
VOLTHOOM. I'M SORRY...
MY FRIEND.
RAMI. I'M SANE AGAIN. LIKE I WAS BEFORE. SO LISTEN TO ME--
VERY CLOSELY.

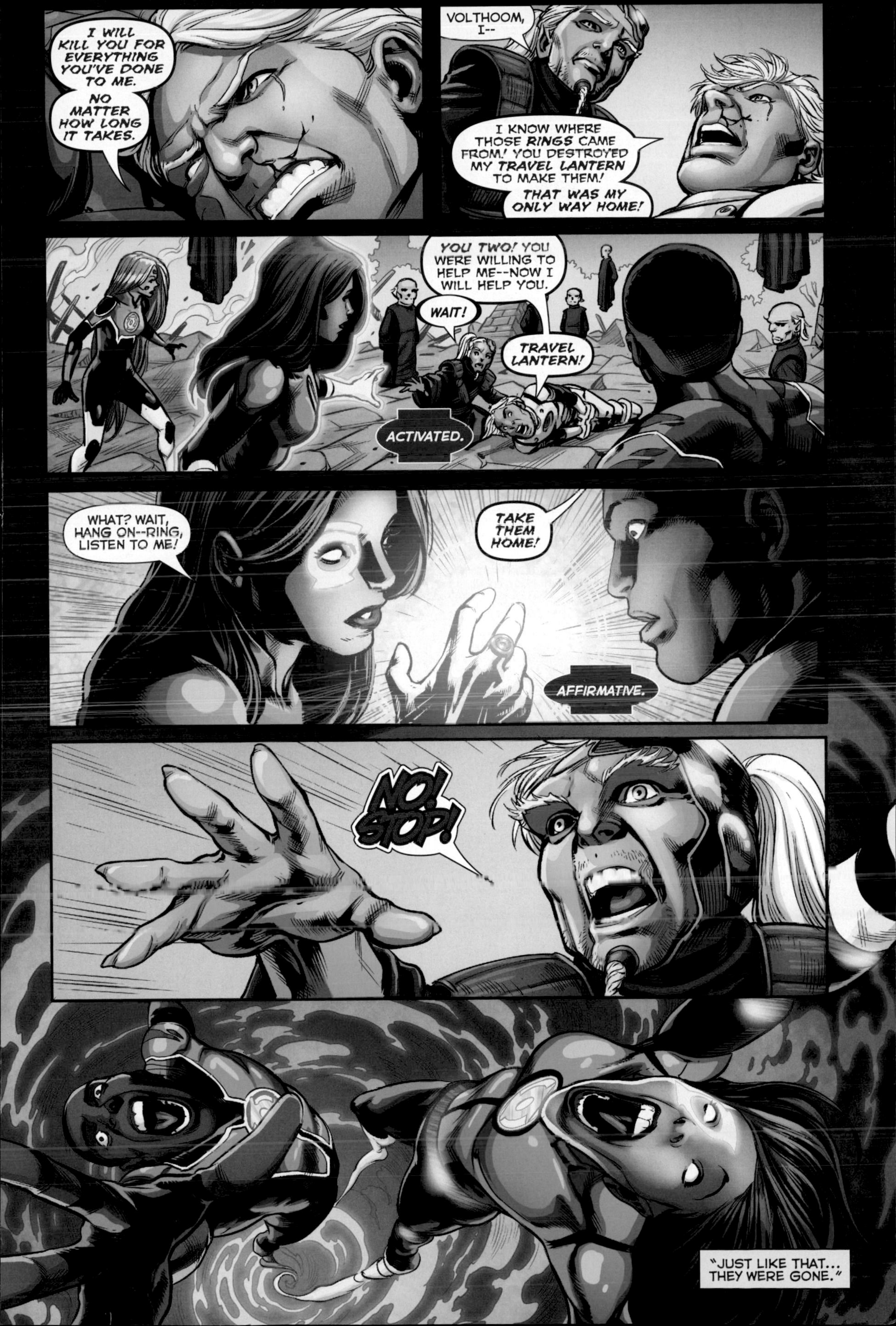
I WILL KILL YOU FOR EVERYTHING YOU'VE DONE TO ME.
NO MATTER HOW LONG IT TAKES.
VOLTHOOM, I--
I KNOW WHERE THOSE RINGS CAME FROM! YOU DESTROYED MY TRAVEL LANTERN TO MAKE THEM!
THAT WAS MY ONLY WAY HOME!
YOU TWO! YOU WERE WILLING TO HELP ME--NOW I WILL HELP YOU.
WAIT!
TRAVEL LANTERN!
ACTIVATED.
WHAT? WAIT, HANG ON--RING, LISTEN TO ME!
TAKE THEM HOME!
AFFIRMATIVE.
NO! STOP!
"JUST LIKE THAT... THEY WERE GONE."

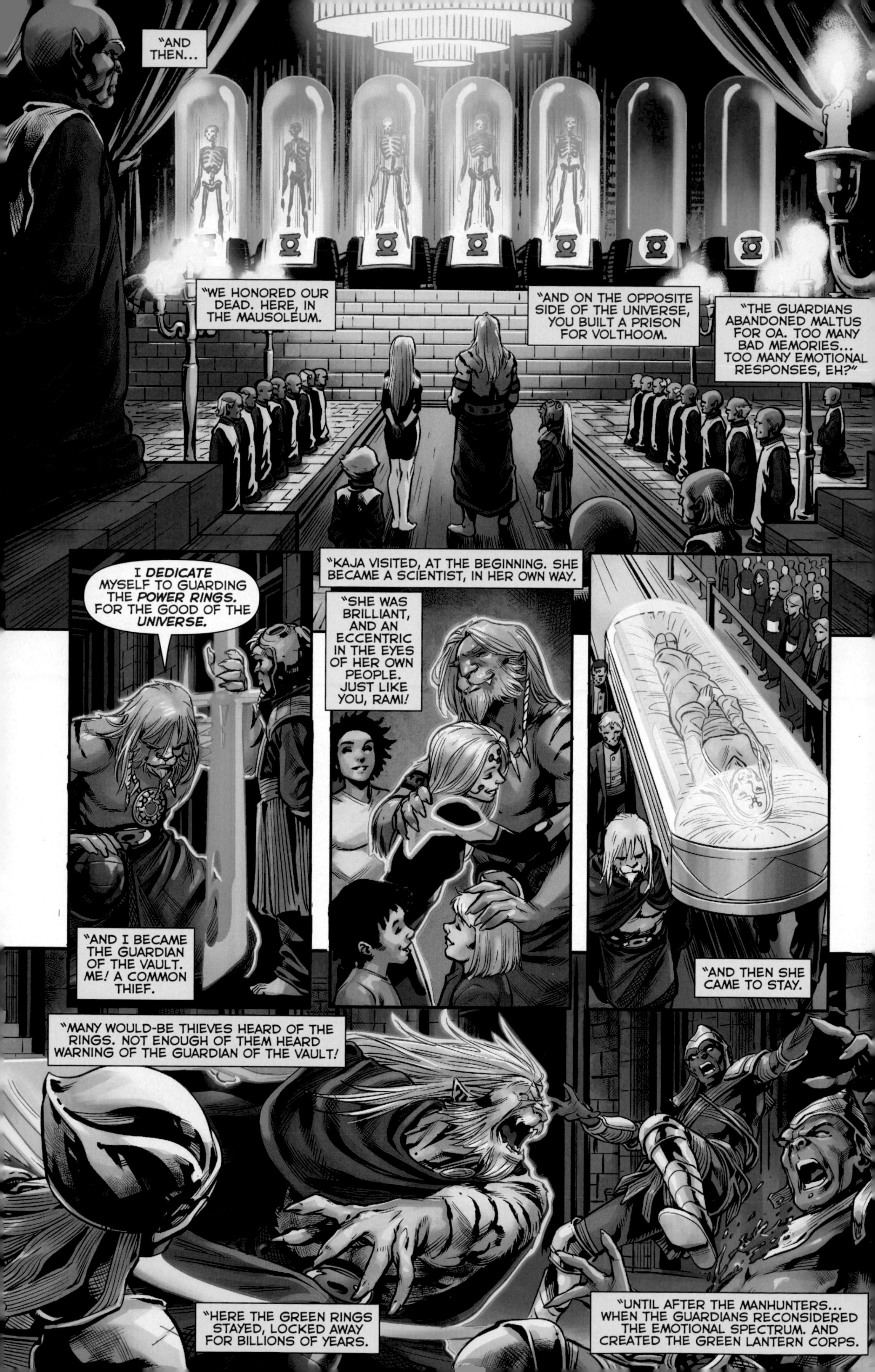
"AND THEN...
"WE HONORED OUR DEAD. HERE, IN THE MAUSOLEUM.
"AND ON THE OPPOSITE SIDE OF THE UNIVERSE, YOU BUILT A PRISON FOR VOLTHOOM.
"THE GUARDIANS ABANDONED MALTUS FOR OA. TOO MANY BAD MEMORIES... TOO MANY EMOTIONAL RESPONSES, EH?"
I *DEDICATE* MYSELF TO GUARDING THE *POWER RINGS.* FOR THE GOOD OF THE *UNIVERSE.*
"AND I BECAME THE GUARDIAN OF THE VAULT. ME*!* A COMMON THIEF.
"KAJA VISITED, AT THE BEGINNING. SHE BECAME A SCIENTIST, IN HER OWN WAY.
"SHE WAS BRILLIANT, AND AN ECCENTRIC IN THE EYES OF HER OWN PEOPLE. JUST LIKE YOU, RAMI*!*
"AND THEN SHE CAME TO STAY.
"MANY WOULD-BE THIEVES HEARD OF THE RINGS. NOT ENOUGH OF THEM HEARD WARNING OF THE GUARDIAN OF THE VAULT*!*
"HERE THE GREEN RINGS STAYED, LOCKED AWAY FOR BILLIONS OF YEARS.
"UNTIL AFTER THE MANHUNTERS... WHEN THE GUARDIANS RECONSIDERED THE EMOTIONAL SPECTRUM. AND CREATED THE GREEN LANTERN CORPS.

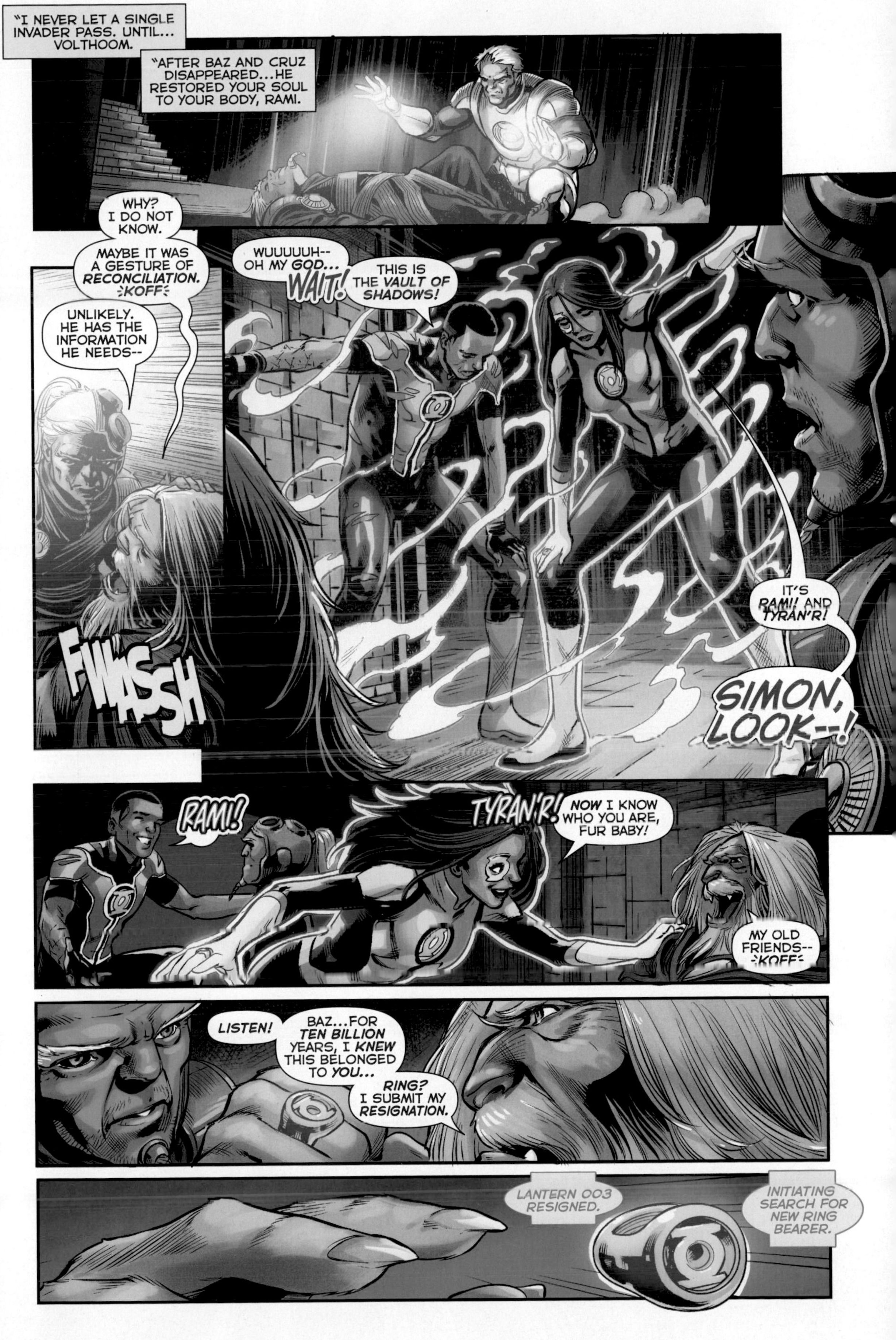
"I NEVER LET A SINGLE INVADER PASS. UNTIL... VOLTHOOM.
"AFTER BAZ AND CRUZ DISAPPEARED...HE RESTORED YOUR SOUL TO YOUR BODY, RAMI.
WHY? I DO NOT KNOW.
MAYBE IT WAS A GESTURE OF RECONCILIATION. KOFF
UNLIKELY. HE HAS THE INFORMATION HE NEEDS--
FWASSH
WUUUUUH-- OH MY GOD... WAIT!
THIS IS THE VAULT OF SHADOWS!
IT'S RAMI! AND TYRAN'R!
SIMON, LOOK--!
RAMI!
TYRAN'R!
NOW I KNOW WHO YOU ARE, FUR BABY!
MY OLD FRIENDS-- KOFF
LISTEN!
BAZ...FOR TEN BILLION YEARS, I KNEW THIS BELONGED TO YOU...
RING? I SUBMIT MY RESIGNATION.
LANTERN 003 RESIGNED.
INITIATING SEARCH FOR NEW RING BEARER.

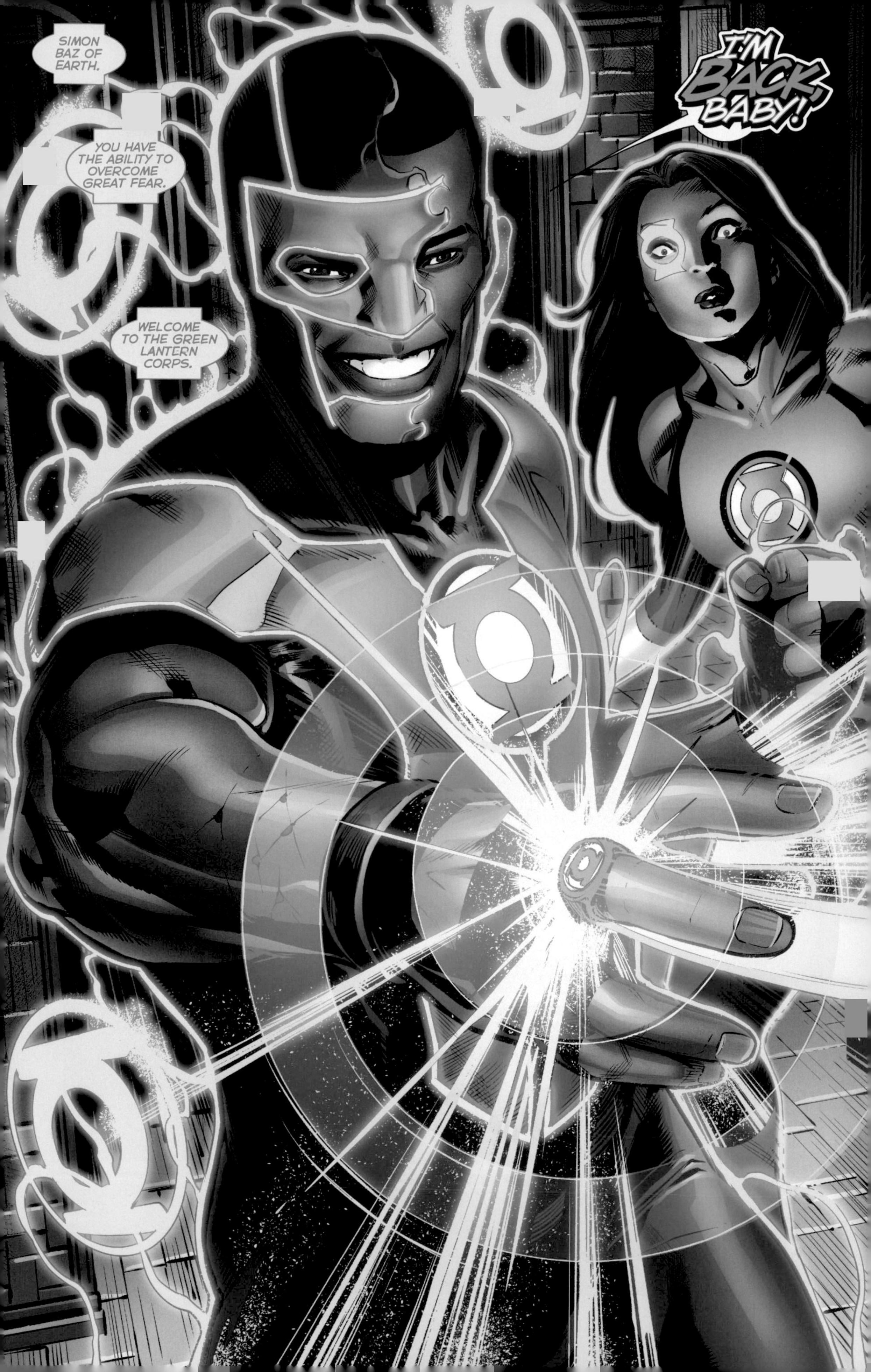
SIMON BAZ OF EARTH.
YOU HAVE THE ABILITY TO OVERCOME GREAT FEAR.
WELCOME TO THE GREEN LANTERN CORPS.
I'M BACK, BABY!

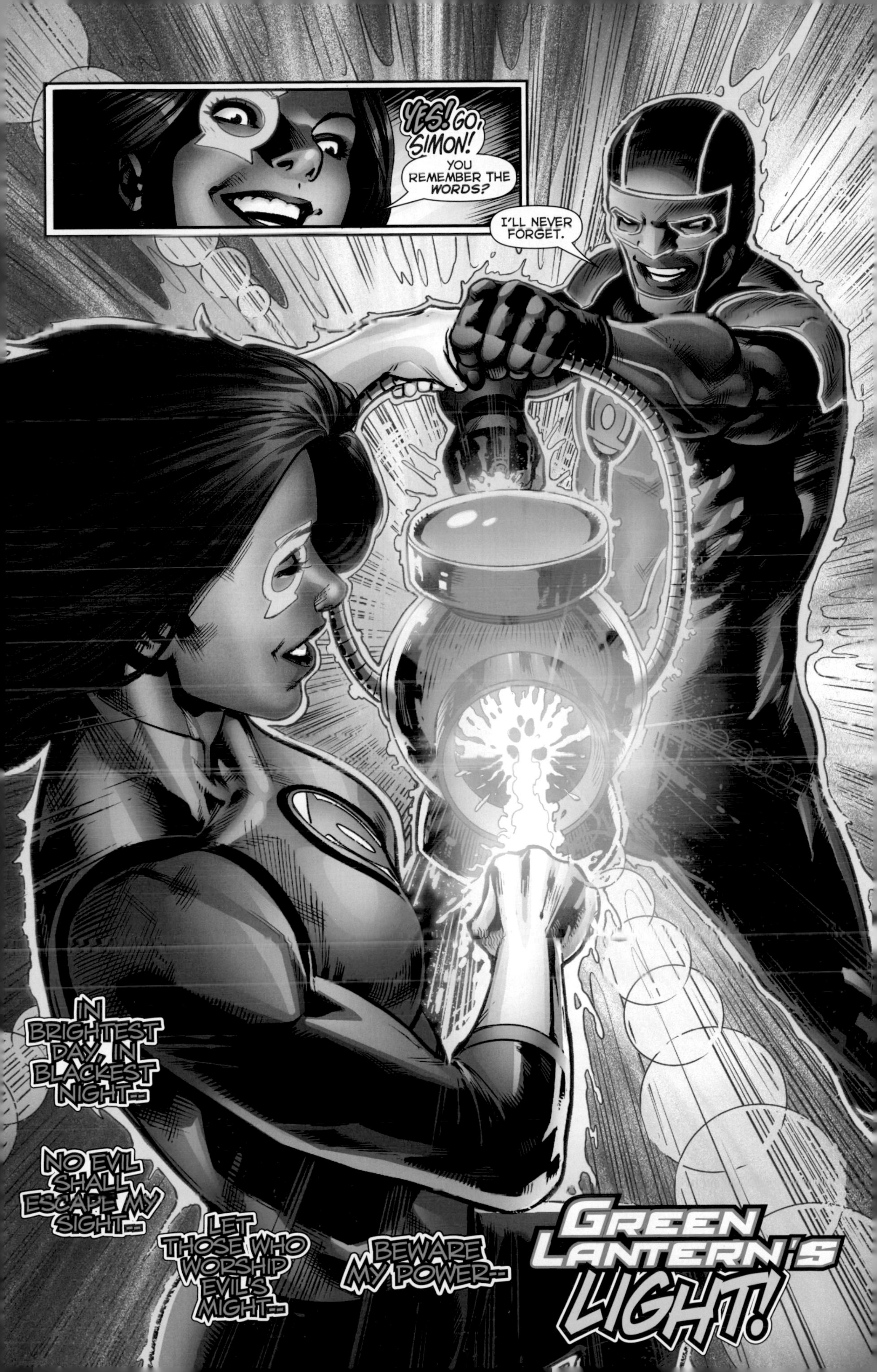
YES! GO, SIMON! YOU REMEMBER THE WORDS?
I'LL NEVER FORGET.
IN BRIGHTEST DAY, IN BLACKEST NIGHT--
NO EVIL SHALL ESCAPE MY SIGHT--
LET THOSE WHO WORSHIP EVIL'S MIGHT--
BEWARE MY POWER--
GREEN LANTERN'S LIGHT!

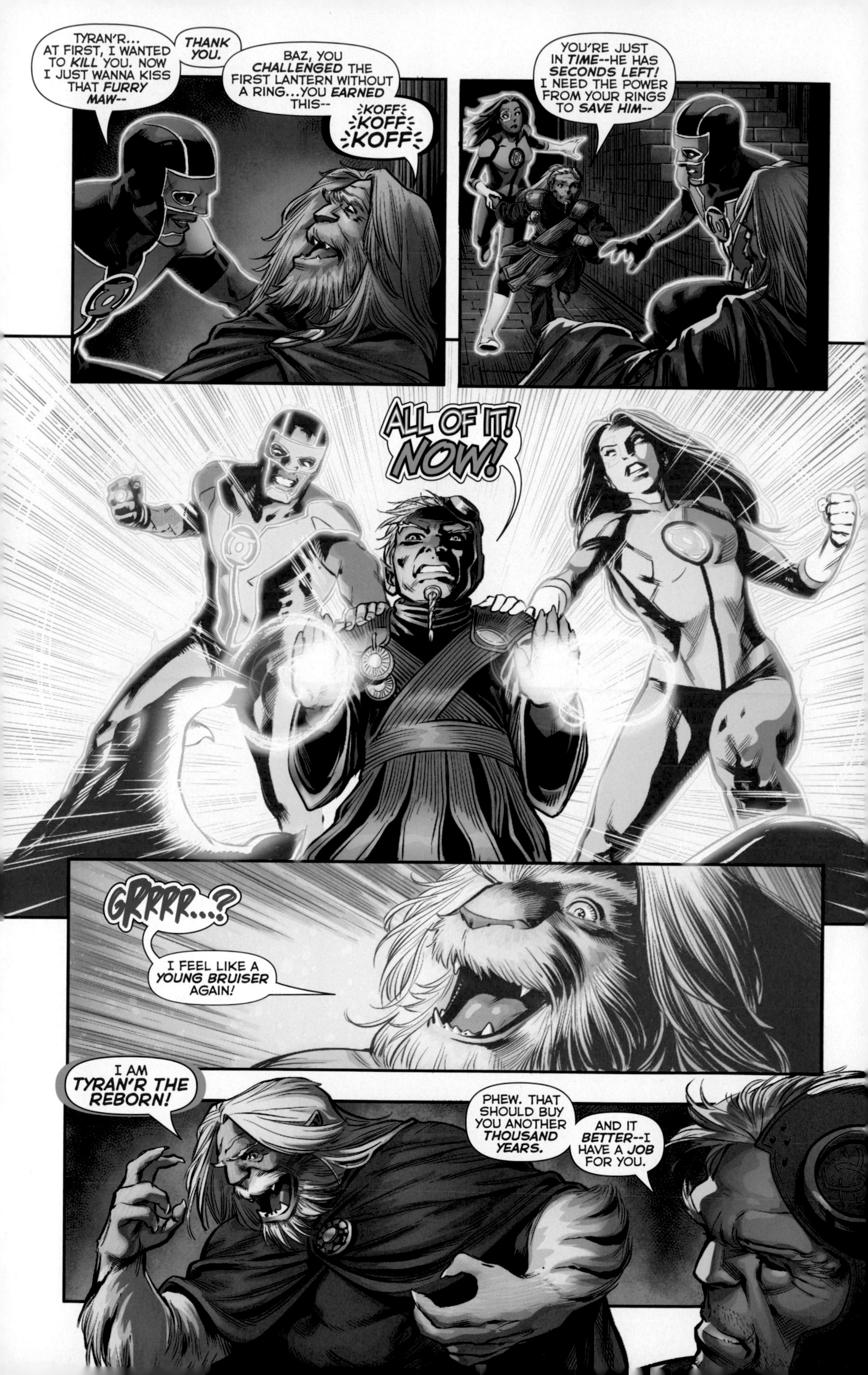
TYRAN'R... AT FIRST, I WANTED TO KILL YOU. NOW I JUST WANNA KISS THAT FURRY MAW--
THANK YOU.
BAZ, YOU CHALLENGED THE FIRST LANTERN WITHOUT A RING...YOU EARNED THIS--
KOFF KOFF KOFF
YOU'RE JUST IN TIME--HE HAS SECONDS LEFT! I NEED THE POWER FROM YOUR RINGS TO SAVE HIM--
ALL OF IT! NOW!
GRRRR...?
I FEEL LIKE A YOUNG BRUISER AGAIN!
I AM TYRAN'R THE REBORN!
PHEW. THAT SHOULD BUY YOU ANOTHER THOUSAND YEARS.
AND IT BETTER--I HAVE A JOB FOR YOU.

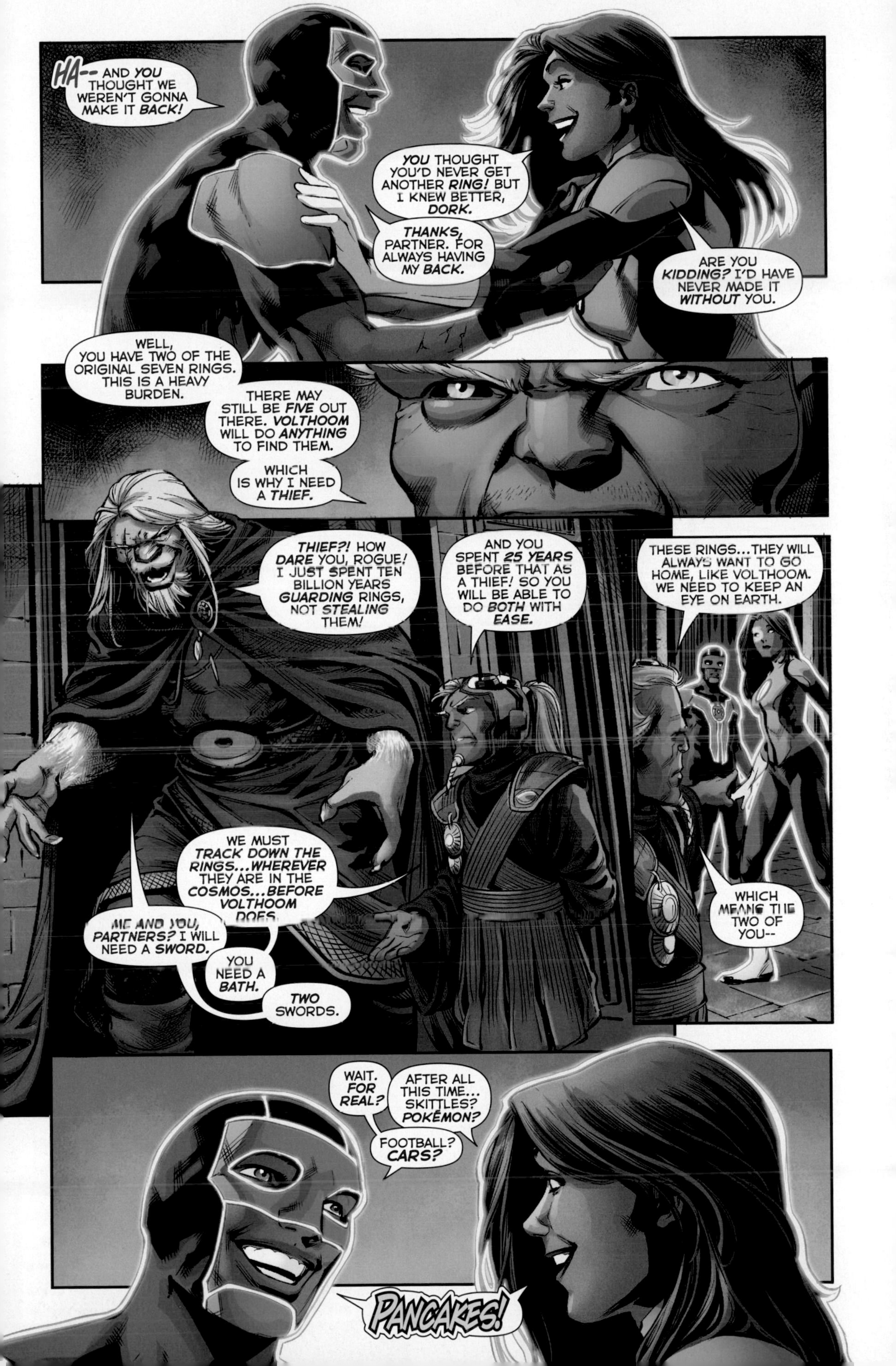
HA-- AND YOU THOUGHT WE WEREN'T GONNA MAKE IT BACK!
YOU THOUGHT YOU'D NEVER GET ANOTHER RING! BUT I KNEW BETTER, DORK.
THANKS, PARTNER. FOR ALWAYS HAVING MY BACK.
ARE YOU KIDDING? I'D HAVE NEVER MADE IT WITHOUT YOU.
WELL, YOU HAVE TWO OF THE ORIGINAL SEVEN RINGS. THIS IS A HEAVY BURDEN.
THERE MAY STILL BE FIVE OUT THERE. VOLTHOOM WILL DO ANYTHING TO FIND THEM.
WHICH IS WHY I NEED A THIEF.
THIEF?! HOW DARE YOU, ROGUE! I JUST SPENT TEN BILLION YEARS GUARDING RINGS, NOT STEALING THEM!
AND YOU SPENT 25 YEARS BEFORE THAT AS A THIEF! SO YOU WILL BE ABLE TO DO BOTH WITH EASE.
WE MUST TRACK DOWN THE RINGS...WHEREVER THEY ARE IN THE COSMOS...BEFORE VOLTHOOM DOES.
ME AND YOU, PARTNERS? I WILL NEED A SWORD.
YOU NEED A BATH.
TWO SWORDS.
THESE RINGS...THEY WILL ALWAYS WANT TO GO HOME, LIKE VOLTHOOM. WE NEED TO KEEP AN EYE ON EARTH.
WHICH MEANS THE TWO OF YOU--
WAIT. FOR REAL?
AFTER ALL THIS TIME... SKITTLES? POKÉMON?
FOOTBALL? CARS?
PANCAKES!

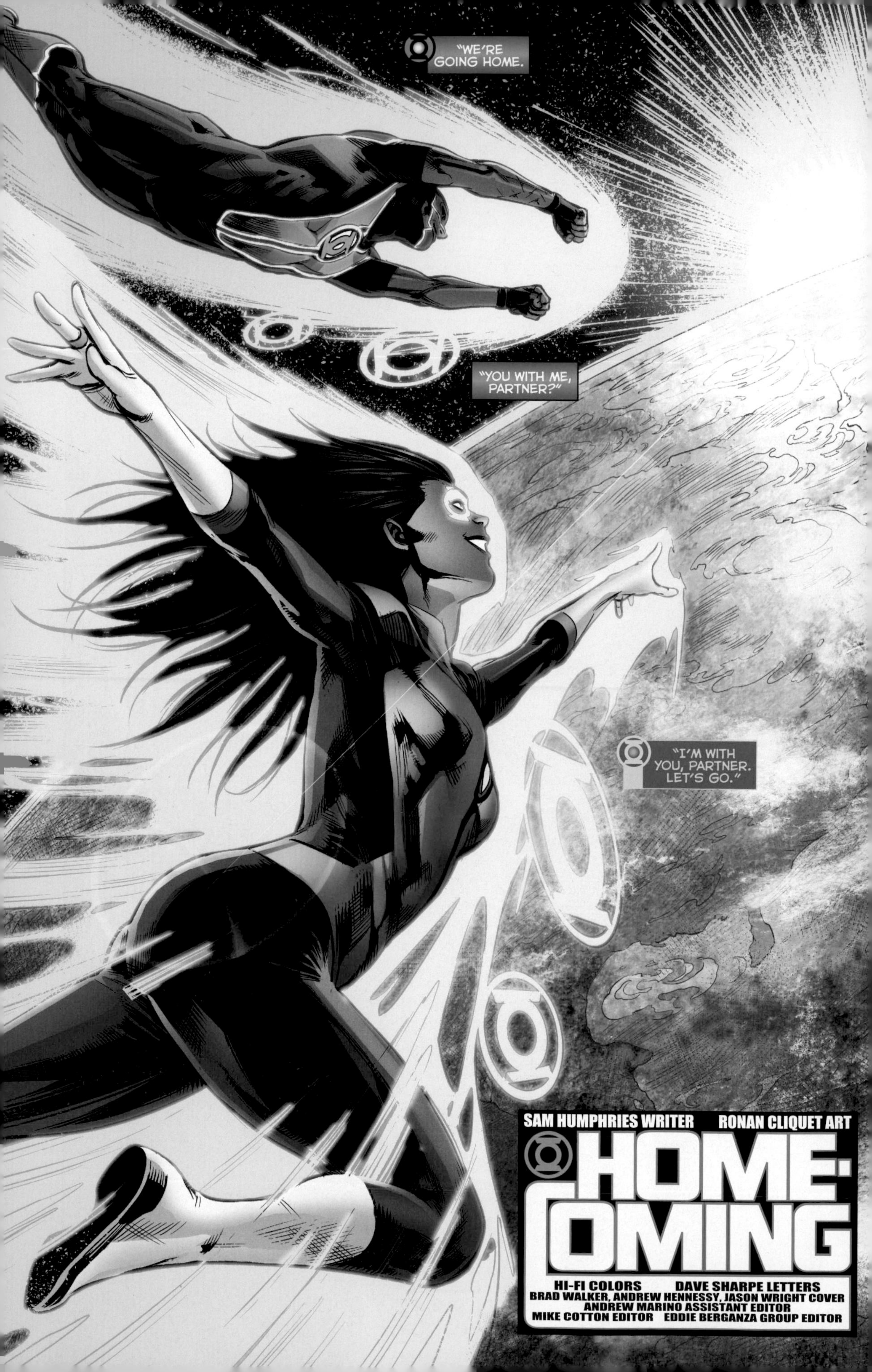
"WE'RE GOING HOME.
"YOU WITH ME, PARTNER?"
"I'M WITH YOU, PARTNER. LET'S GO."
SAM HUMPHRIES WRITER
RONAN CLIQUET ART
HOME-COMING
HI-FI COLORS
DAVE SHARPE LETTERS
BRAD WALKER, ANDREW HENNESSY, JASON WRIGHT COVER
ANDREW MARINO ASSISTANT EDITOR
MIKE COTTON EDITOR
EDDIE BERGANZA GROUP EDITOR

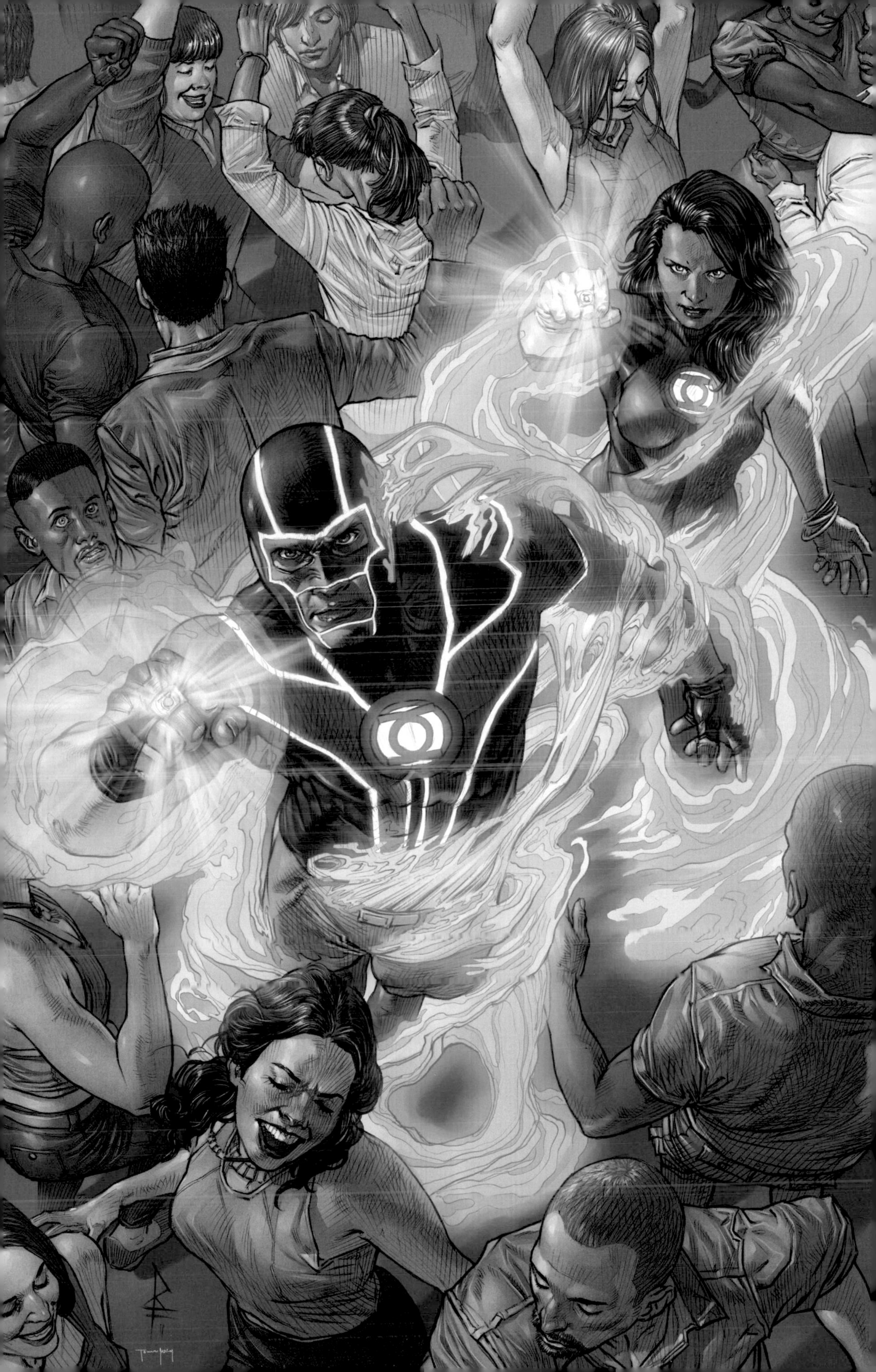

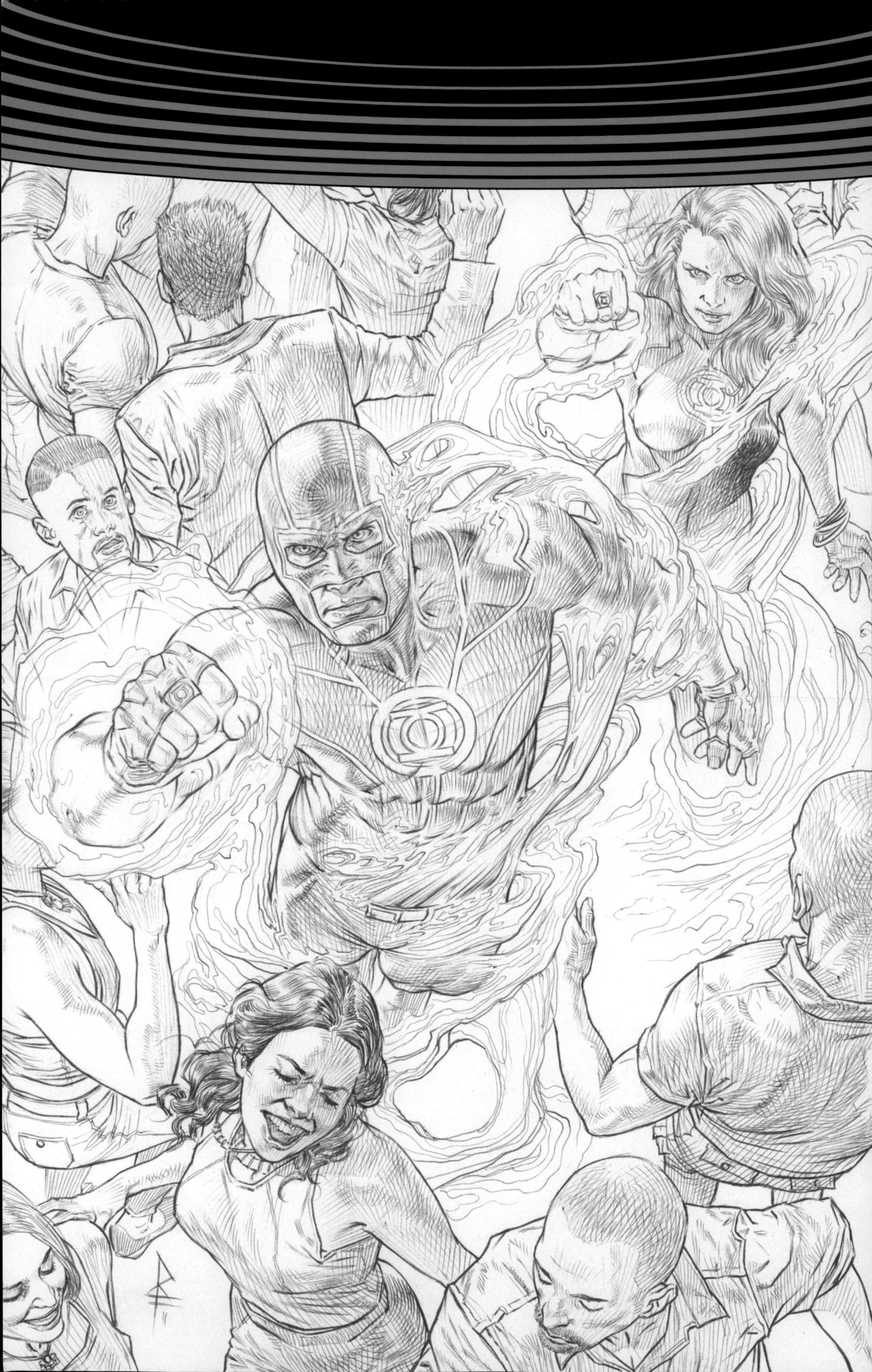

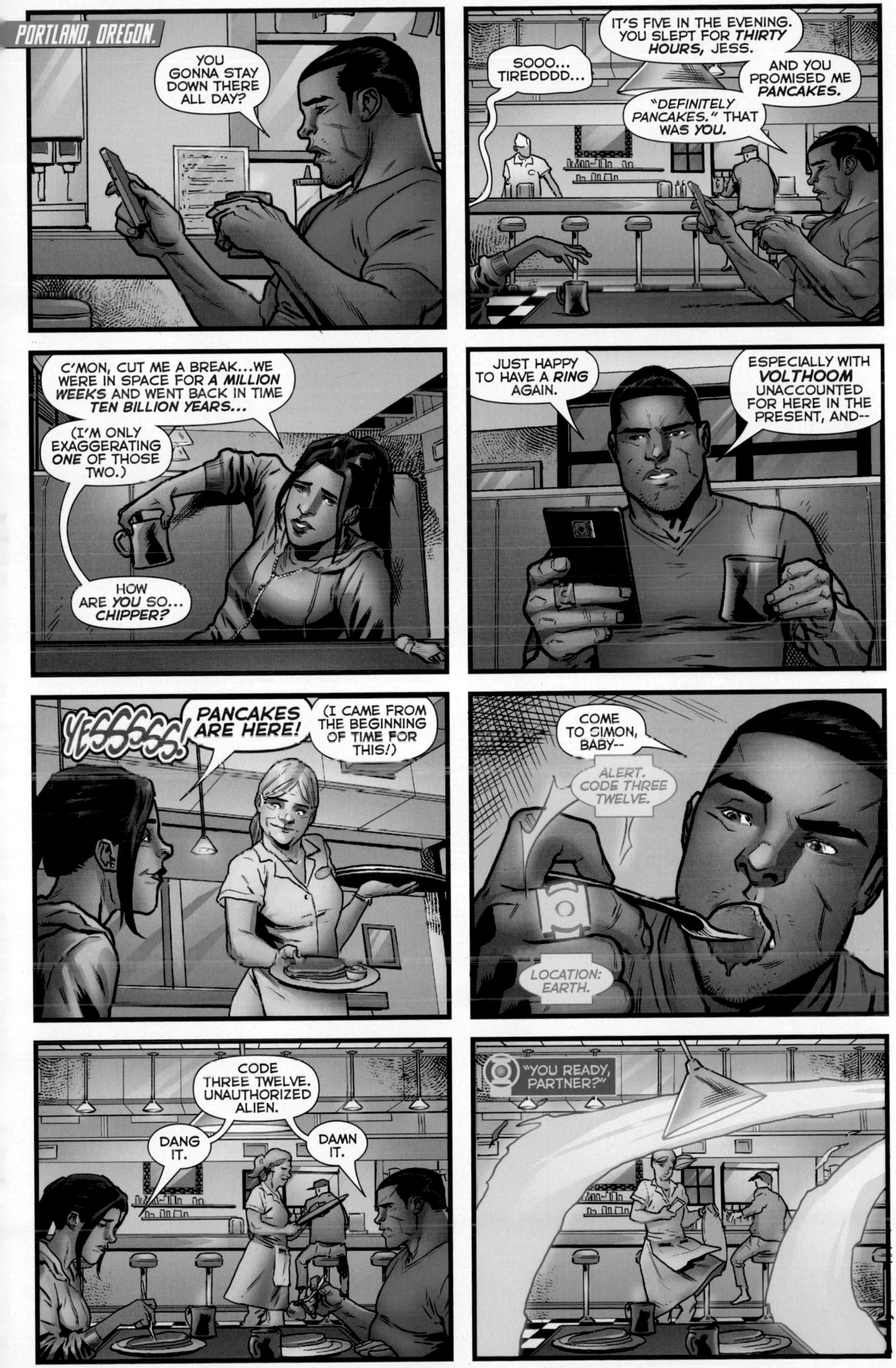
PORTLAND, OREGON.
YOU GONNA STAY DOWN THERE ALL DAY?
SOOO... TIREDDDD...
IT'S FIVE IN THE EVENING. YOU SLEPT FOR THIRTY HOURS, JESS.
AND YOU PROMISED ME PANCAKES.
"DEFINITELY PANCAKES." THAT WAS YOU.
C'MON, CUT ME A BREAK...WE WERE IN SPACE FOR A MILLION WEEKS AND WENT BACK IN TIME TEN BILLION YEARS...
(I'M ONLY EXAGGERATING ONE OF THOSE TWO.)
HOW ARE YOU SO... CHIPPER?
JUST HAPPY TO HAVE A RING AGAIN.
ESPECIALLY WITH VOLTHOOM UNACCOUNTED FOR HERE IN THE PRESENT, AND--
YESSSSS!
PANCAKES ARE HERE!
(I CAME FROM THE BEGINNING OF TIME FOR THIS!)
COME TO SIMON, BABY--
ALERT. CODE THREE TWELVE.
LOCATION: EARTH.
CODE THREE TWELVE. UNAUTHORIZED ALIEN.
DANG IT.
DAMN IT.
"YOU READY, PARTNER?"

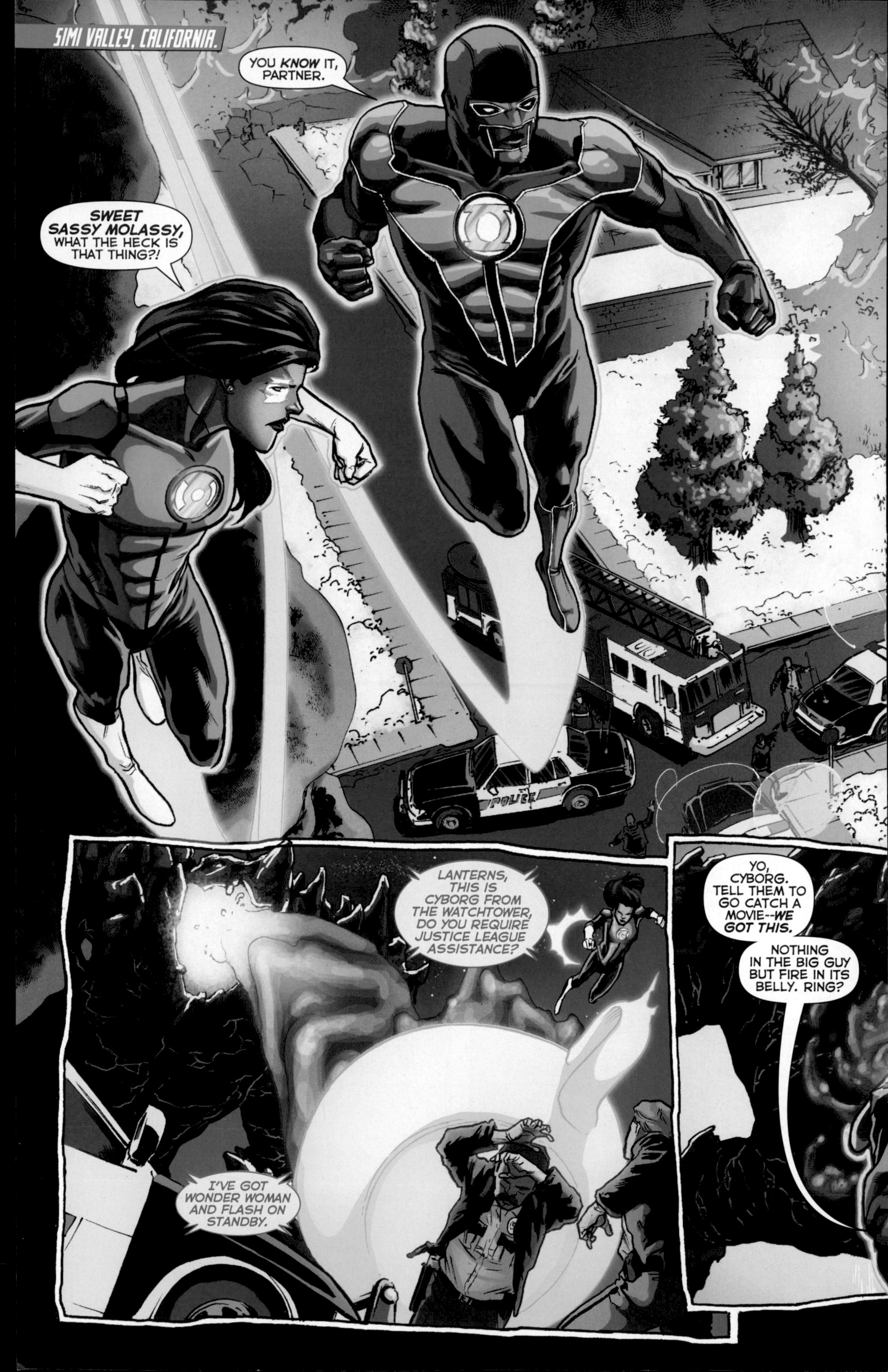
SIMI VALLEY, CALIFORNIA.
YOU KNOW IT, PARTNER.
SWEET SASSY MOLASSY, WHAT THE HECK IS THAT THING?!
LANTERNS, THIS IS CYBORG FROM THE WATCHTOWER, DO YOU REQUIRE JUSTICE LEAGUE ASSISTANCE?
I'VE GOT WONDER WOMAN AND FLASH ON STANDBY.
YO, CYBORG. TELL THEM TO GO CATCH A MOVIE--WE GOT THIS.
NOTHING IN THE BIG GUY BUT FIRE IN ITS BELLY. RING?
POLICE

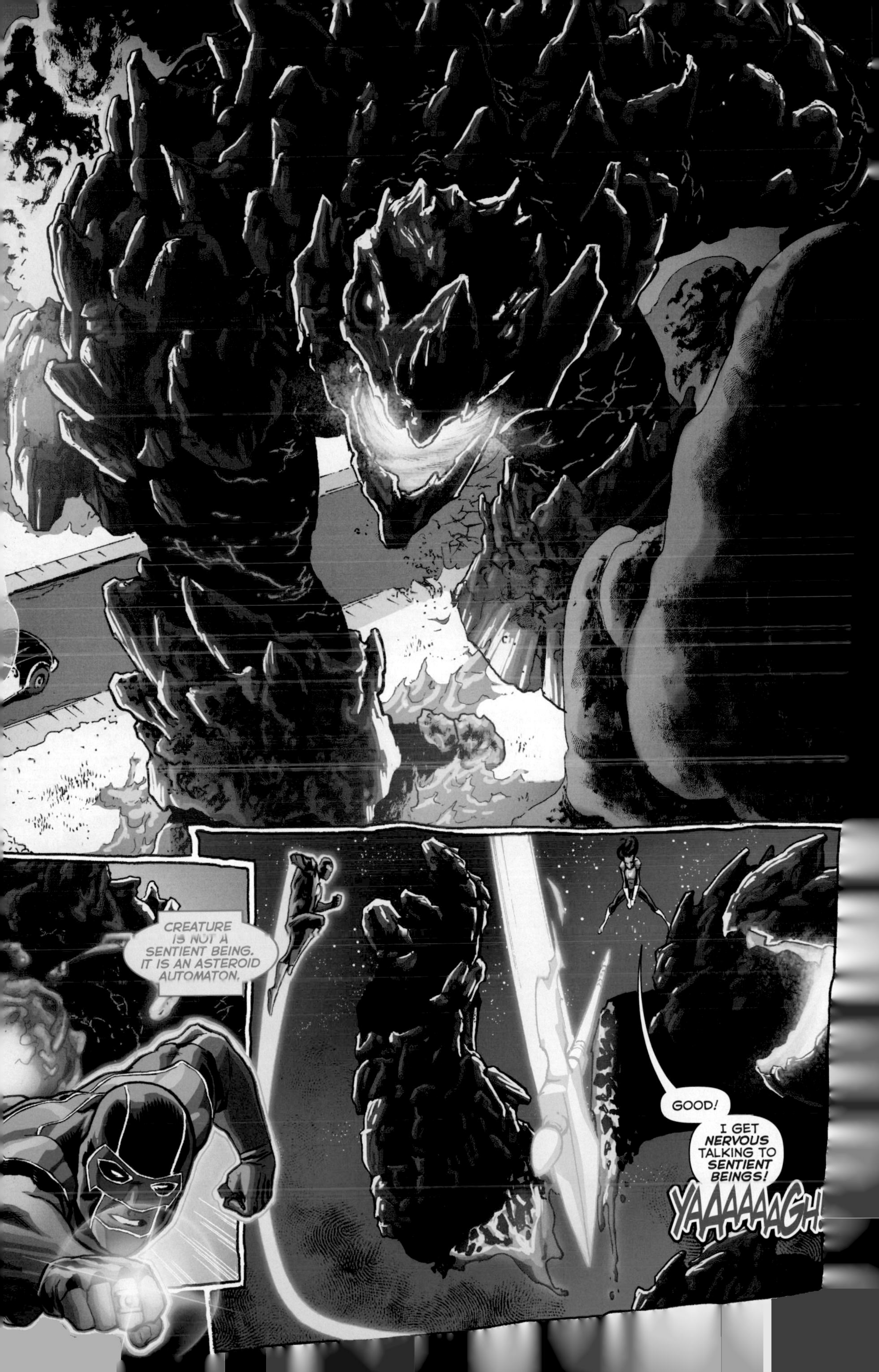
CREATURE IS NOT A SENTIENT BEING. IT IS AN ASTEROID AUTOMATON.
GOOD!
I GET NERVOUS TALKING TO SENTIENT BEINGS!
YAAAAAAGH!

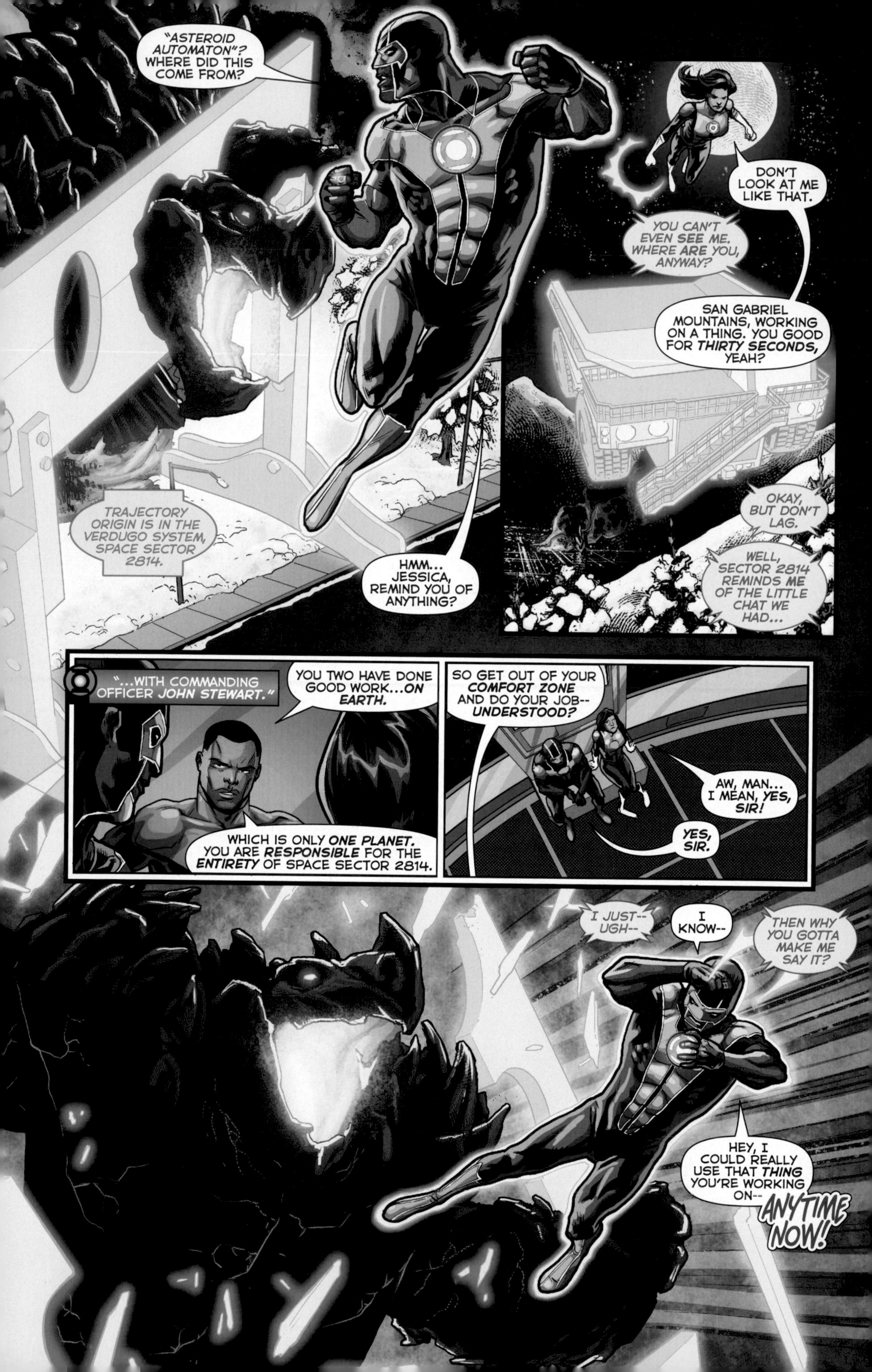
"ASTEROID AUTOMATON"? WHERE DID THIS COME FROM?
TRAJECTORY ORIGIN IS IN THE VERDUGO SYSTEM, SPACE SECTOR 2814.
HMM... JESSICA, REMIND YOU OF ANYTHING?
DON'T LOOK AT ME LIKE THAT.
YOU CAN'T EVEN SEE ME. WHERE ARE YOU, ANYWAY?
SAN GABRIEL MOUNTAINS, WORKING ON A THING. YOU GOOD FOR THIRTY SECONDS, YEAH?
OKAY, BUT DON'T LAG.
WELL, SECTOR 2814 REMINDS ME OF THE LITTLE CHAT WE HAD...
"...WITH COMMANDING OFFICER JOHN STEWART."
YOU TWO HAVE DONE GOOD WORK...ON EARTH.
WHICH IS ONLY ONE PLANET. YOU ARE RESPONSIBLE FOR THE ENTIRETY OF SPACE SECTOR 2814.
SO GET OUT OF YOUR COMFORT ZONE AND DO YOUR JOB--UNDERSTOOD?
AW, MAN... I MEAN, YES, SIR!
YES, SIR.
I JUST-- UGH--
I KNOW--
THEN WHY YOU GOTTA MAKE ME SAY IT?
HEY, I COULD REALLY USE THAT THING YOU'RE WORKING ON--
ANYTIME NOW!

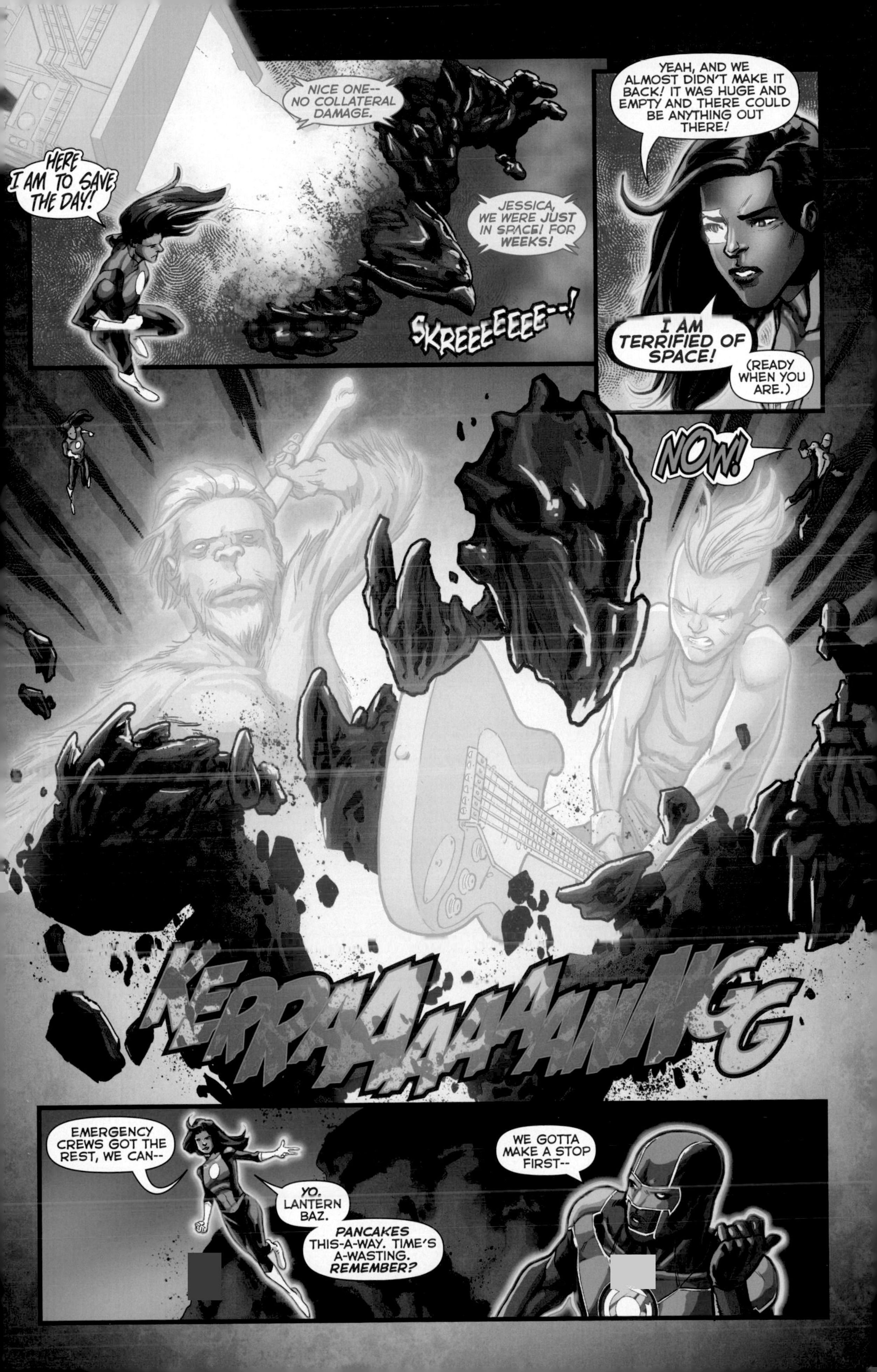
HERE I AM TO SAVE THE DAY!
NICE ONE-- NO COLLATERAL DAMAGE.
JESSICA, WE WERE JUST IN SPACE! FOR WEEKS!
SKREEEEEEE--!
YEAH, AND WE ALMOST DIDN'T MAKE IT BACK! IT WAS HUGE AND EMPTY AND THERE COULD BE ANYTHING OUT THERE!
I AM TERRIFIED OF SPACE!
(READY WHEN YOU ARE.)
NOW!
KERRAAAAAAANNNGG
EMERGENCY CREWS GOT THE REST, WE CAN--
YO. LANTERN BAZ.
PANCAKES THIS-A-WAY. TIME'S A-WASTING. REMEMBER?
WE GOTTA MAKE A STOP FIRST--

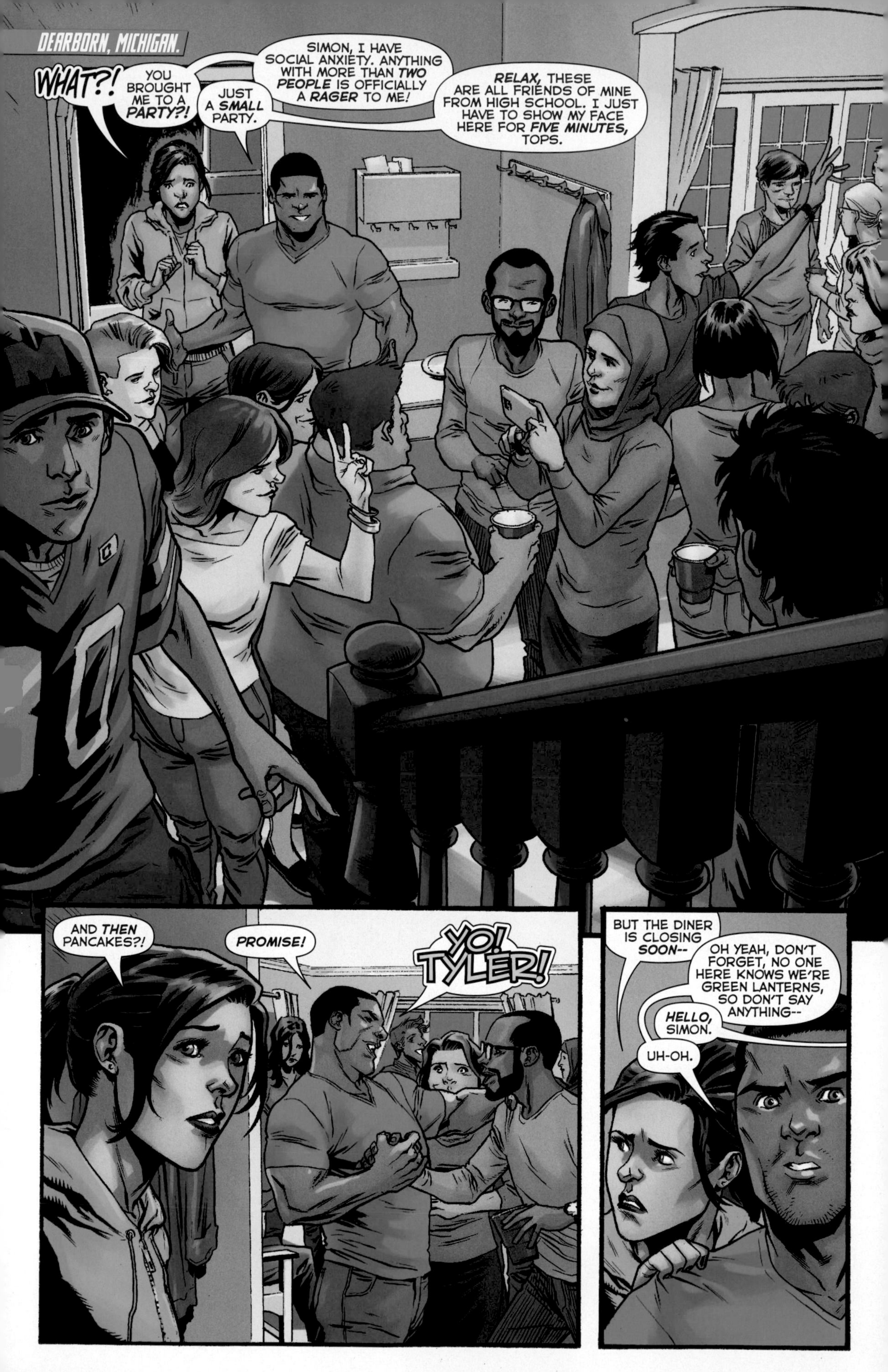
DEARBORN, MICHIGAN.
WHAT?!
YOU BROUGHT ME TO A PARTY?!
JUST A SMALL PARTY.
SIMON, I HAVE SOCIAL ANXIETY. ANYTHING WITH MORE THAN TWO PEOPLE IS OFFICIALLY A RAGER TO ME!
RELAX, THESE ARE ALL FRIENDS OF MINE FROM HIGH SCHOOL. I JUST HAVE TO SHOW MY FACE HERE FOR FIVE MINUTES, TOPS.
AND THEN PANCAKES?!
PROMISE!
YO! TYLER!
BUT THE DINER IS CLOSING SOON--
OH YEAH, DON'T FORGET, NO ONE HERE KNOWS WE'RE GREEN LANTERNS, SO DON'T SAY ANYTHING--
HELLO, SIMON.
UH-OH.

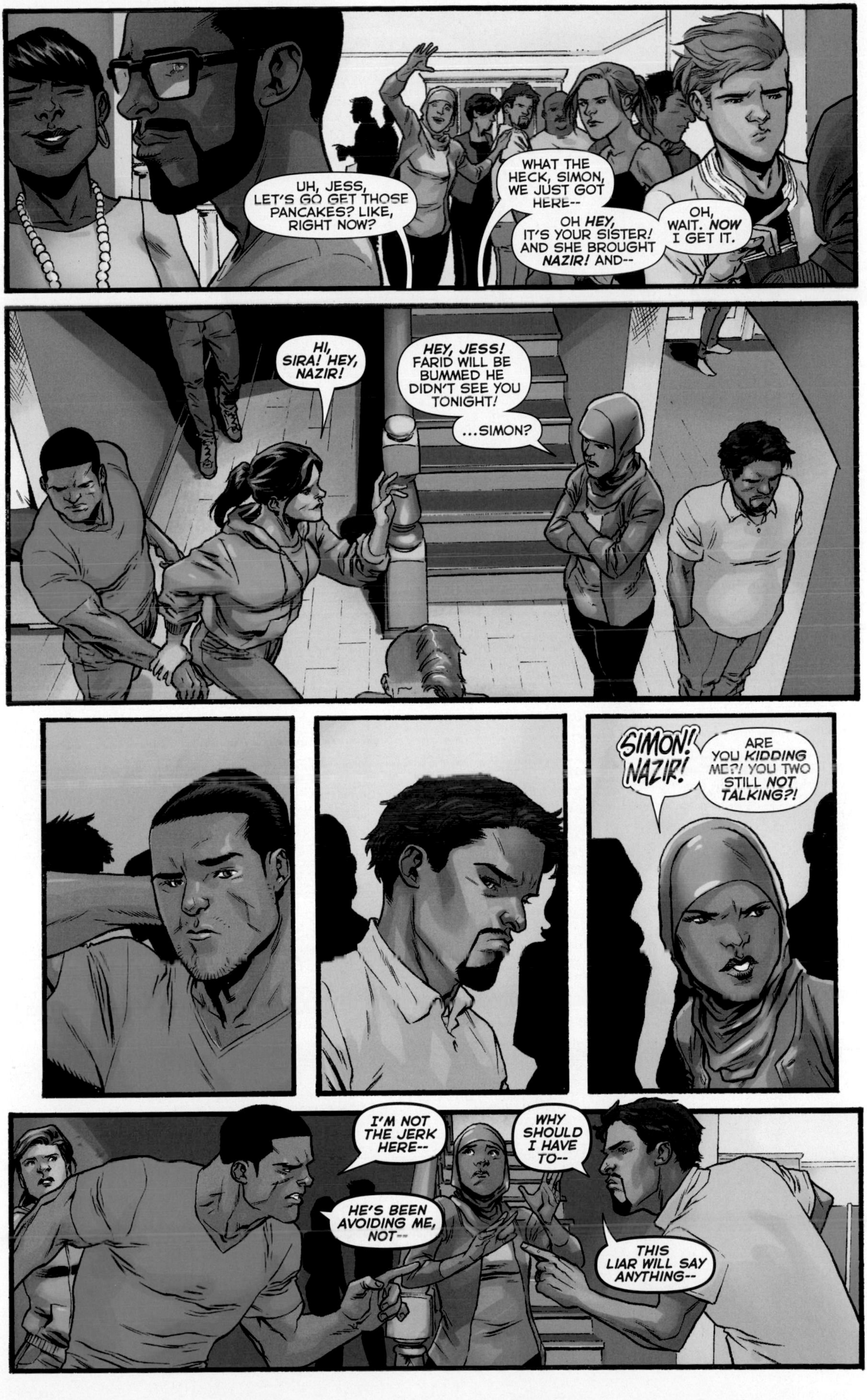
UH, JESS, LET'S GO GET THOSE PANCAKES? LIKE, RIGHT NOW?
WHAT THE HECK, SIMON, WE JUST GOT HERE--
OH HEY, IT'S YOUR SISTER! AND SHE BROUGHT NAZIR! AND--
OH, WAIT. NOW I GET IT.
HI, SIRA! HEY, NAZIR!
HEY, JESS! FARID WILL BE BUMMED HE DIDN'T SEE YOU TONIGHT!
...SIMON?
SIMON! NAZIR!
ARE YOU KIDDING ME?! YOU TWO STILL NOT TALKING?!
I'M NOT THE JERK HERE--
HE'S BEEN AVOIDING ME, NOT--
WHY SHOULD I HAVE TO--
THIS LIAR WILL SAY ANYTHING--

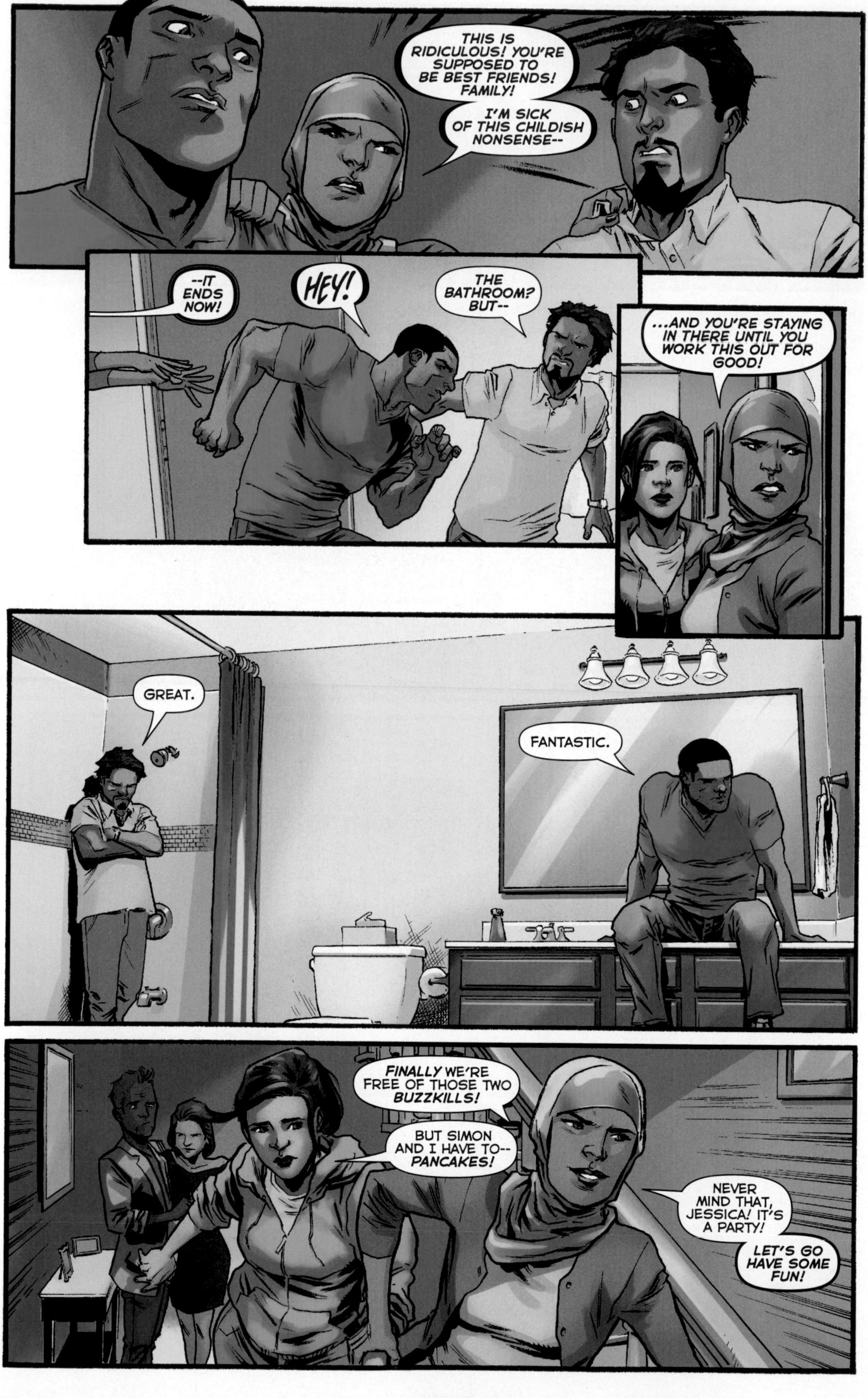
THIS IS RIDICULOUS! YOU'RE SUPPOSED TO BE BEST FRIENDS! FAMILY!
I'M SICK OF THIS CHILDISH NONSENSE--
--IT ENDS NOW!
HEY!
THE BATHROOM? BUT--
...AND YOU'RE STAYING IN THERE UNTIL YOU WORK THIS OUT FOR GOOD!
GREAT.
FANTASTIC.
FINALLY WE'RE FREE OF THOSE TWO BUZZKILLS!
BUT SIMON AND I HAVE TO-- PANCAKES!
NEVER MIND THAT, JESSICA! IT'S A PARTY!
LET'S GO HAVE SOME FUN!

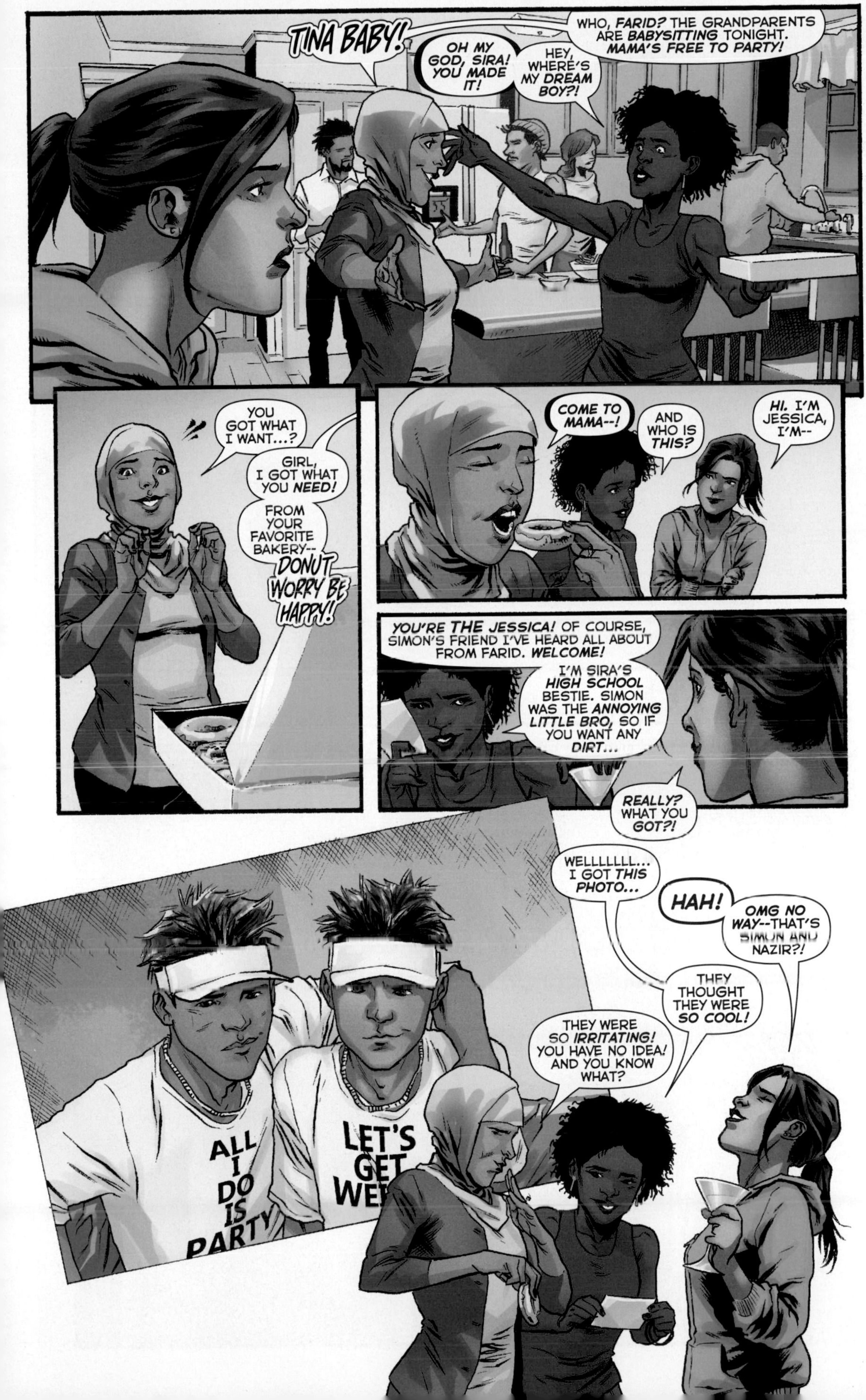
TINA BABY!
OH MY GOD, SIRA! YOU MADE IT!
HEY, WHERE'S MY DREAM BOY?!
WHO, FARID? THE GRANDPARENTS ARE BABYSITTING TONIGHT. MAMA'S FREE TO PARTY!
YOU GOT WHAT I WANT...?
GIRL, I GOT WHAT YOU NEED!
FROM YOUR FAVORITE BAKERY--
DONUT WORRY BE HAPPY!
COME TO MAMA--!
AND WHO IS THIS?
HI. I'M JESSICA, I'M--
YOU'RE THE JESSICA! OF COURSE, SIMON'S FRIEND I'VE HEARD ALL ABOUT FROM FARID. WELCOME!
I'M SIRA'S HIGH SCHOOL BESTIE. SIMON WAS THE ANNOYING LITTLE BRO, SO IF YOU WANT ANY DIRT...
REALLY? WHAT YOU GOT?!
WELLLLLLLL... I GOT THIS PHOTO...
HAH!
OMG NO WAY--THAT'S SIMON AND NAZIR?!
THEY THOUGHT THEY WERE SO COOL!
THEY WERE SO IRRITATING! YOU HAVE NO IDEA! AND YOU KNOW WHAT?
ALL I DO IS PARTY
LET'S GET WE

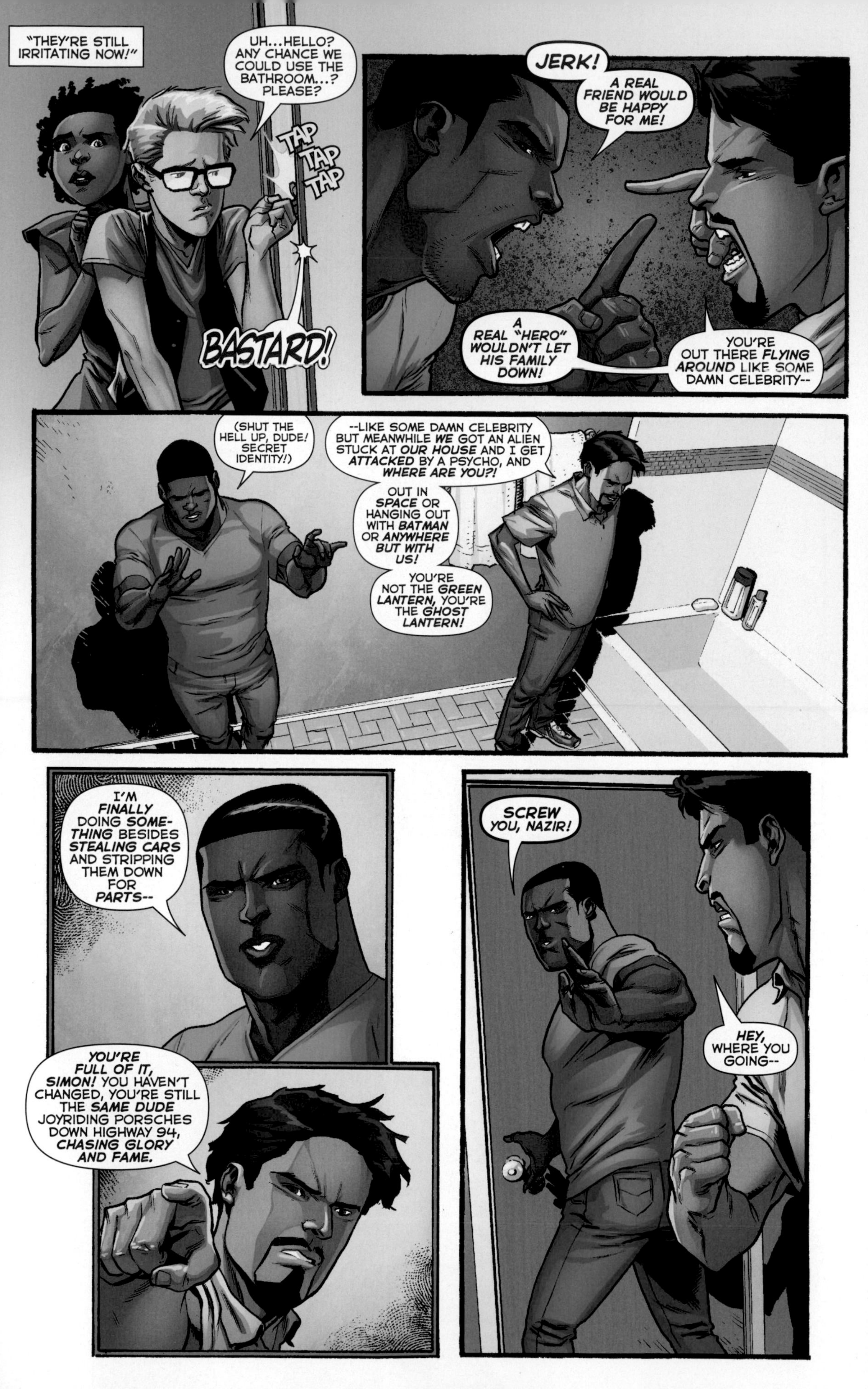
"THEY'RE STILL IRRITATING NOW!"
UH...HELLO? ANY CHANCE WE COULD USE THE BATHROOM...? PLEASE?
TAP TAP TAP
BASTARD!
JERK!
A REAL FRIEND WOULD BE HAPPY FOR ME!
A REAL "HERO" WOULDN'T LET HIS FAMILY DOWN!
YOU'RE OUT THERE FLYING AROUND LIKE SOME DAMN CELEBRITY--
(SHUT THE HELL UP, DUDE! SECRET IDENTITY!)
--LIKE SOME DAMN CELEBRITY BUT MEANWHILE WE GOT AN ALIEN STUCK AT OUR HOUSE AND I GET ATTACKED BY A PSYCHO, AND WHERE ARE YOU?!
OUT IN SPACE OR HANGING OUT WITH BATMAN OR ANYWHERE BUT WITH US!
YOU'RE NOT THE GREEN LANTERN, YOU'RE THE GHOST LANTERN!
I'M FINALLY DOING SOMETHING BESIDES STEALING CARS AND STRIPPING THEM DOWN FOR PARTS--
YOU'RE FULL OF IT, SIMON! YOU HAVEN'T CHANGED, YOU'RE STILL THE SAME DUDE JOYRIDING PORSCHES DOWN HIGHWAY 94, CHASING GLORY AND FAME.
SCREW YOU, NAZIR!
HEY, WHERE YOU GOING--

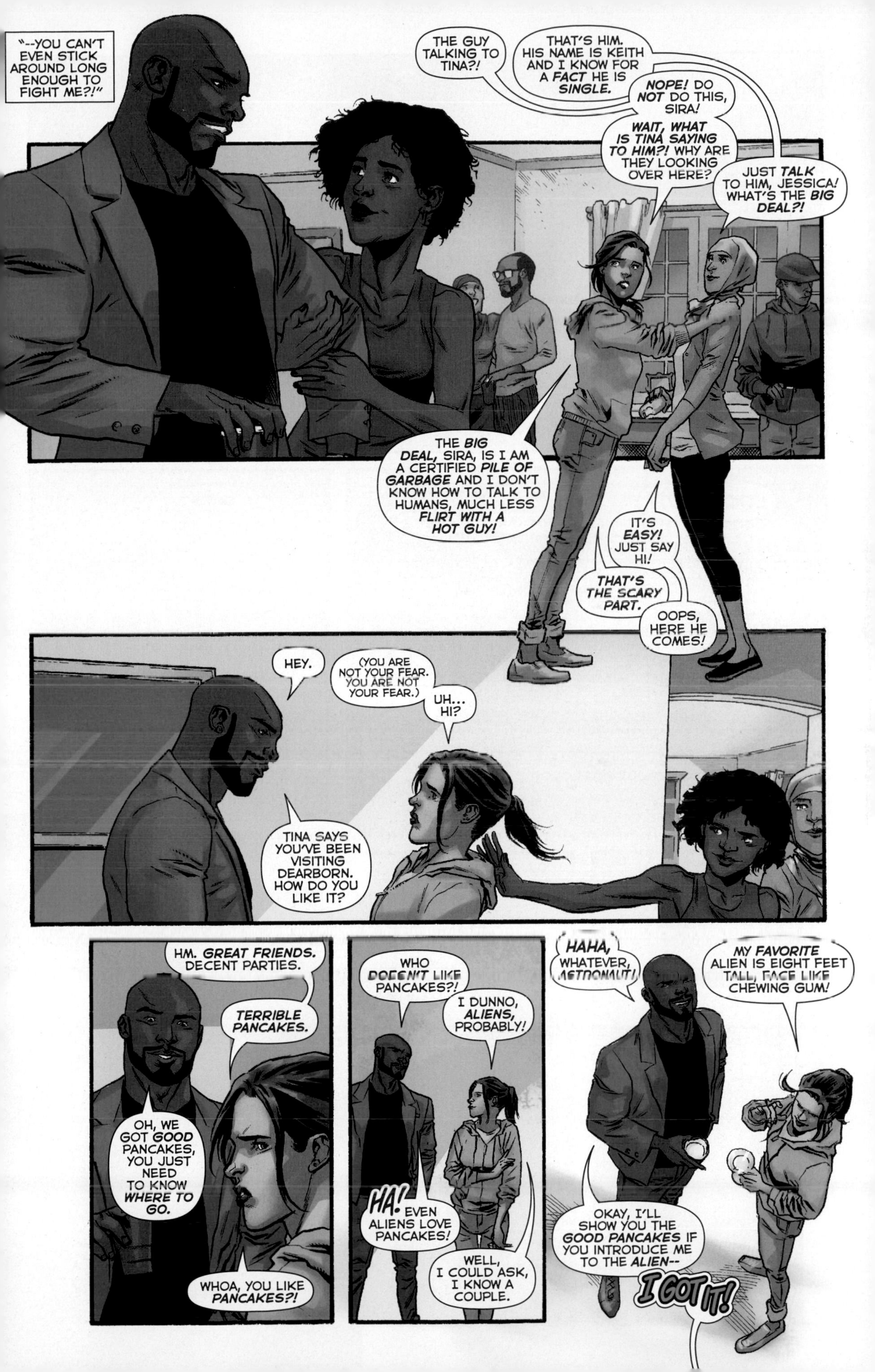
"--YOU CAN'T EVEN STICK AROUND LONG ENOUGH TO FIGHT ME?!"
THE GUY TALKING TO TINA?!
THAT'S HIM. HIS NAME IS KEITH AND I KNOW FOR A FACT HE IS SINGLE.
NOPE! DO NOT DO THIS, SIRA!
WAIT, WHAT IS TINA SAYING TO HIM?! WHY ARE THEY LOOKING OVER HERE?
JUST TALK TO HIM, JESSICA! WHAT'S THE BIG DEAL?!
THE BIG DEAL, SIRA, IS I AM A CERTIFIED PILE OF GARBAGE AND I DON'T KNOW HOW TO TALK TO HUMANS, MUCH LESS FLIRT WITH A HOT GUY!
IT'S EASY! JUST SAY HI!
THAT'S THE SCARY PART.
OOPS, HERE HE COMES!
HEY.
(YOU ARE NOT YOUR FEAR. YOU ARE NOT YOUR FEAR.)
UH... HI?
TINA SAYS YOU'VE BEEN VISITING DEARBORN. HOW DO YOU LIKE IT?
HM. GREAT FRIENDS. DECENT PARTIES.
TERRIBLE PANCAKES.
OH, WE GOT GOOD PANCAKES, YOU JUST NEED TO KNOW WHERE TO GO.
WHOA, YOU LIKE PANCAKES?!
WHO DOESN'T LIKE PANCAKES?!
I DUNNO, ALIENS, PROBABLY!
HA! EVEN ALIENS LOVE PANCAKES!
WELL, I COULD ASK, I KNOW A COUPLE.
HAHA, WHATEVER, ASTRONAUT!
MY FAVORITE ALIEN IS EIGHT FEET TALL, FACE LIKE CHEWING GUM!
OKAY, I'LL SHOW YOU THE GOOD PANCAKES IF YOU INTRODUCE ME TO THE ALIEN--
I GOT IT!

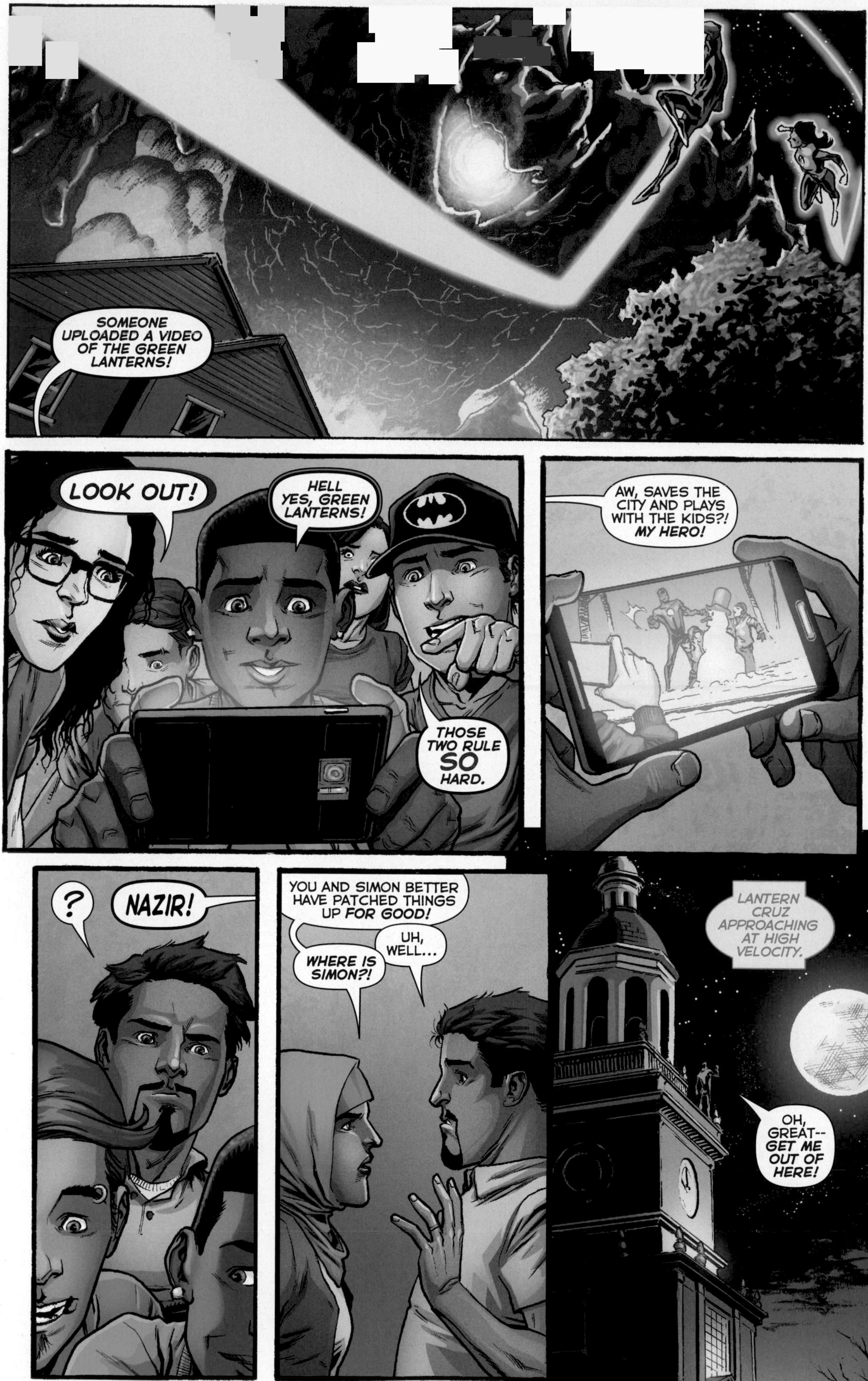
SOMEONE UPLOADED A VIDEO OF THE GREEN LANTERNS!
LOOK OUT!
HELL YES, GREEN LANTERNS!
THOSE TWO RULE SO HARD.
AW, SAVES THE CITY AND PLAYS WITH THE KIDS?! MY HERO!
?
NAZIR!
YOU AND SIMON BETTER HAVE PATCHED THINGS UP FOR GOOD!
UH, WELL...
WHERE IS SIMON?!
LANTERN CRUZ APPROACHING AT HIGH VELOCITY.
OH, GREAT-- GET ME OUT OF HERE!

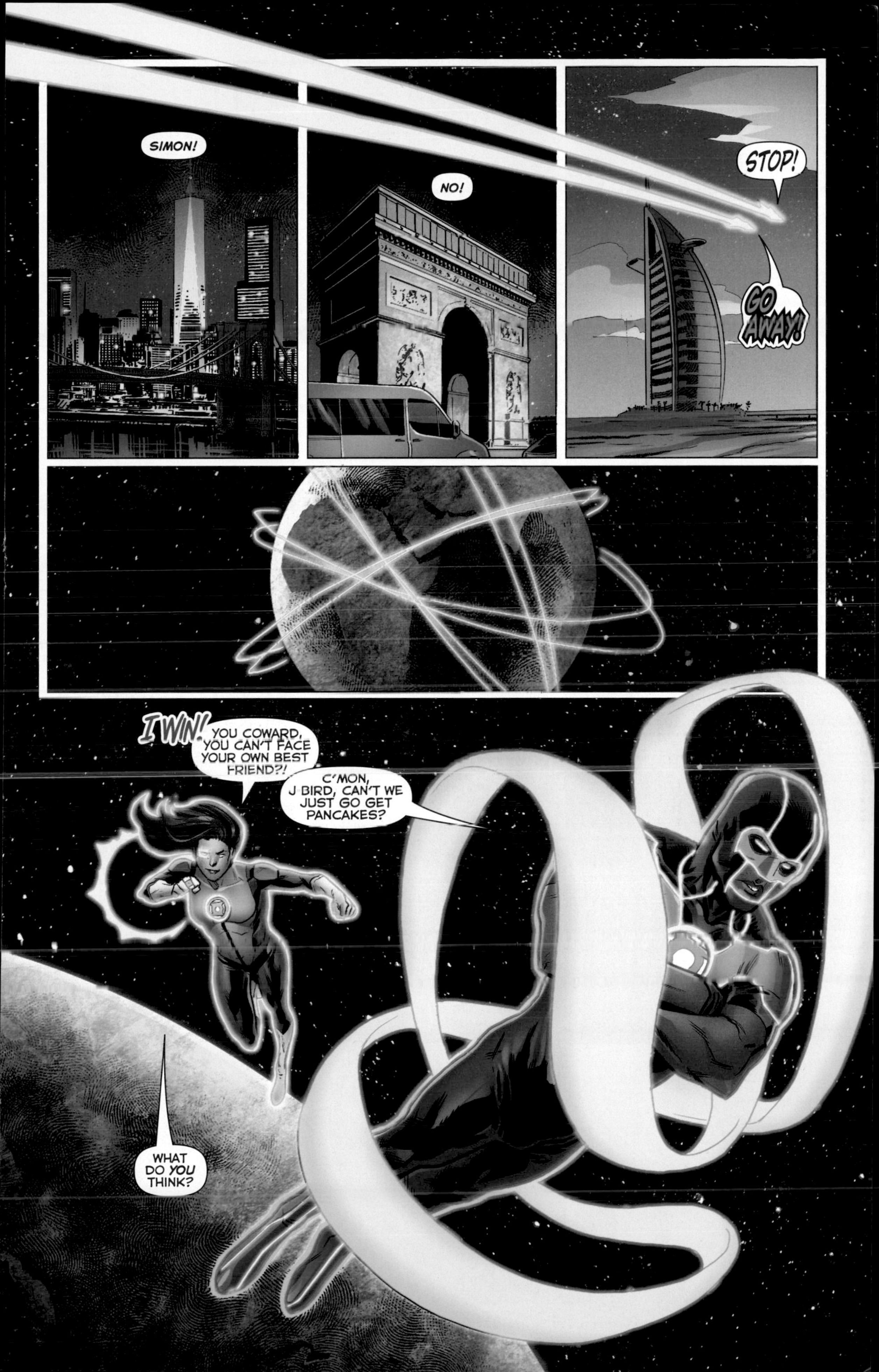
SIMON!
NO!
STOP!
GO AWAY!
I WIN!
YOU COWARD, YOU CAN'T FACE YOUR OWN BEST FRIEND?!
C'MON, J BIRD, CAN'T WE JUST GO GET PANCAKES?
WHAT DO YOU THINK?

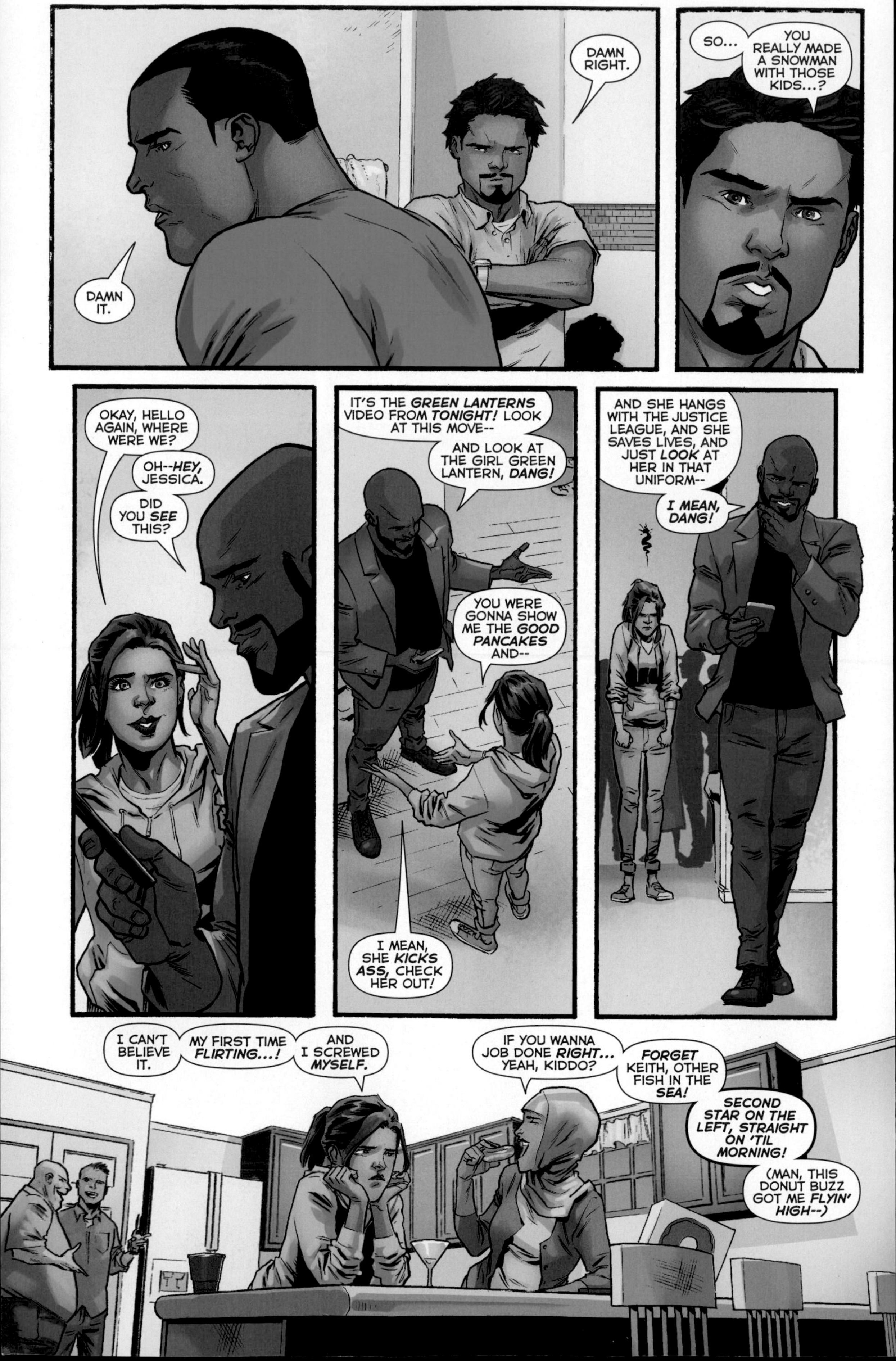
DAMN IT.
DAMN RIGHT.
SO...
YOU REALLY MADE A SNOWMAN WITH THOSE KIDS...?
OKAY, HELLO AGAIN, WHERE WERE WE?
OH--HEY, JESSICA.
DID YOU SEE THIS?
IT'S THE GREEN LANTERNS VIDEO FROM TONIGHT! LOOK AT THIS MOVE--
AND LOOK AT THE GIRL GREEN LANTERN, DANG!
YOU WERE GONNA SHOW ME THE GOOD PANCAKES AND--
I MEAN, SHE KICKS ASS, CHECK HER OUT!
AND SHE HANGS WITH THE JUSTICE LEAGUE, AND SHE SAVES LIVES, AND JUST LOOK AT HER IN THAT UNIFORM--
I MEAN, DANG!
I CAN'T BELIEVE IT.
MY FIRST TIME FLIRTING...!
AND I SCREWED MYSELF.
IF YOU WANNA JOB DONE RIGHT... YEAH, KIDDO?
FORGET KEITH, OTHER FISH IN THE SEA!
SECOND STAR ON THE LEFT, STRAIGHT ON 'TIL MORNING!
(MAN, THIS DONUT BUZZ GOT ME FLYIN' HIGH--)

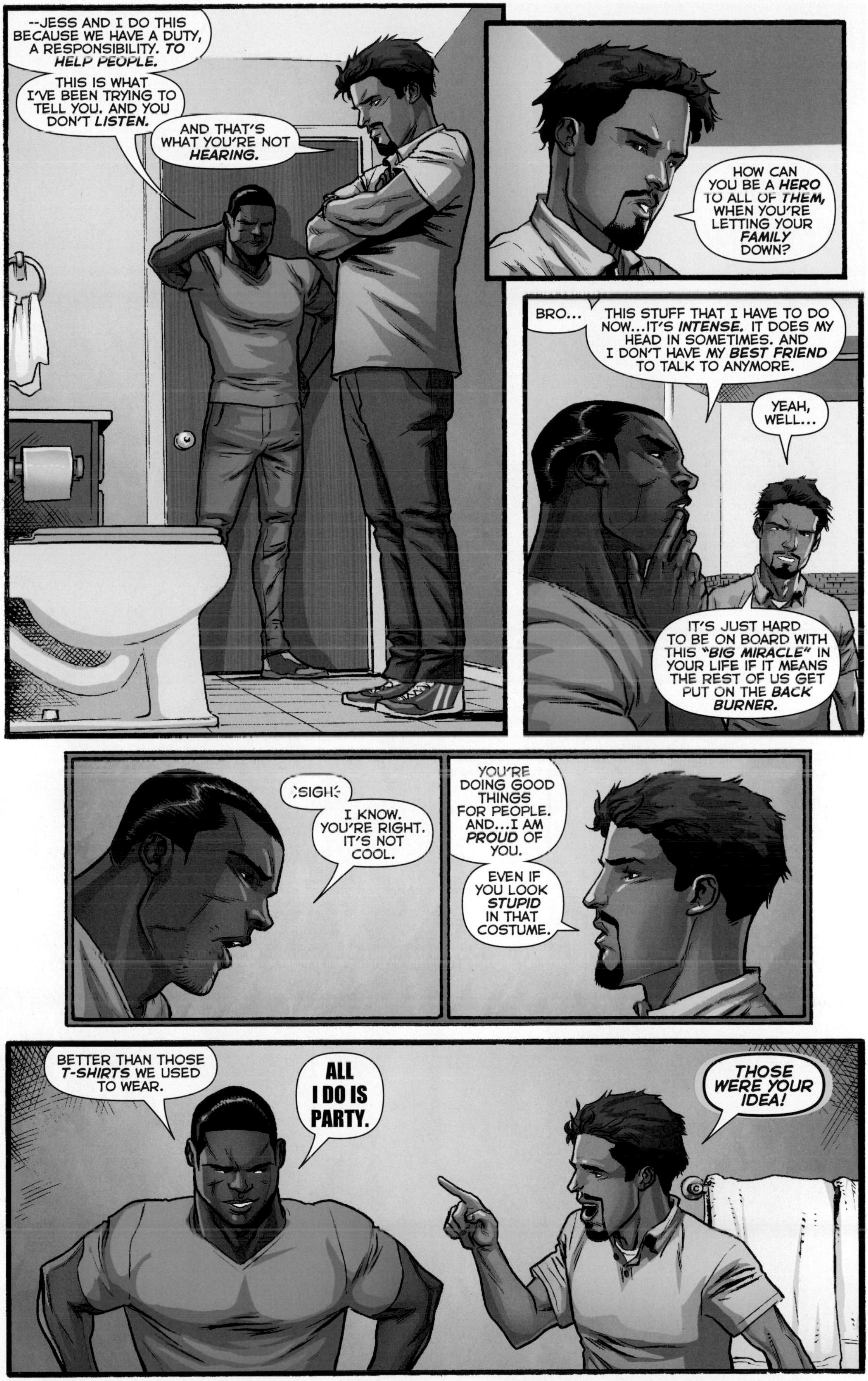
--JESS AND I DO THIS BECAUSE WE HAVE A DUTY, A RESPONSIBILITY. *TO HELP PEOPLE.*
THIS IS WHAT I'VE BEEN TRYING TO TELL YOU. AND YOU DON'T *LISTEN.*
AND THAT'S WHAT YOU'RE NOT *HEARING.*
HOW CAN YOU BE A *HERO* TO ALL OF *THEM,* WHEN YOU'RE LETTING YOUR *FAMILY* DOWN?
BRO...
THIS STUFF THAT I HAVE TO DO NOW...IT'S *INTENSE.* IT DOES MY HEAD IN SOMETIMES. AND I DON'T HAVE MY *BEST FRIEND* TO TALK TO ANYMORE.
YEAH, WELL...
IT'S JUST HARD TO BE ON BOARD WITH THIS *"BIG MIRACLE"* IN YOUR LIFE IF IT MEANS THE REST OF US GET PUT ON THE *BACK BURNER.*
SIGH
I KNOW. YOU'RE RIGHT. IT'S NOT COOL.
YOU'RE DOING GOOD THINGS FOR PEOPLE. AND...I AM *PROUD* OF YOU.
EVEN IF YOU LOOK *STUPID* IN THAT COSTUME.
BETTER THAN THOSE *T-SHIRTS* WE USED TO WEAR.
ALL I DO IS PARTY.
THOSE WERE YOUR IDEA!

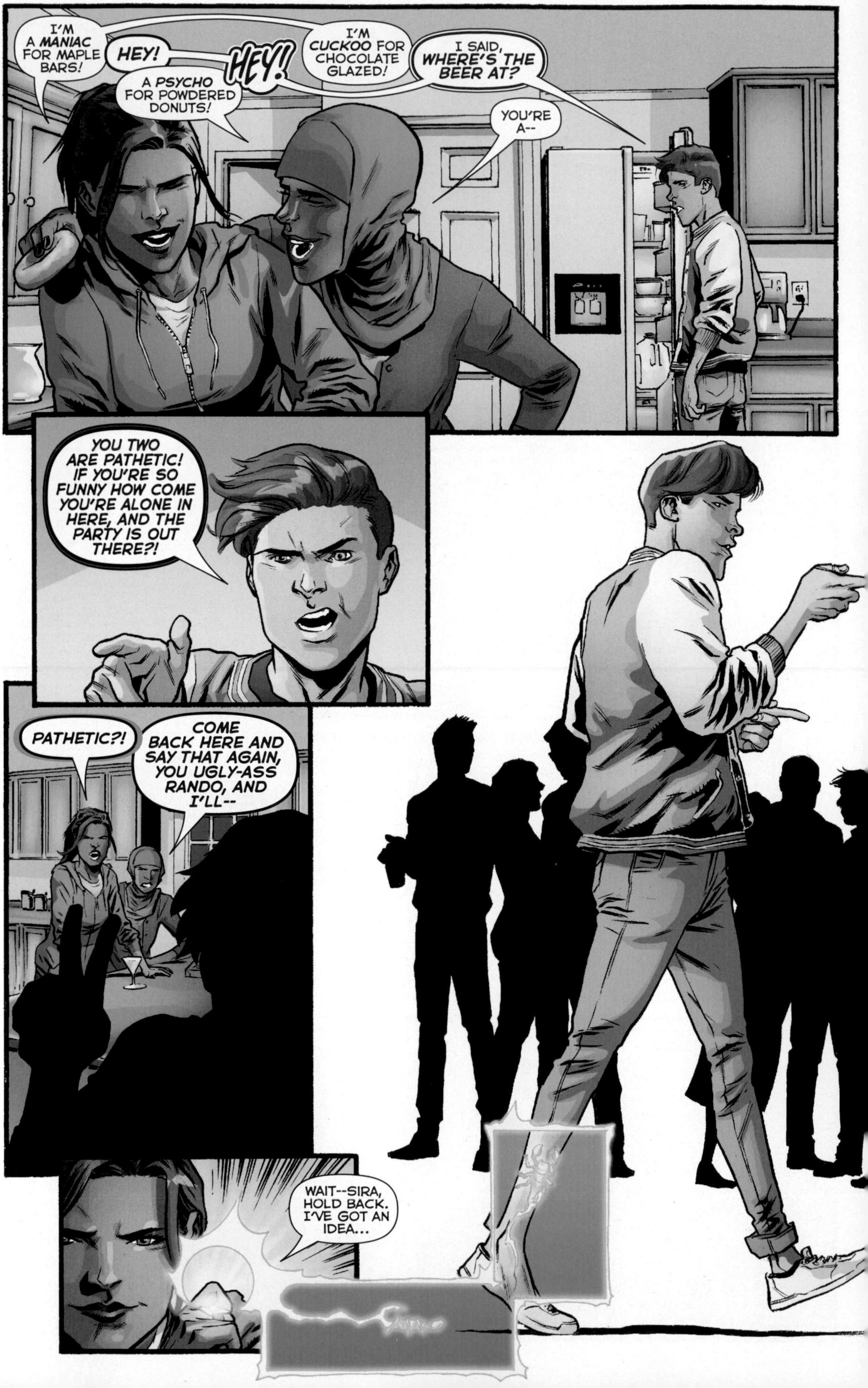
I'M A MANIAC FOR MAPLE BARS!
HEY!
A PSYCHO FOR POWDERED DONUTS!
HEY!
I'M CUCKOO FOR CHOCOLATE GLAZED!
I SAID, WHERE'S THE BEER AT?
YOU'RE A--
YOU TWO ARE PATHETIC! IF YOU'RE SO FUNNY HOW COME YOU'RE ALONE IN HERE, AND THE PARTY IS OUT THERE?!
PATHETIC?!
COME BACK HERE AND SAY THAT AGAIN, YOU UGLY-ASS RANDO, AND I'LL--
WAIT--SIRA, HOLD BACK. I'VE GOT AN IDEA...

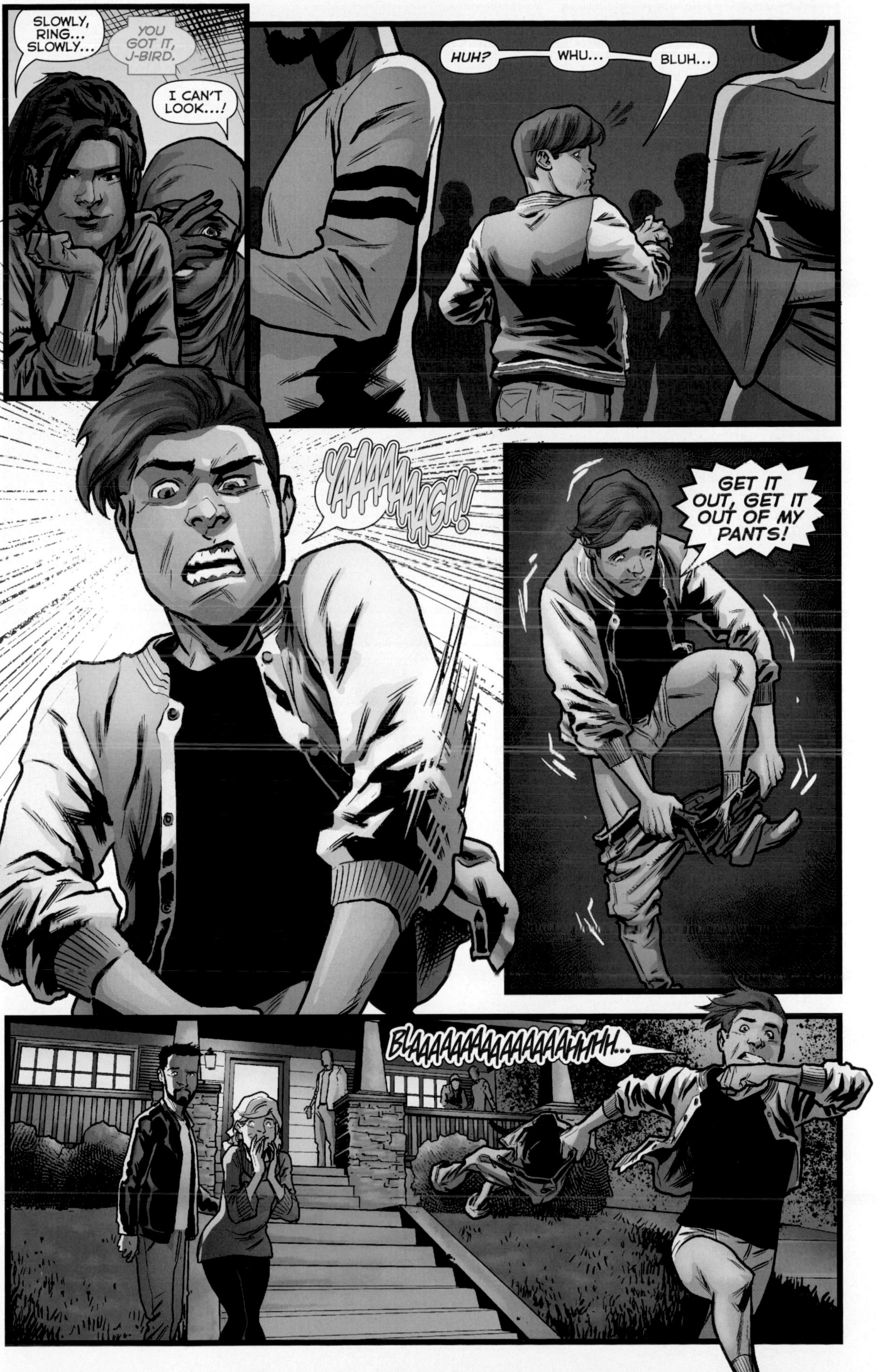
SLOWLY, RING... SLOWLY...
YOU GOT IT, J-BIRD.
I CAN'T LOOK...!
HUH?
WHU...
BLUH...
YAAAAAAAAGH!
GET IT OUT, GET IT OUT OF MY PANTS!
BLAAAAAAAAAAAAAAAHHHH...

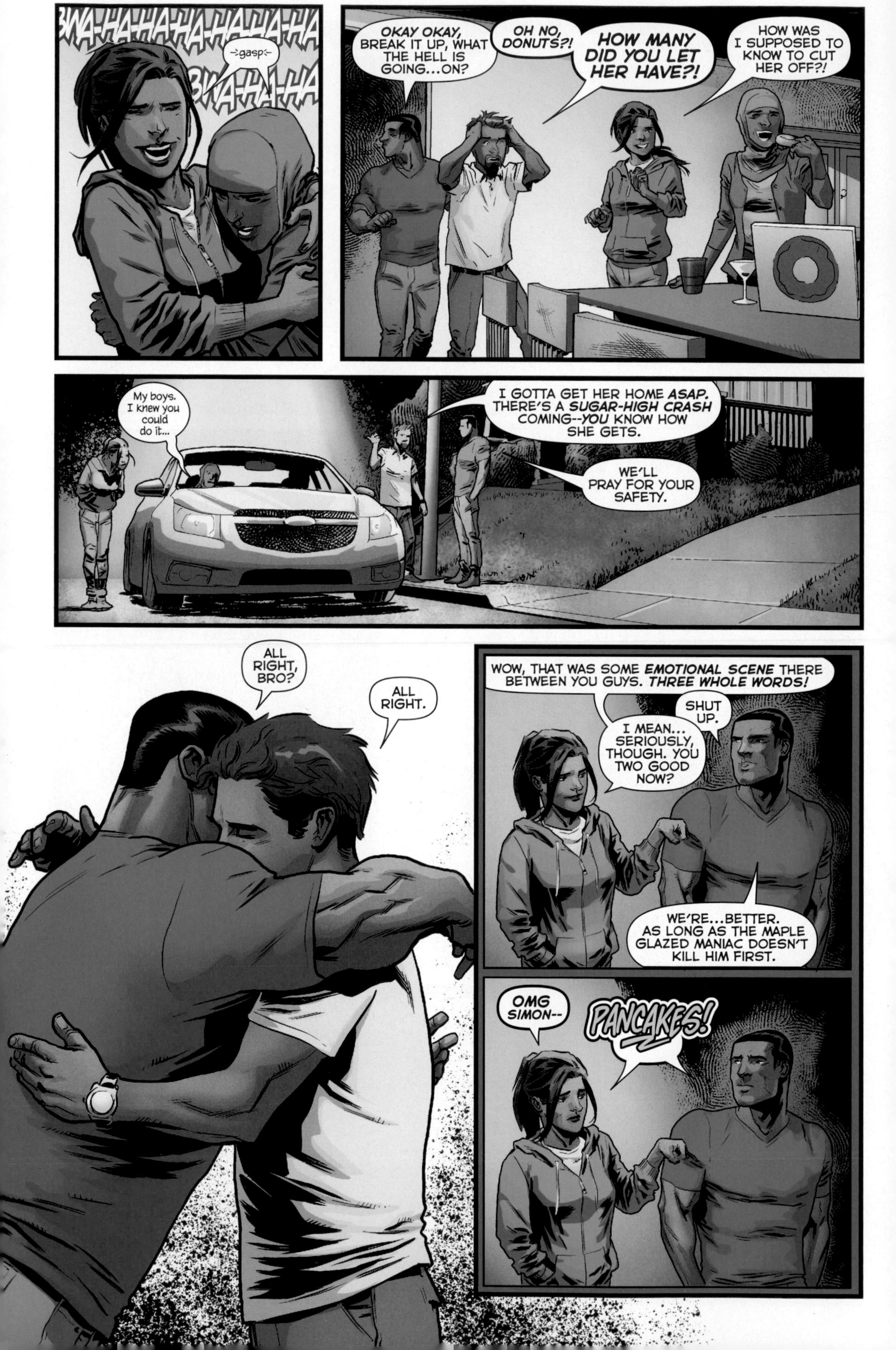
BWA-HA-HA-HA-HA-HA-HA
-gasp-
BWA-HA-HA
OKAY OKAY, BREAK IT UP, WHAT THE HELL IS GOING...ON?
OH NO, DONUTS?!
HOW MANY DID YOU LET HER HAVE?!
HOW WAS I SUPPOSED TO KNOW TO CUT HER OFF?!
My boys. I knew you could do it...
I GOTTA GET HER HOME ASAP. THERE'S A SUGAR-HIGH CRASH COMING--YOU KNOW HOW SHE GETS.
WE'LL PRAY FOR YOUR SAFETY.
ALL RIGHT, BRO?
ALL RIGHT.
WOW, THAT WAS SOME EMOTIONAL SCENE THERE BETWEEN YOU GUYS. THREE WHOLE WORDS!
SHUT UP.
I MEAN... SERIOUSLY, THOUGH. YOU TWO GOOD NOW?
WE'RE...BETTER. AS LONG AS THE MAPLE GLAZED MANIAC DOESN'T KILL HIM FIRST.
OMG SIMON--
PANCAKES!

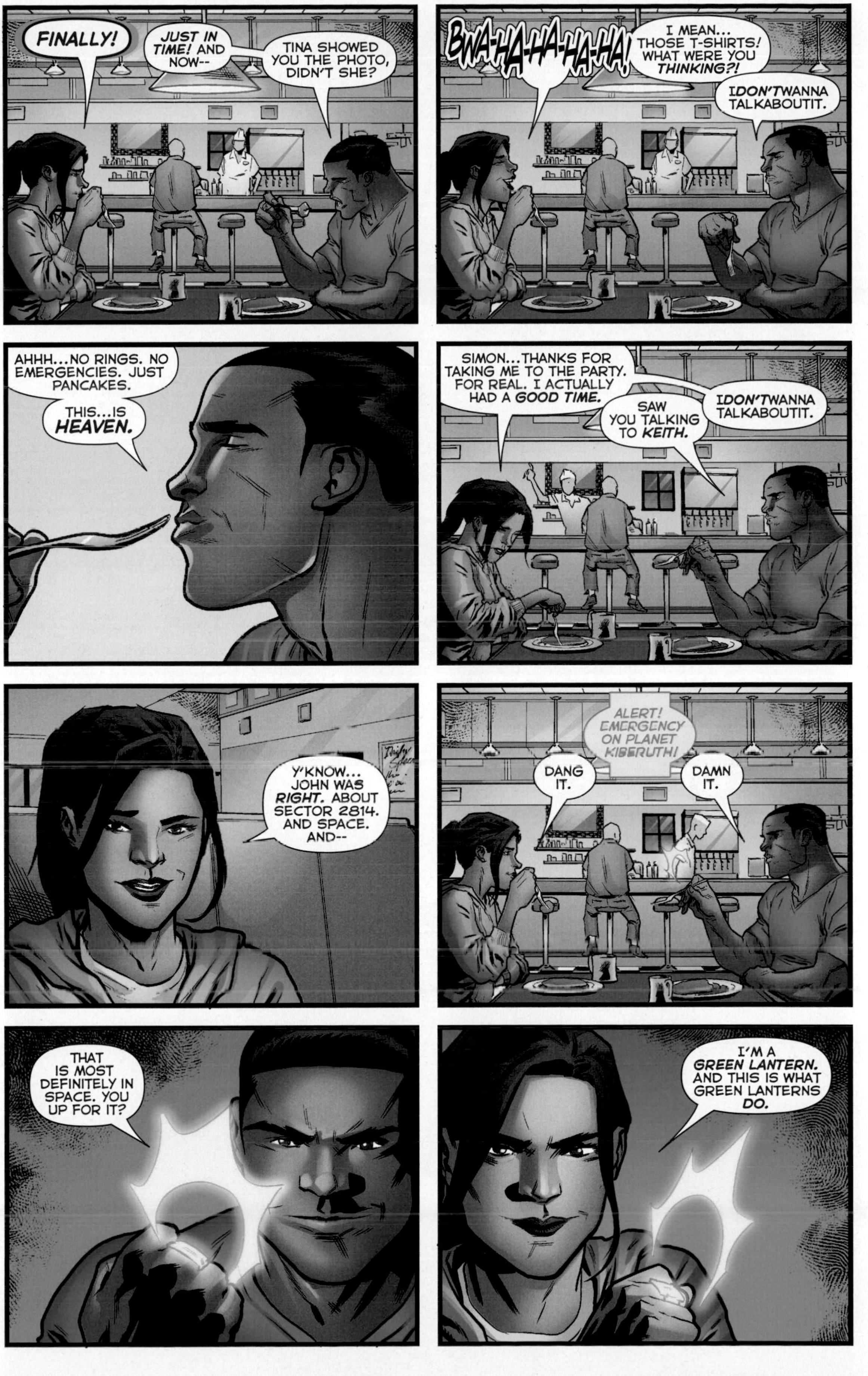
FINALLY!
JUST IN TIME! AND NOW--
TINA SHOWED YOU THE PHOTO, DIDN'T SHE?
BWA-HA-HA-HA-HA!
I MEAN... THOSE T-SHIRTS! WHAT WERE YOU THINKING?!
IDON'TWANNA TALKABOUTIT.
AHHH...NO RINGS. NO EMERGENCIES. JUST PANCAKES.
THIS...IS HEAVEN.
SIMON...THANKS FOR TAKING ME TO THE PARTY. FOR REAL. I ACTUALLY HAD A GOOD TIME.
IDON'TWANNA TALKABOUTIT.
SAW YOU TALKING TO KEITH.
Y'KNOW... JOHN WAS RIGHT. ABOUT SECTOR 2814. AND SPACE. AND--
ALERT! EMERGENCY ON PLANET KIBERUTH!
DANG IT.
DAMN IT.
THAT IS MOST DEFINITELY IN SPACE. YOU UP FOR IT?
I'M A GREEN LANTERN. AND THIS IS WHAT GREEN LANTERNS DO.

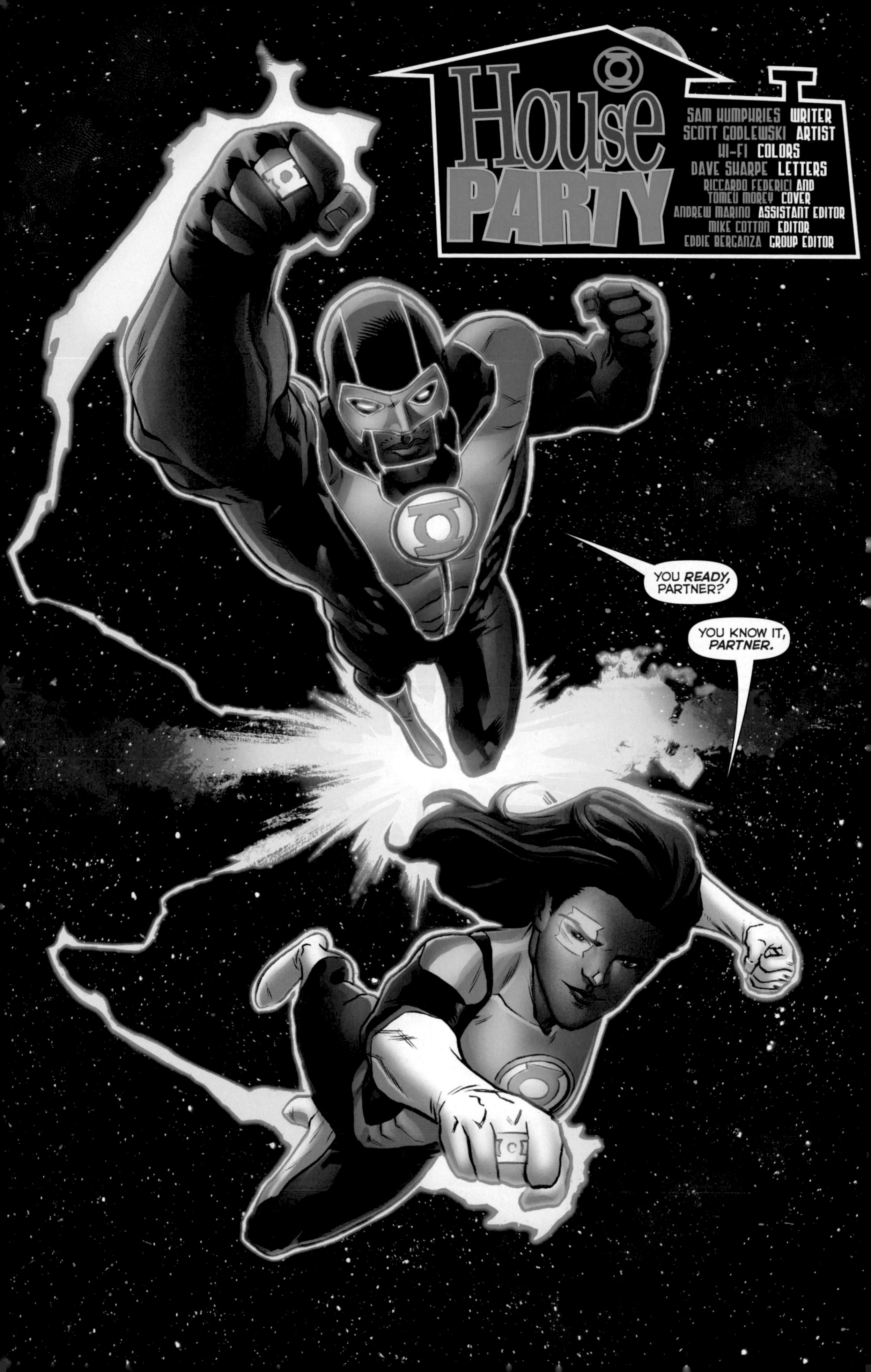
House Party
SAM HUMPHRIES WRITER
SCOTT GODLEWSKI ARTIST
HI-FI COLORS
DAVE SHARPE LETTERS
RICCARDO FEDERICI AND TOMEU MOREY COVER
ANDREW MARINO ASSISTANT EDITOR
MIKE COTTON EDITOR
EDDIE BERGANZA GROUP EDITOR
YOU READY, PARTNER?
YOU KNOW IT, PARTNER.

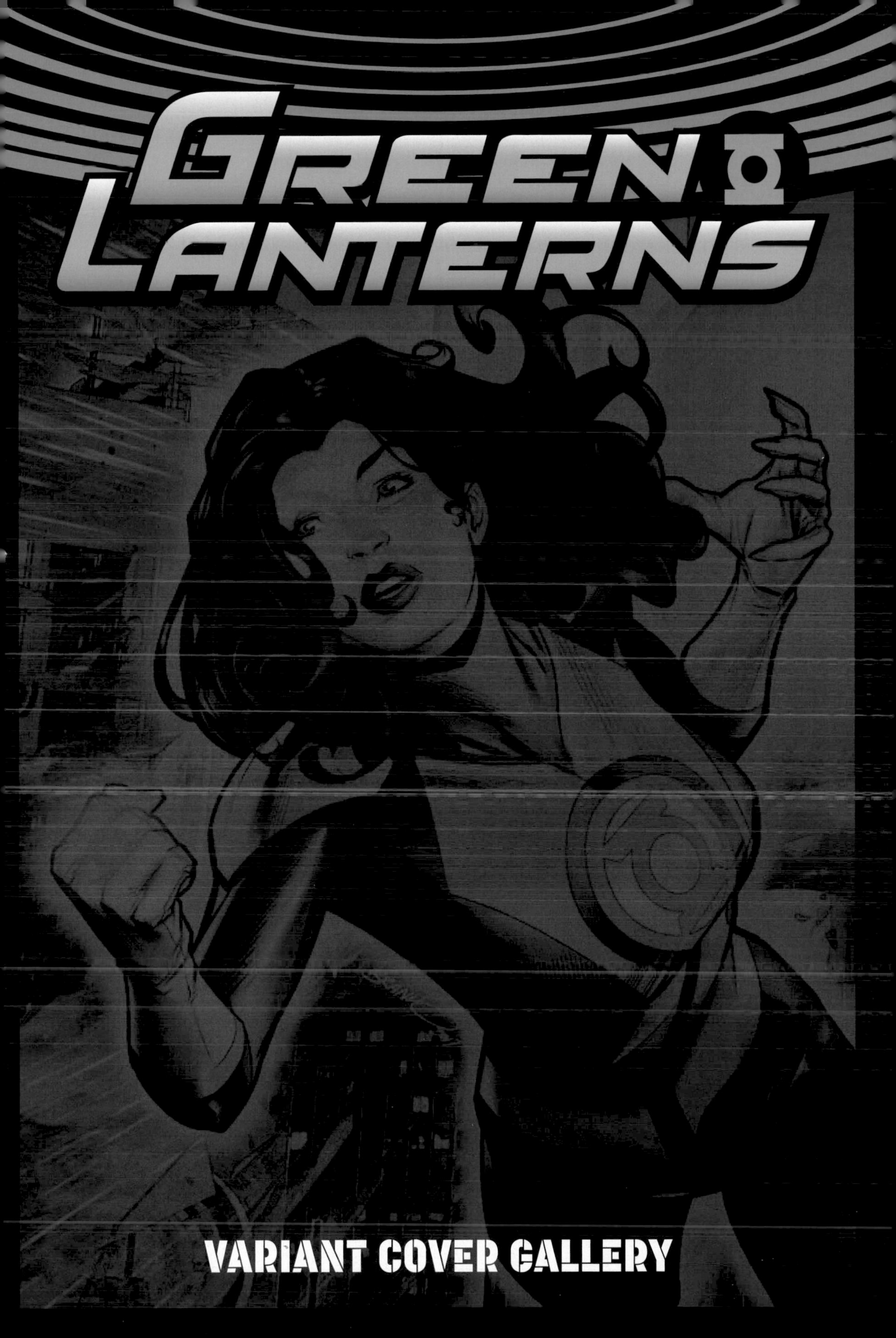
GREEN LANTERNS
VARIANT COVER GALLERY

GREEN LANTERNS #27 variant cover by BRANDON PETERSON

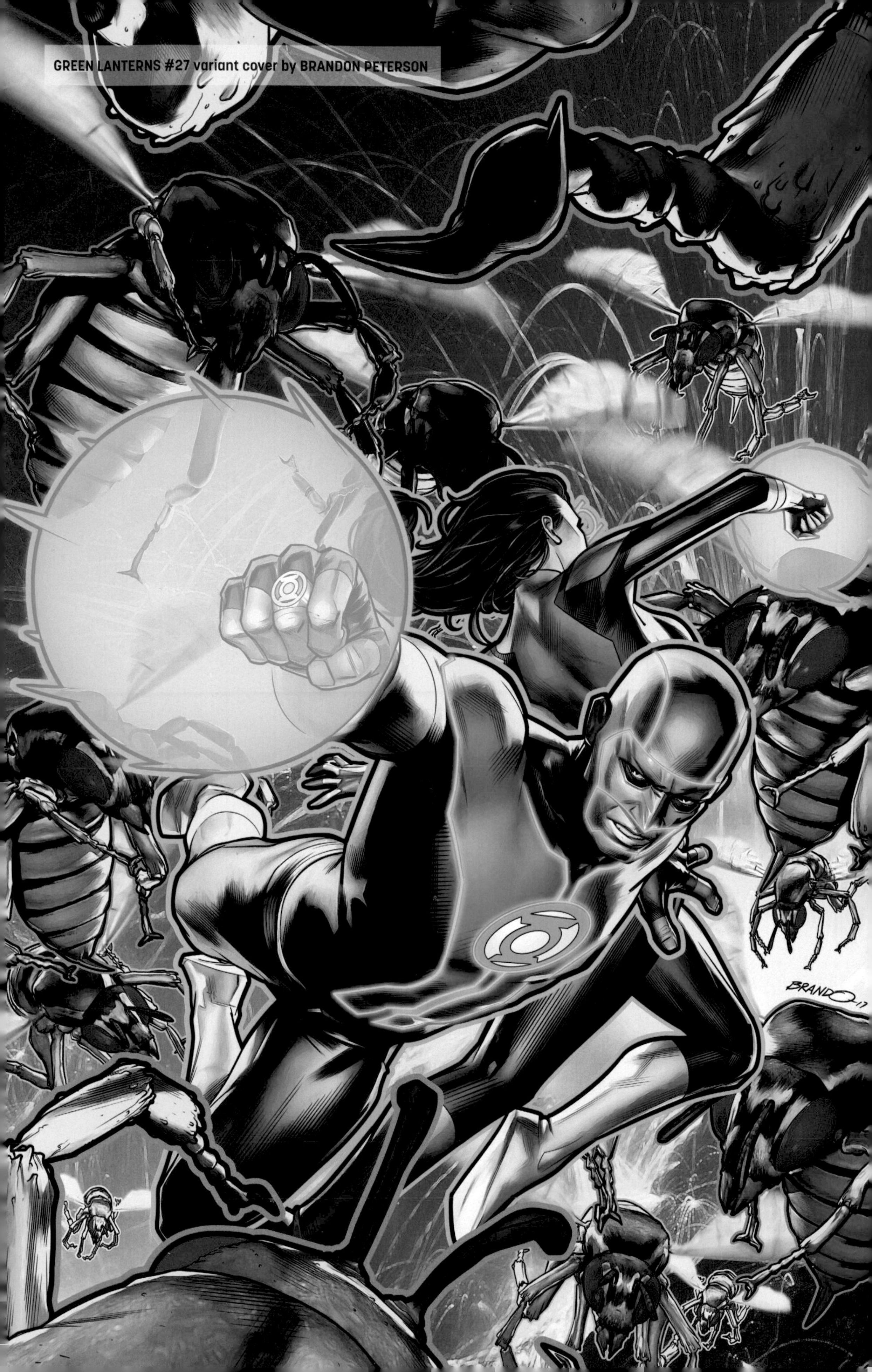
BRANDO-17

GREEN LANTERNS #28 variant cover by BRANDON PETERSON

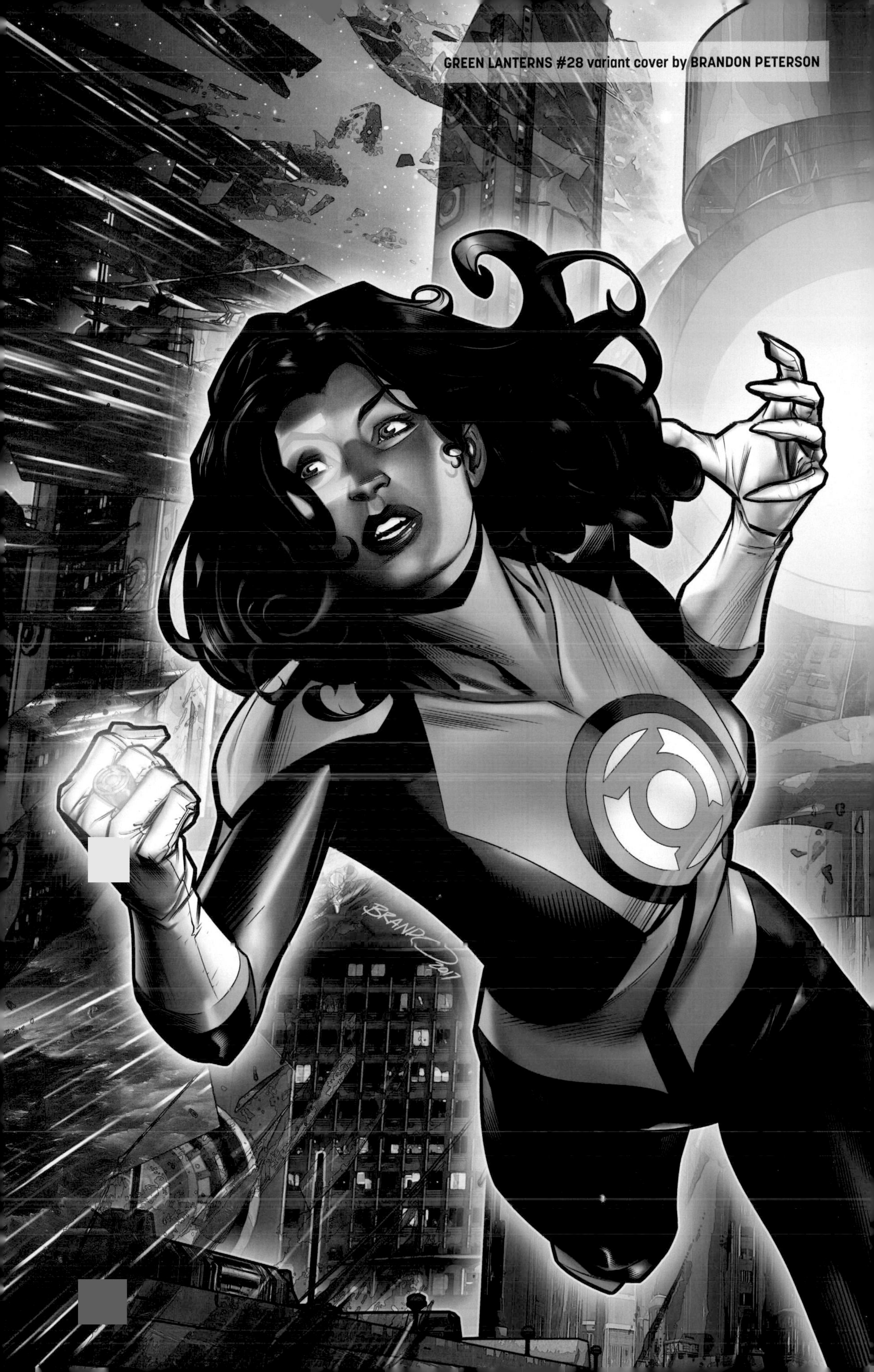

GREEN LANTERNS #29 variant cover by BRANDON PETERSON

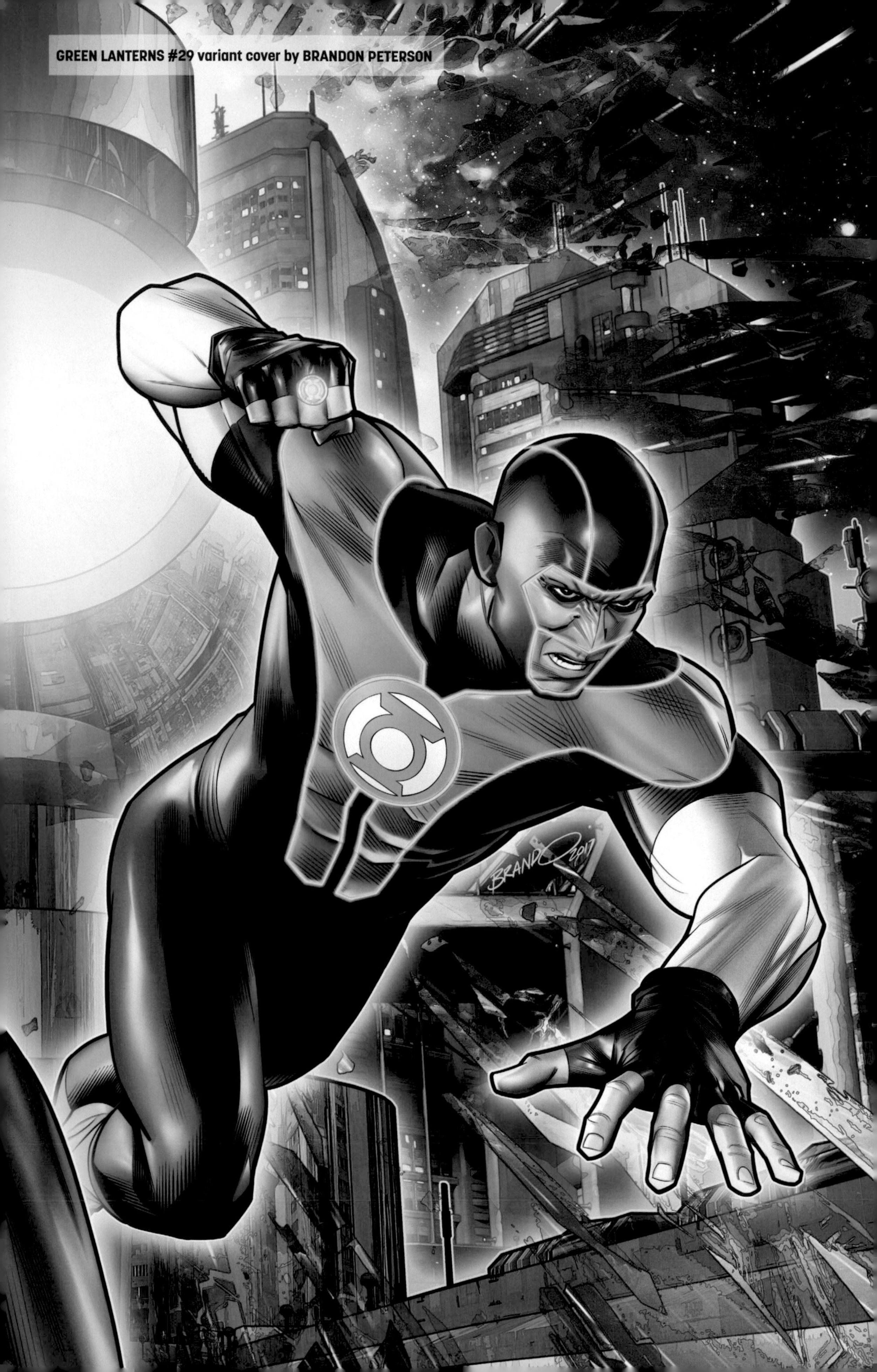
BRANDON 2017

GREEN LANTERNS #30 variant cover by BRANDON PETERSON

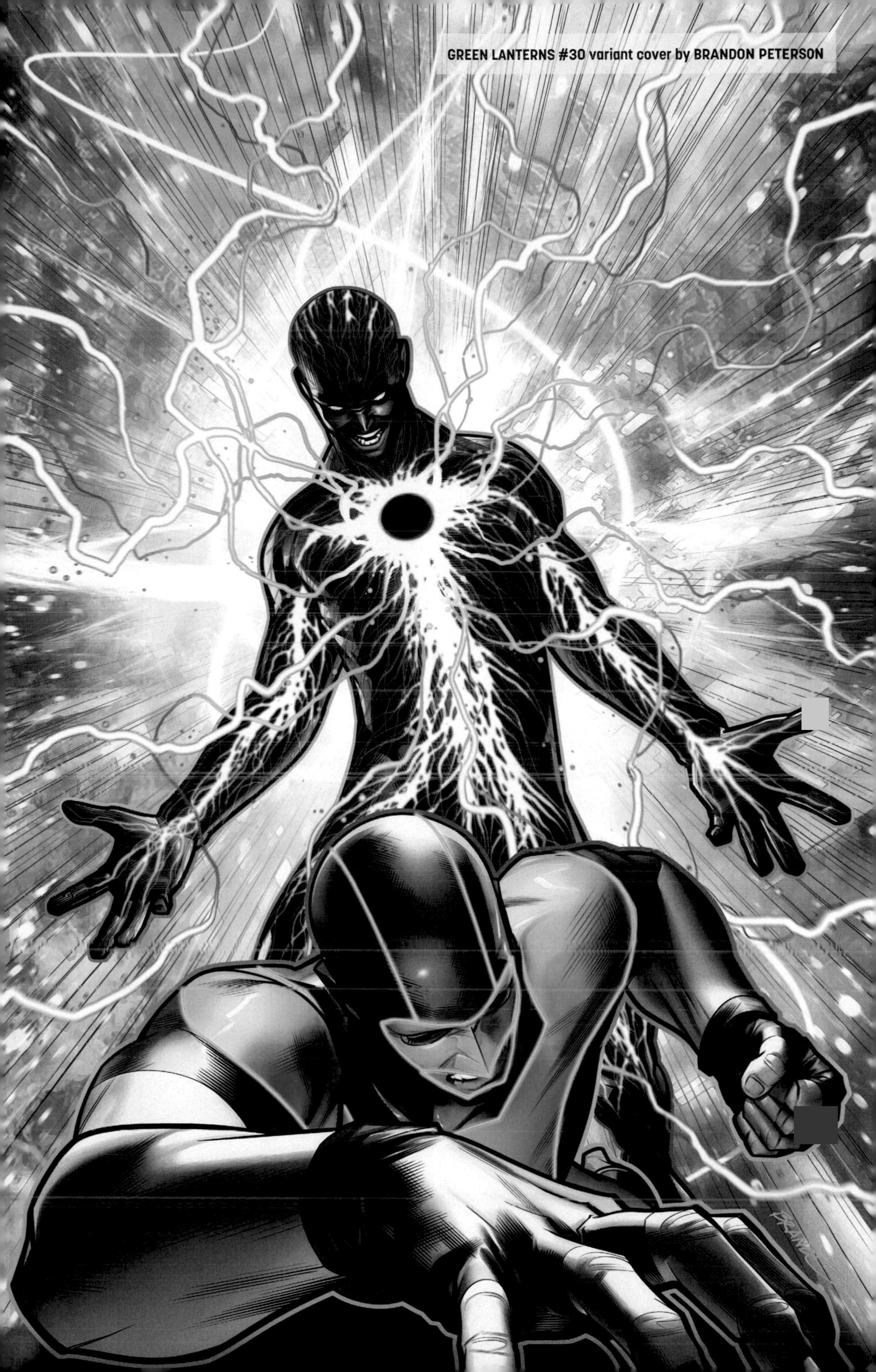

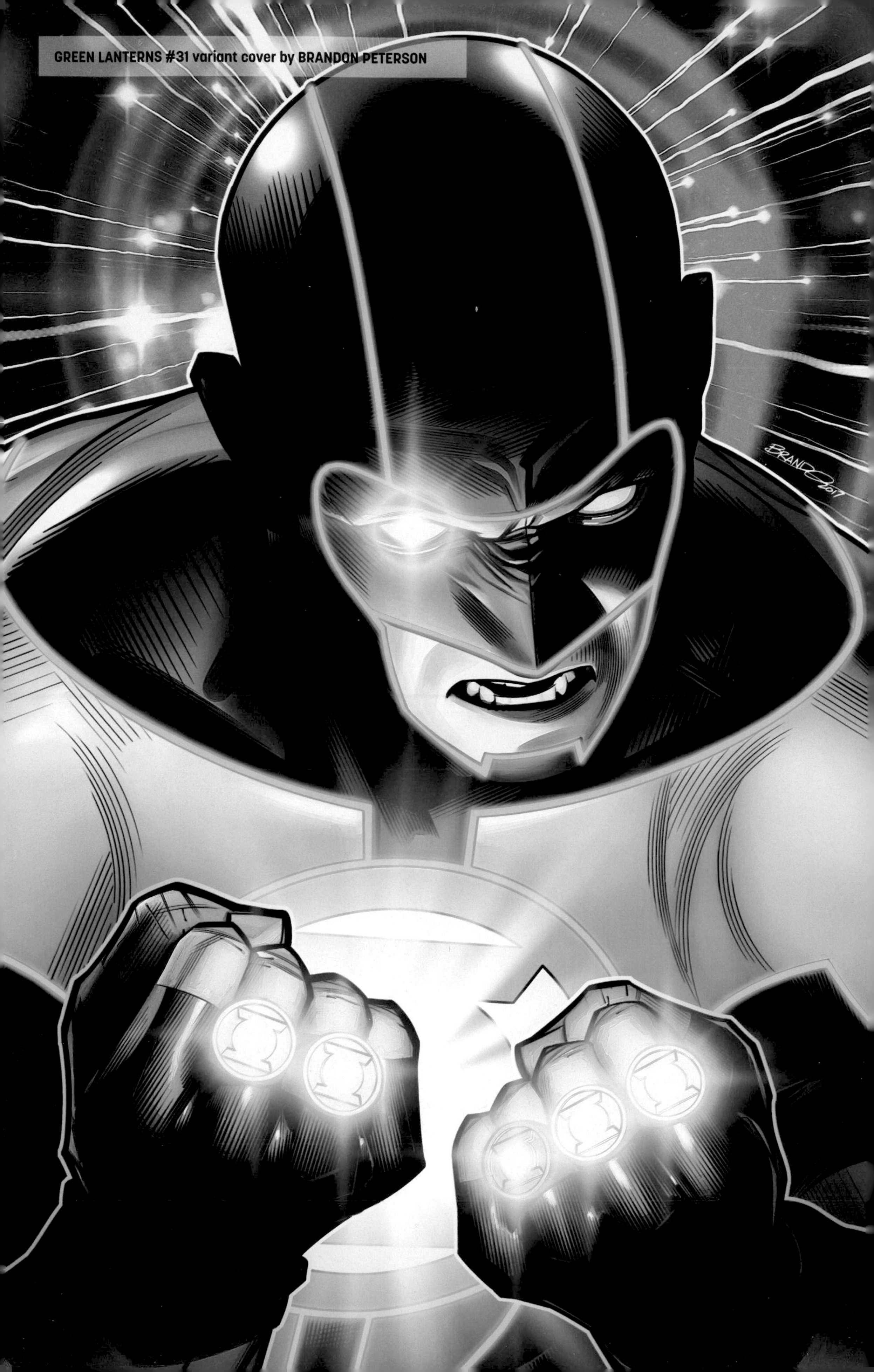

GREEN LANTERNS #31 variant cover by BRANDON PETERSON

GREEN LANTERNS #32 variant cover by BRANDON PETERSON

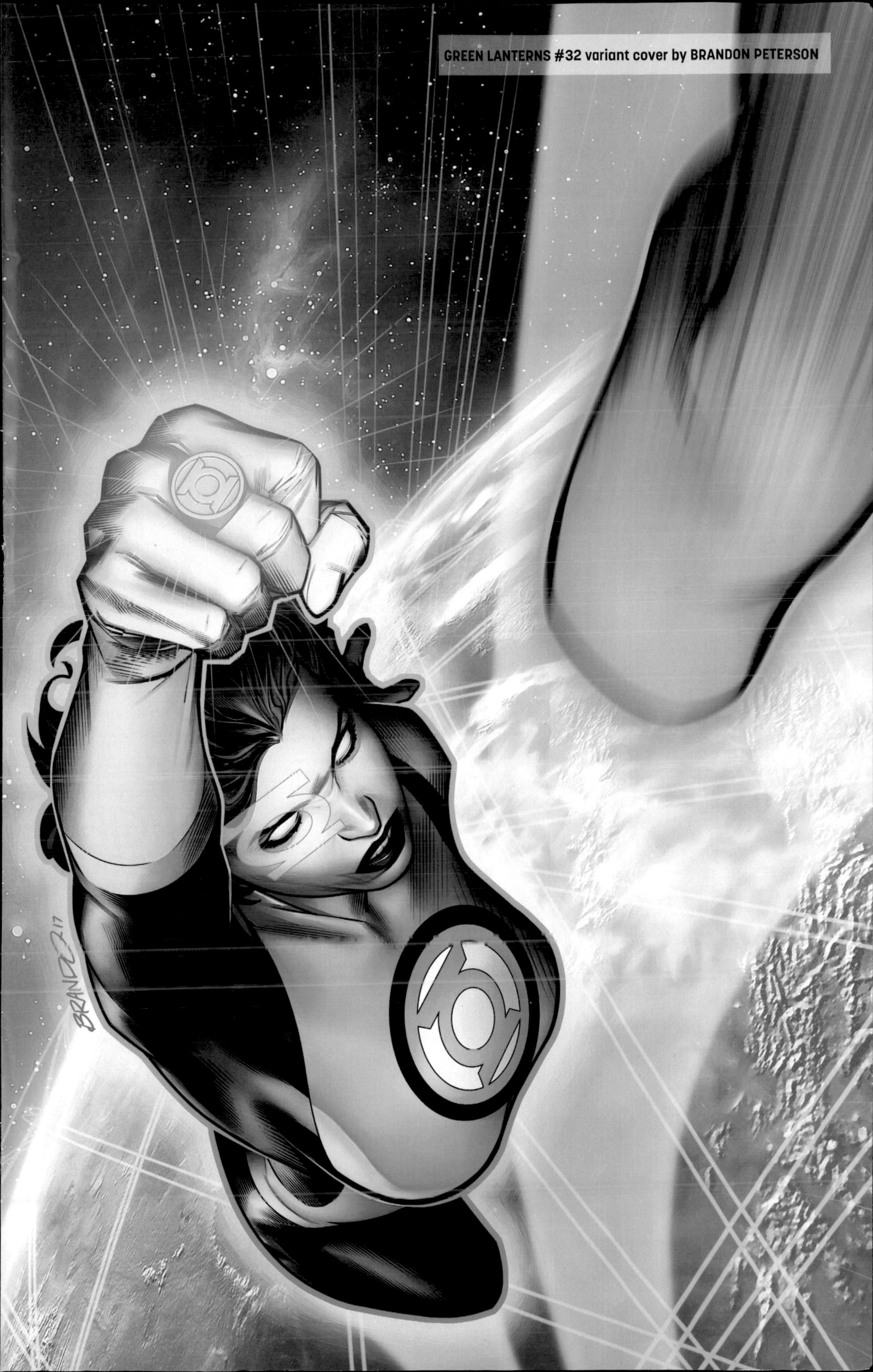
BRANDON '17

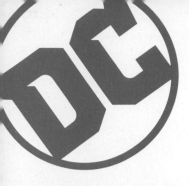

"Sam Humphries and artist Ethan Van Sciver debut a new era of emerald greatness!"
– COMIC BOOK RESOURCES

"...it's hard not to walk away impressed."
– IGN

DC UNIVERSE REBIRTH

GREEN LANTERNS

VOL. 1: RAGE PLANET

SAM HUMPHRIES
with ETHAN VAN SCIVER

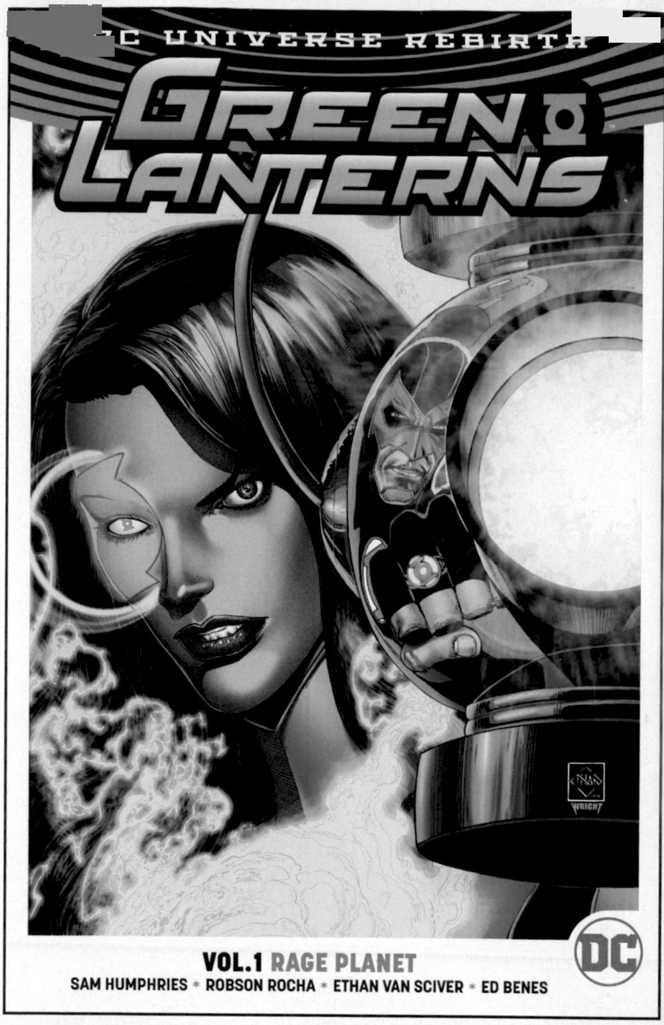
C UNIVERSE REBIRTH
GREEN LANTERNS
VOL.1 RAGE PLANET
SAM HUMPHRIES * ROBSON ROCHA * ETHAN VAN SCIVER * ED BENES

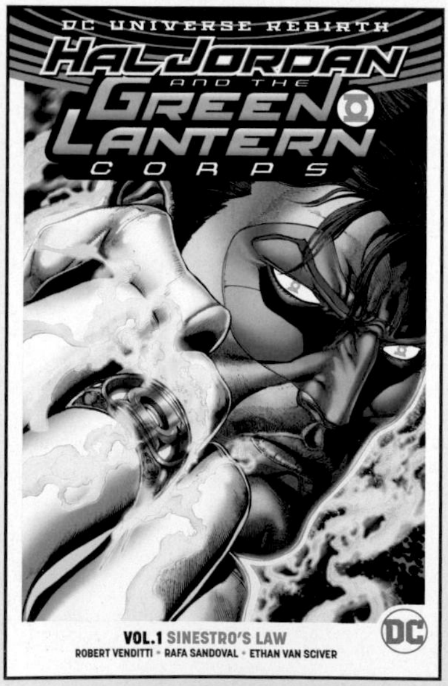
DC UNIVERSE REBIRTH
HAL JORDAN AND THE GREEN LANTERN CORPS
VOL.1 SINESTRO'S LAW
ROBERT VENDITTI * RAFA SANDOVAL * ETHAN VAN SCIVER

HAL JORDAN AND THE GREEN LANTERN CORPS VOL. 1: SINESTRO'S LAW

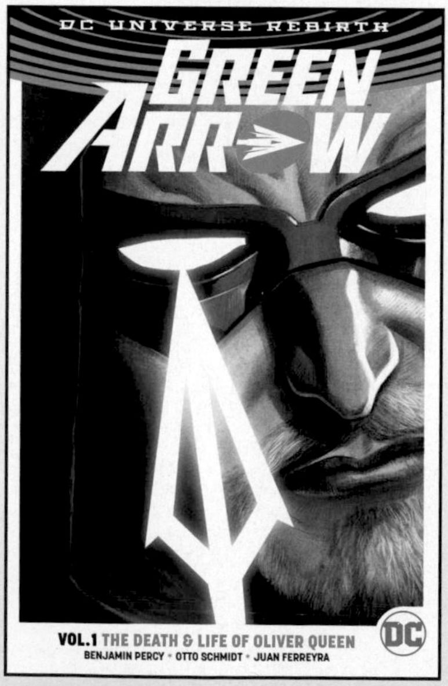
DC UNIVERSE REBIRTH
GREEN ARROW
VOL.1 THE DEATH & LIFE OF OLIVER QUEEN
BENJAMIN PERCY * OTTO SCHMIDT * JUAN FERREYRA

GREEN ARROW VOL. 1: THE DEATH & LIFE OF OLIVER QUEEN

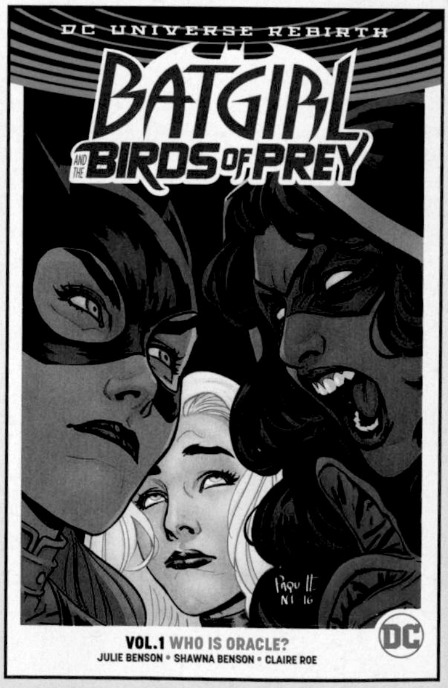
DC UNIVERSE REBIRTH
BATGIRL AND THE BIRDS OF PREY
VOL.1 WHO IS ORACLE?
JULIE BENSON * SHAWNA BENSON * CLAIRE ROE

BATGIRL AND THE BIRDS OF PREY VOL. 1: WHO IS ORACLE?